X-MEN ORIGINS II

I0406794

X-MEN ORIGINS II. Contains material originally published in magazine form as X-MEN ORIGINS CYCLOPS, NIGHTCRAWLER, ICEMAN, EMMA FROST and DEADPOOL. First printing 2011. ISBN# 978-0-7851-4670-4. Published by MARVEL WORLDWIDE, INC., a subsidiary of MARVEL ENTERTAINMENT, LLC. OFFICE OF PUBLICATION: 135 West 50th Street, New York, NY 10020. Copyright © 2010 and 2011 Marvel Characters, Inc. All rights reserved. $19.99 per copy in the U.S. and $21.99 in Canada (GST #R127032852): Canadian Agreement #40668537. All characters featured in this issue and the distinctive names and likenesses thereof, and all related indicia are trademarks of Marvel Characters, Inc. No similarity between any of the names, characters, persons, and/or institutions in this magazine with those of any living or dead person or institution is intended, and any such similarity which may exist is purely coincidental. **Printed in the U.S.A.** ALAN FINE, EVP - Office of the President, Marvel Worldwide, Inc. and EVP & CMO Marvel Characters B.V.; DAN BUCKLEY, Publisher & President - Print, Animation & Digital Divisions: JOE QUESADA, Chief Creative Officer; JIM SOKOLOWSKI, Chief Operating Officer; DAVID BOGART, SVP of Business Affairs & Talent Management; TOM BREVOORT, SVP of Publishing; C.B. CEBULSKI, SVP of Creator & Content Development; DAVID GABRIEL, SVP of Publishing Sales & Circulation; MICHAEL PASCIULLO, SVP of Brand Planning & Communications; JIM O'KEEFE, VP of Operations & Logistics; DAN CARR, Executive Director of Publishing Technology; SUSAN CRESPI, Editorial Operations Manager; ALEX MORALES, Publishing Operations Manager; STAN LEE, Chairman Emeritus. For information regarding advertising in Marvel Comics or on Marvel.com, please contact John Dokes, SVP Integrated Sales and Marketing, at jdokes@marvel.com. For Marvel subscription inquiries, please call 800-217-9158. **Manufactured between 8/18/2011 and 9/6/2011 by QUAD/GRAPHICS, DUBUQUE, IA, USA.**

10987654321

X-MEN ORIGINS II

Writers: STUART MOORE, ROBERTO AGUIRRE-SACASA,
VALERIE D'ORAZIO, ADAM FREEMAN & MARC BERNARDIN
AND DUANE SWIERCZYNSKI
Artists: JESSE DELPERDANG & ANDY LANNING;
PHIL NOTO; KARL MOLINE & RICK MAGYAR;
CARY NORD & JAMES HARREN; AND LEANDRO FERNANDEZ
Colorists: MATT HOLLINGSWORTH, PHIL NOTO,
MORRY HOLLOWELL, CHRIS SOTOMAYOR
AND STEVE BUCCELLATO
Letterers: ROB STEEN, DAVE SHARPE
AND JEFF ECKLEBERRY
Cover Art: ADI GRANOV, PHIL NOTO,
BENJAMIN ZHANG BIN, CARY NORD & EMILY WARREN
AND MARK BROOKS
Assistant Editor: SEBASTIAN GIRNER
Associate Editor: DANIEL KETCHUM
Editors: NICK LOWE AND AXEL ALONSO

Collection Editor: JENNIFER GRÜNWALD
Editorial Assistants: JAMES EMMETT & JOE HOCHSTEIN
Assistant Editors: ALEX STARBUCK & NELSON RIBEIRO
Editor, Special Projects: MARK D. BEAZLEY
Senior Editor, Special Projects: JEFF YOUNGQUIST
Senior Vice President of Sales: DAVID GABRIEL
SVP of Brand Planning & Communications: MICHAEL PASCIULLO

Editor in Chief: AXEL ALONSO
Chief Creative Officer: JOE QUESADA
Publisher: DAN BUCKLEY
Executive Producer: ALAN FINE

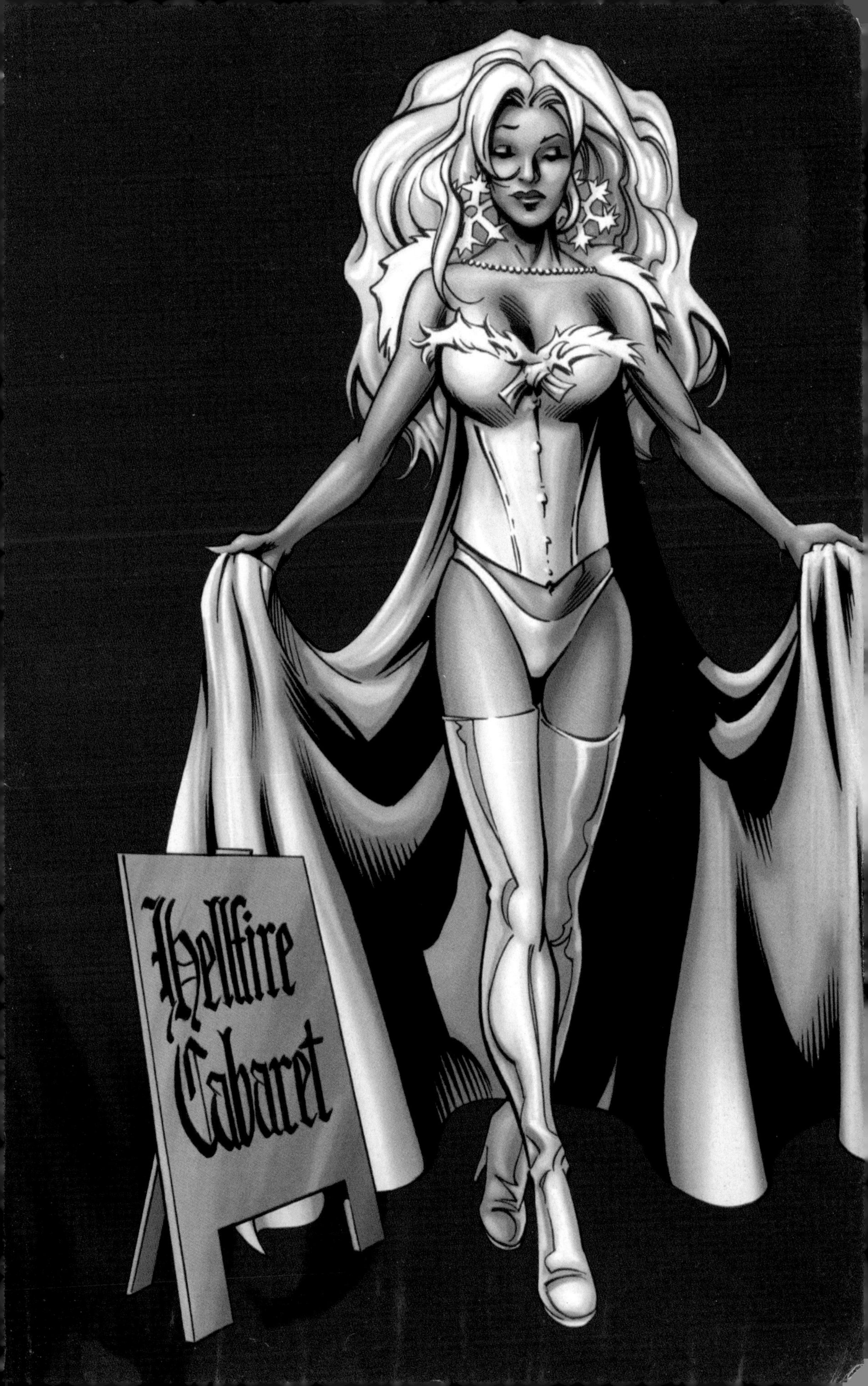
Hellfire
Cabaret

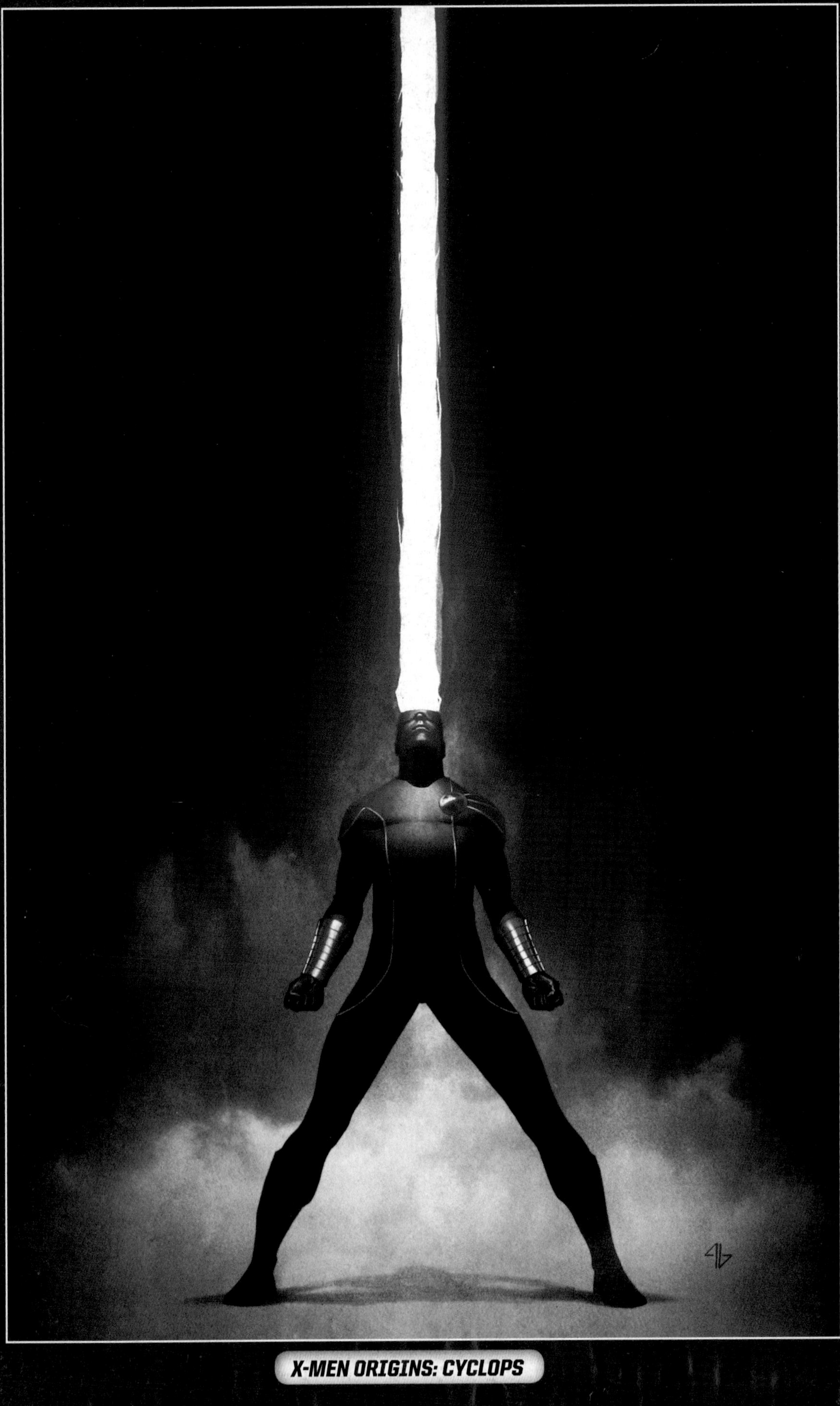

X-MEN ORIGINS: CYCLOPS

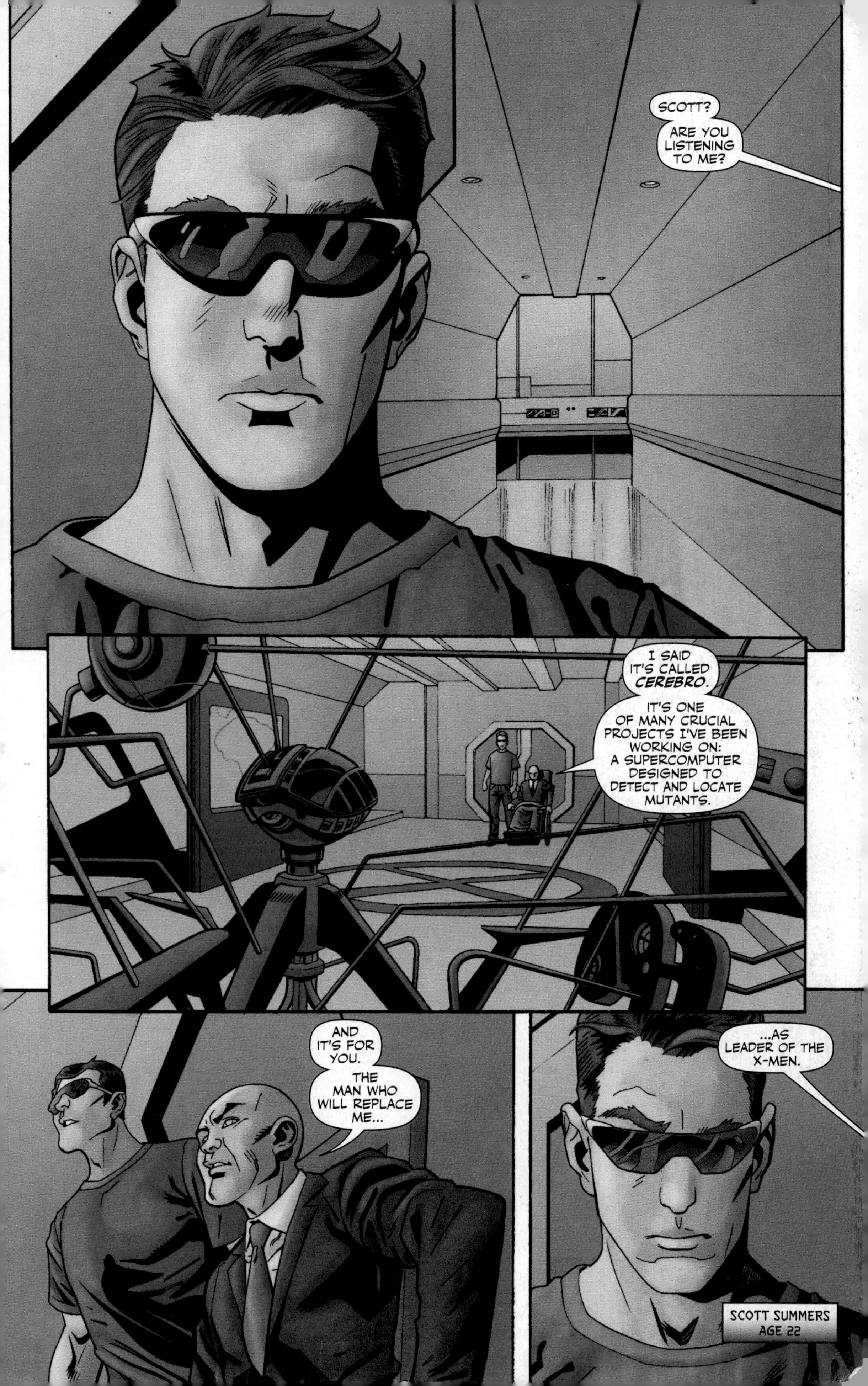
SCOTT?
ARE YOU LISTENING TO ME?
I SAID IT'S CALLED *CEREBRO*.
IT'S ONE OF MANY CRUCIAL PROJECTS I'VE BEEN WORKING ON: A SUPERCOMPUTER DESIGNED TO DETECT AND LOCATE MUTANTS.
AND IT'S FOR YOU.
THE MAN WHO WILL REPLACE ME...
...AS LEADER OF THE X-MEN.
SCOTT SUMMERS AGE 22

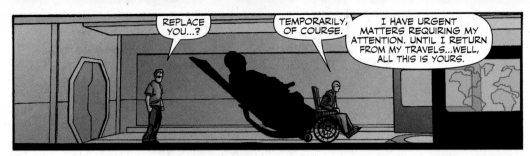

REPLACE YOU...?

TEMPORARILY, OF COURSE.

I HAVE URGENT MATTERS REQUIRING MY ATTENTION. UNTIL I RETURN FROM MY TRAVELS...WELL, ALL THIS IS YOURS.

PROFESSOR, I--I'M NOT SURE I CAN ACCEPT.

I WASN'T SURE HOW TO TELL YOU THIS-- BUT I'VE BEEN THINKING OF LEAVING THE X-MEN.

I'VE... MADE INQUIRIES WITH A FEW DOCTORS. ABOUT CURING ME OF MY EYE-BEAM POWER...

AH, YES.

DOCTOR STATHIS AND I DISCUSSED THE MATTER. HE BELIEVES A "CURE" IS HIGHLY UNLIKELY-- AS DO I.

SIR. YOU KNOW DOCTOR STATHIS?

YES. HE'S A MUTANT HIMSELF, YOU KNOW.

I FOUND HIM WITH THIS.

SCOTT.

I NEED YOU TO LISTEN, NOW...

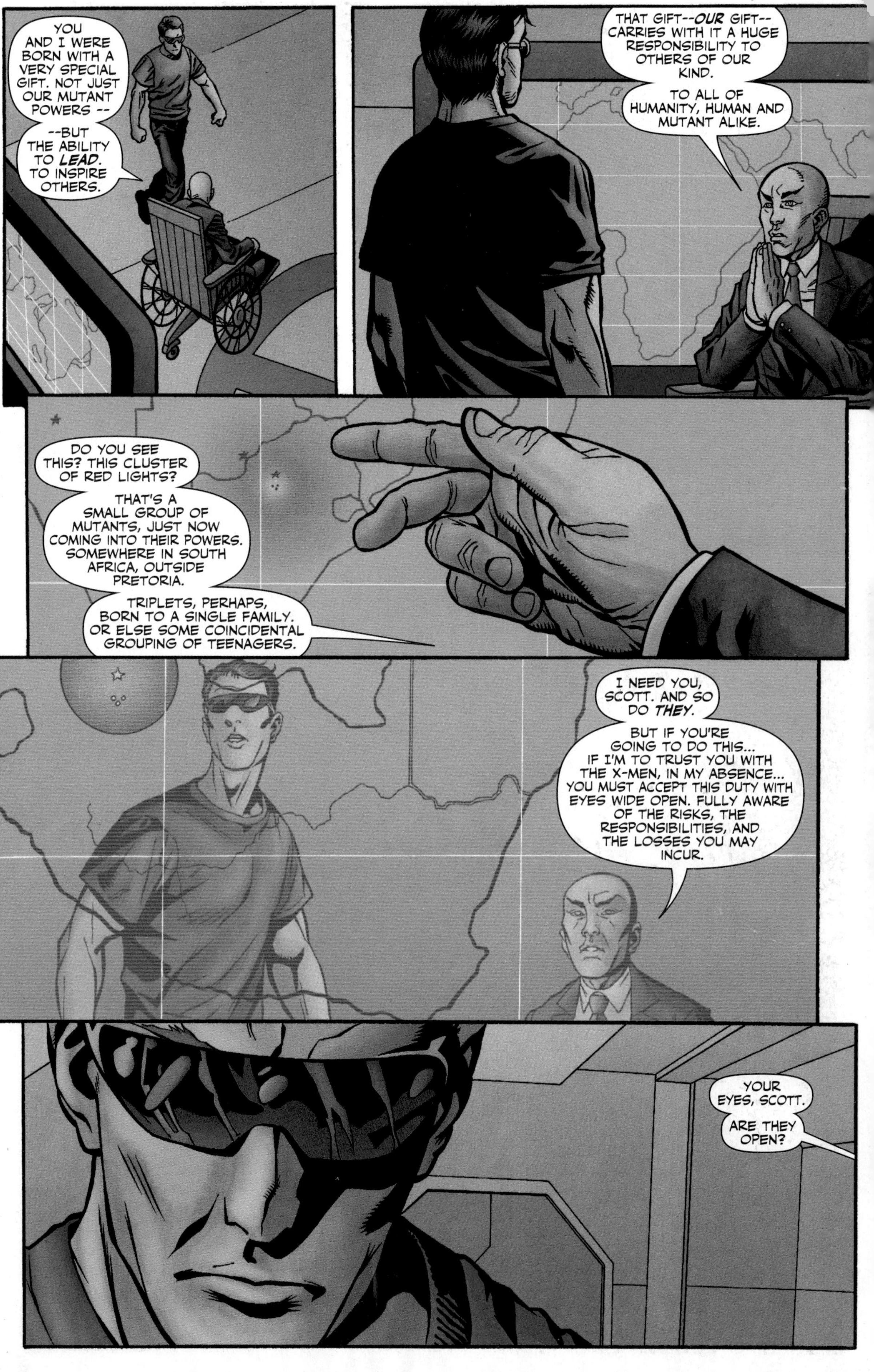
YOU AND I WERE BORN WITH A VERY SPECIAL GIFT. NOT JUST OUR MUTANT POWERS --
--BUT THE ABILITY TO LEAD. TO INSPIRE OTHERS.
THAT GIFT--OUR GIFT-- CARRIES WITH IT A HUGE RESPONSIBILITY TO OTHERS OF OUR KIND.
TO ALL OF HUMANITY, HUMAN AND MUTANT ALIKE.
DO YOU SEE THIS? THIS CLUSTER OF RED LIGHTS?
THAT'S A SMALL GROUP OF MUTANTS, JUST NOW COMING INTO THEIR POWERS. SOMEWHERE IN SOUTH AFRICA, OUTSIDE PRETORIA.
TRIPLETS, PERHAPS, BORN TO A SINGLE FAMILY. OR ELSE SOME COINCIDENTAL GROUPING OF TEENAGERS.
I NEED YOU, SCOTT. AND SO DO THEY.
BUT IF YOU'RE GOING TO DO THIS... IF I'M TO TRUST YOU WITH THE X-MEN, IN MY ABSENCE... YOU MUST ACCEPT THIS DUTY WITH EYES WIDE OPEN. FULLY AWARE OF THE RISKS, THE RESPONSIBILITIES, AND THE LOSSES YOU MAY INCUR.
YOUR EYES, SCOTT.
ARE THEY OPEN?

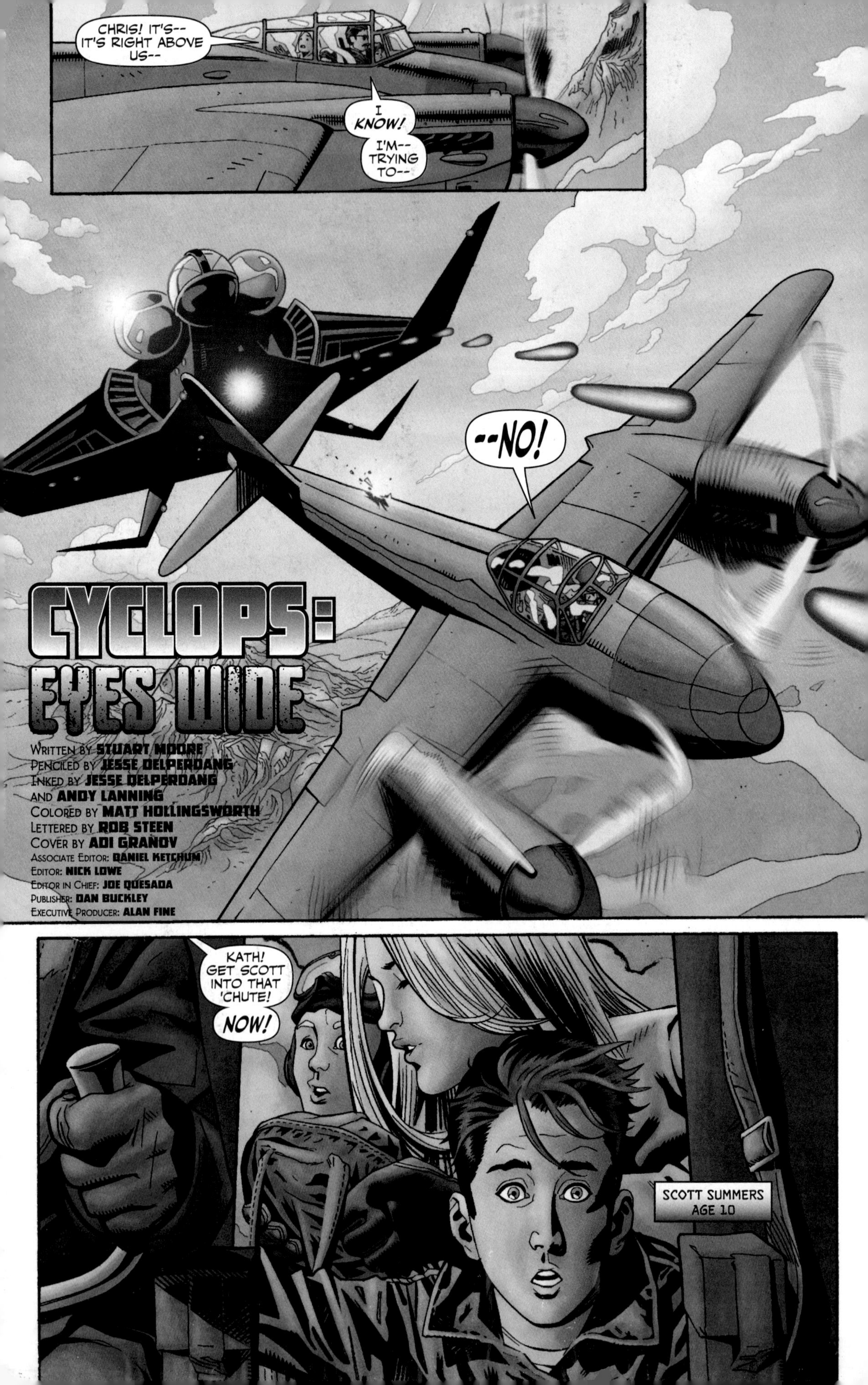
CHRIS! IT'S-- IT'S RIGHT ABOVE US--
I KNOW! I'M-- TRYING TO--
--NO!
CYCLOPS: EYES WIDE
WRITTEN BY STUART MOORE
PENCILED BY JESSE DELPERDANG
INKED BY JESSE DELPERDANG AND ANDY LANNING
COLORED BY MATT HOLLINGSWORTH
LETTERED BY ROB STEEN
COVER BY ADI GRANOV
ASSOCIATE EDITOR: DANIEL KETCHUM
EDITOR: NICK LOWE
EDITOR IN CHIEF: JOE QUESADA
PUBLISHER: DAN BUCKLEY
EXECUTIVE PRODUCER: ALAN FINE
KATH! GET SCOTT INTO THAT 'CHUTE! NOW!
SCOTT SUMMERS AGE 10

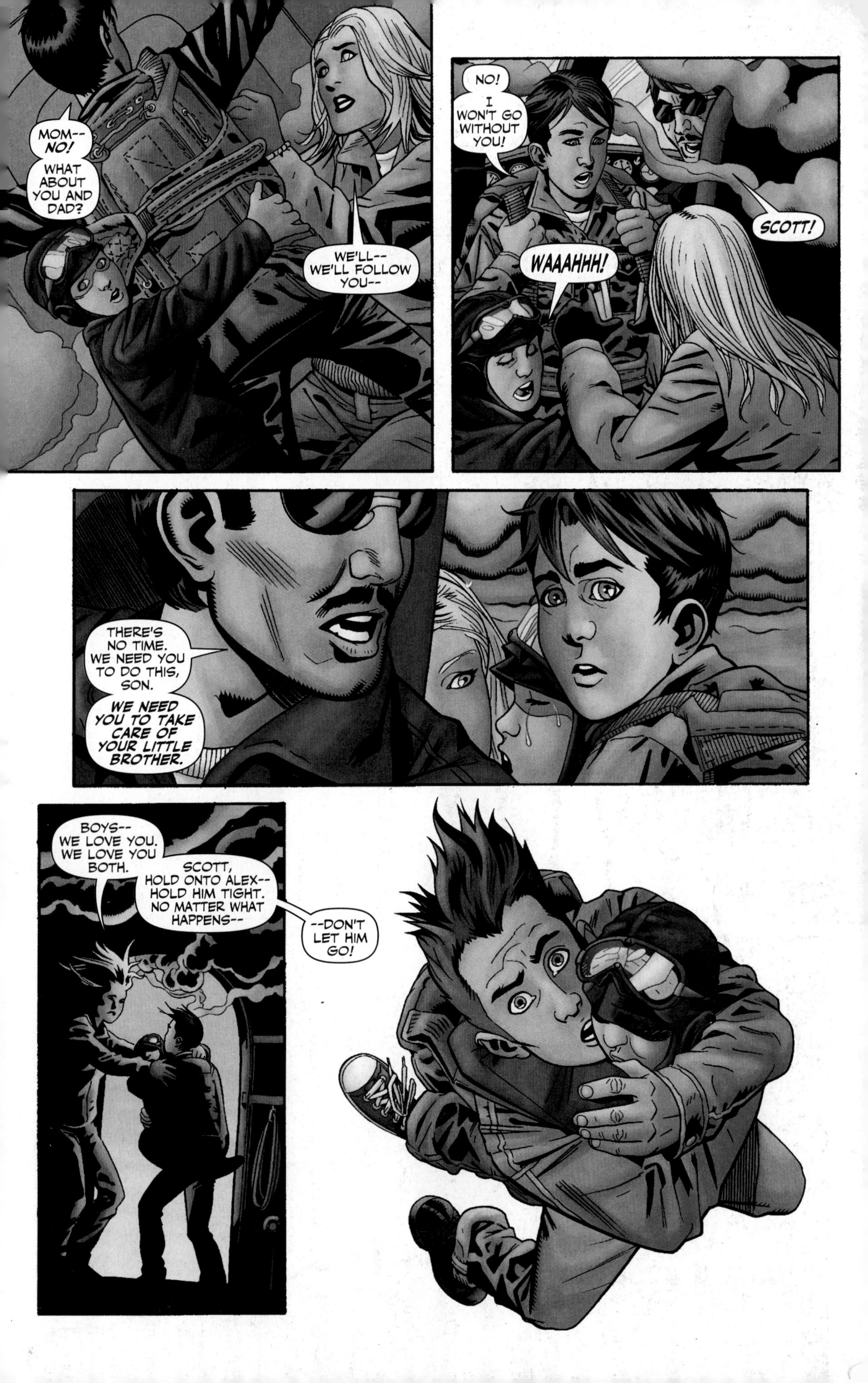
MOM-- NO! WHAT ABOUT YOU AND DAD?
WE'LL-- WE'LL FOLLOW YOU--
NO! I WON'T GO WITHOUT YOU!
SCOTT!
WAAAHHH!
THERE'S NO TIME. WE NEED YOU TO DO THIS, SON.
WE NEED YOU TO TAKE CARE OF YOUR LITTLE BROTHER.
BOYS-- WE LOVE YOU. WE LOVE YOU BOTH.
SCOTT, HOLD ONTO ALEX-- HOLD HIM TIGHT. NO MATTER WHAT HAPPENS--
--DON'T LET HIM GO!

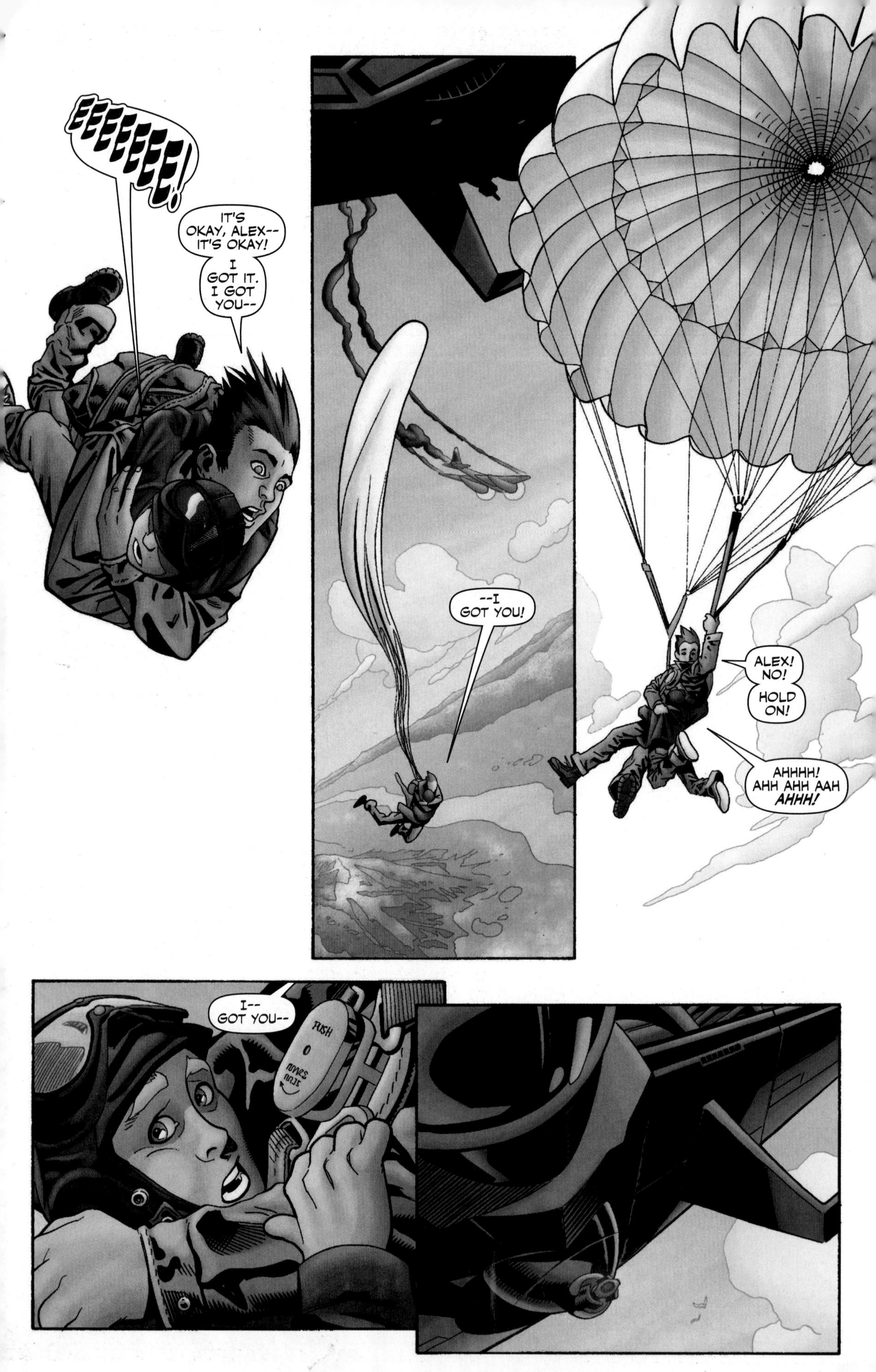
EEEEEEE!
IT'S OKAY, ALEX-- IT'S OKAY!
I GOT IT. I GOT YOU--
--I GOT YOU!
ALEX! NO!
HOLD ON!
AHHHH! AHH AHH AAH *AHHH!*
I-- GOT YOU--
PUSH

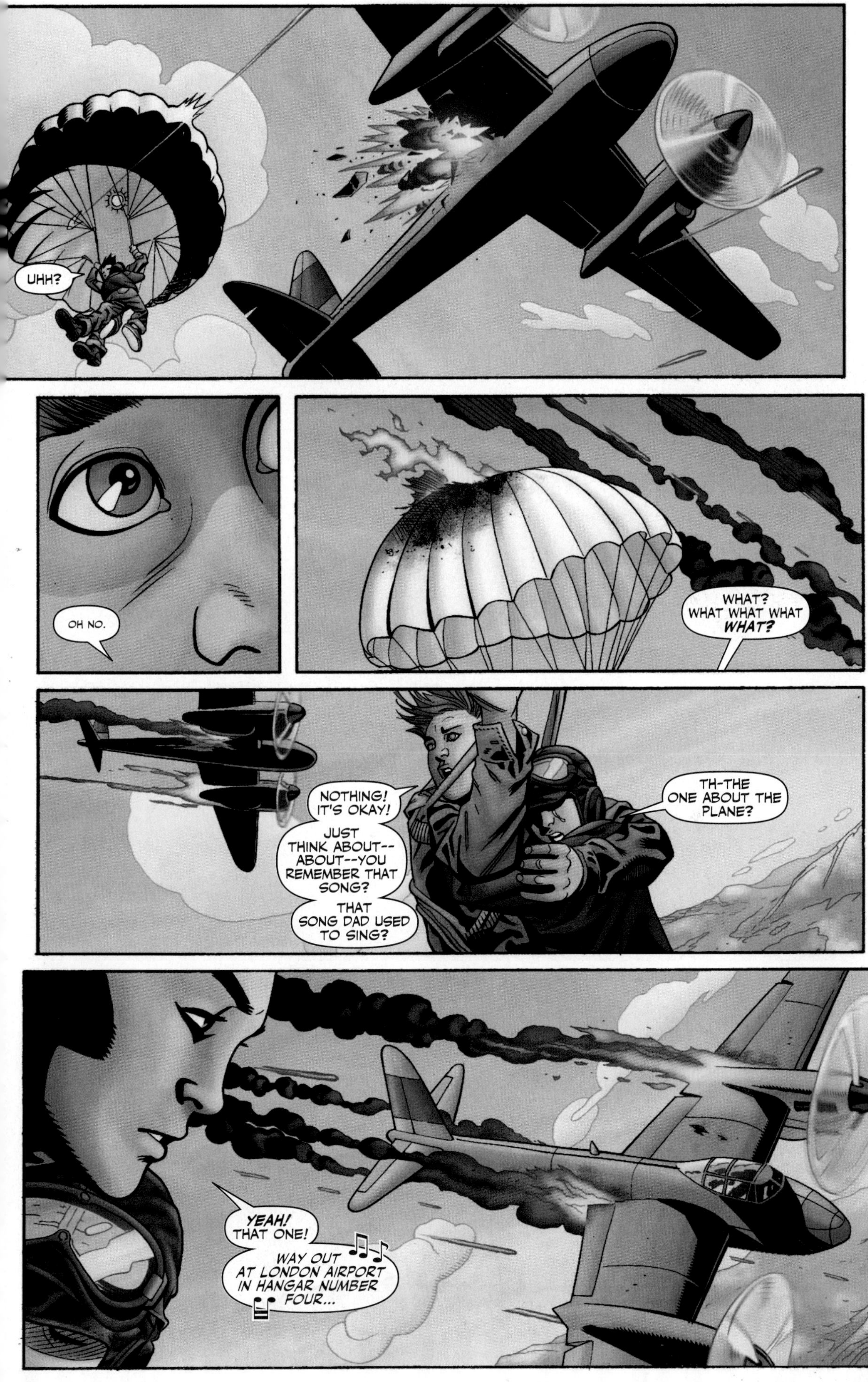
UHH?
OH NO.
WHAT? WHAT WHAT WHAT WHAT?
NOTHING! IT'S OKAY!
JUST THINK ABOUT-- ABOUT--YOU REMEMBER THAT SONG?
THAT SONG DAD USED TO SING?
TH-THE ONE ABOUT THE PLANE?
YEAH! THAT ONE!
WAY OUT AT LONDON AIRPORT IN HANGAR NUMBER FOUR...

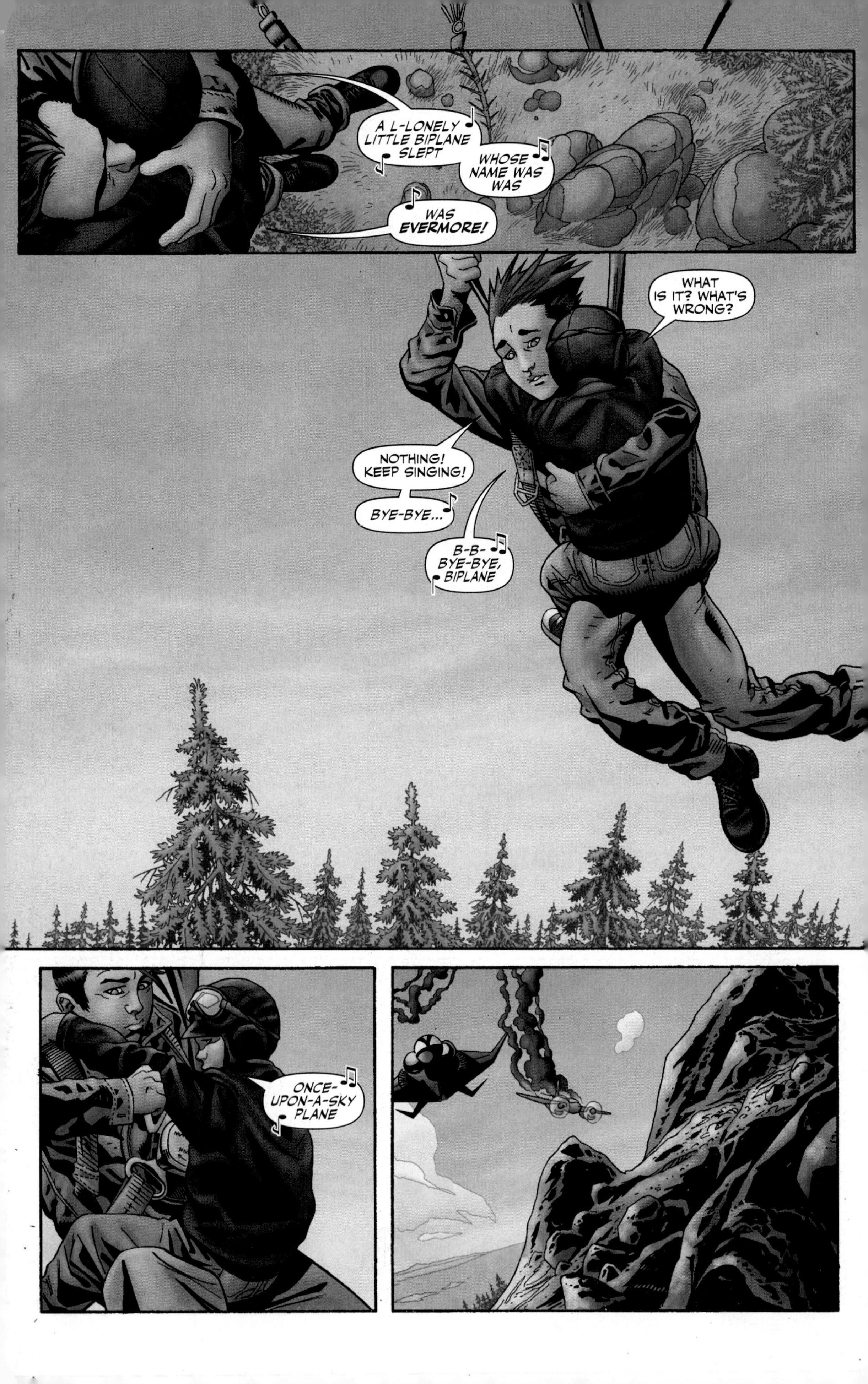
A L-LONELY LITTLE BIPLANE SLEPT
WHOSE NAME WAS WAS
WAS EVERMORE!
WHAT IS IT? WHAT'S WRONG?
NOTHING! KEEP SINGING!
BYE-BYE...
B-B-BYE-BYE, BIPLANE
ONCE-UPON-A-SKY PLANE

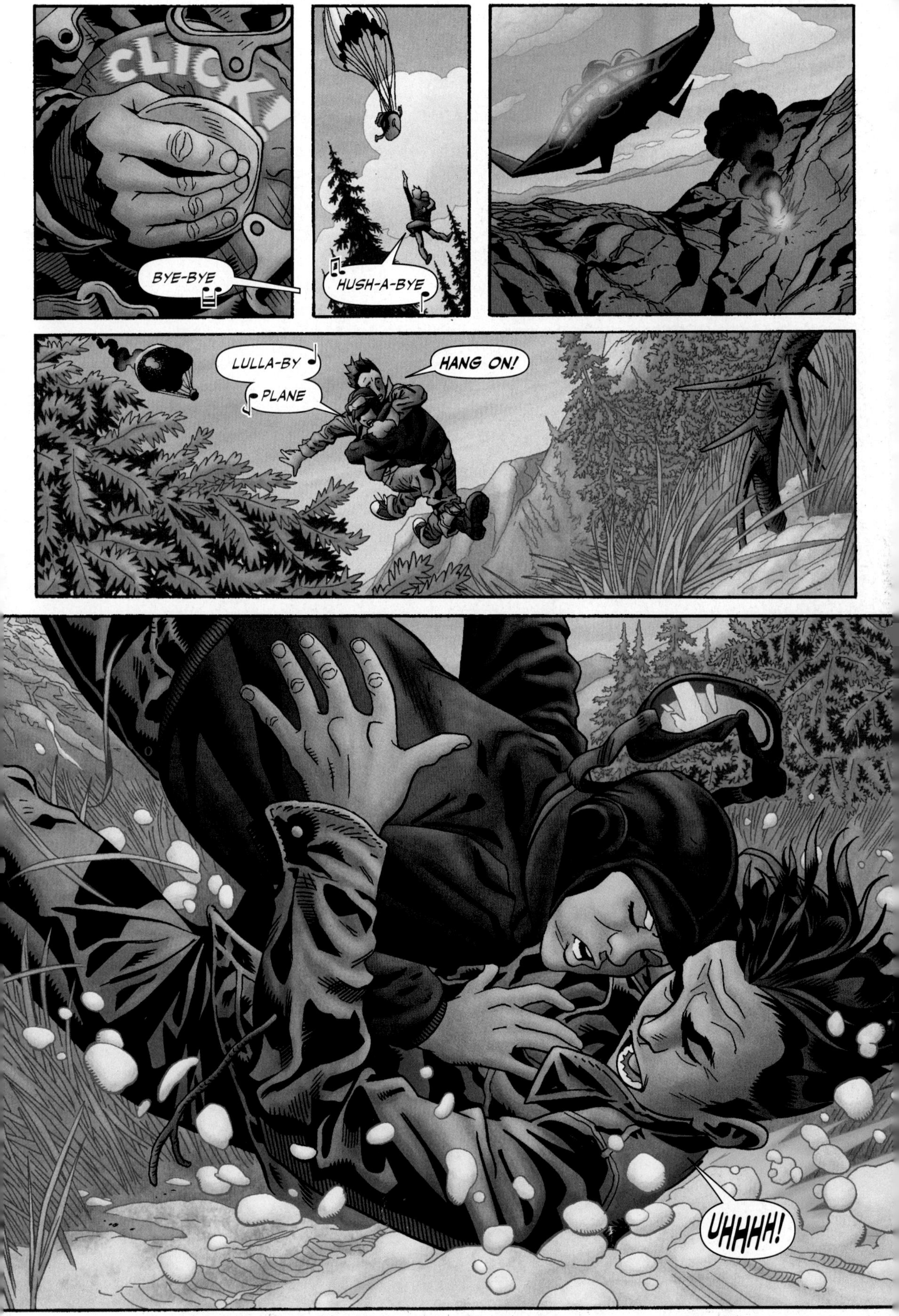
CLICK
BYE-BYE
HUSH-A-BYE
LULLA-BY
PLANE
HANG ON!
UHHHH!

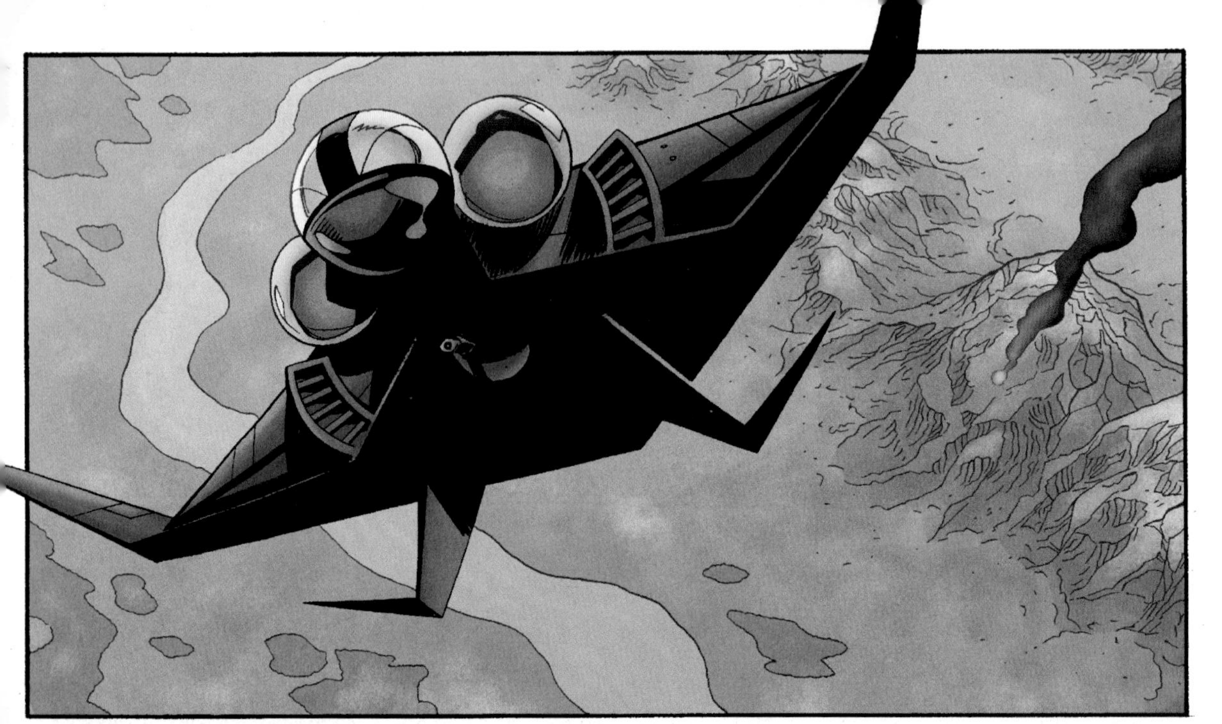

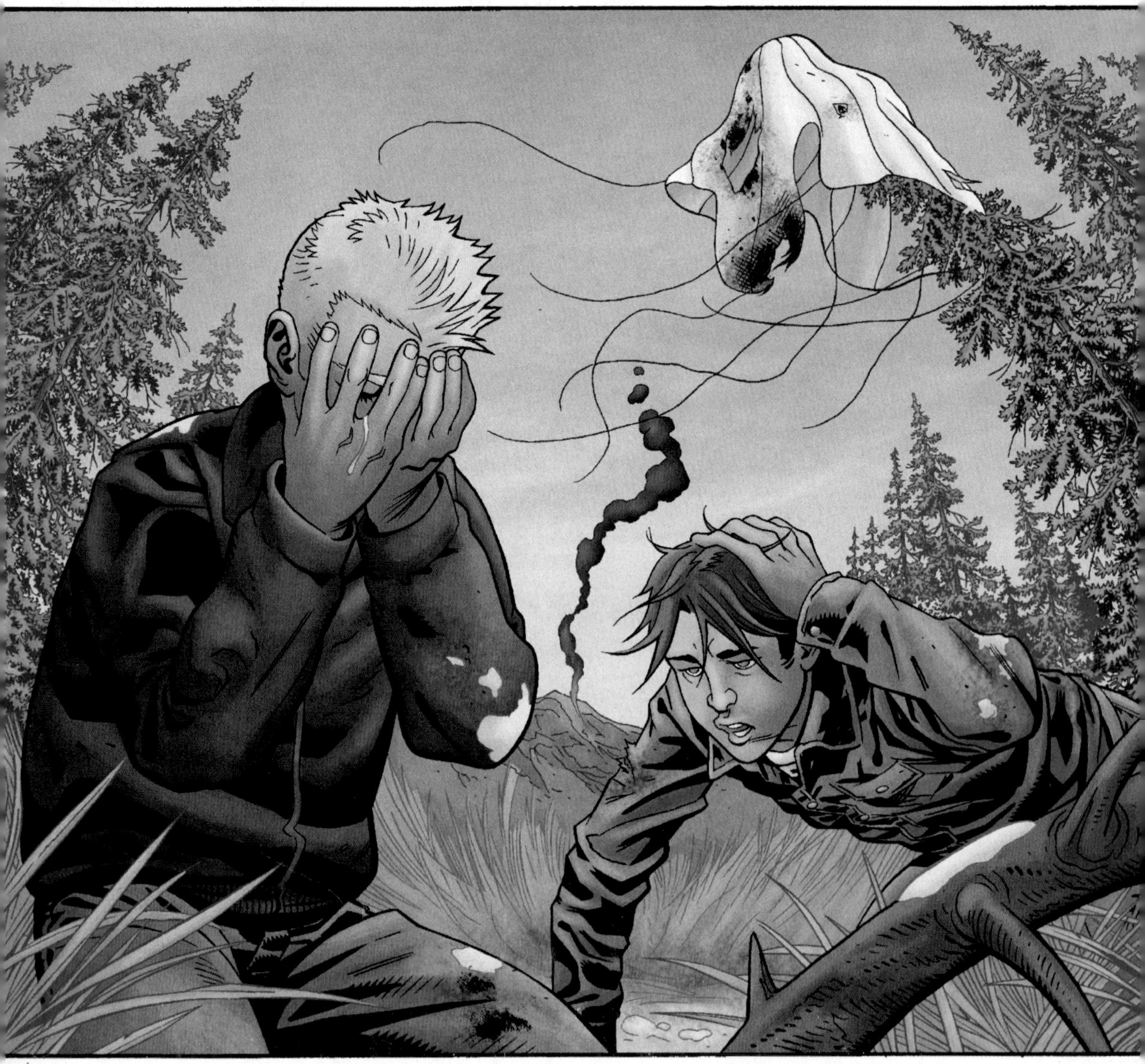

THAT NIGHT

SCOTT?

SCOTTY?!

ARE YOU OKAY?

I'M--I'M FINE, ALEX. IT'S JUST A HEADACHE.

MUST HAVE HIT MY HEAD IN THE FALL.

DON'T WORRY ABOUT ME. LET'S--LET'S SING ANOTHER SONG--

YOU HAD A HEADACHE YESTERDAY. BEFORE, BEFORE... EVERYTHING.

AND THE DAY BEFORE, TOO.

DO YOU HAVE A TUMOR? ARE YOU GONNA DIE?

ALEX!

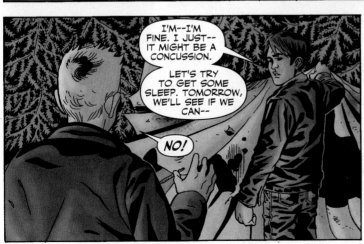

I'M--I'M FINE. I JUST-- IT MIGHT BE A CONCUSSION.

LET'S TRY TO GET SOME SLEEP. TOMORROW, WE'LL SEE IF WE CAN--

NO!

IF YOU GO TO SLEEP, YOU'RE GONNA DIE!

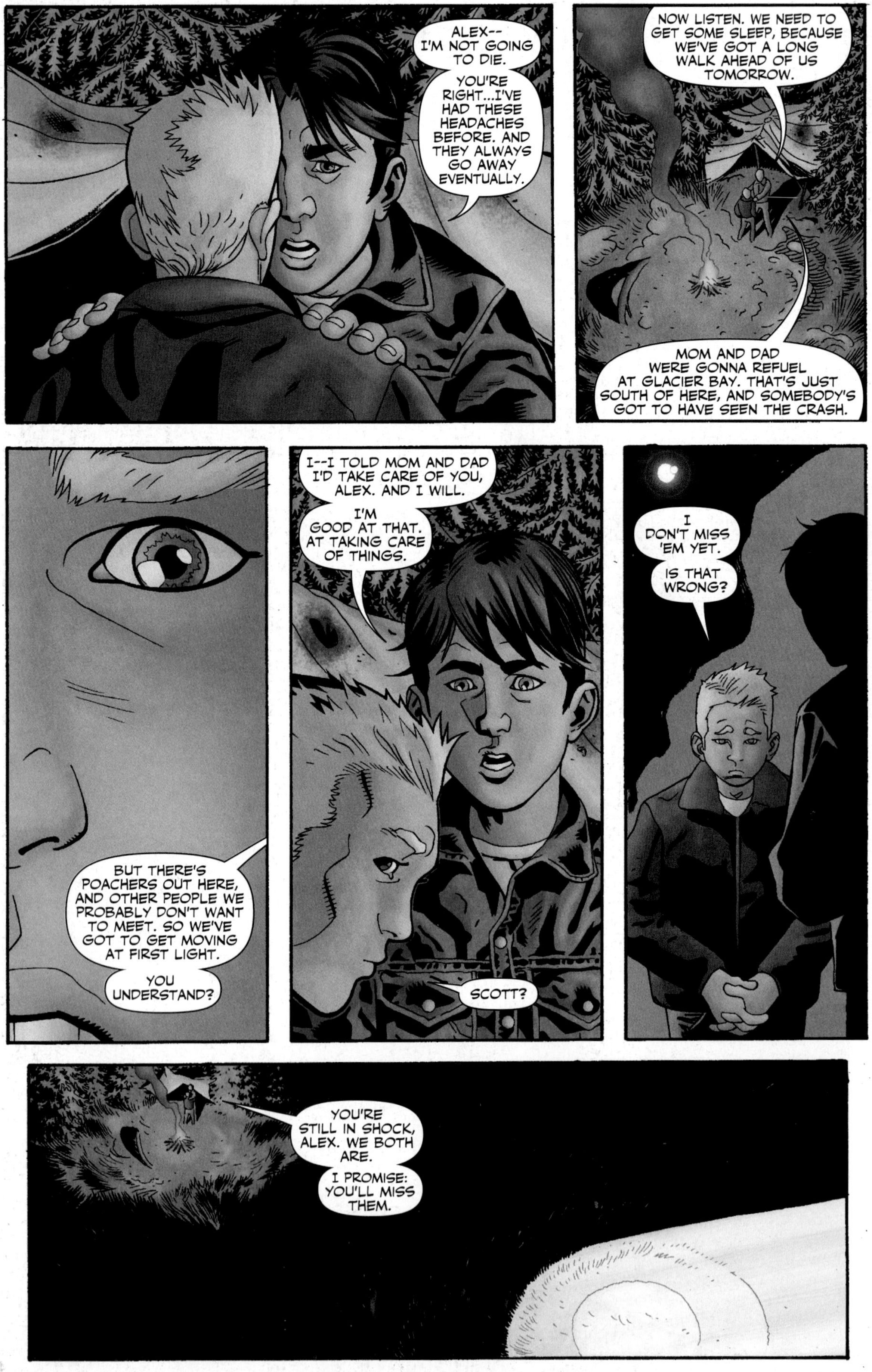
ALEX-- I'M NOT GOING TO DIE.
YOU'RE RIGHT...I'VE HAD THESE HEADACHES BEFORE. AND THEY ALWAYS GO AWAY EVENTUALLY.
NOW LISTEN. WE NEED TO GET SOME SLEEP, BECAUSE WE'VE GOT A LONG WALK AHEAD OF US TOMORROW.
MOM AND DAD WERE GONNA REFUEL AT GLACIER BAY. THAT'S JUST SOUTH OF HERE, AND SOMEBODY'S GOT TO HAVE SEEN THE CRASH.
BUT THERE'S POACHERS OUT HERE, AND OTHER PEOPLE WE PROBABLY DON'T WANT TO MEET. SO WE'VE GOT TO GET MOVING AT FIRST LIGHT.
YOU UNDERSTAND?
I--I TOLD MOM AND DAD I'D TAKE CARE OF YOU, ALEX. AND I WILL.
I'M GOOD AT THAT. AT TAKING CARE OF THINGS.
SCOTT?
I DON'T MISS 'EM YET.
IS THAT WRONG?
YOU'RE STILL IN SHOCK, ALEX. WE BOTH ARE.
I PROMISE: YOU'LL MISS THEM.

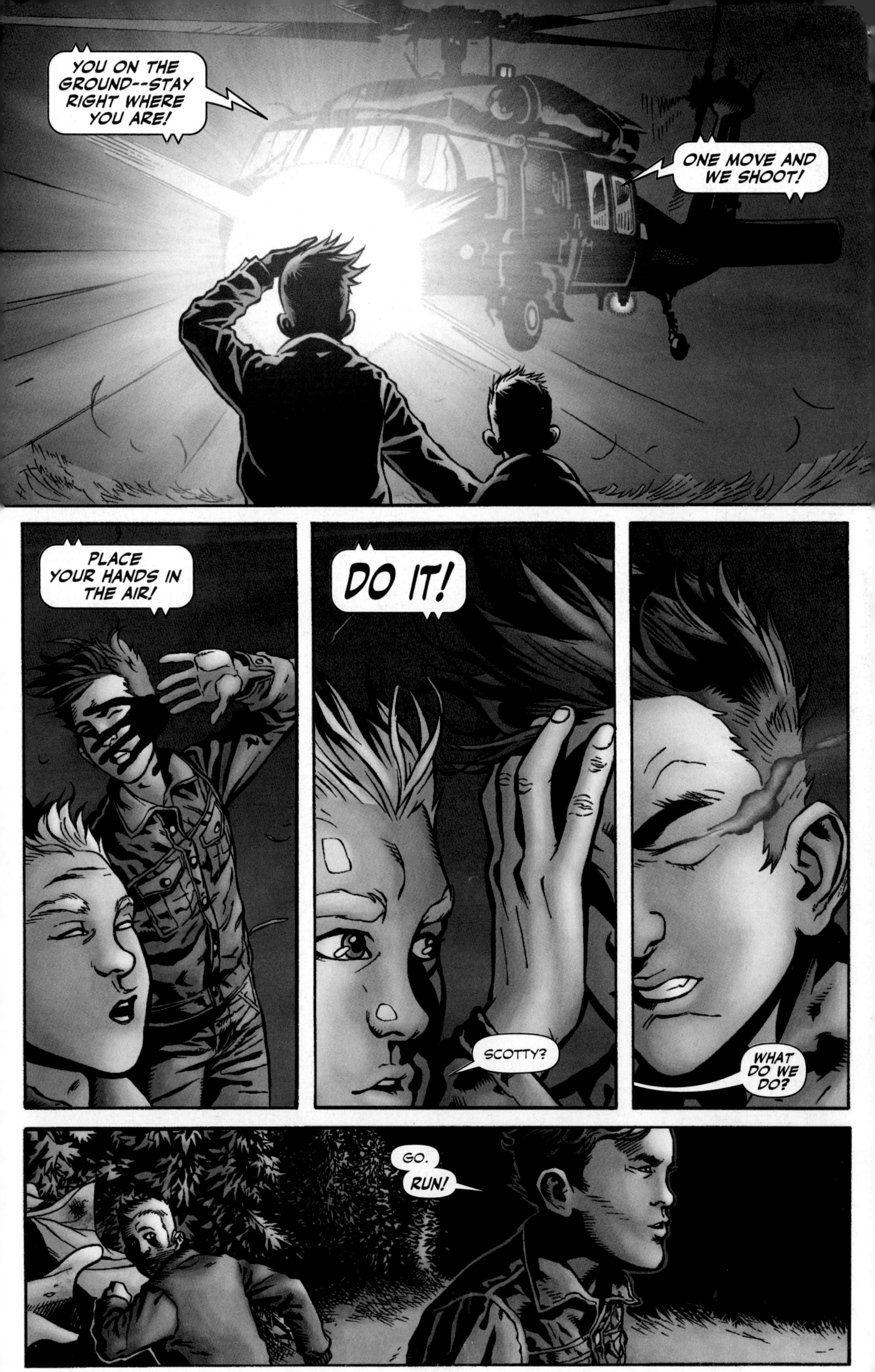
YOU ON THE GROUND--STAY RIGHT WHERE YOU ARE!
ONE MOVE AND WE SHOOT!
PLACE YOUR HANDS IN THE AIR!
DO IT!
SCOTTY?
WHAT DO WE DO?
GO.
RUN!

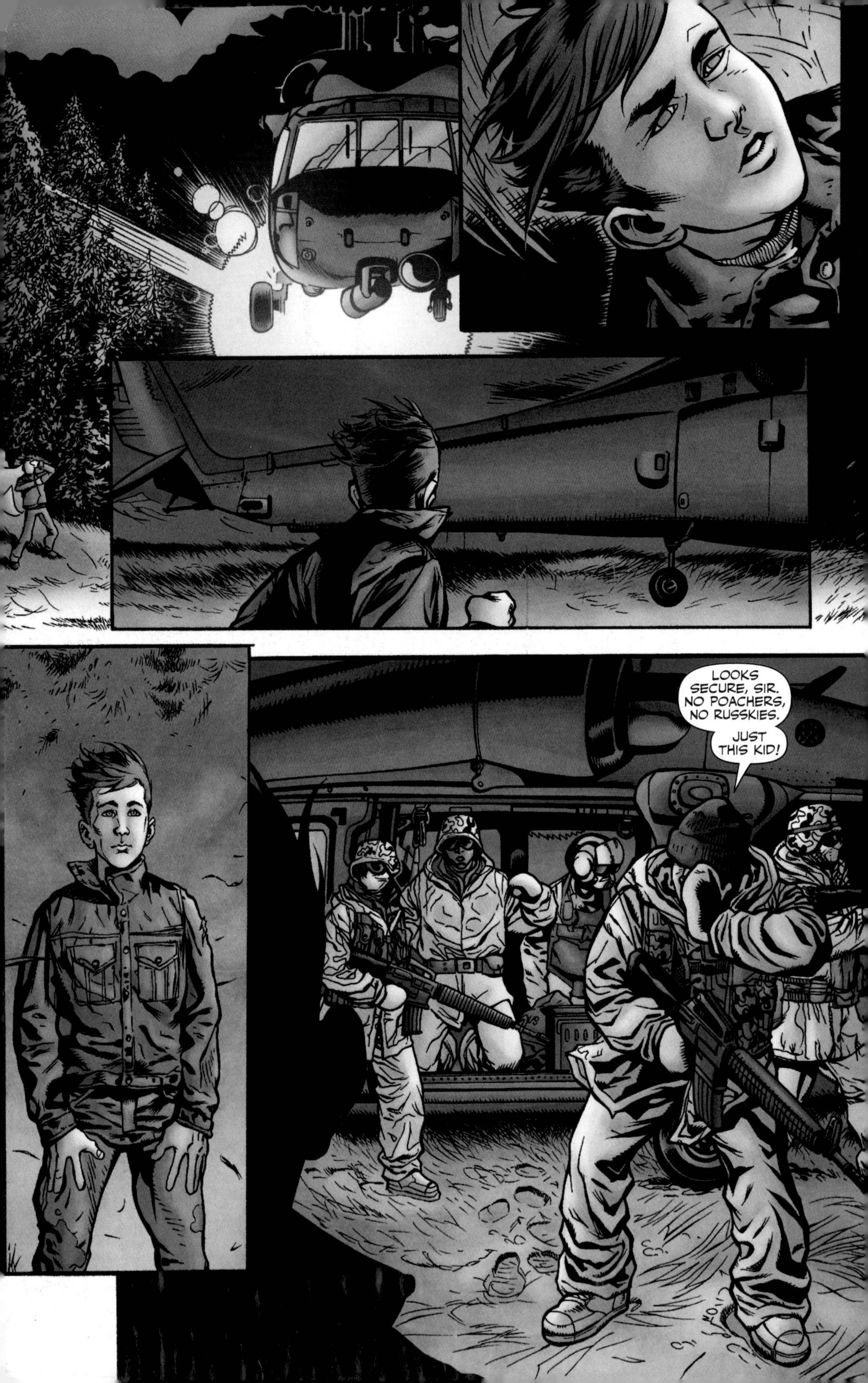
LOOKS SECURE, SIR. NO POACHERS, NO RUSSKIES.
JUST THIS KID!

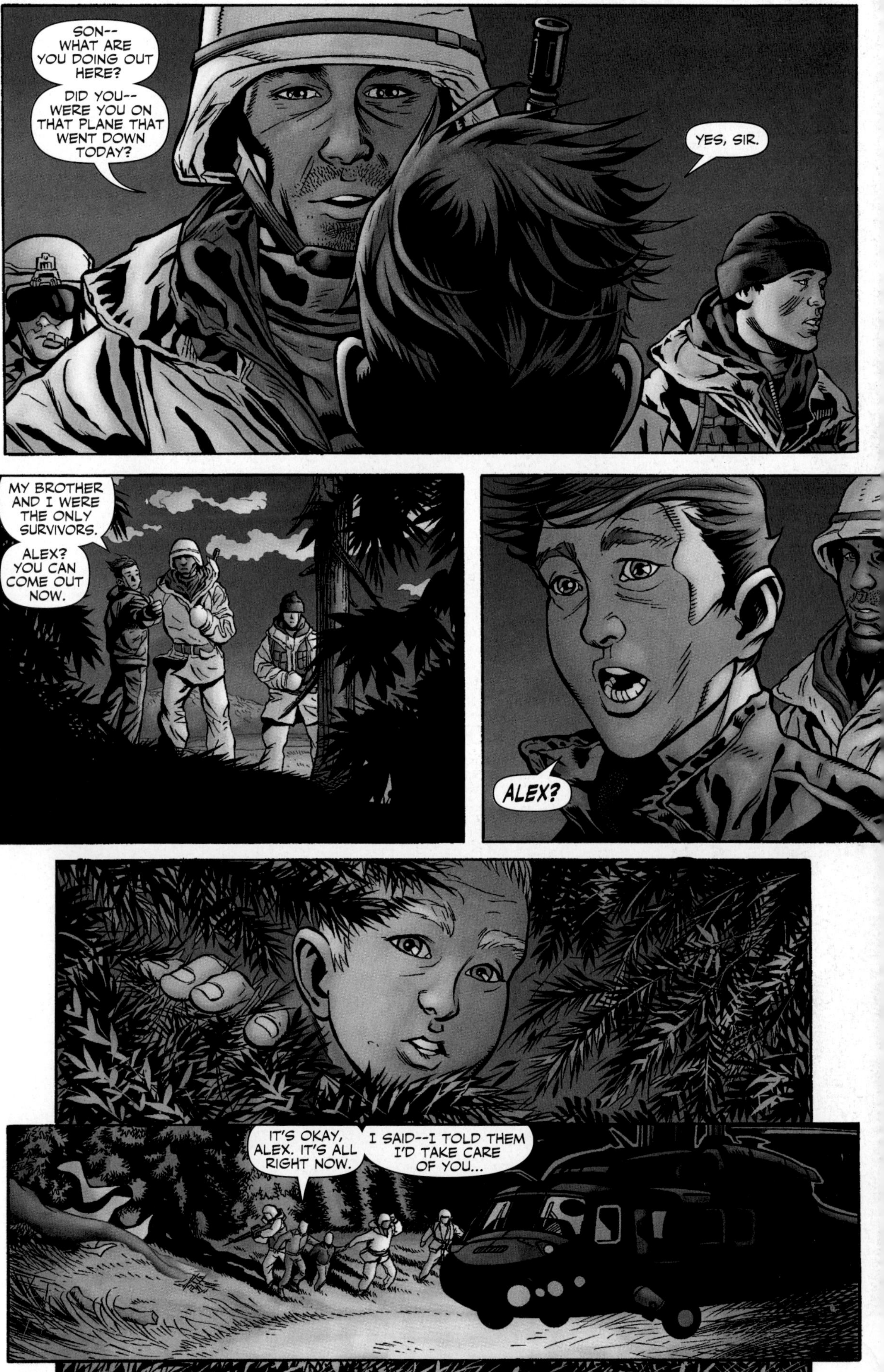
SON-- WHAT ARE YOU DOING OUT HERE?
DID YOU-- WERE YOU ON THAT PLANE THAT WENT DOWN TODAY?
YES, SIR.
MY BROTHER AND I WERE THE ONLY SURVIVORS.
ALEX? YOU CAN COME OUT NOW.
ALEX?
IT'S OKAY, ALEX. IT'S ALL RIGHT NOW.
I SAID--I TOLD THEM I'D TAKE CARE OF YOU...

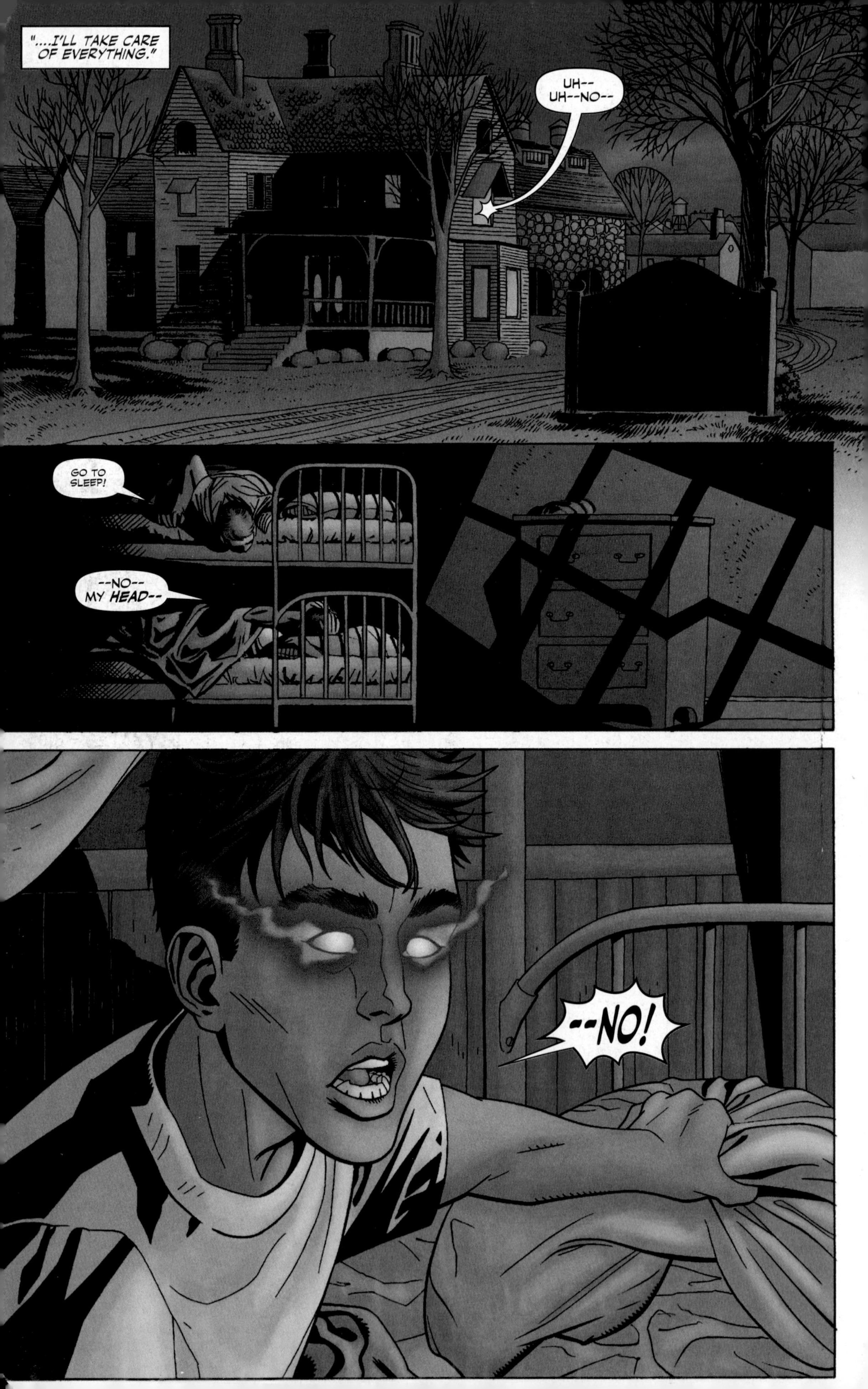
"....I'LL TAKE CARE OF EVERYTHING."
UH-- UH--NO--
GO TO SLEEP!
--NO-- MY HEAD--
--NO!

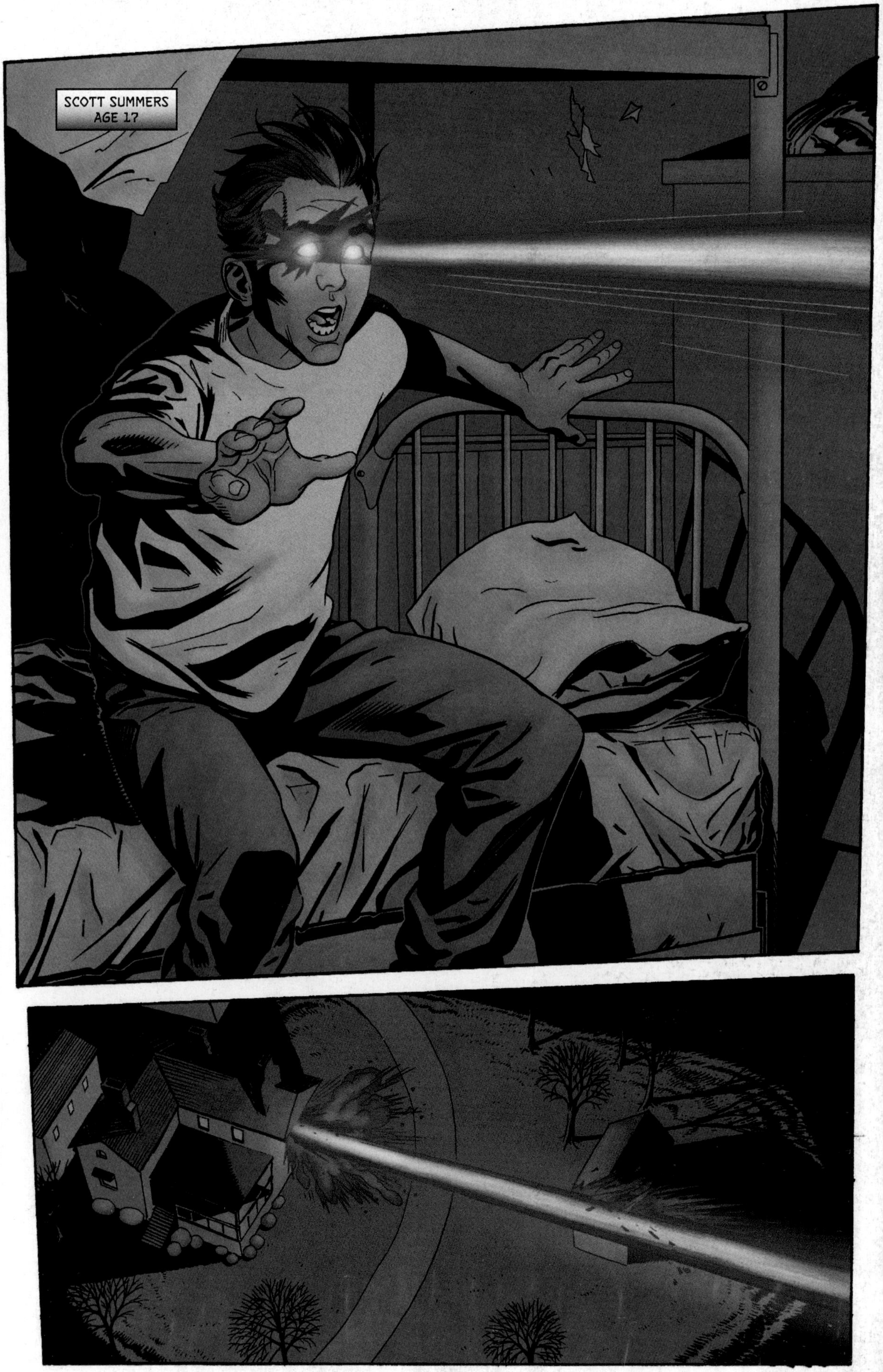
SCOTT SUMMERS
AGE 17

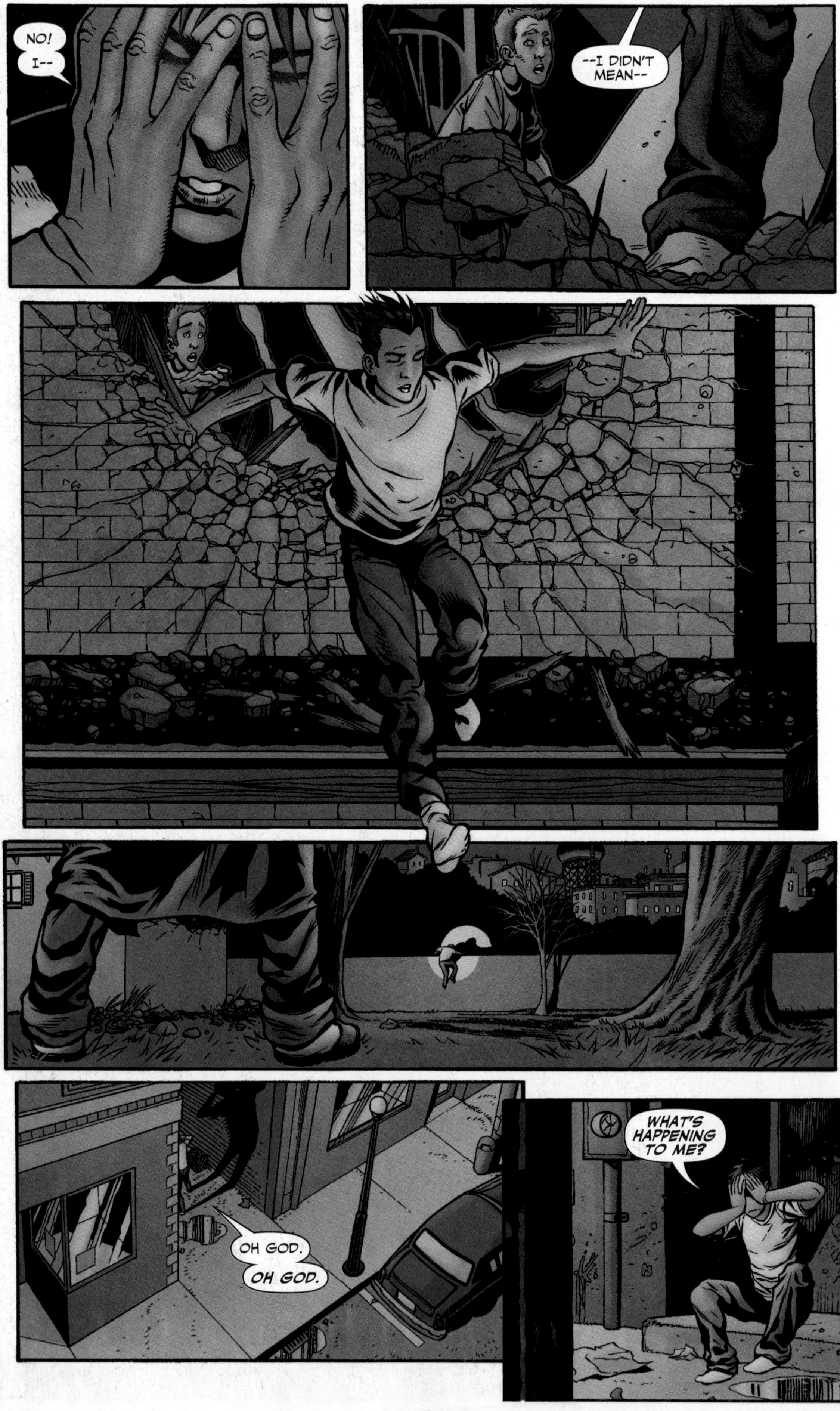
NO! I--
--I DIDN'T MEAN--
OH GOD.
OH GOD.
WHAT'S HAPPENING TO ME?

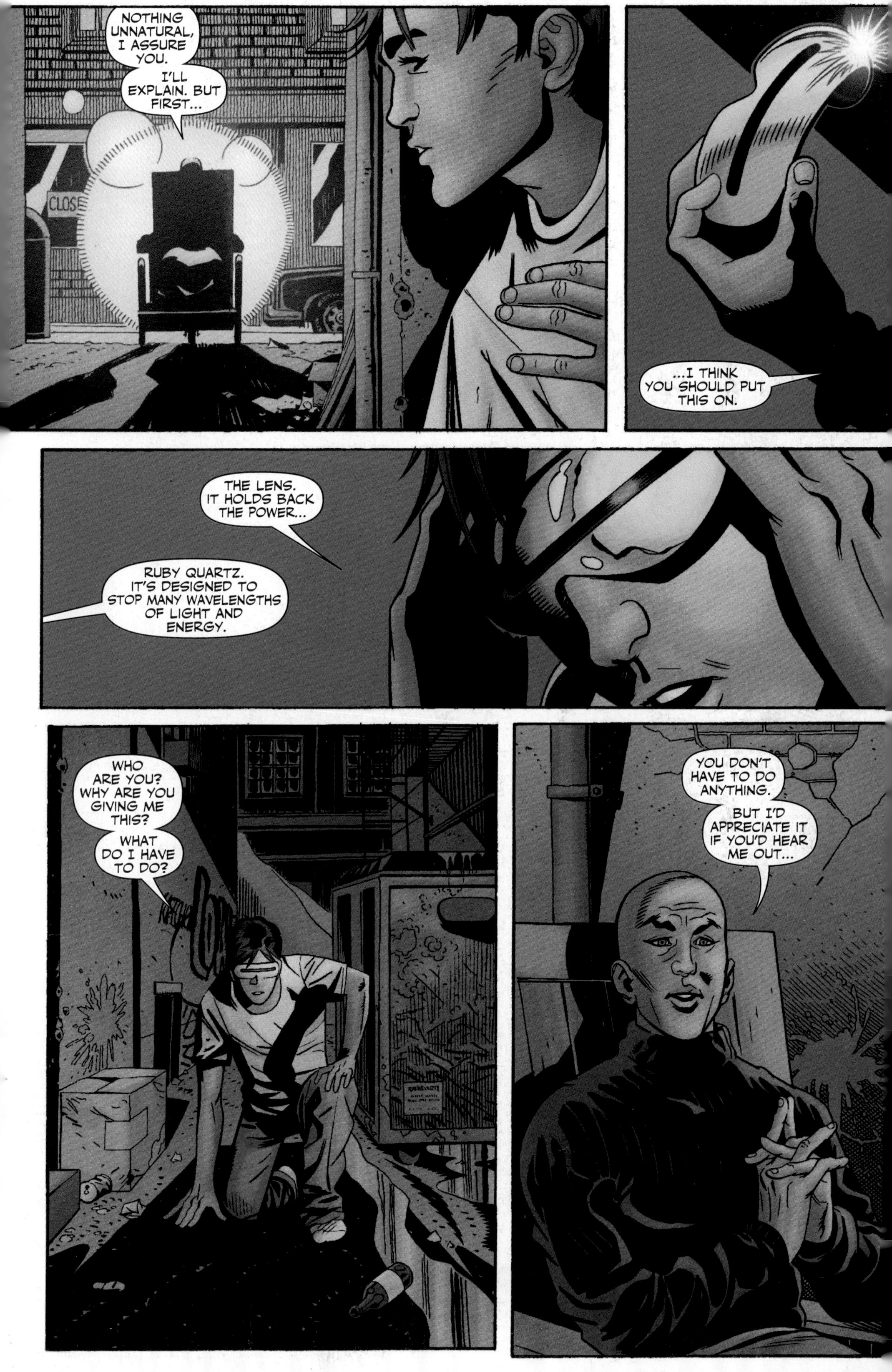
NOTHING UNNATURAL, I ASSURE YOU.
I'LL EXPLAIN. BUT FIRST...
CLOSE
...I THINK YOU SHOULD PUT THIS ON.
THE LENS. IT HOLDS BACK THE POWER...
RUBY QUARTZ. IT'S DESIGNED TO STOP MANY WAVELENGTHS OF LIGHT AND ENERGY.
WHO ARE YOU? WHY ARE YOU GIVING ME THIS?
WHAT DO I HAVE TO DO?
YOU DON'T HAVE TO DO ANYTHING.
BUT I'D APPRECIATE IT IF YOU'D HEAR ME OUT...

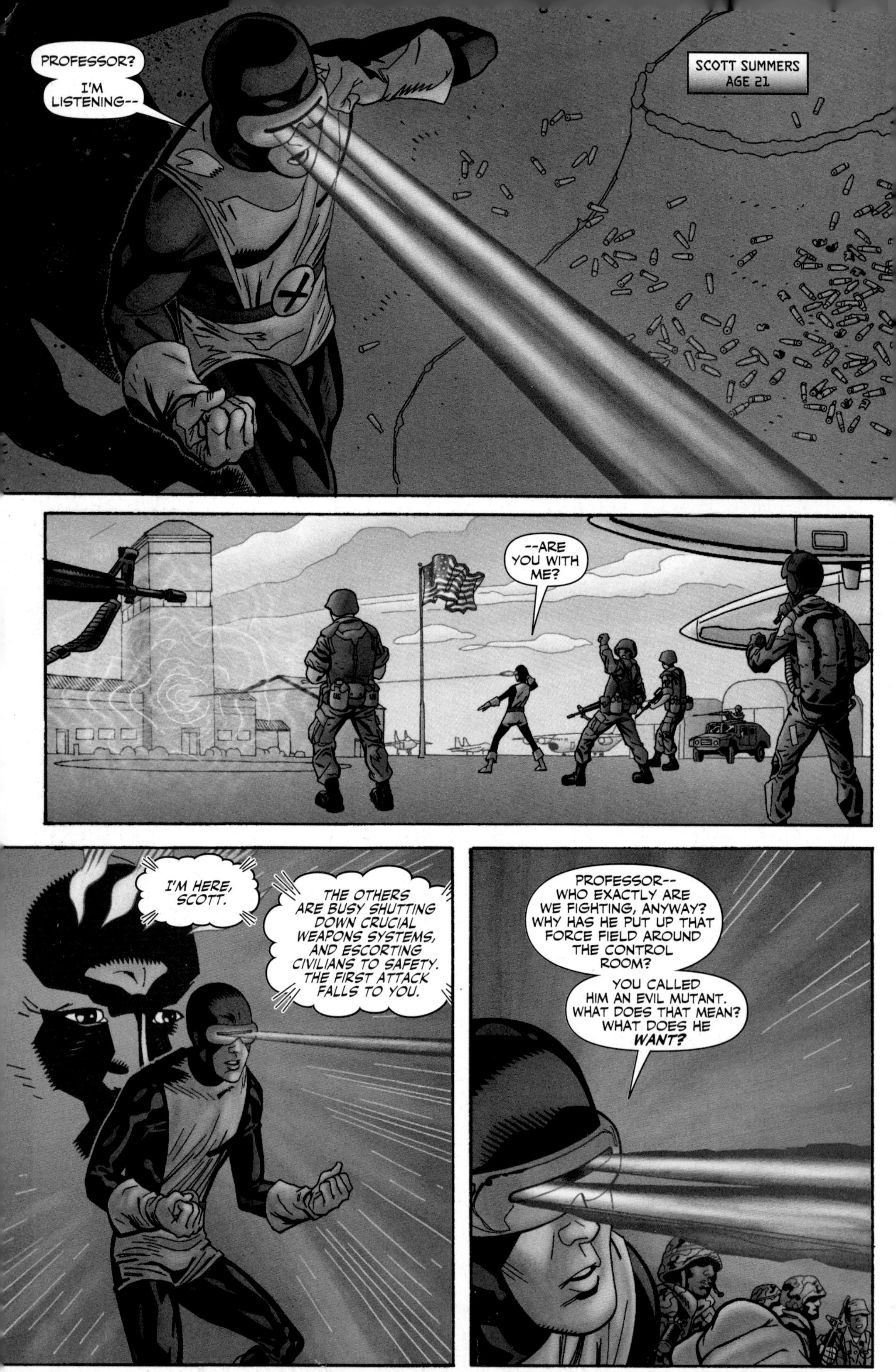
PROFESSOR?
I'M LISTENING--
SCOTT SUMMERS AGE 21
--ARE YOU WITH ME?
I'M HERE, SCOTT.
THE OTHERS ARE BUSY SHUTTING DOWN CRUCIAL WEAPONS SYSTEMS, AND ESCORTING CIVILIANS TO SAFETY. THE FIRST ATTACK FALLS TO YOU.
PROFESSOR-- WHO EXACTLY ARE WE FIGHTING, ANYWAY? WHY HAS HE PUT UP THAT FORCE FIELD AROUND THE CONTROL ROOM?
YOU CALLED HIM AN EVIL MUTANT. WHAT DOES THAT MEAN? WHAT DOES HE *WANT?*

SCOTT-- THIS IS HARDLY THE TIME FOR PSYCHOANALYSIS.

PLEASE CONCENTRATE ON TACTICS.

THAT FORCE FIELD IS MAGNETIC.

LINK YOUR MIND WITH MINE... SEE WHAT I SEE, ON THE MANSION'S COMPUTER SCREEN...

CAN YOU SEE IT? THE DIRECTION OF THE CURRENT?

YES.

GOOD. FIRE OFF A BEAM DIRECTLY PARALLEL TO THE FORCE LINES...

GOT IT.

JUST A THIN BURST DOWN ALONG THE CURRENT LINE... THEN A WIDER BEAM RUNNING PERPENDICULAR TO THE--

PROFESSOR!

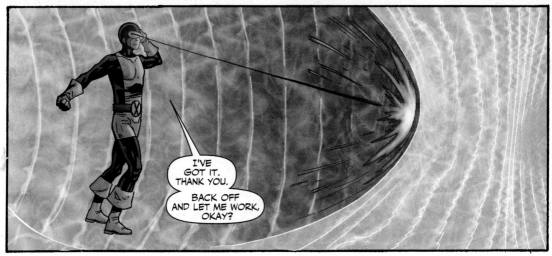

I'VE GOT IT. THANK YOU.

BACK OFF AND LET ME WORK, OKAY?

AS YOU WISH, SCOTT...

...LESSON OVER.

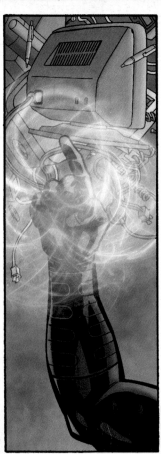

UHHH!

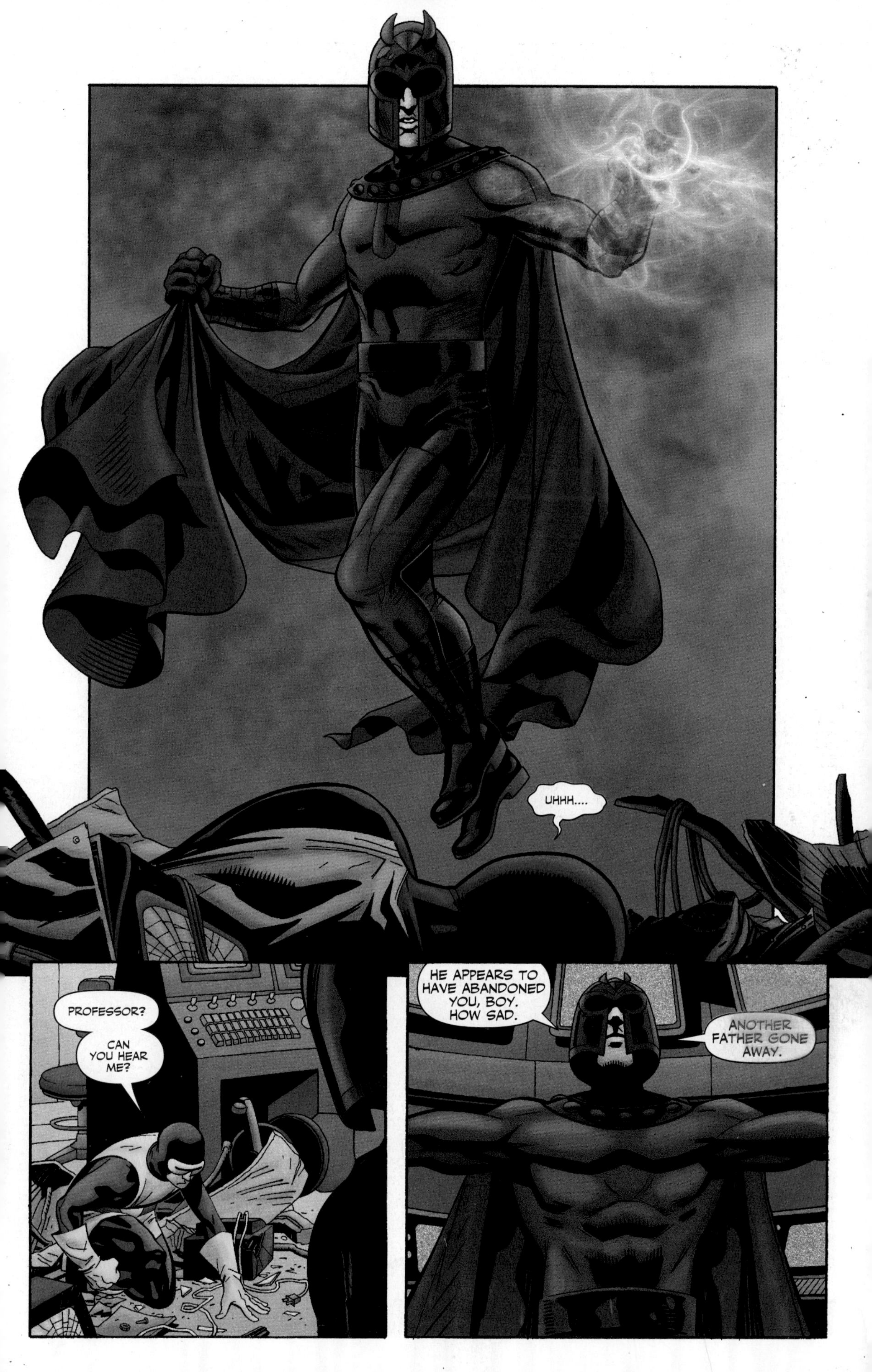
UHHH....
PROFESSOR?
CAN YOU HEAR ME?
HE APPEARS TO HAVE ABANDONED YOU, BOY. HOW SAD.
ANOTHER FATHER GONE AWAY.

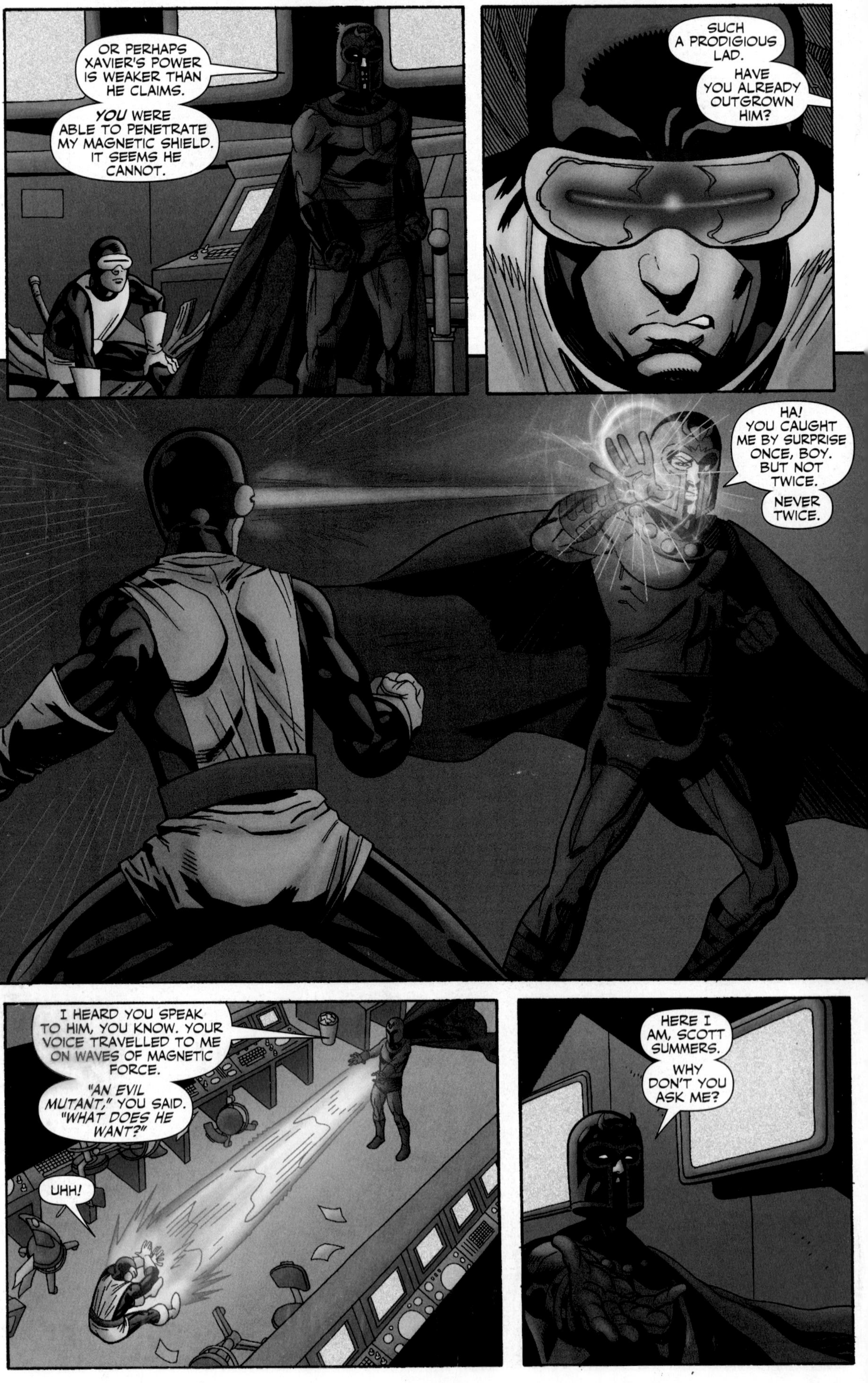
OR PERHAPS XAVIER'S POWER IS WEAKER THAN HE CLAIMS.
YOU WERE ABLE TO PENETRATE MY MAGNETIC SHIELD. IT SEEMS HE CANNOT.
SUCH A PRODIGIOUS LAD.
HAVE YOU ALREADY OUTGROWN HIM?
HA! YOU CAUGHT ME BY SURPRISE ONCE, BOY. BUT NOT TWICE.
NEVER TWICE.
I HEARD YOU SPEAK TO HIM, YOU KNOW. YOUR VOICE TRAVELLED TO ME ON WAVES OF MAGNETIC FORCE.
"AN EVIL MUTANT," YOU SAID. "WHAT DOES HE WANT?"
UHH!
HERE I AM, SCOTT SUMMERS.
WHY DON'T YOU ASK ME?

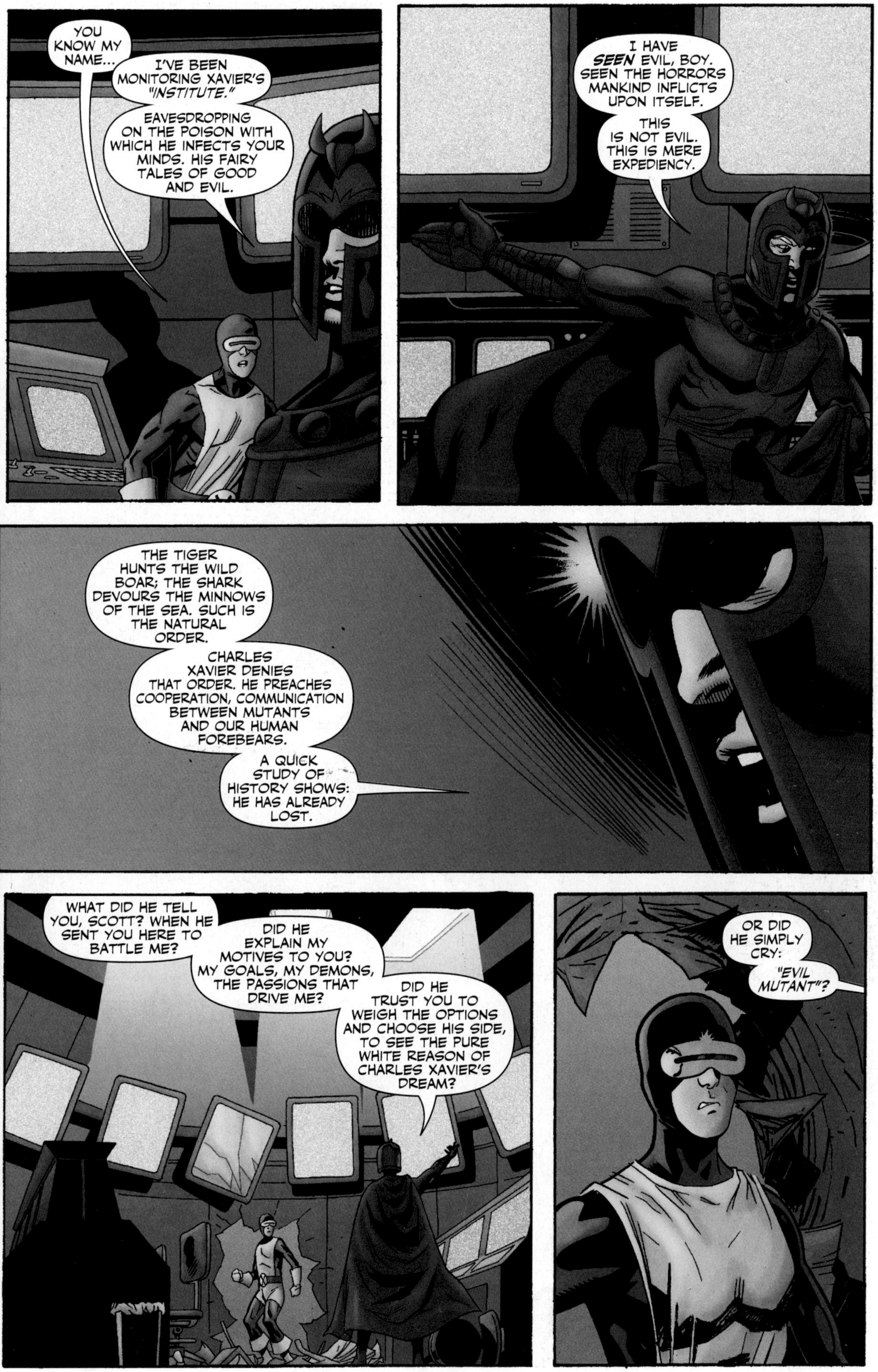
YOU KNOW MY NAME...
I'VE BEEN MONITORING XAVIER'S "INSTITUTE."
EAVESDROPPING ON THE POISON WITH WHICH HE INFECTS YOUR MINDS. HIS FAIRY TALES OF GOOD AND EVIL.
I HAVE *SEEN* EVIL, BOY. SEEN THE HORRORS MANKIND INFLICTS UPON ITSELF.
THIS IS NOT EVIL. THIS IS MERE EXPEDIENCY.
THE TIGER HUNTS THE WILD BOAR; THE SHARK DEVOURS THE MINNOWS OF THE SEA. SUCH IS THE NATURAL ORDER.
CHARLES XAVIER DENIES THAT ORDER. HE PREACHES COOPERATION, COMMUNICATION BETWEEN MUTANTS AND OUR HUMAN FOREBEARS.
A QUICK STUDY OF HISTORY SHOWS: HE HAS ALREADY LOST.
WHAT DID HE TELL YOU, SCOTT? WHEN HE SENT YOU HERE TO BATTLE ME?
DID HE EXPLAIN MY MOTIVES TO YOU? MY GOALS, MY DEMONS, THE PASSIONS THAT DRIVE ME?
DID HE TRUST YOU TO WEIGH THE OPTIONS AND CHOOSE HIS SIDE, TO SEE THE PURE WHITE REASON OF CHARLES XAVIER'S DREAM?
OR DID HE SIMPLY CRY:
"EVIL MUTANT"?

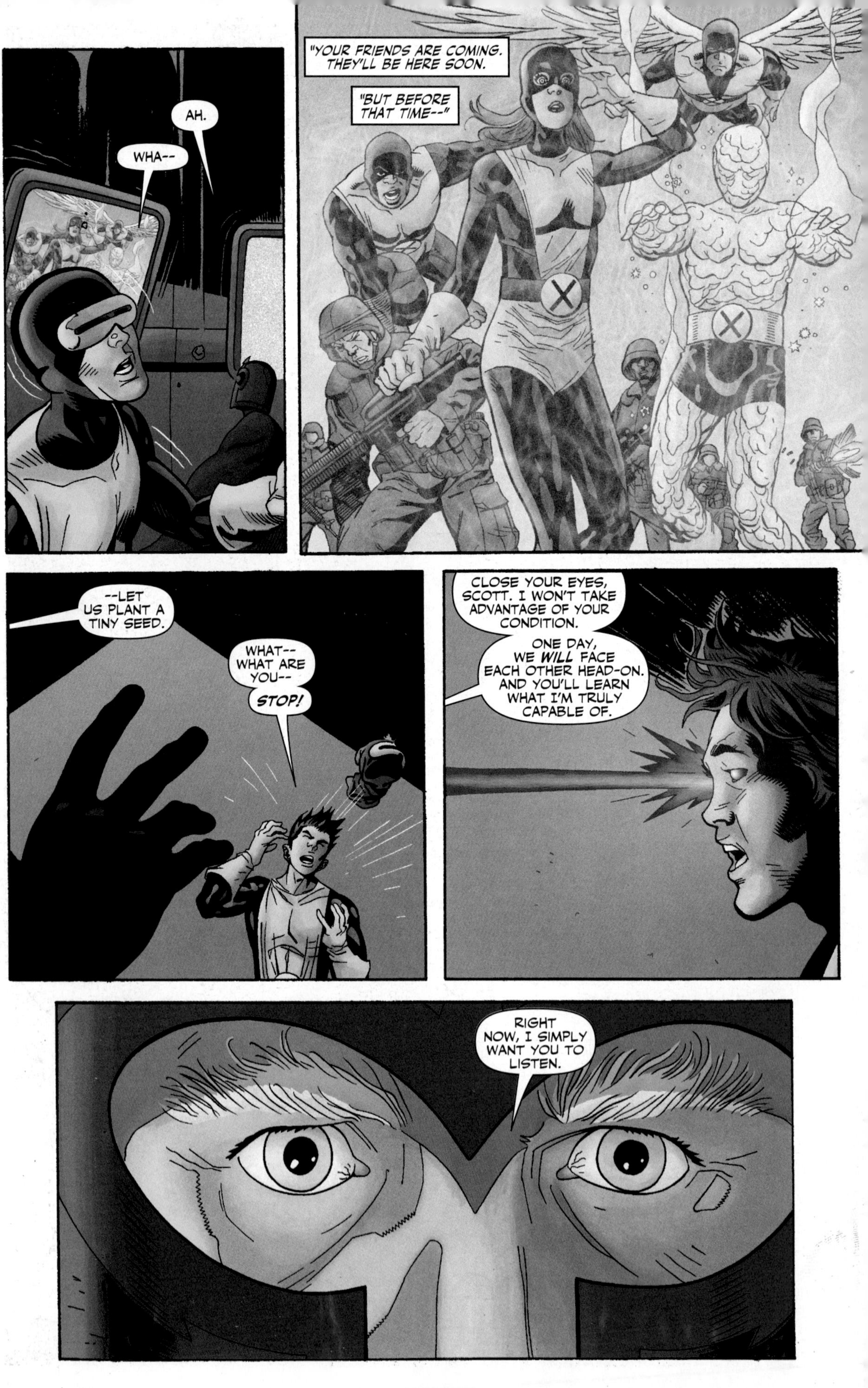
AH.
WHA--
"YOUR FRIENDS ARE COMING. THEY'LL BE HERE SOON.
"BUT BEFORE THAT TIME--"
--LET US PLANT A TINY SEED.
WHAT-- WHAT ARE YOU--
STOP!
CLOSE YOUR EYES, SCOTT. I WON'T TAKE ADVANTAGE OF YOUR CONDITION.
ONE DAY, WE WILL FACE EACH OTHER HEAD-ON. AND YOU'LL LEARN WHAT I'M TRULY CAPABLE OF.
RIGHT NOW, I SIMPLY WANT YOU TO LISTEN.

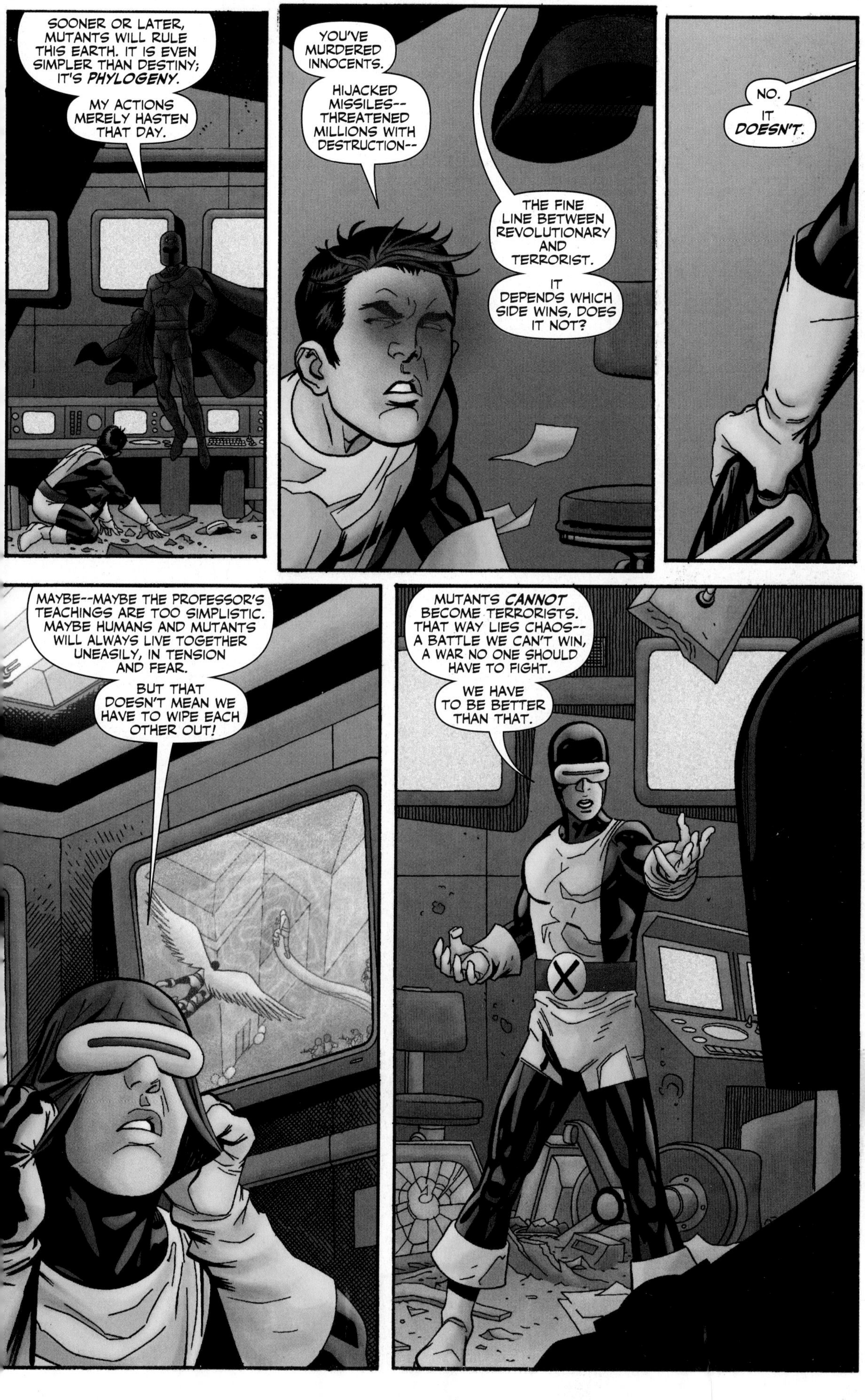
SOONER OR LATER, MUTANTS WILL RULE THIS EARTH. IT IS EVEN SIMPLER THAN DESTINY; IT'S PHYLOGENY.
MY ACTIONS MERELY HASTEN THAT DAY.
YOU'VE MURDERED INNOCENTS.
HIJACKED MISSILES--THREATENED MILLIONS WITH DESTRUCTION--
THE FINE LINE BETWEEN REVOLUTIONARY AND TERRORIST.
IT DEPENDS WHICH SIDE WINS, DOES IT NOT?
NO.
IT DOESN'T.
MAYBE--MAYBE THE PROFESSOR'S TEACHINGS ARE TOO SIMPLISTIC. MAYBE HUMANS AND MUTANTS WILL ALWAYS LIVE TOGETHER UNEASILY, IN TENSION AND FEAR.
BUT THAT DOESN'T MEAN WE HAVE TO WIPE EACH OTHER OUT!
MUTANTS CANNOT BECOME TERRORISTS. THAT WAY LIES CHAOS--A BATTLE WE CAN'T WIN, A WAR NO ONE SHOULD HAVE TO FIGHT.
WE HAVE TO BE BETTER THAN THAT.

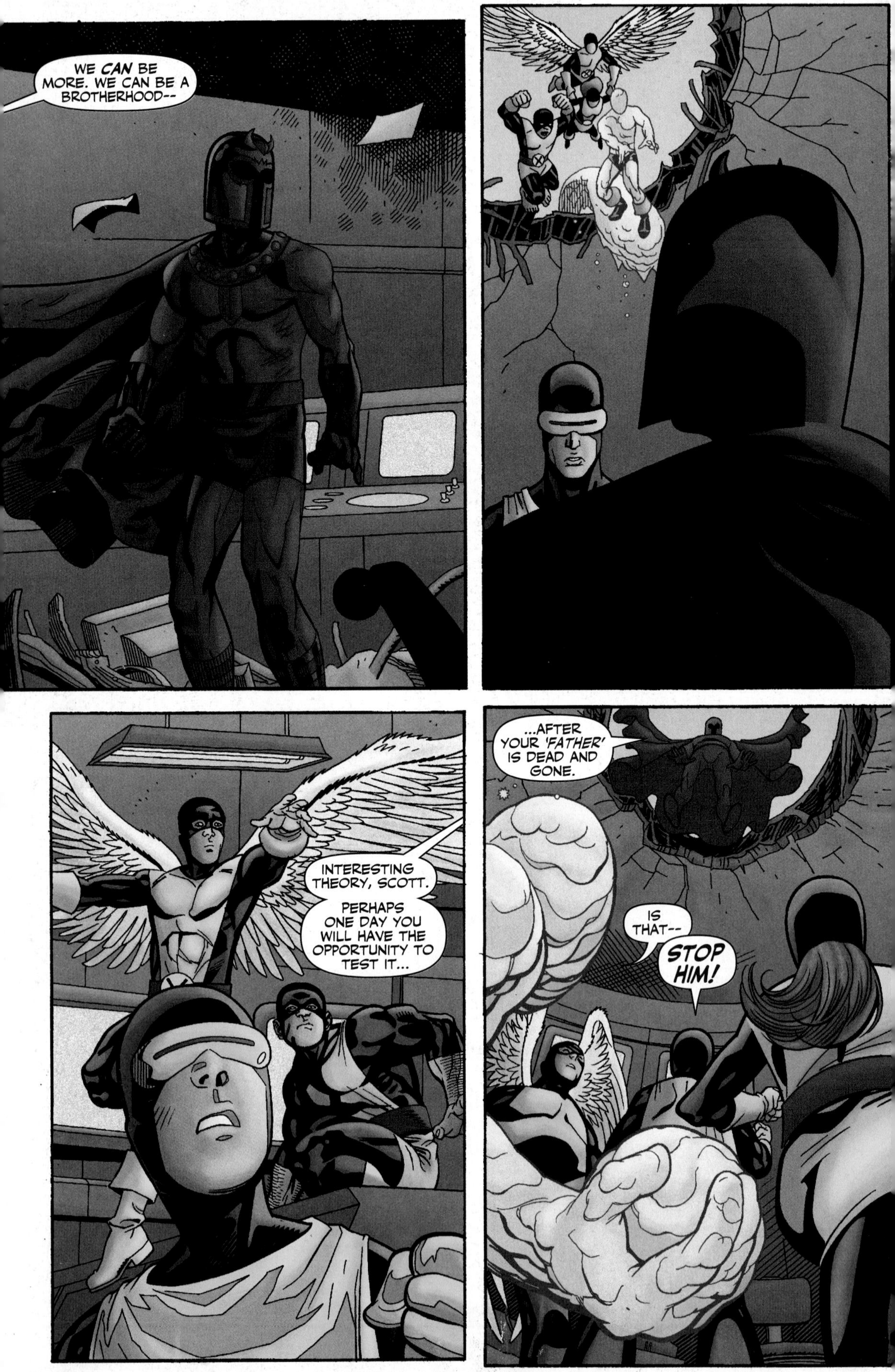
WE CAN BE MORE. WE CAN BE A BROTHERHOOD--
INTERESTING THEORY, SCOTT.
PERHAPS ONE DAY YOU WILL HAVE THE OPPORTUNITY TO TEST IT...
...AFTER YOUR 'FATHER' IS DEAD AND GONE.
IS THAT--
STOP HIM!

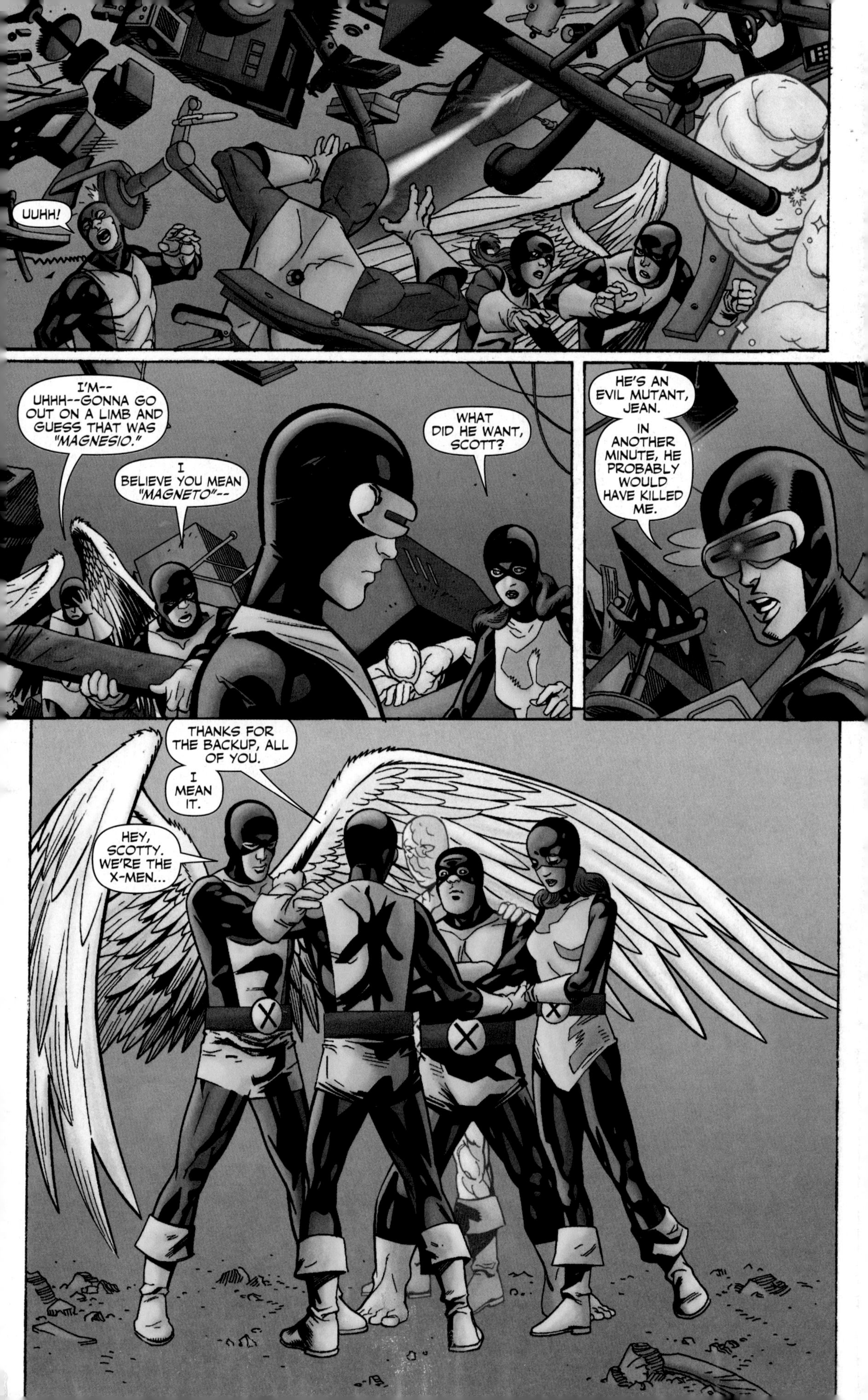
UUHH!
I'M--UHHH--GONNA GO OUT ON A LIMB AND GUESS THAT WAS "MAGNESIO."
I BELIEVE YOU MEAN "MAGNETO"--
WHAT DID HE WANT, SCOTT?
HE'S AN EVIL MUTANT, JEAN.
IN ANOTHER MINUTE, HE PROBABLY WOULD HAVE KILLED ME.
THANKS FOR THE BACKUP, ALL OF YOU.
I MEAN IT.
HEY, SCOTTY. WE'RE THE X-MEN...

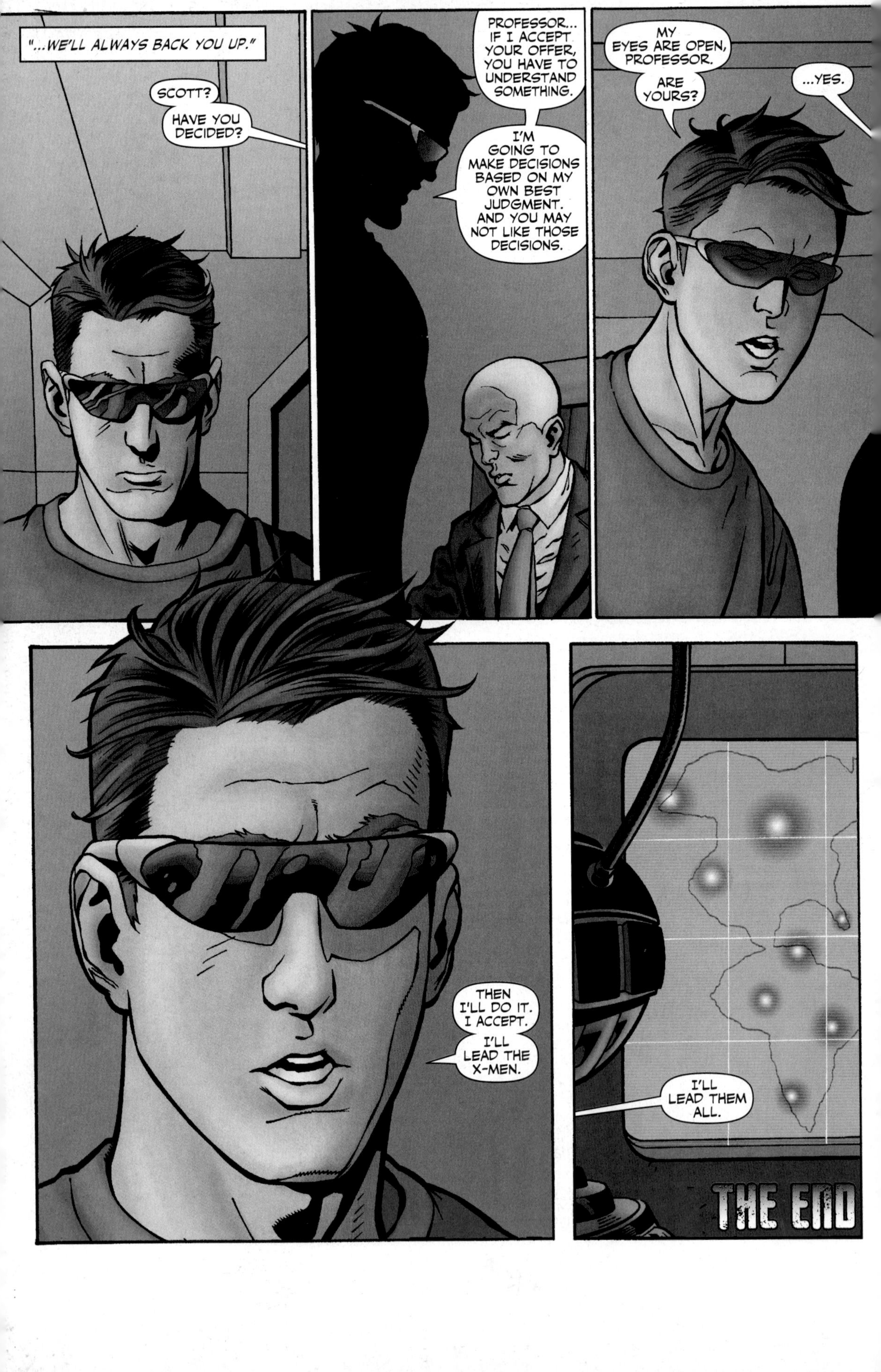
"...WE'LL ALWAYS BACK YOU UP."
SCOTT?
HAVE YOU DECIDED?
PROFESSOR... IF I ACCEPT YOUR OFFER, YOU HAVE TO UNDERSTAND SOMETHING.
I'M GOING TO MAKE DECISIONS BASED ON MY OWN BEST JUDGMENT. AND YOU MAY NOT LIKE THOSE DECISIONS.
MY EYES ARE OPEN, PROFESSOR.
ARE YOURS?
...YES.
THEN I'LL DO IT. I ACCEPT.
I'LL LEAD THE X-MEN.
I'LL LEAD THEM ALL.
THE END

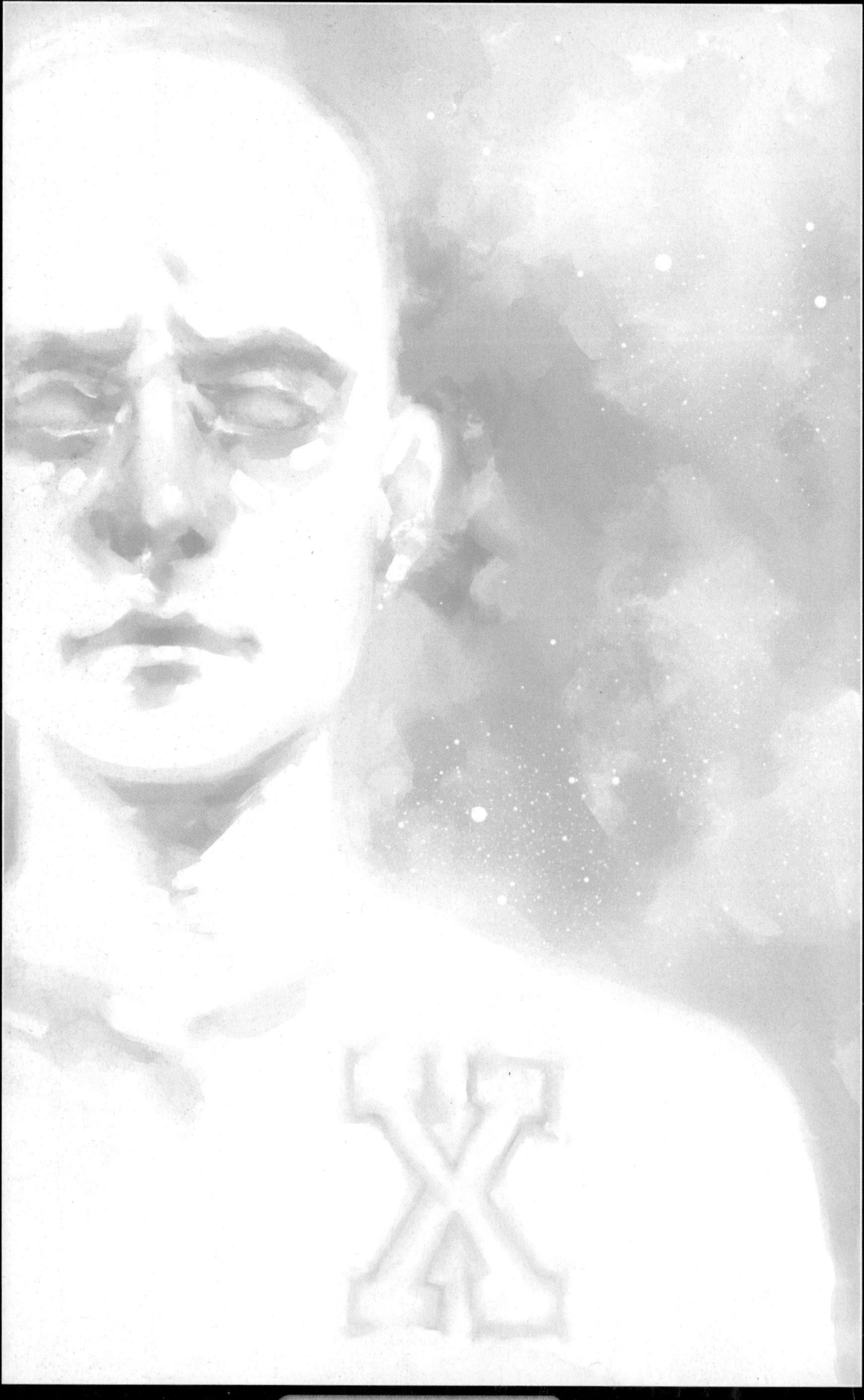

X-MEN ORIGINS: ICEMAN

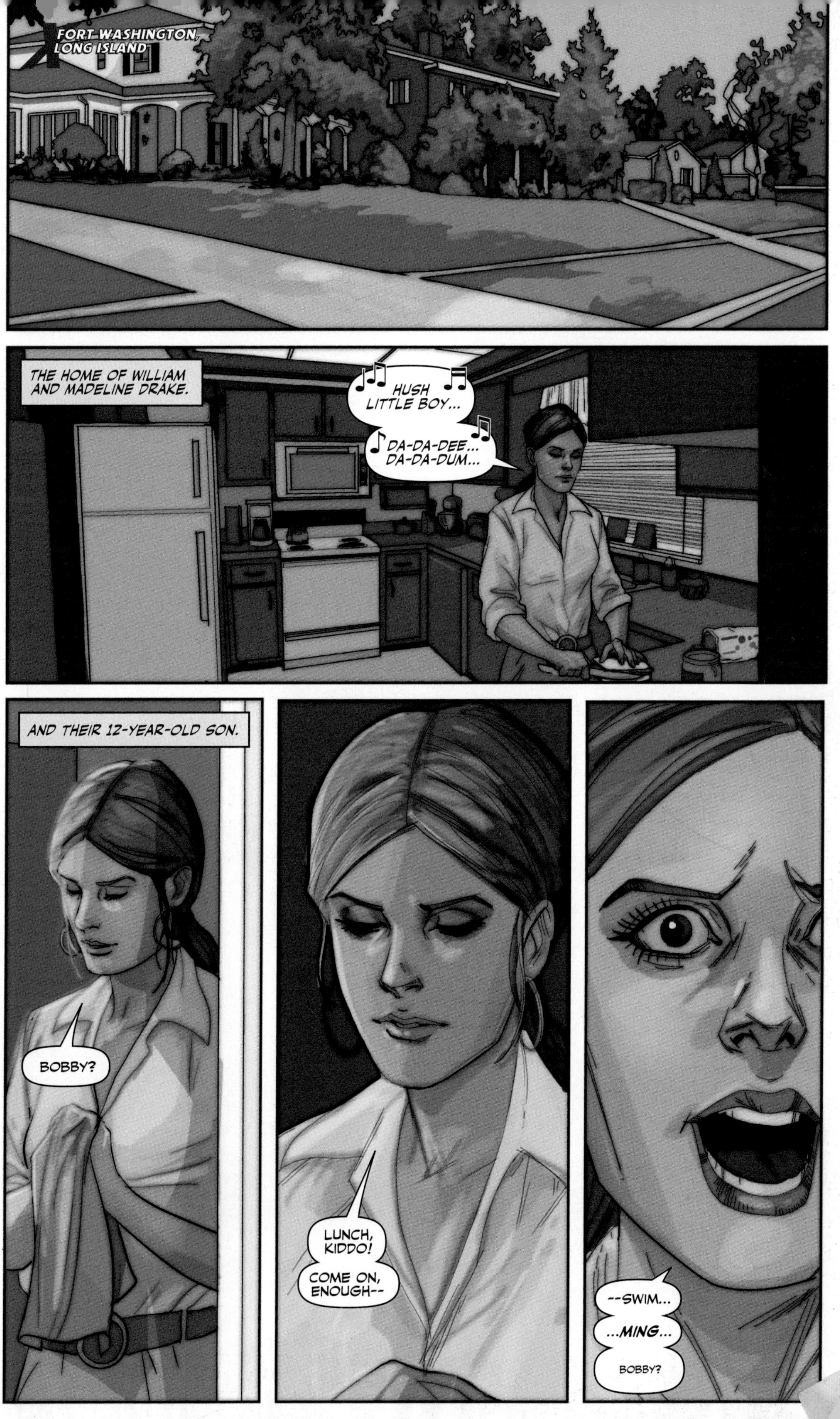
FORT WASHINGTON, LONG ISLAND
THE HOME OF WILLIAM AND MADELINE DRAKE.
HUSH LITTLE BOY...
DA-DA-DEE... DA-DA-DUM...
AND THEIR 12-YEAR-OLD SON.
BOBBY?
LUNCH, KIDDO!
COME ON, ENOUGH--
--SWIM...
...MING...
BOBBY?

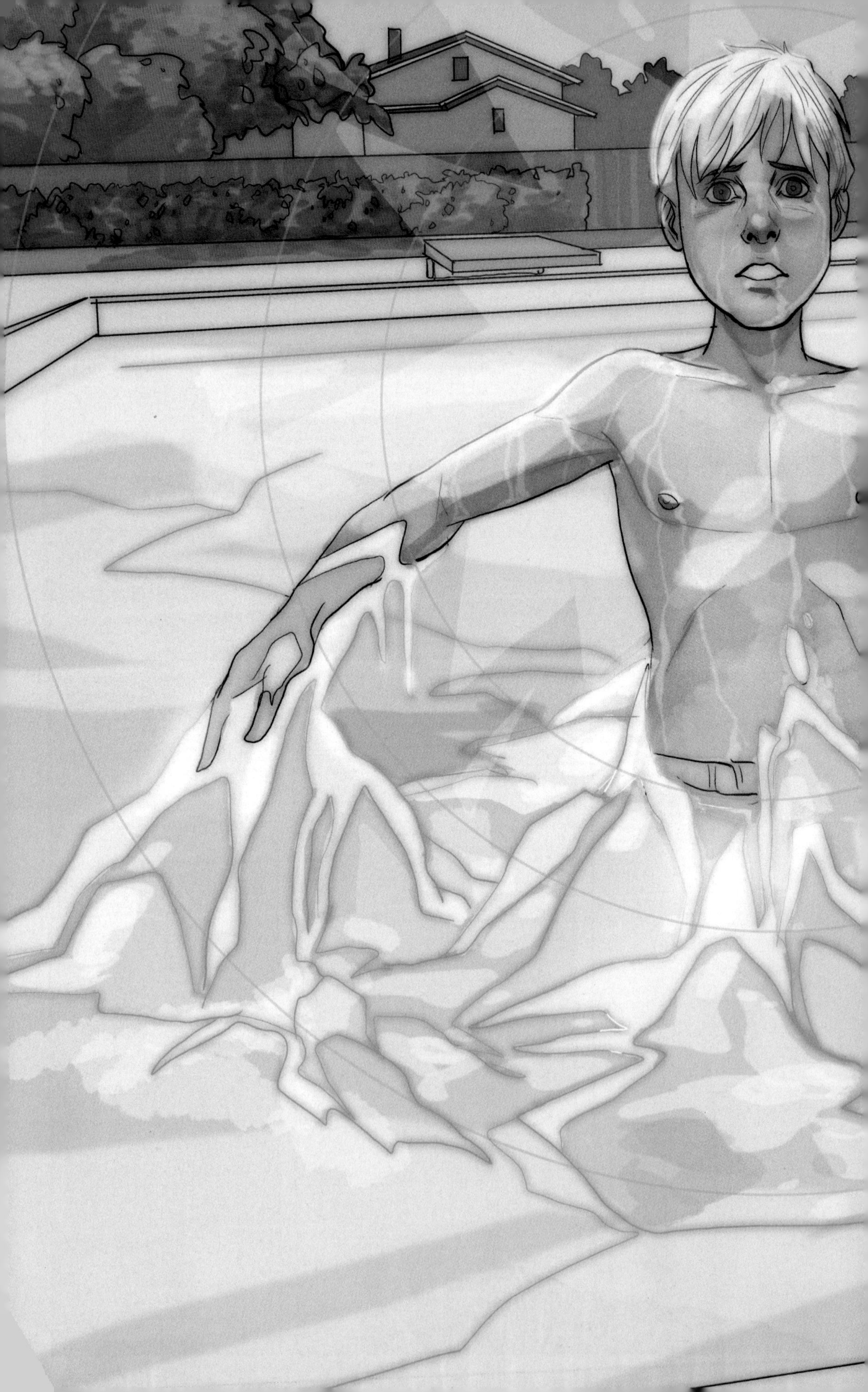

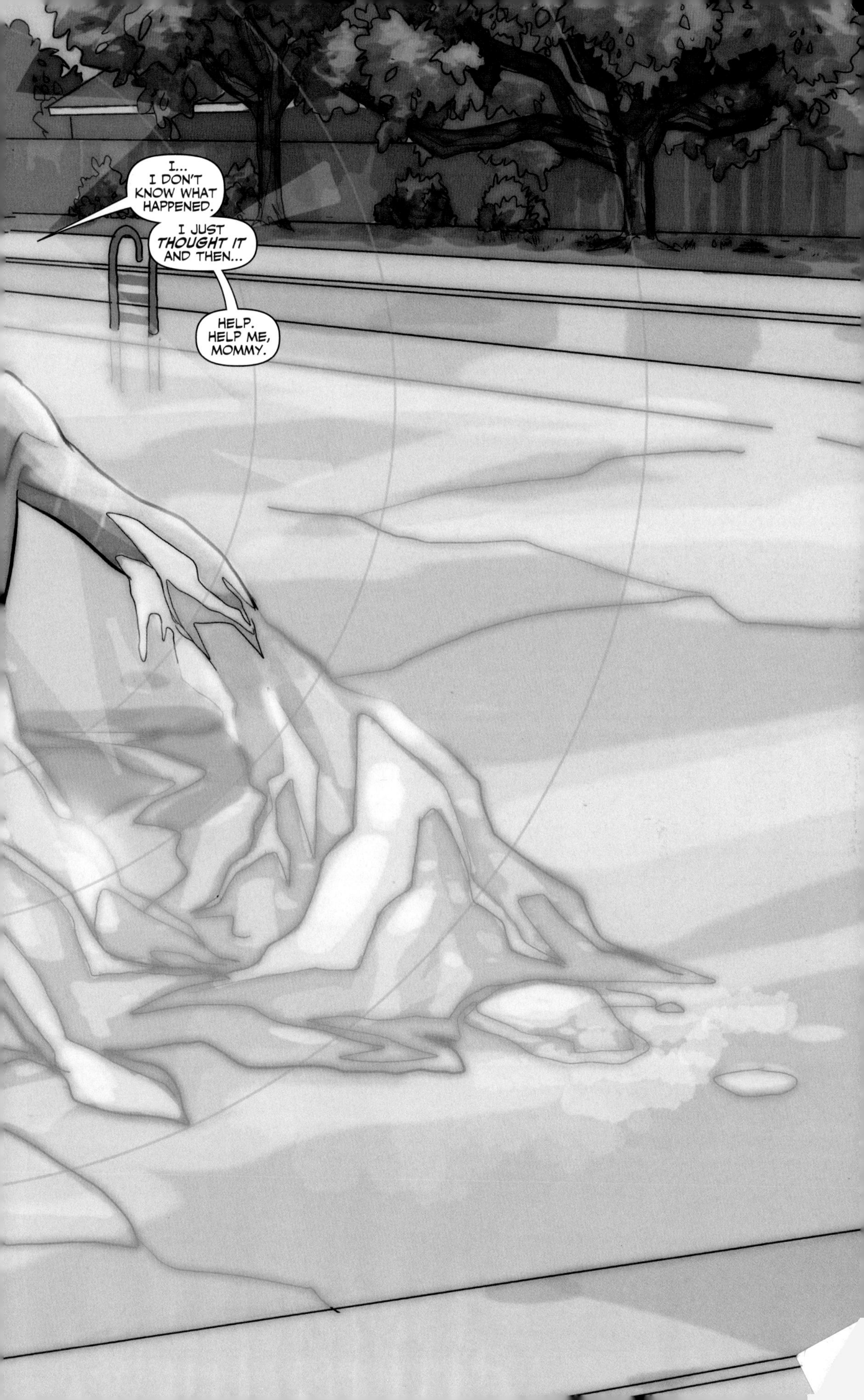
I... I DON'T KNOW WHAT HAPPENED.
I JUST *THOUGHT IT* AND THEN...
HELP. HELP ME, MOMMY.

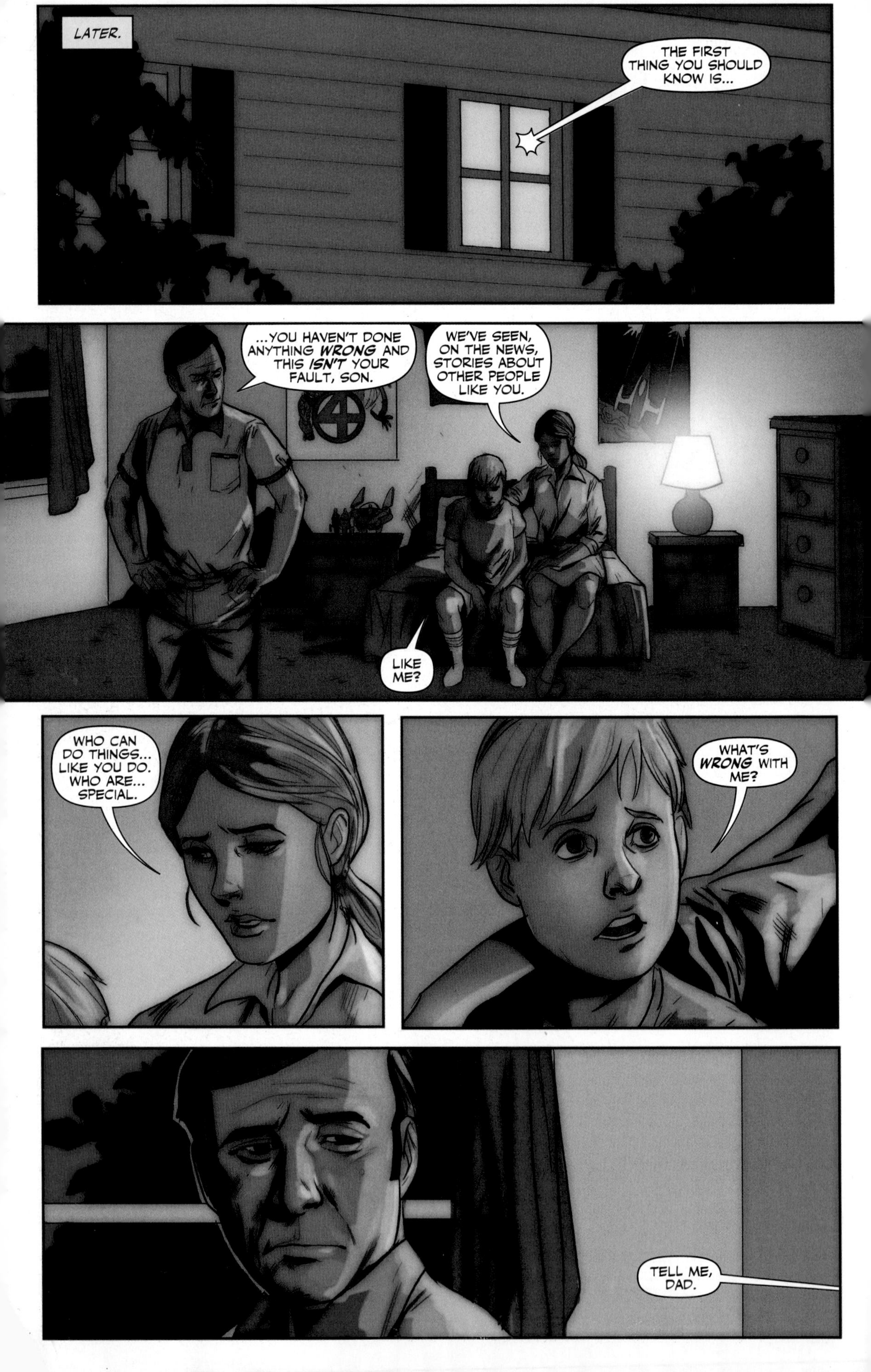
LATER.
THE FIRST THING YOU SHOULD KNOW IS...
...YOU HAVEN'T DONE ANYTHING *WRONG* AND THIS *ISN'T* YOUR FAULT, SON.
WE'VE SEEN, ON THE NEWS, STORIES ABOUT OTHER PEOPLE LIKE YOU.
LIKE ME?
WHO CAN DO THINGS... LIKE YOU DO. WHO ARE... SPECIAL.
WHAT'S *WRONG* WITH ME?
TELL ME, DAD.

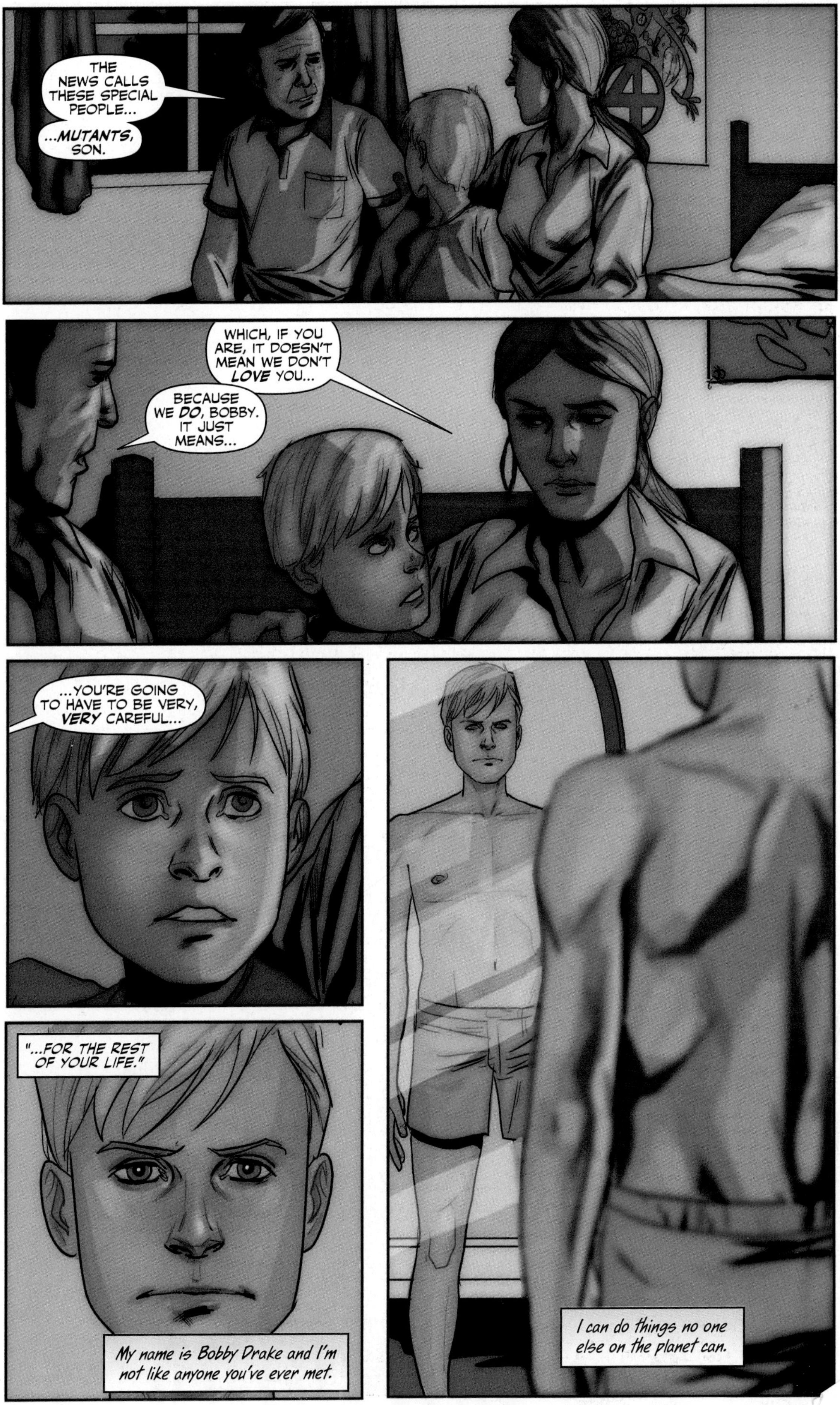
THE NEWS CALLS THESE SPECIAL PEOPLE...
...MUTANTS, SON.
WHICH, IF YOU ARE, IT DOESN'T MEAN WE DON'T LOVE YOU...
BECAUSE WE DO, BOBBY. IT JUST MEANS...
...YOU'RE GOING TO HAVE TO BE VERY, VERY CAREFUL...
"...FOR THE REST OF YOUR LIFE."
My name is Bobby Drake and I'm not like anyone you've ever met.
I can do things no one else on the planet can.

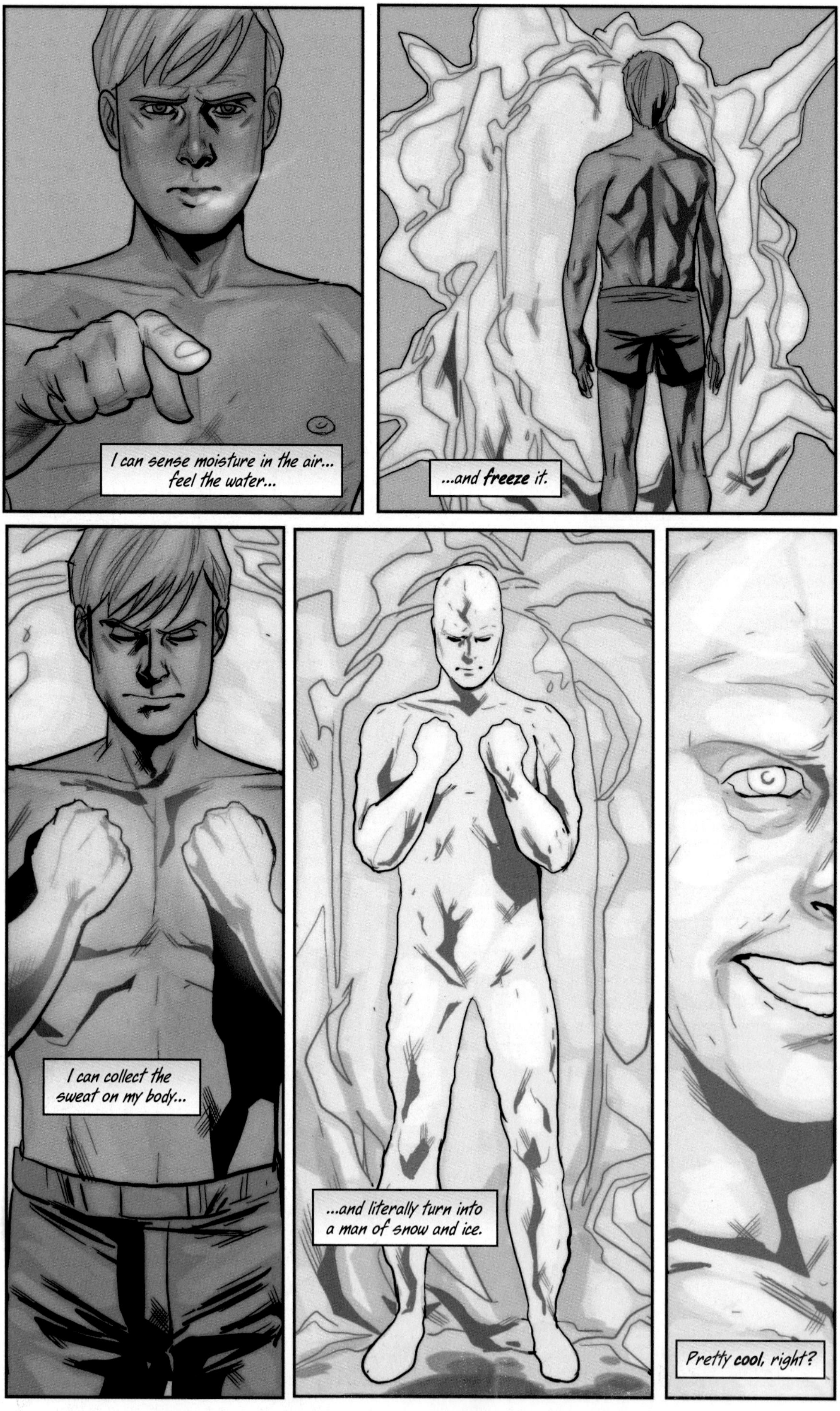
I can sense moisture in the air... feel the water...
...and freeze it.
I can collect the sweat on my body...
...and literally turn into a man of snow and ice.
Pretty cool, right?

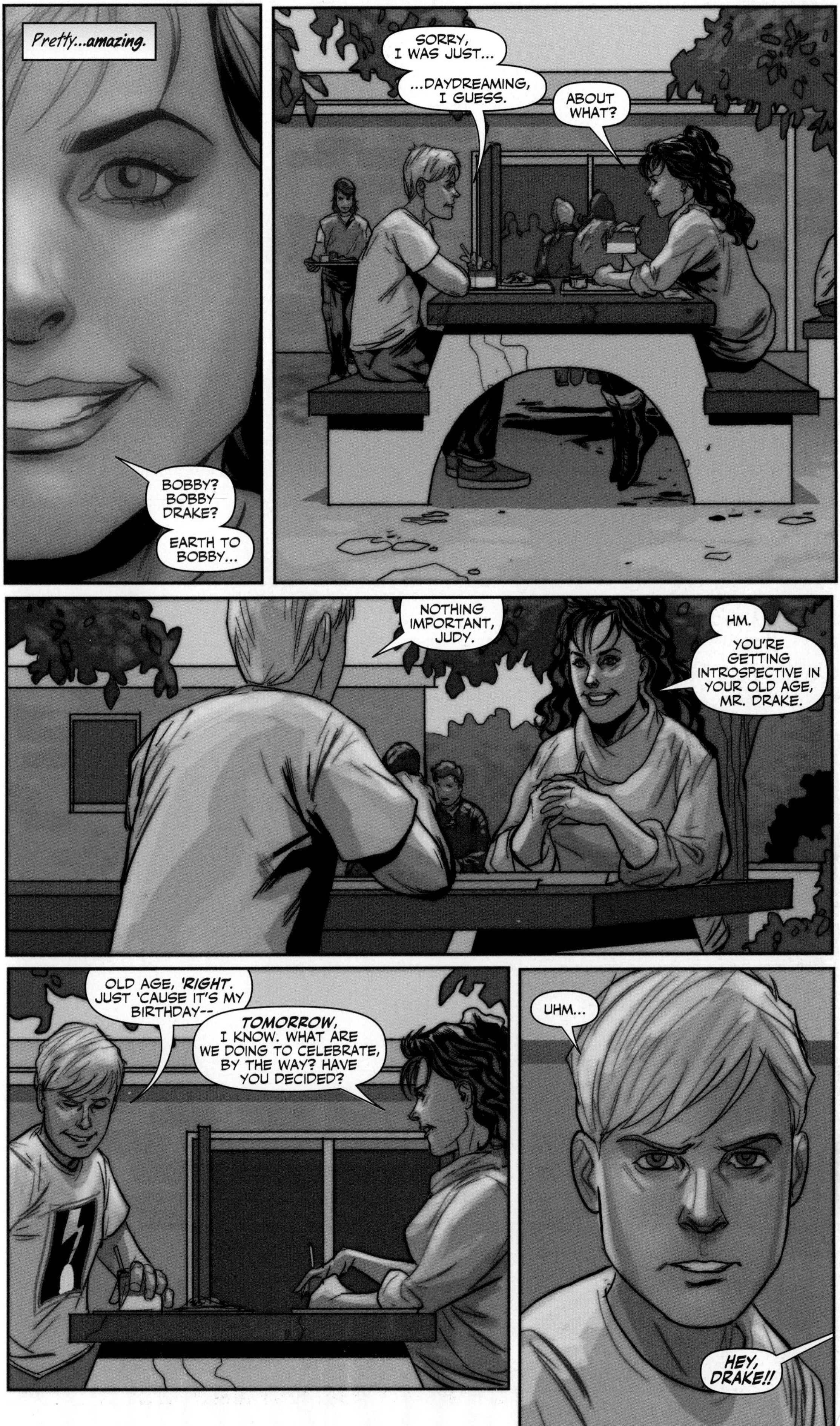
Pretty...amazing.
BOBBY? BOBBY DRAKE?
EARTH TO BOBBY...
SORRY, I WAS JUST...
...DAYDREAMING, I GUESS.
ABOUT WHAT?
NOTHING IMPORTANT, JUDY.
HM.
YOU'RE GETTING INTROSPECTIVE IN YOUR OLD AGE, MR. DRAKE.
OLD AGE, 'RIGHT. JUST 'CAUSE IT'S MY BIRTHDAY--
TOMORROW, I KNOW. WHAT ARE WE DOING TO CELEBRATE, BY THE WAY? HAVE YOU DECIDED?
UHM...
HEY, DRAKE!!

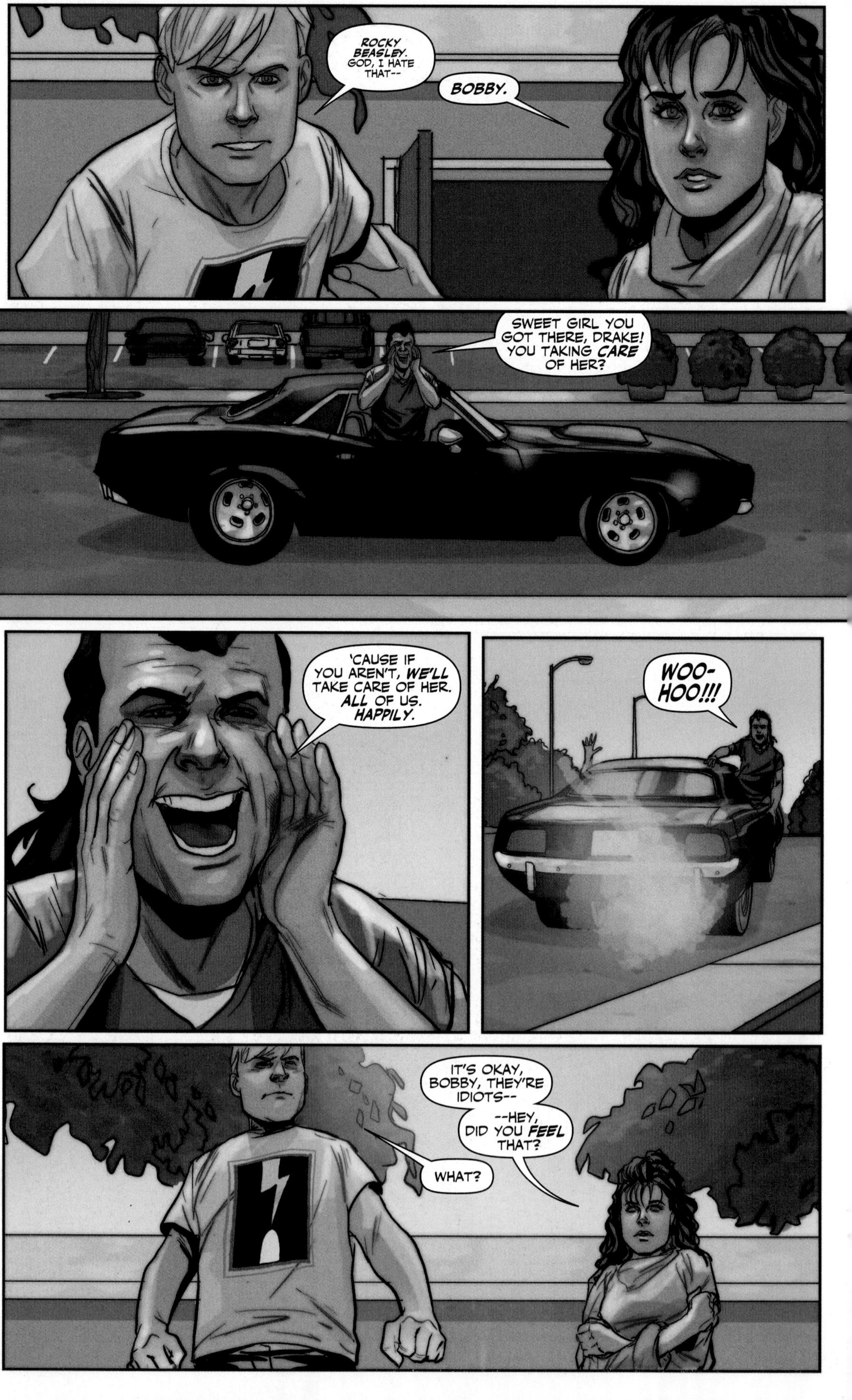
ROCKY BEASLEY. GOD, I HATE THAT--
BOBBY.
SWEET GIRL YOU GOT THERE, DRAKE! YOU TAKING CARE OF HER?
'CAUSE IF YOU AREN'T, WE'LL TAKE CARE OF HER. ALL OF US. HAPPILY.
WOO-HOO!!!
IT'S OKAY, BOBBY, THEY'RE IDIOTS--
--HEY, DID YOU FEEL THAT?
WHAT?

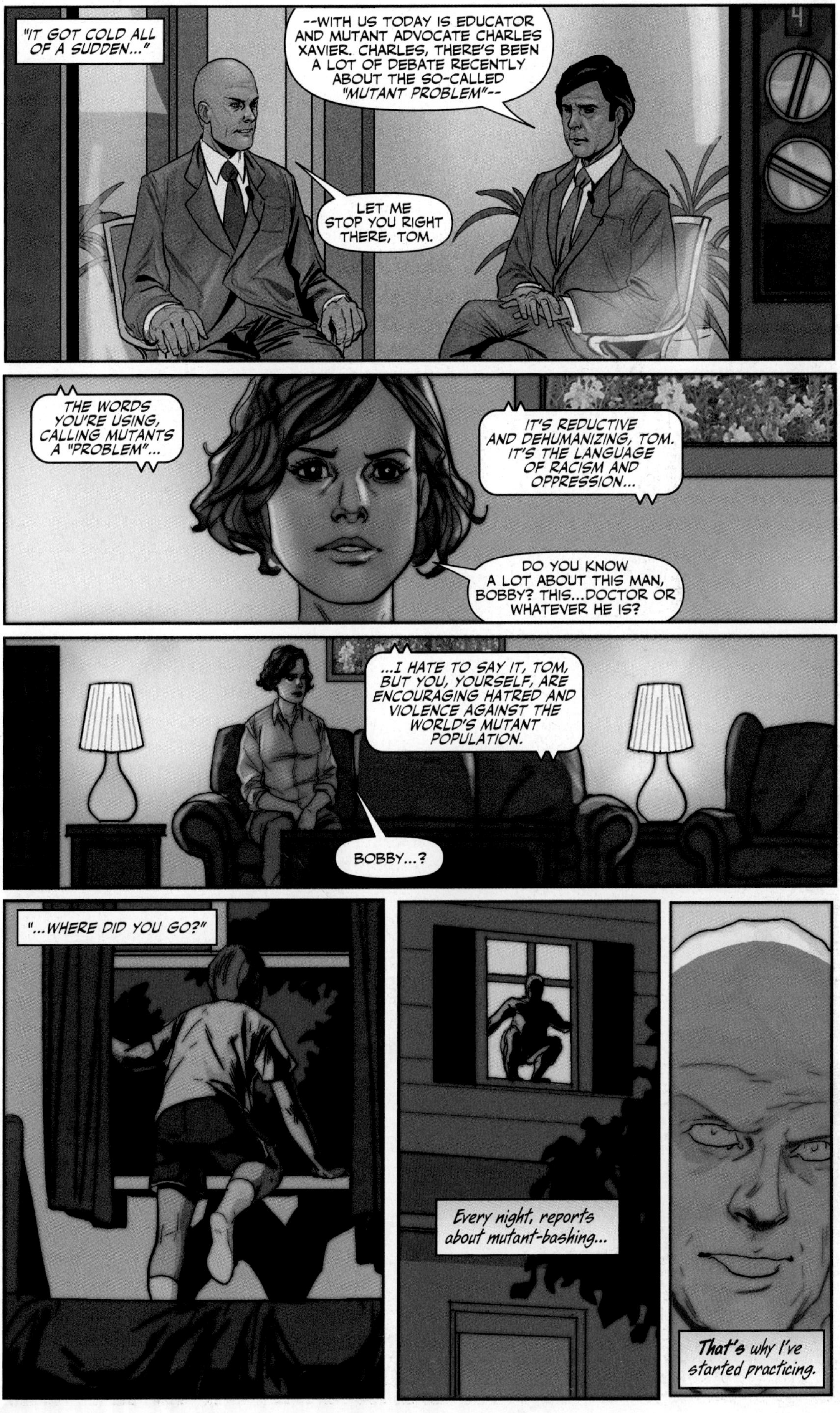
"IT GOT COLD ALL OF A SUDDEN..."
--WITH US TODAY IS EDUCATOR AND MUTANT ADVOCATE CHARLES XAVIER. CHARLES, THERE'S BEEN A LOT OF DEBATE RECENTLY ABOUT THE SO-CALLED "MUTANT PROBLEM"--
LET ME STOP YOU RIGHT THERE, TOM.
THE WORDS YOU'RE USING, CALLING MUTANTS A "PROBLEM"...
IT'S REDUCTIVE AND DEHUMANIZING, TOM. IT'S THE LANGUAGE OF RACISM AND OPPRESSION...
DO YOU KNOW A LOT ABOUT THIS MAN, BOBBY? THIS...DOCTOR OR WHATEVER HE IS?
...I HATE TO SAY IT, TOM, BUT YOU, YOURSELF, ARE ENCOURAGING HATRED AND VIOLENCE AGAINST THE WORLD'S MUTANT POPULATION.
BOBBY...?
"...WHERE DID YOU GO?"
Every night, reports about mutant-bashing...
That's why I've started practicing.

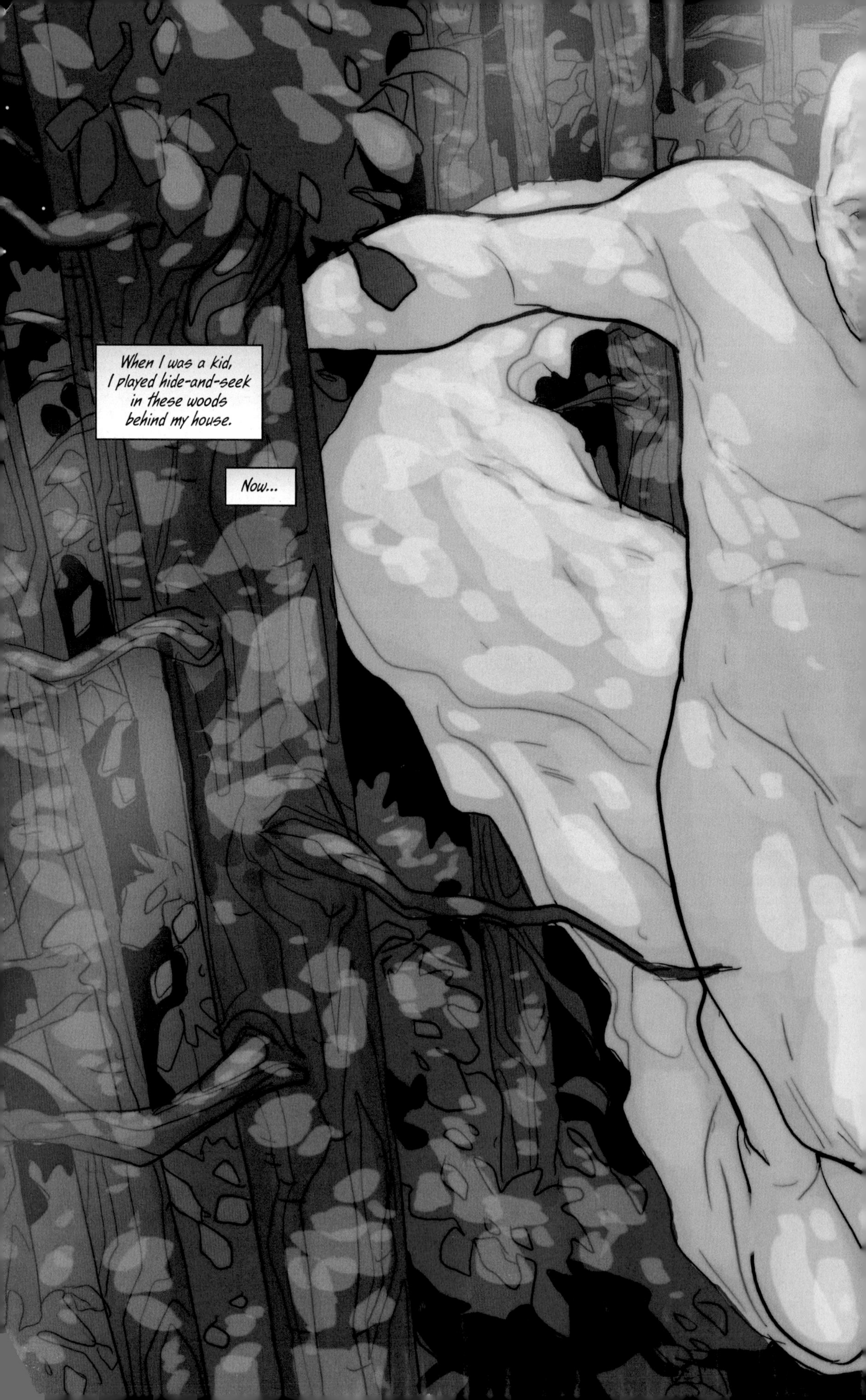
When I was a kid, I played hide-and-seek in these woods behind my house.
Now...

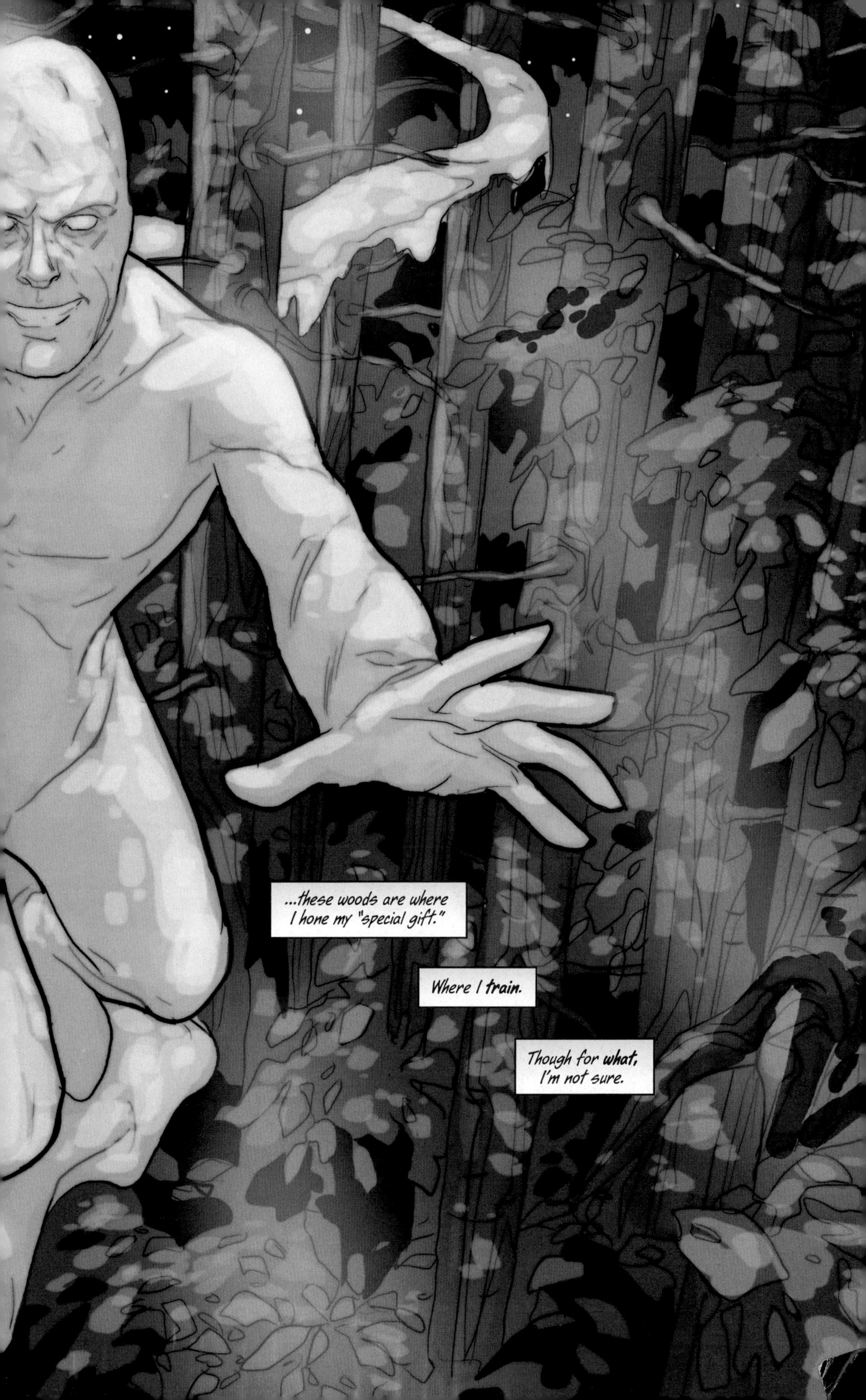
...these woods are where I hone my "special gift."
Where I **train.**
Though for **what,** I'm not sure.

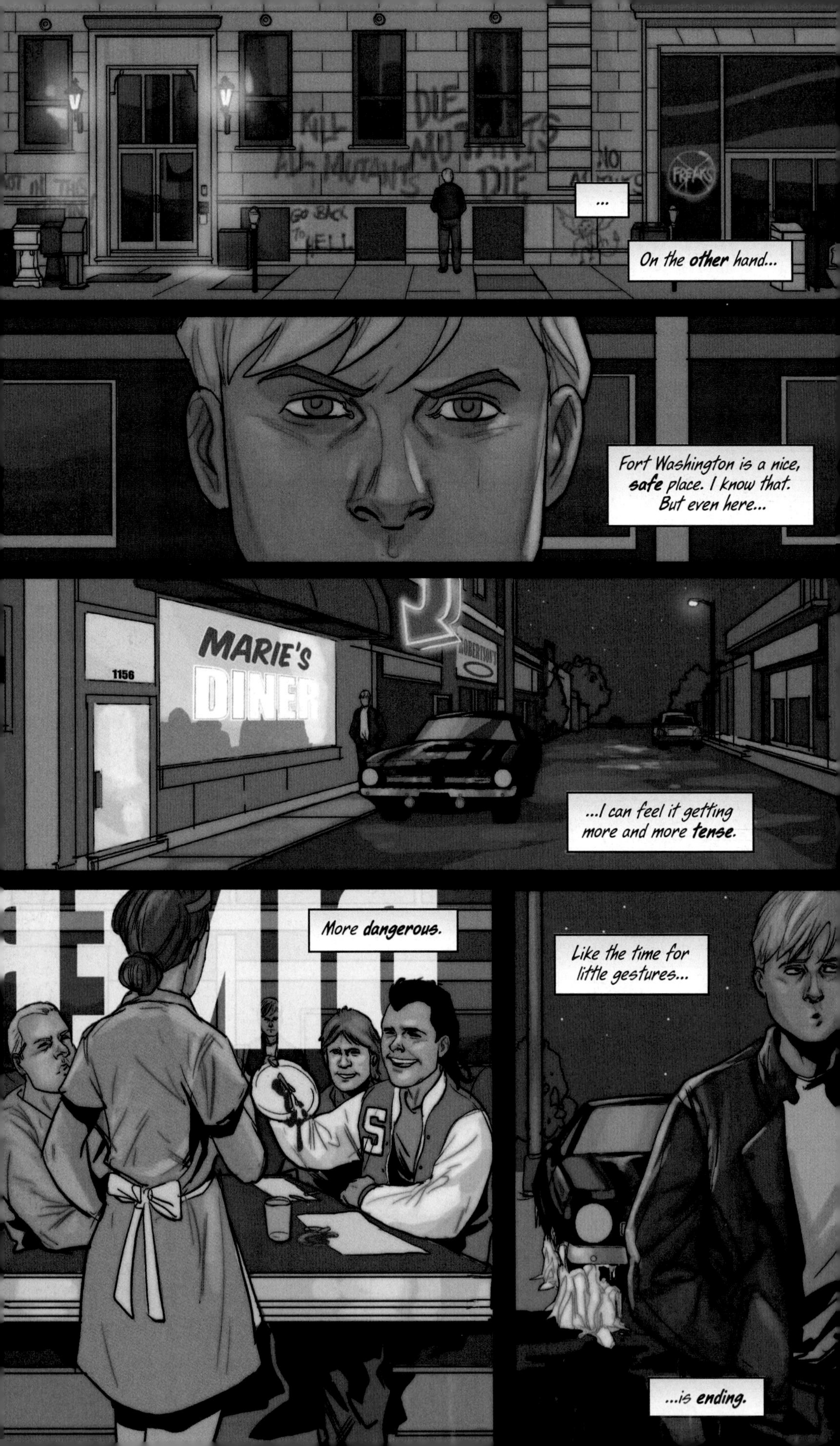
KILL ALL MUTANTS
DIE MUTANTS DIE
GO BACK TO HELL
FREAKS
...
On the other hand...
Fort Washington is a nice, safe place. I know that. But even here...
MARIE'S DINER
1156
ROBERTSON'S
...I can feel it getting more and more tense.
More dangerous.
Like the time for little gestures...
...is ending.

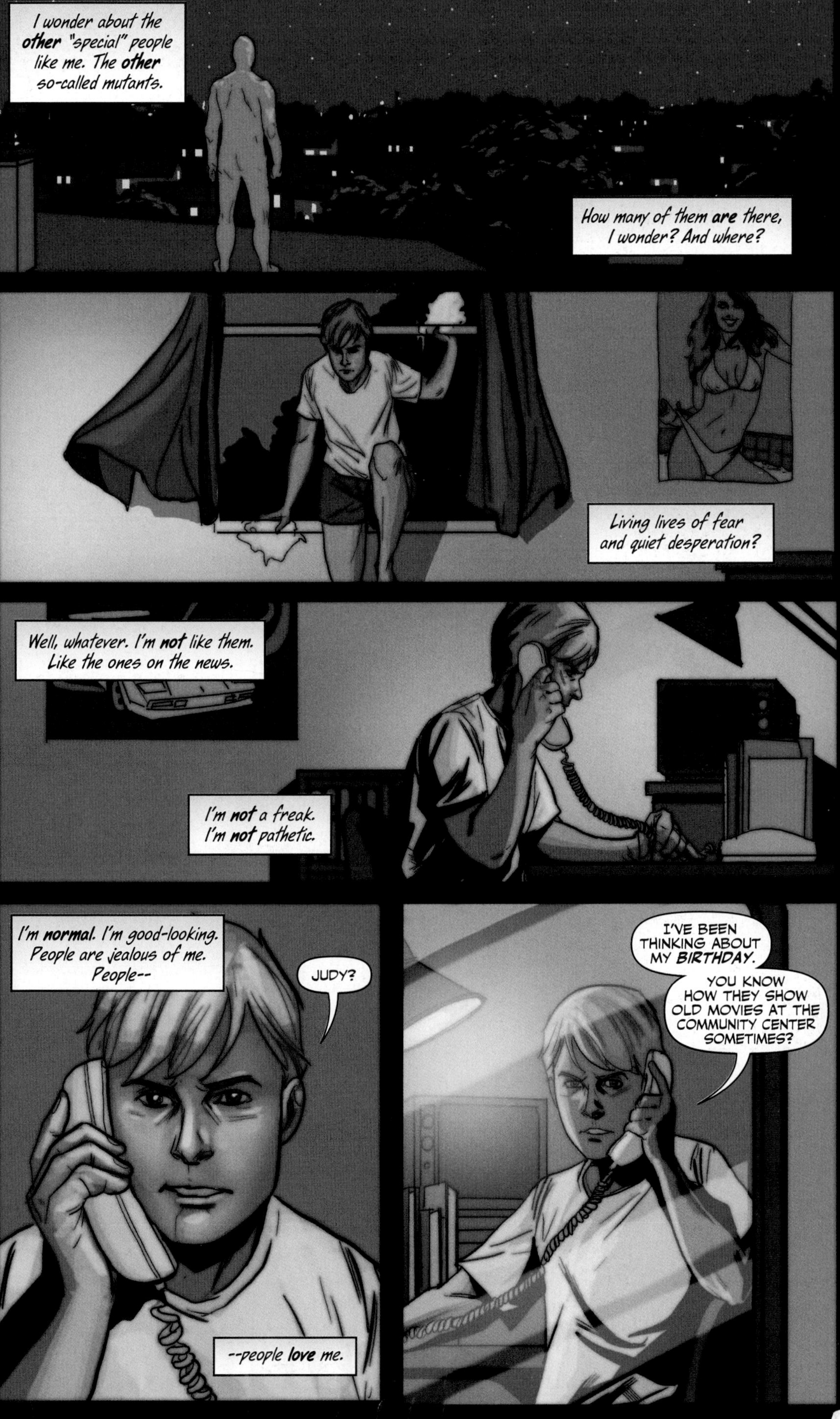
I wonder about the other "special" people like me. The other so-called mutants.
How many of them are there, I wonder? And where?
Living lives of fear and quiet desperation?
Well, whatever. I'm not like them. Like the ones on the news.
I'm not a freak. I'm not pathetic.
I'm normal. I'm good-looking. People are jealous of me. People--
JUDY?
--people love me.
I'VE BEEN THINKING ABOUT MY BIRTHDAY.
YOU KNOW HOW THEY SHOW OLD MOVIES AT THE COMMUNITY CENTER SOMETIMES?

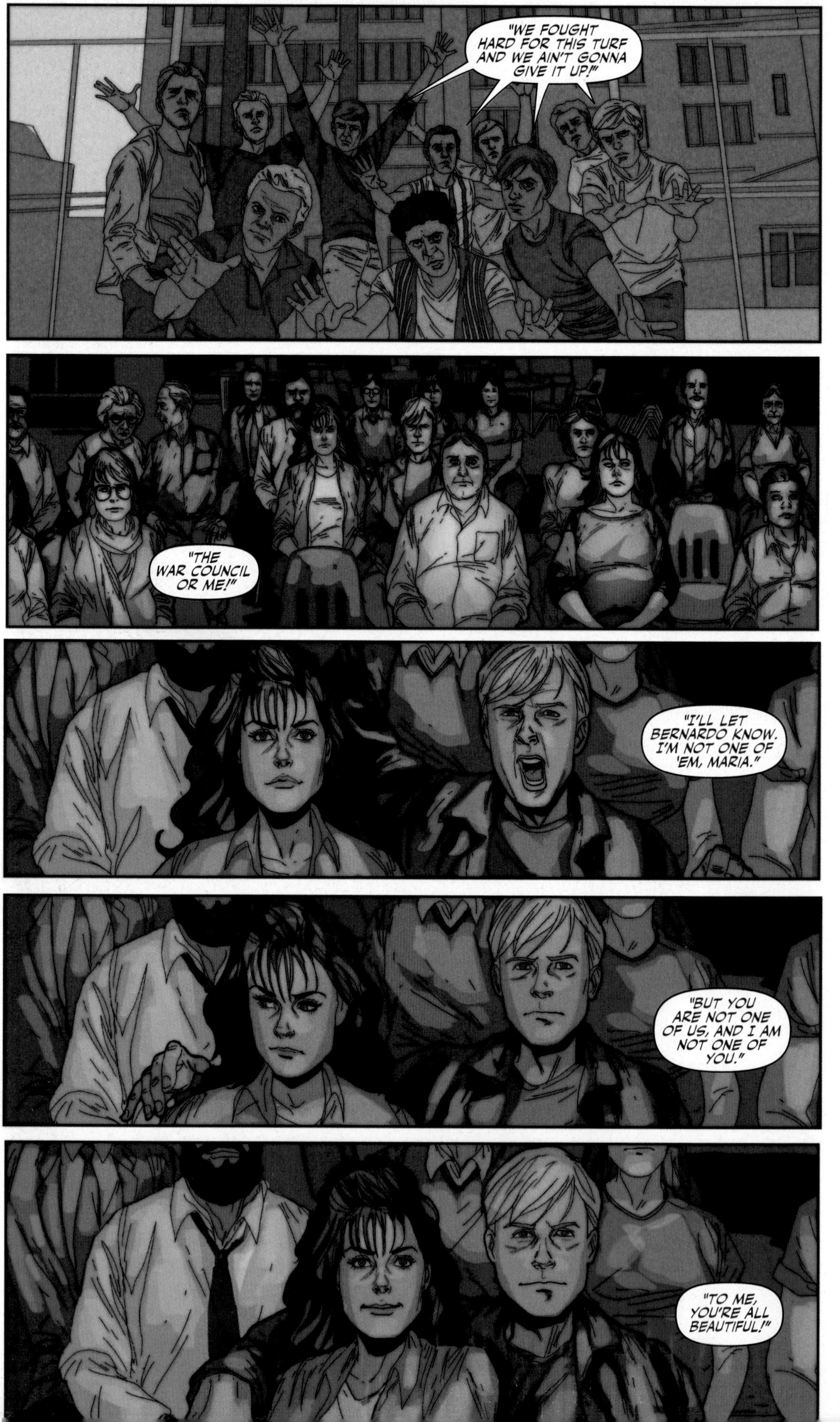
"WE FOUGHT HARD FOR THIS TURF AND WE AIN'T GONNA GIVE IT UP!"
"THE WAR COUNCIL OR ME!"
"I'LL LET BERNARDO KNOW. I'M NOT ONE OF 'EM, MARIA."
"BUT YOU ARE NOT ONE OF US, AND I AM NOT ONE OF YOU."
"TO ME, YOU'RE ALL BEAUTIFUL!"

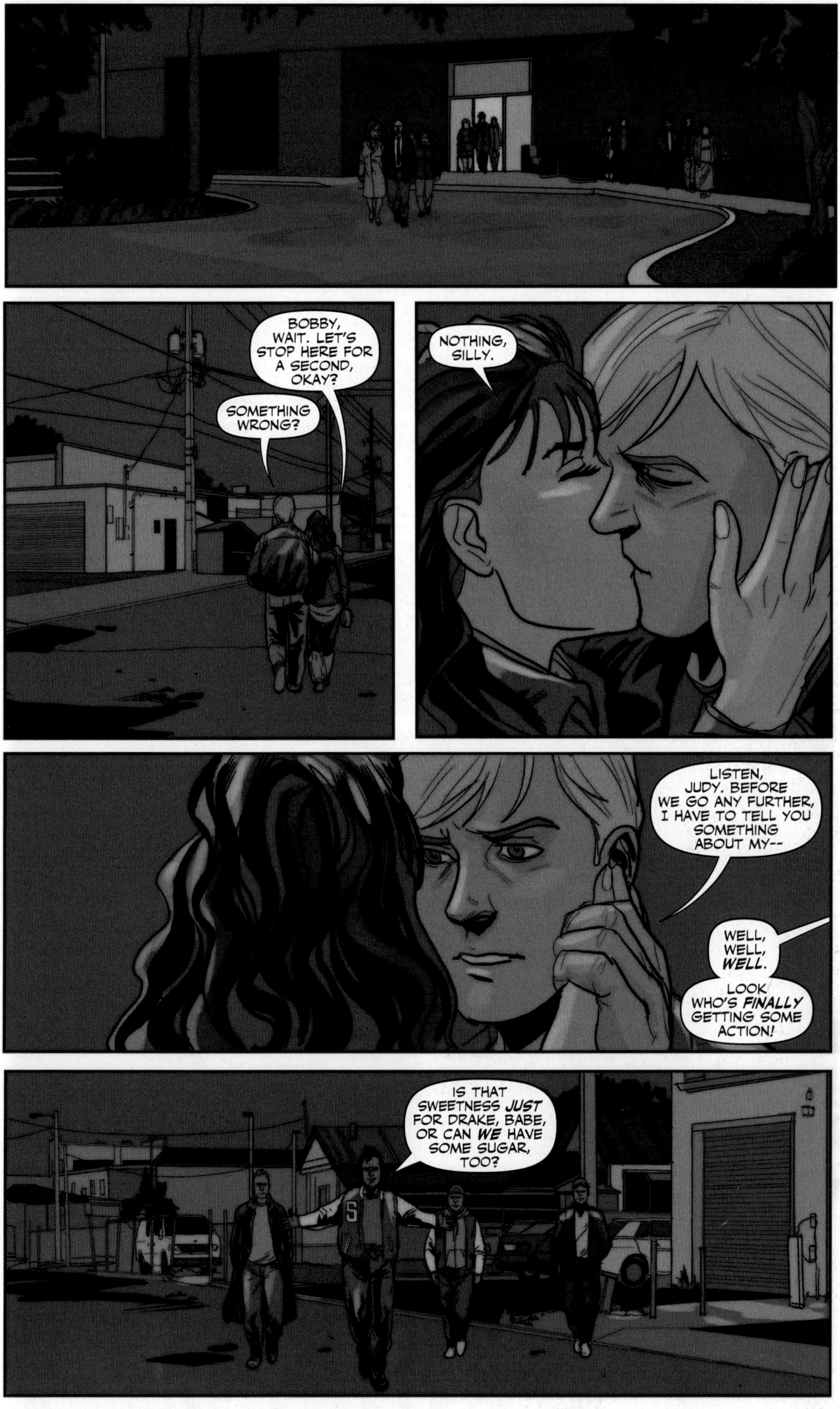
BOBBY, WAIT. LET'S STOP HERE FOR A SECOND, OKAY?
SOMETHING WRONG?
NOTHING, SILLY.
LISTEN, JUDY. BEFORE WE GO ANY FURTHER, I HAVE TO TELL YOU SOMETHING ABOUT MY--
WELL, WELL, **WELL**.
LOOK WHO'S ***FINALLY*** GETTING SOME ACTION!
IS THAT SWEETNESS ***JUST*** FOR DRAKE, BABE, OR CAN ***WE*** HAVE SOME SUGAR, TOO?

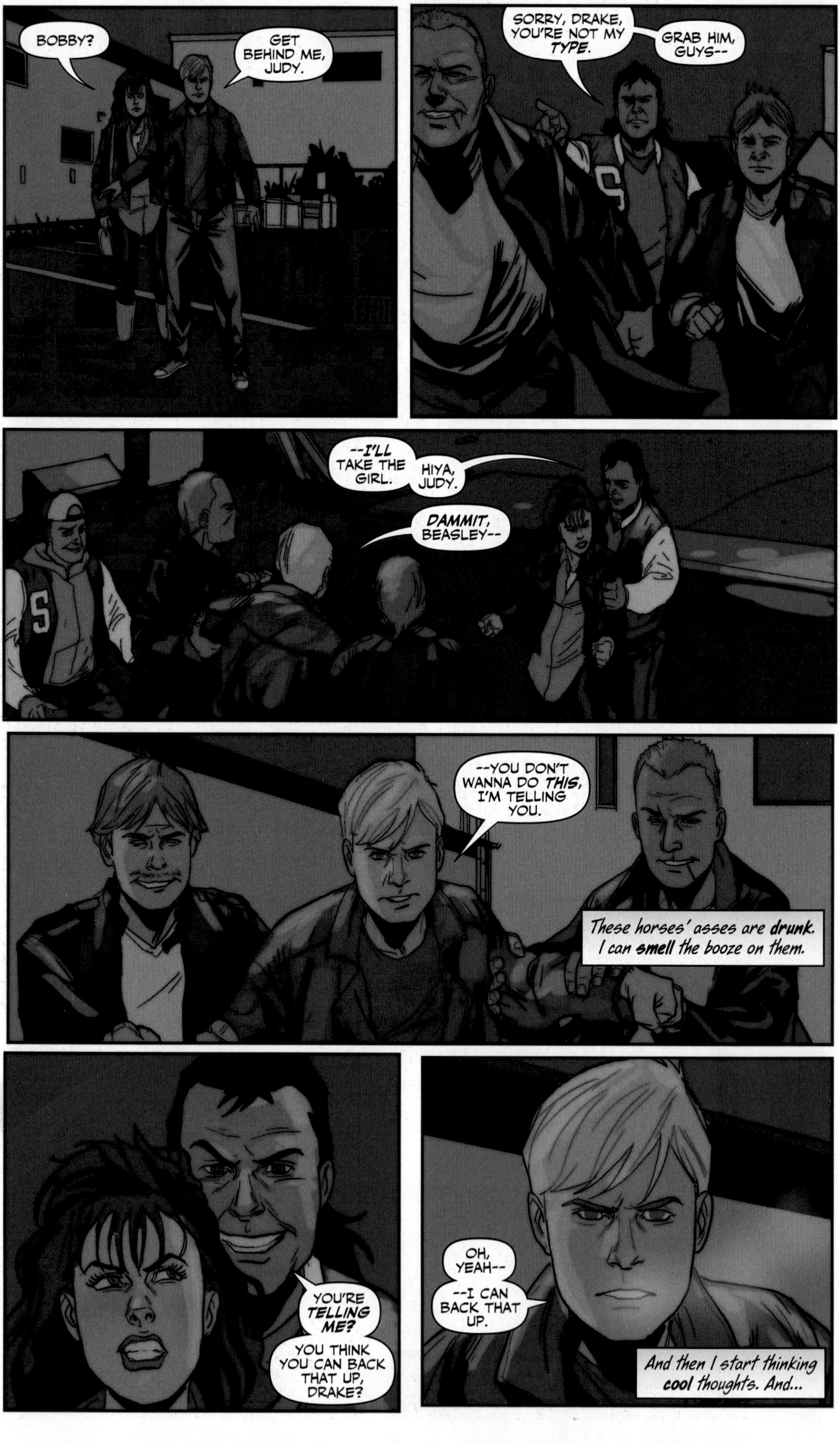
BOBBY?
GET BEHIND ME, JUDY.
SORRY, DRAKE, YOU'RE NOT MY *TYPE*.
GRAB HIM, GUYS--
--*I'LL* TAKE THE GIRL.
HIYA, JUDY.
DAMMIT, BEASLEY--
--YOU DON'T WANNA DO *THIS*, I'M TELLING YOU.
These horses' asses are ***drunk****. I can* ***smell*** *the booze on them.*
YOU'RE ***TELLING ME?***
YOU THINK YOU CAN BACK THAT UP, DRAKE?
OH, YEAH--
--I CAN BACK THAT UP.
And then I start thinking ***cool*** *thoughts. And...*

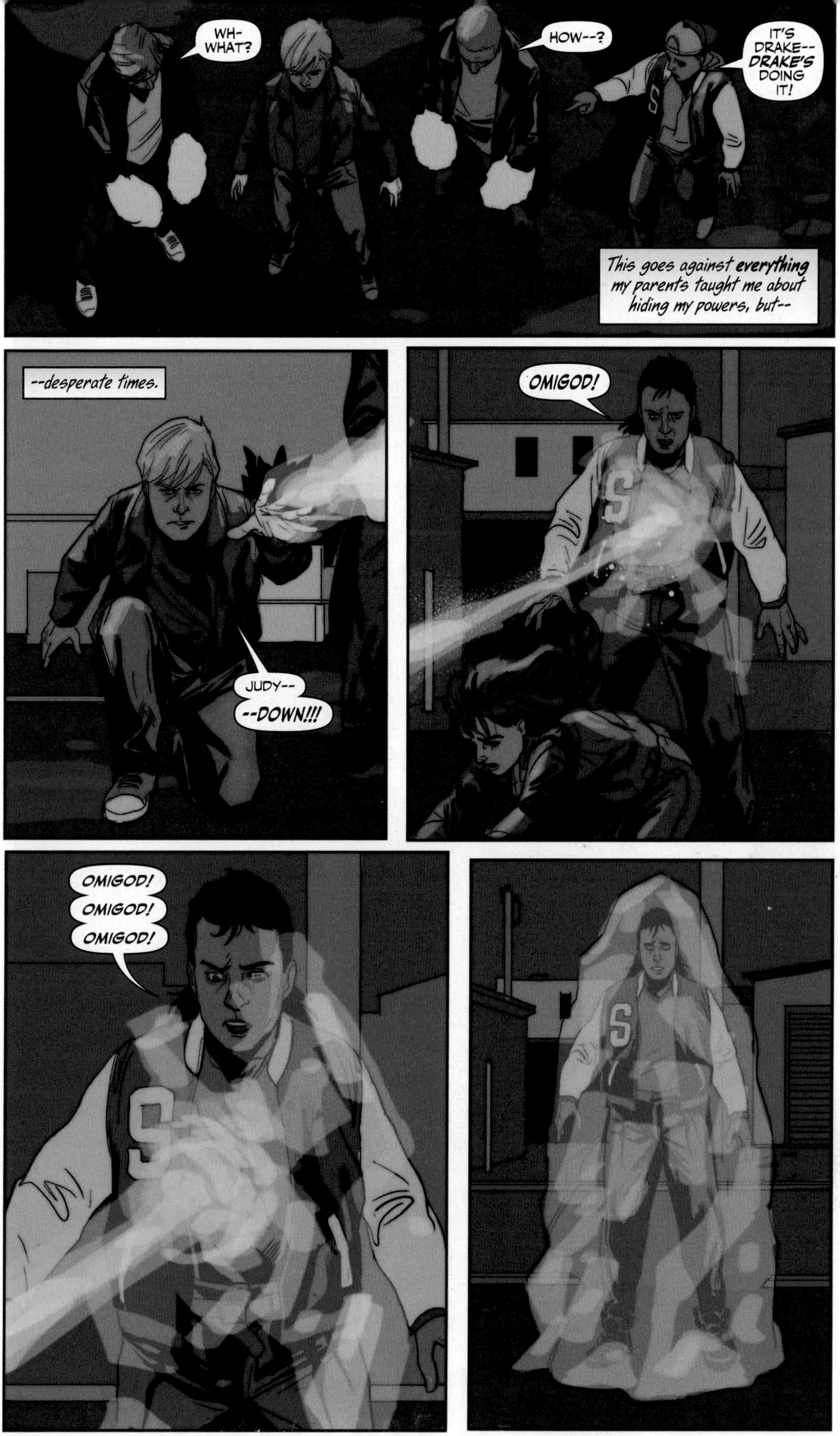
WH-WHAT?
HOW--?
IT'S DRAKE--DRAKE'S DOING IT!
This goes against everything my parents taught me about hiding my powers, but--
--desperate times.
JUDY--
--DOWN!!!
OMIGOD!
OMIGOD!
OMIGOD!
OMIGOD!

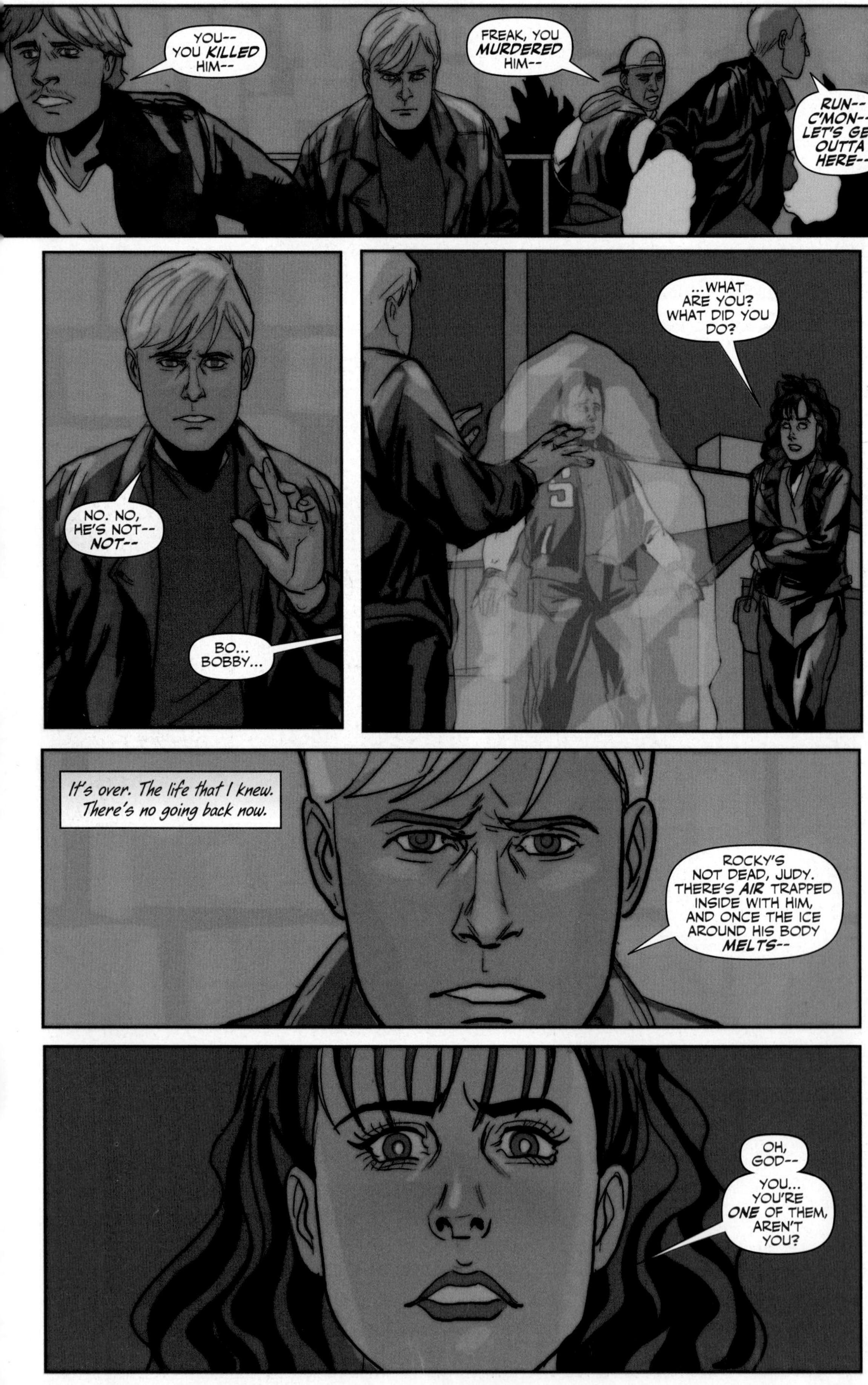

YOU-- YOU KILLED HIM--
FREAK, YOU MURDERED HIM--
RUN-- C'MON-- LET'S GET OUTTA HERE--
NO. NO, HE'S NOT-- NOT--
BO... BOBBY...
...WHAT ARE YOU? WHAT DID YOU DO?
It's over. The life that I knew. There's no going back now.
ROCKY'S NOT DEAD, JUDY. THERE'S AIR TRAPPED INSIDE WITH HIM, AND ONCE THE ICE AROUND HIS BODY MELTS--
OH, GOD--
YOU... YOU'RE ONE OF THEM, AREN'T YOU?

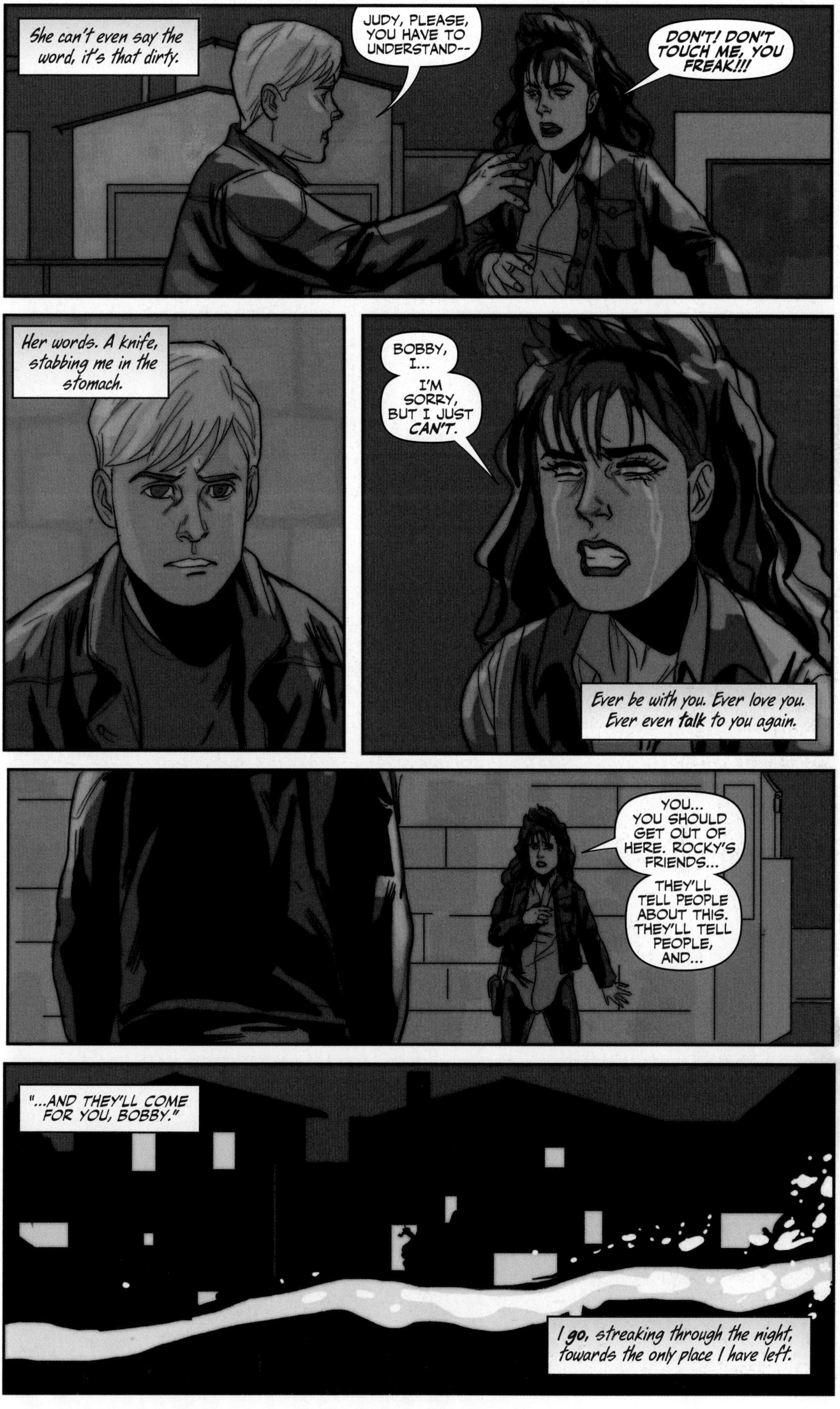
She can't even say the word, it's that dirty.
JUDY, PLEASE, YOU HAVE TO UNDERSTAND--
DON'T! DON'T TOUCH ME, YOU FREAK!!!
Her words. A knife, stabbing me in the stomach.
BOBBY, I...
I'M SORRY, BUT I JUST CAN'T.
Ever be with you. Ever love you. Ever even talk to you again.
YOU... YOU SHOULD GET OUT OF HERE. ROCKY'S FRIENDS...
THEY'LL TELL PEOPLE ABOUT THIS. THEY'LL TELL PEOPLE, AND...
"...AND THEY'LL COME FOR YOU, BOBBY."
I go, streaking through the night, towards the only place I have left.

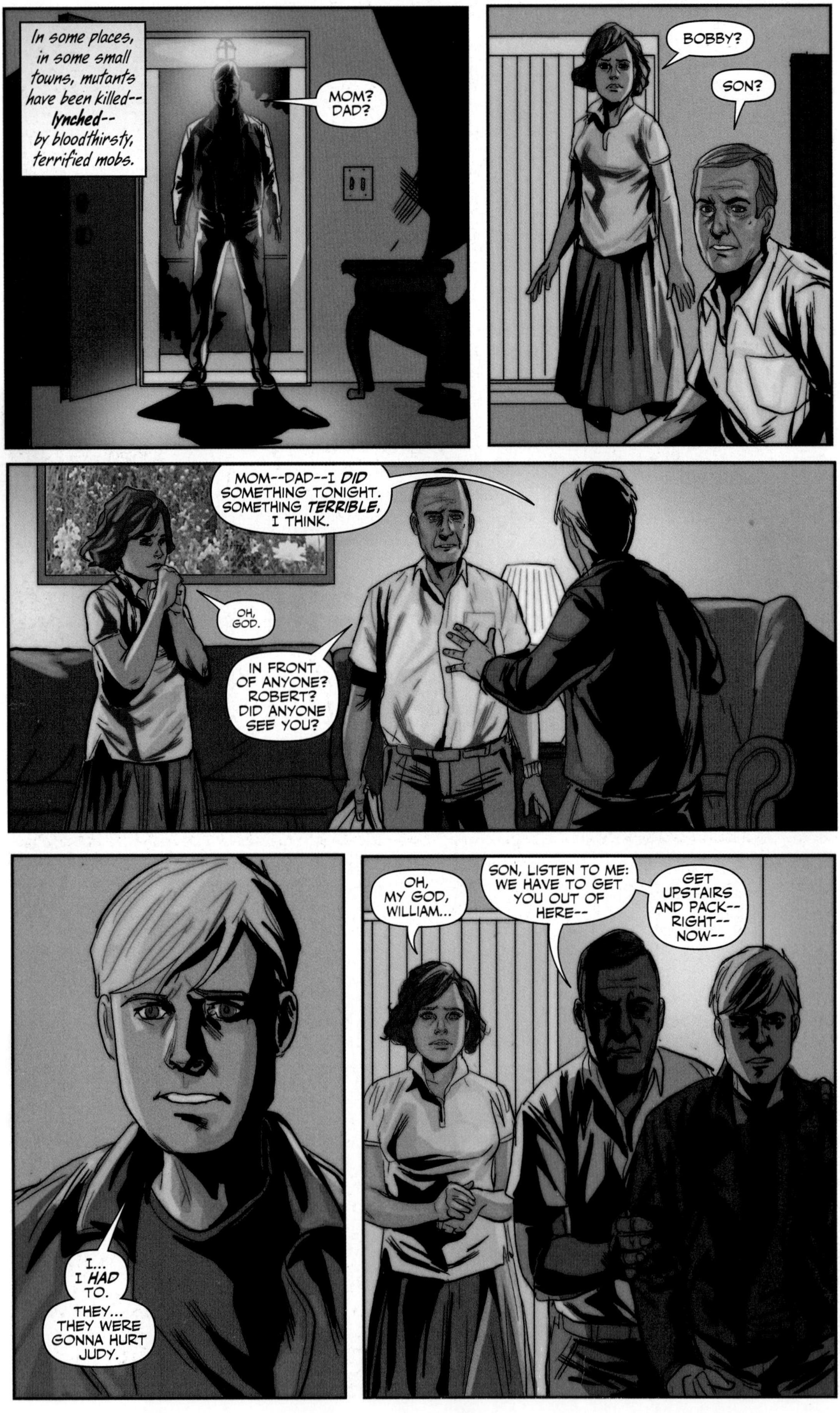
In some places, in some small towns, mutants have been killed-- **lynched**-- by bloodthirsty, terrified mobs.
MOM? DAD?
BOBBY?
SON?
MOM--DAD--I *DID* SOMETHING TONIGHT. SOMETHING *TERRIBLE*, I THINK.
OH, GOD.
IN FRONT OF ANYONE? ROBERT? DID ANYONE SEE YOU?
I... I *HAD* TO. THEY... THEY WERE GONNA HURT JUDY.
OH, MY GOD, WILLIAM...
SON, LISTEN TO ME: WE HAVE TO GET YOU OUT OF HERE--
GET UPSTAIRS AND PACK-- RIGHT-- NOW--

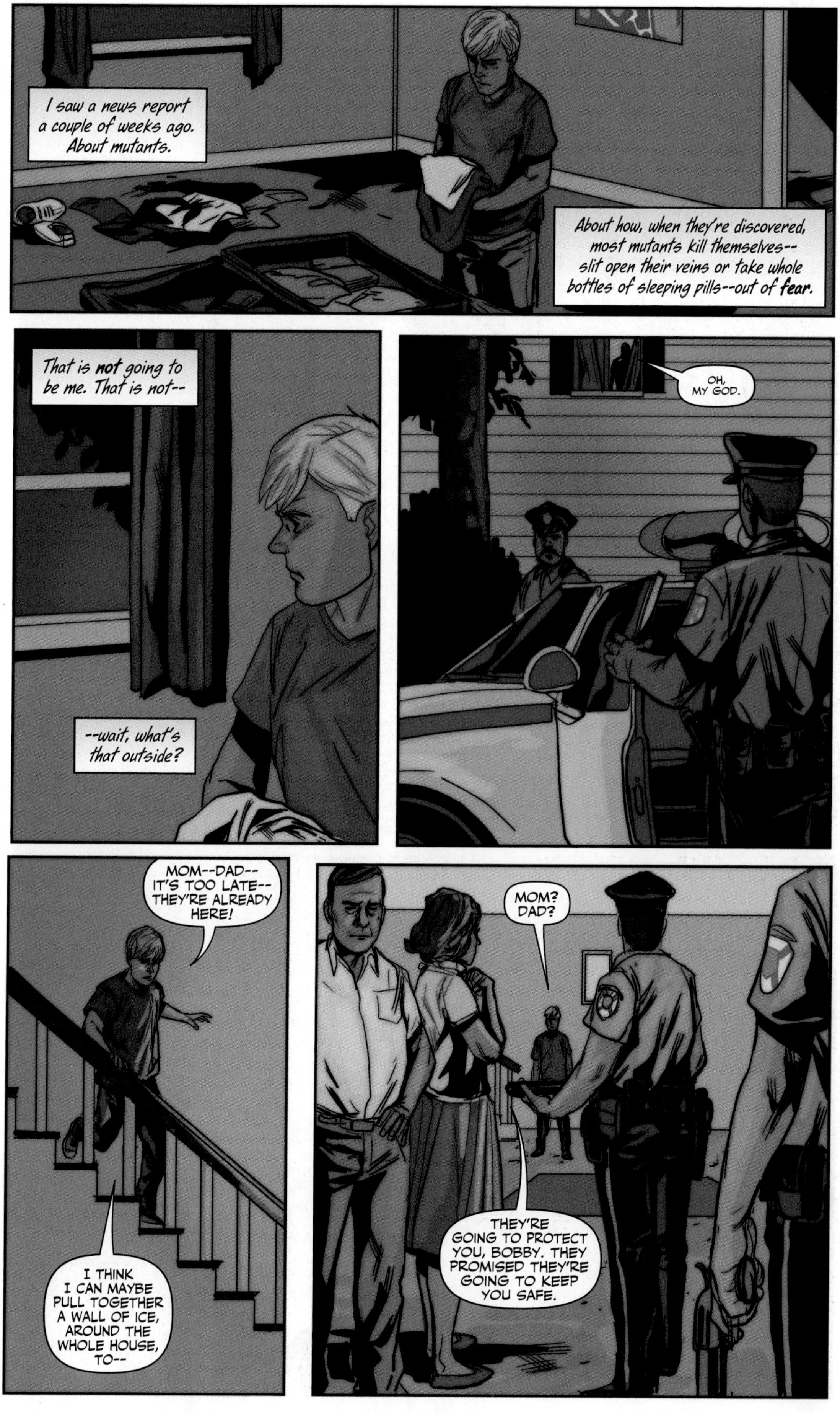

I saw a news report a couple of weeks ago. About mutants.
About how, when they're discovered, most mutants kill themselves--slit open their veins or take whole bottles of sleeping pills--out of **fear**.
That is **not** going to be me. That is not--
--wait, what's that outside?
OH, MY GOD.
MOM--DAD--IT'S TOO LATE--THEY'RE ALREADY HERE!
I THINK I CAN MAYBE PULL TOGETHER A WALL OF ICE, AROUND THE WHOLE HOUSE, TO--
MOM? DAD?
THEY'RE GOING TO PROTECT YOU, BOBBY. THEY PROMISED THEY'RE GOING TO KEEP YOU SAFE.

"Safe." Right...

...tell that to the **mob** outside my cell.

MY GOD, WILLIAM, THEY WANT TO **KILL** HIM! WE **SHOULDN'T** HAVE HANDED HIM OVER!

OVER MY DEAD BODY WILL THEY TOUCH A HAIR ON BOBBY'S HEAD!

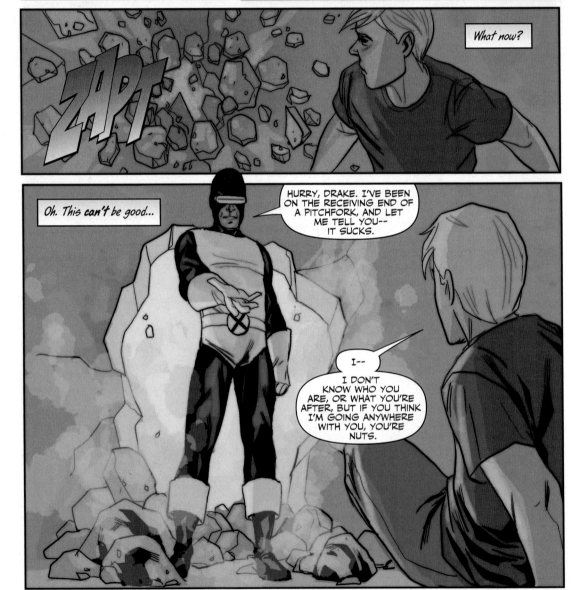

What now?

Oh. This **can't** be good...

HURRY, DRAKE. I'VE BEEN ON THE RECEIVING END OF A PITCHFORK, AND LET ME TELL YOU-- IT SUCKS.

I-- I DON'T KNOW WHO YOU ARE, OR WHAT YOU'RE AFTER, BUT IF YOU THINK I'M GOING ANYWHERE WITH YOU, YOU'RE NUTS.

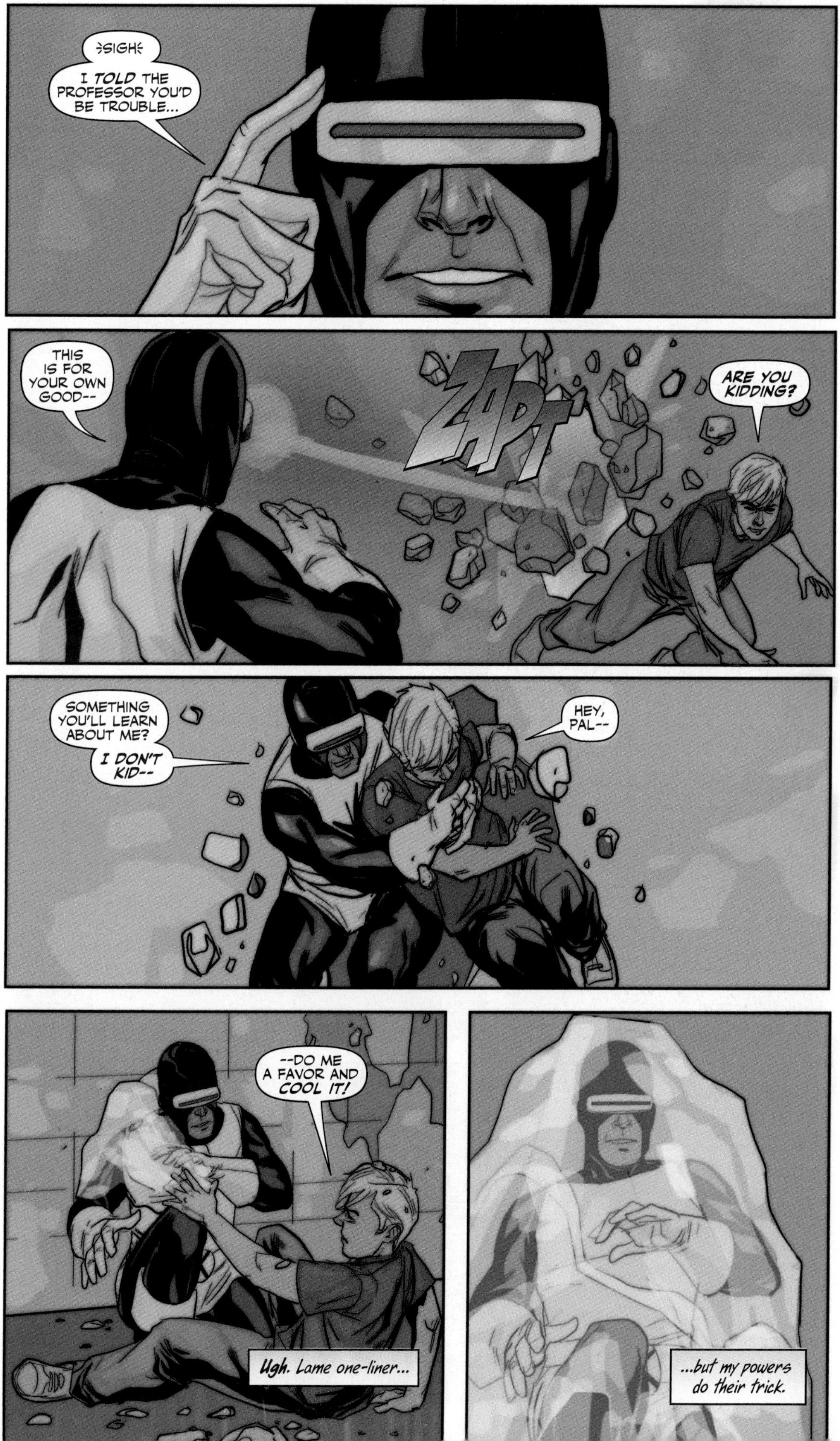

SIGH
I TOLD THE PROFESSOR YOU'D BE TROUBLE...
THIS IS FOR YOUR OWN GOOD--
ZAPT
ARE YOU KIDDING?
SOMETHING YOU'LL LEARN ABOUT ME? I DON'T KID--
HEY, PAL--
--DO ME A FAVOR AND COOL IT!
Ugh. Lame one-liner...
...but my powers do their trick.

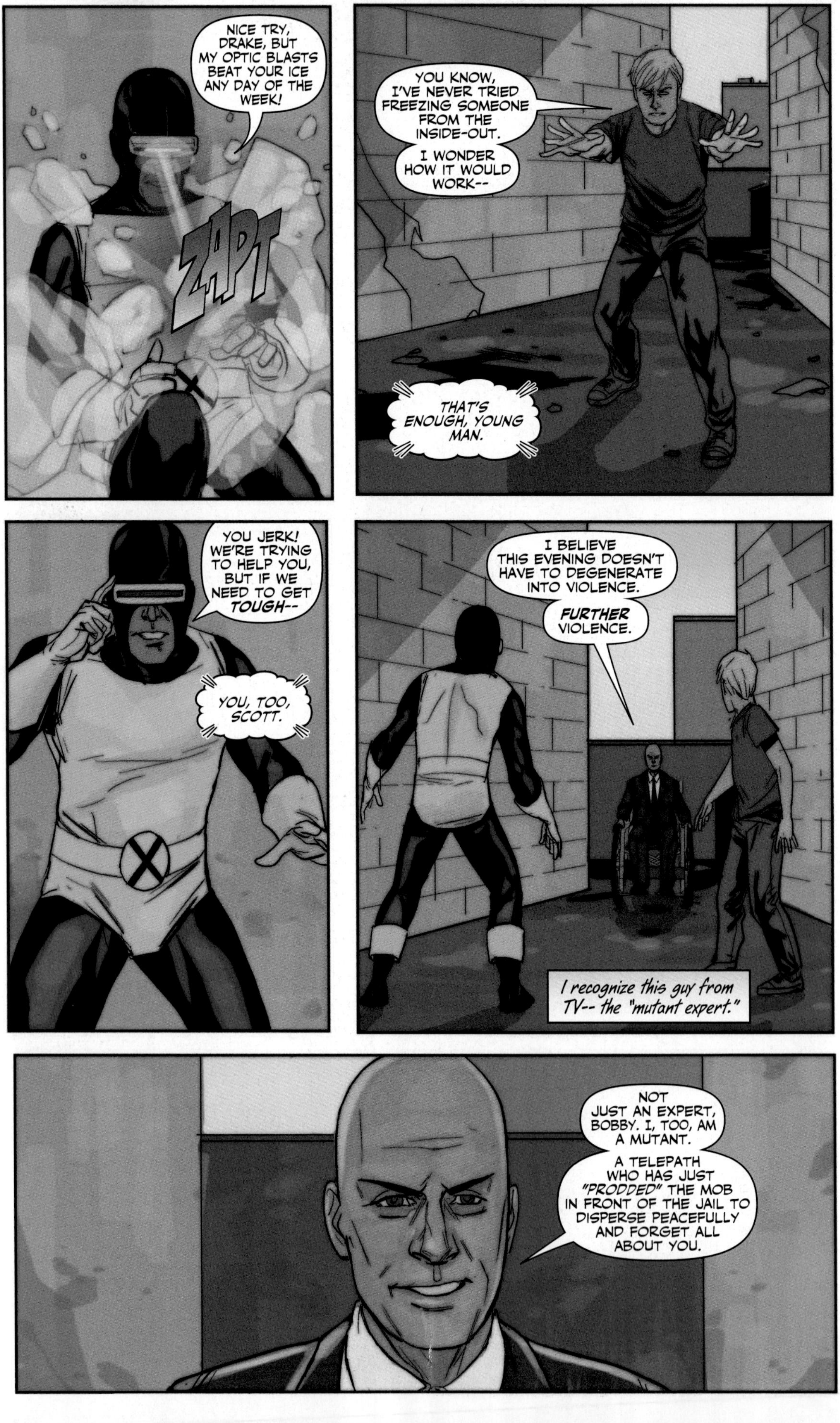
NICE TRY, DRAKE, BUT MY OPTIC BLASTS BEAT YOUR ICE ANY DAY OF THE WEEK!
ZAPT
YOU KNOW, I'VE NEVER TRIED FREEZING SOMEONE FROM THE INSIDE-OUT.
I WONDER HOW IT WOULD WORK--
THAT'S ENOUGH, YOUNG MAN.
YOU JERK! WE'RE TRYING TO HELP YOU, BUT IF WE NEED TO GET TOUGH--
YOU, TOO, SCOTT.
I BELIEVE THIS EVENING DOESN'T HAVE TO DEGENERATE INTO VIOLENCE.
FURTHER VIOLENCE.
I recognize this guy from TV-- the "mutant expert."
NOT JUST AN EXPERT, BOBBY. I, TOO, AM A MUTANT.
A TELEPATH WHO HAS JUST "PRODDED" THE MOB IN FRONT OF THE JAIL TO DISPERSE PEACEFULLY AND FORGET ALL ABOUT YOU.

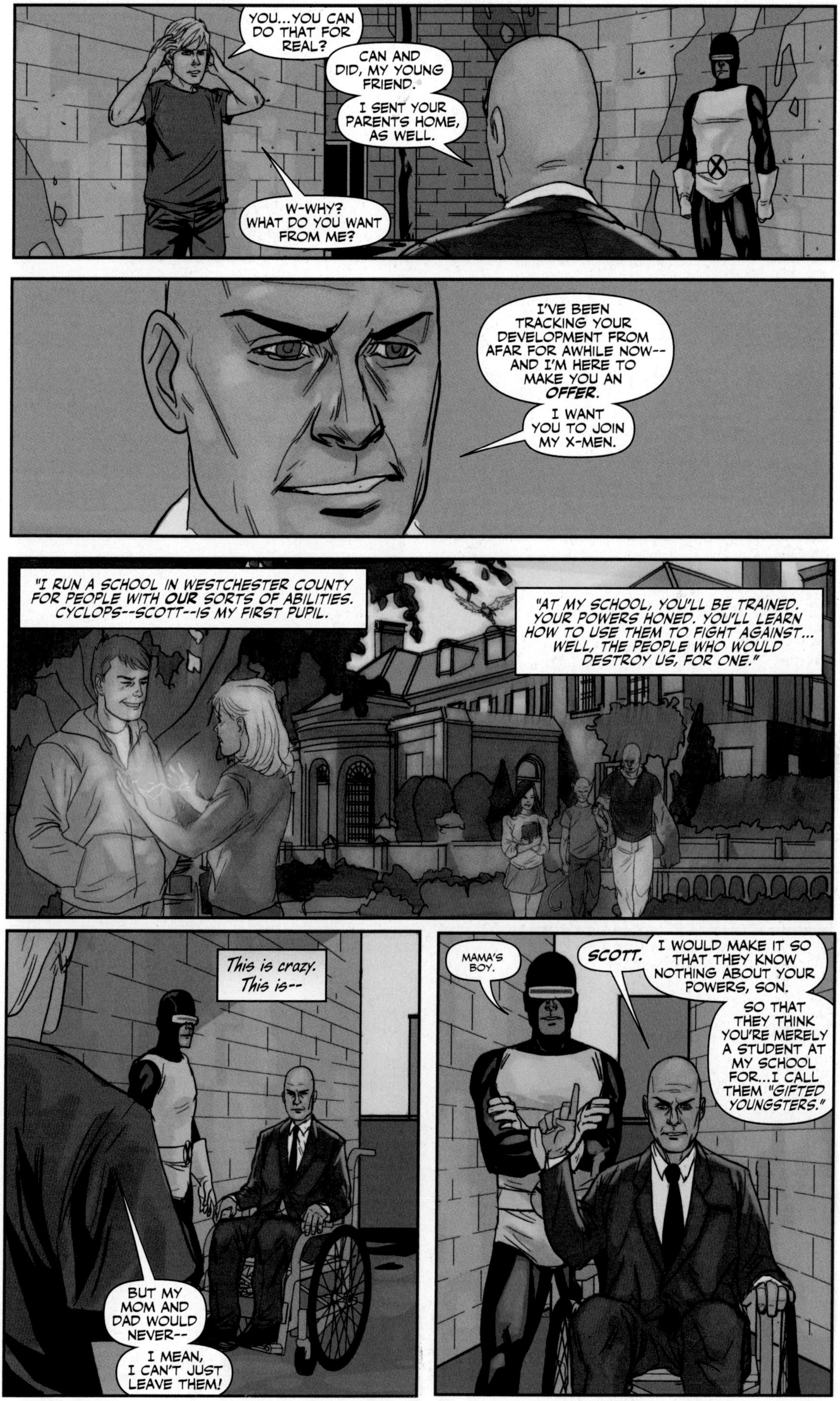
YOU...YOU CAN DO THAT FOR REAL?
CAN AND DID, MY YOUNG FRIEND.
I SENT YOUR PARENTS HOME, AS WELL.
W-WHY? WHAT DO YOU WANT FROM ME?
I'VE BEEN TRACKING YOUR DEVELOPMENT FROM AFAR FOR AWHILE NOW-- AND I'M HERE TO MAKE YOU AN OFFER.
I WANT YOU TO JOIN MY X-MEN.
"I RUN A SCHOOL IN WESTCHESTER COUNTY FOR PEOPLE WITH OUR SORTS OF ABILITIES. CYCLOPS--SCOTT--IS MY FIRST PUPIL.
"AT MY SCHOOL, YOU'LL BE TRAINED. YOUR POWERS HONED. YOU'LL LEARN HOW TO USE THEM TO FIGHT AGAINST... WELL, THE PEOPLE WHO WOULD DESTROY US, FOR ONE."
This is crazy. This is--
BUT MY MOM AND DAD WOULD NEVER--
I MEAN, I CAN'T JUST LEAVE THEM!
MAMA'S BOY.
SCOTT.
I WOULD MAKE IT SO THAT THEY KNOW NOTHING ABOUT YOUR POWERS, SON.
SO THAT THEY THINK YOU'RE MERELY A STUDENT AT MY SCHOOL FOR...I CALL THEM "GIFTED YOUNGSTERS."

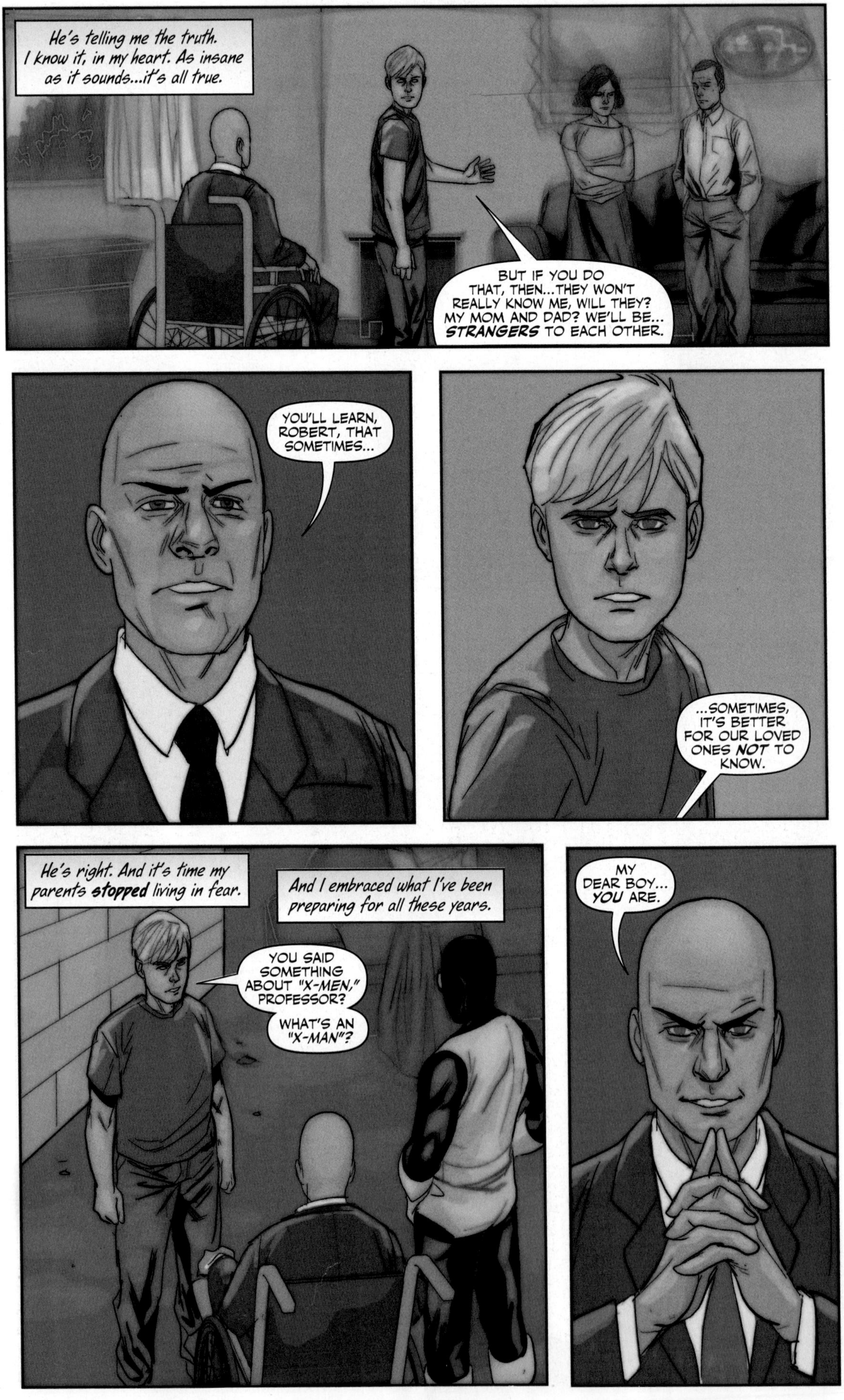
He's telling me the truth. I know it, in my heart. As insane as it sounds...it's all true.
BUT IF YOU DO THAT, THEN...THEY WON'T REALLY KNOW ME, WILL THEY? MY MOM AND DAD? WE'LL BE... STRANGERS TO EACH OTHER.
YOU'LL LEARN, ROBERT, THAT SOMETIMES...
...SOMETIMES, IT'S BETTER FOR OUR LOVED ONES NOT TO KNOW.
He's right. And it's time my parents stopped living in fear.
And I embraced what I've been preparing for all these years.
YOU SAID SOMETHING ABOUT "X-MEN," PROFESSOR?
WHAT'S AN "X-MAN"?
MY DEAR BOY... YOU ARE.

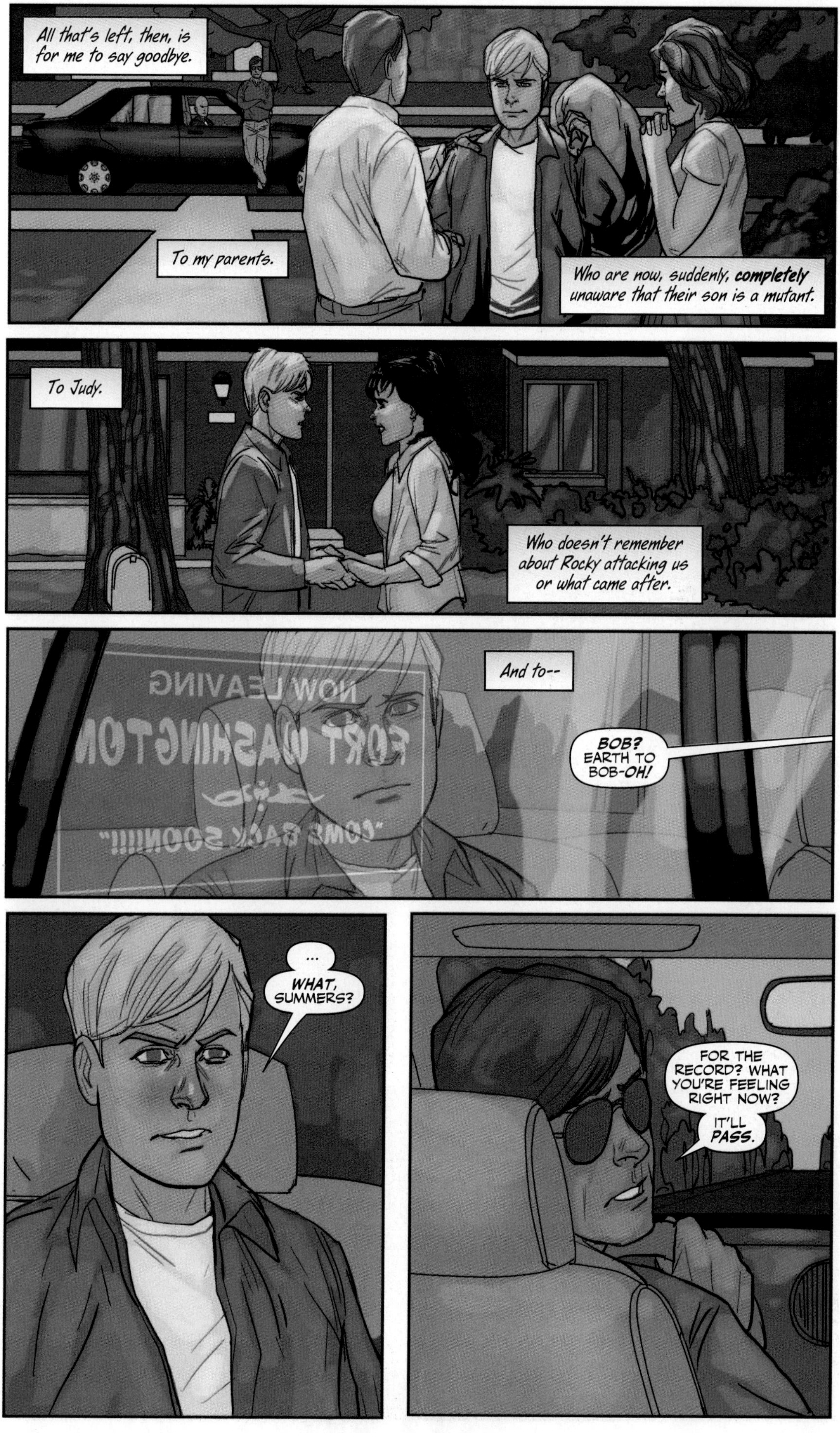
All that's left, then, is for me to say goodbye.
To my parents.
Who are now, suddenly, **completely** unaware that their son is a mutant.
To Judy.
Who doesn't remember about Rocky attacking us or what came after.
And to--
BOB? EARTH TO BOB-**OH!**
...
WHAT, SUMMERS?
FOR THE RECORD? WHAT YOU'RE FEELING RIGHT NOW?
IT'LL **PASS.**

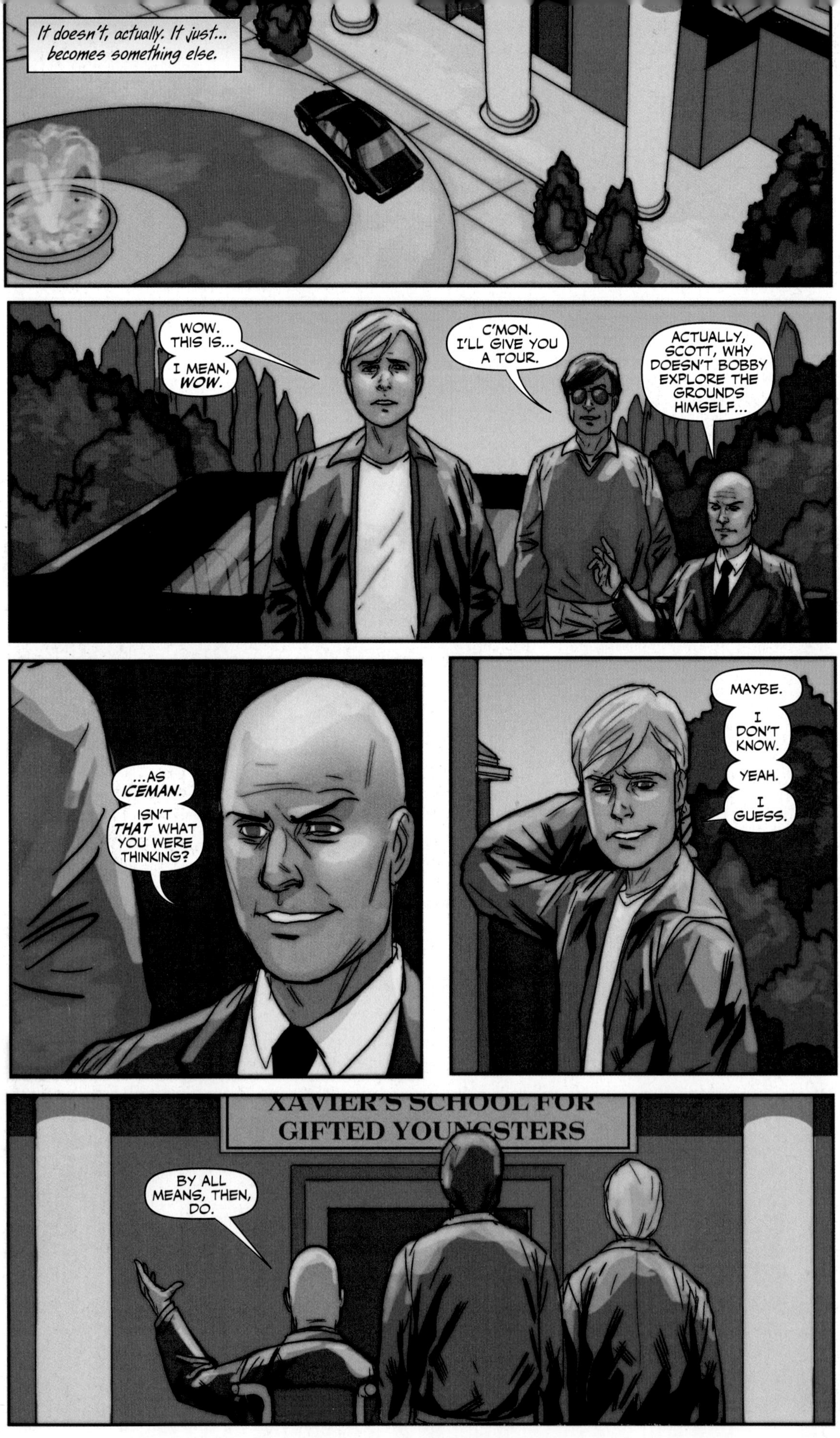
It doesn't, actually. It just... becomes something else.
WOW. THIS IS...
I MEAN, WOW.
C'MON. I'LL GIVE YOU A TOUR.
ACTUALLY, SCOTT, WHY DOESN'T BOBBY EXPLORE THE GROUNDS HIMSELF...
...AS ICEMAN.
ISN'T THAT WHAT YOU WERE THINKING?
MAYBE.
I DON'T KNOW.
YEAH.
I GUESS.
XAVIER'S SCHOOL FOR GIFTED YOUNGSTERS
BY ALL MEANS, THEN, DO.

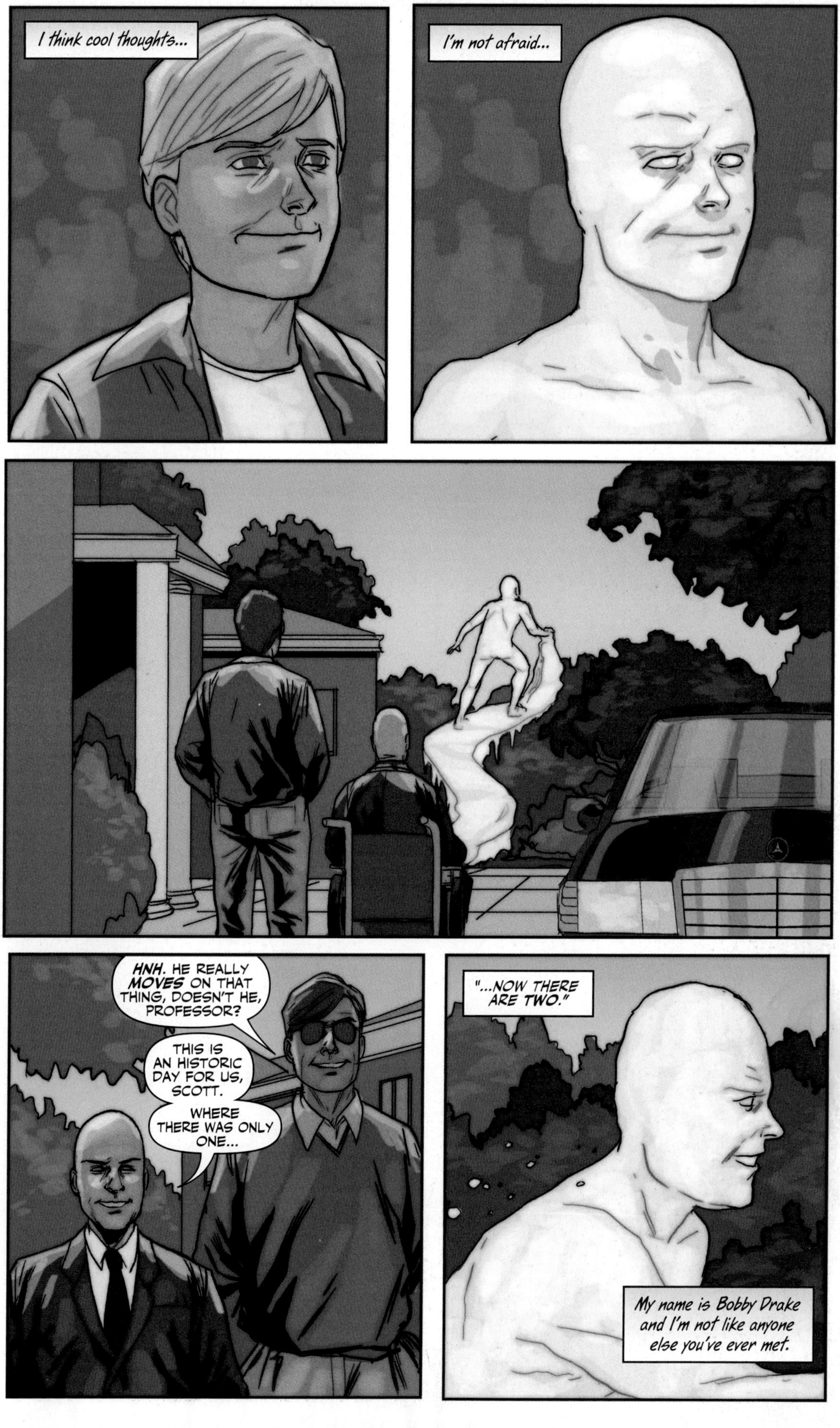
I think cool thoughts...
I'm not afraid...
HNH. HE REALLY MOVES ON THAT THING, DOESN'T HE, PROFESSOR?
THIS IS AN HISTORIC DAY FOR US, SCOTT.
WHERE THERE WAS ONLY ONE...
"...NOW THERE ARE TWO."
My name is Bobby Drake and I'm not like anyone else you've ever met.

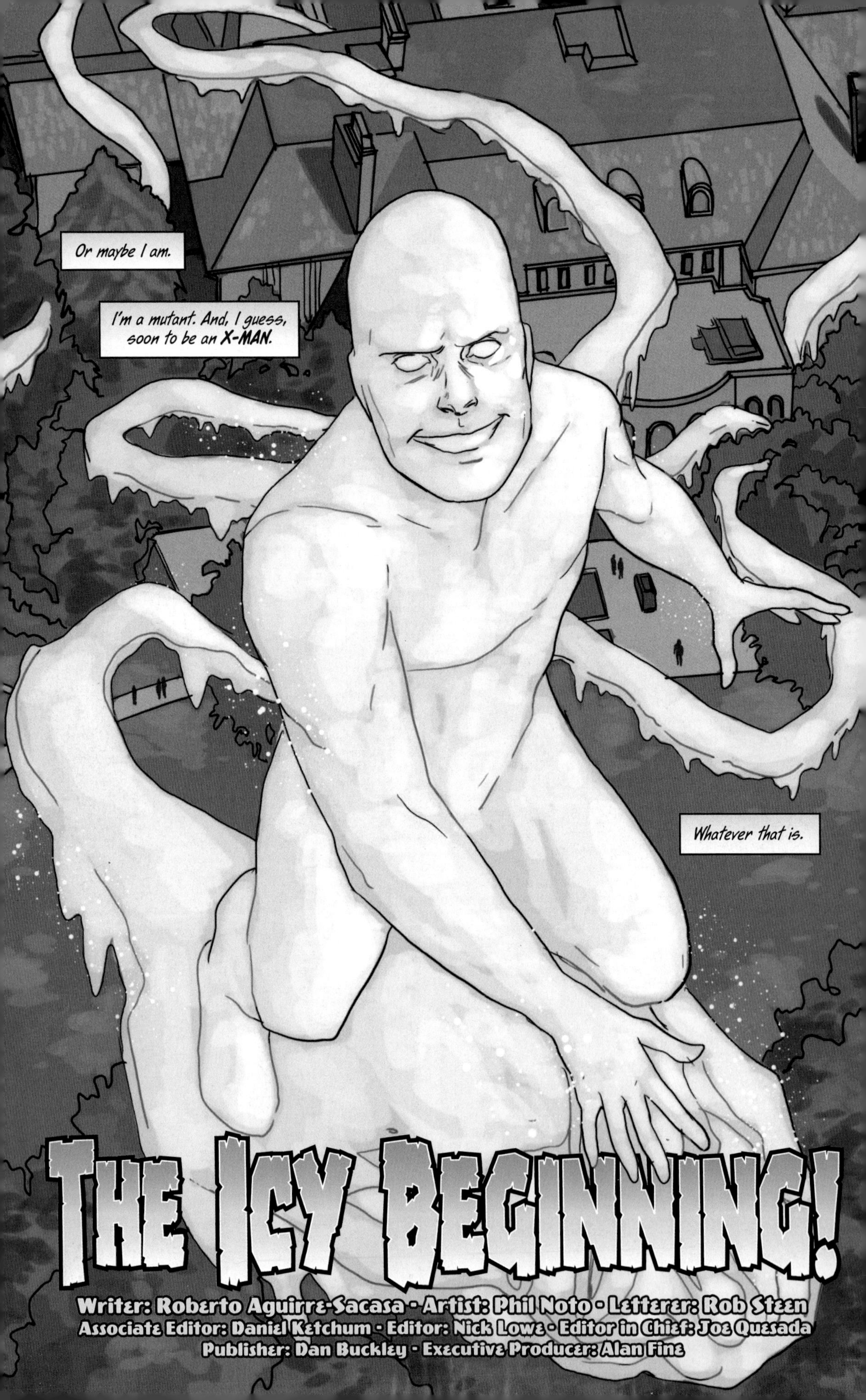
Or maybe I am.
I'm a mutant. And, I guess, soon to be an X-MAN.
Whatever that is.
THE ICY BEGINNING!
Writer: Roberto Aguirre-Sacasa - Artist: Phil Noto - Letterer: Rob Steen
Associate Editor: Daniel Ketchum - Editor: Nick Lowe - Editor in Chief: Joe Quesada
Publisher: Dan Buckley - Executive Producer: Alan Fine

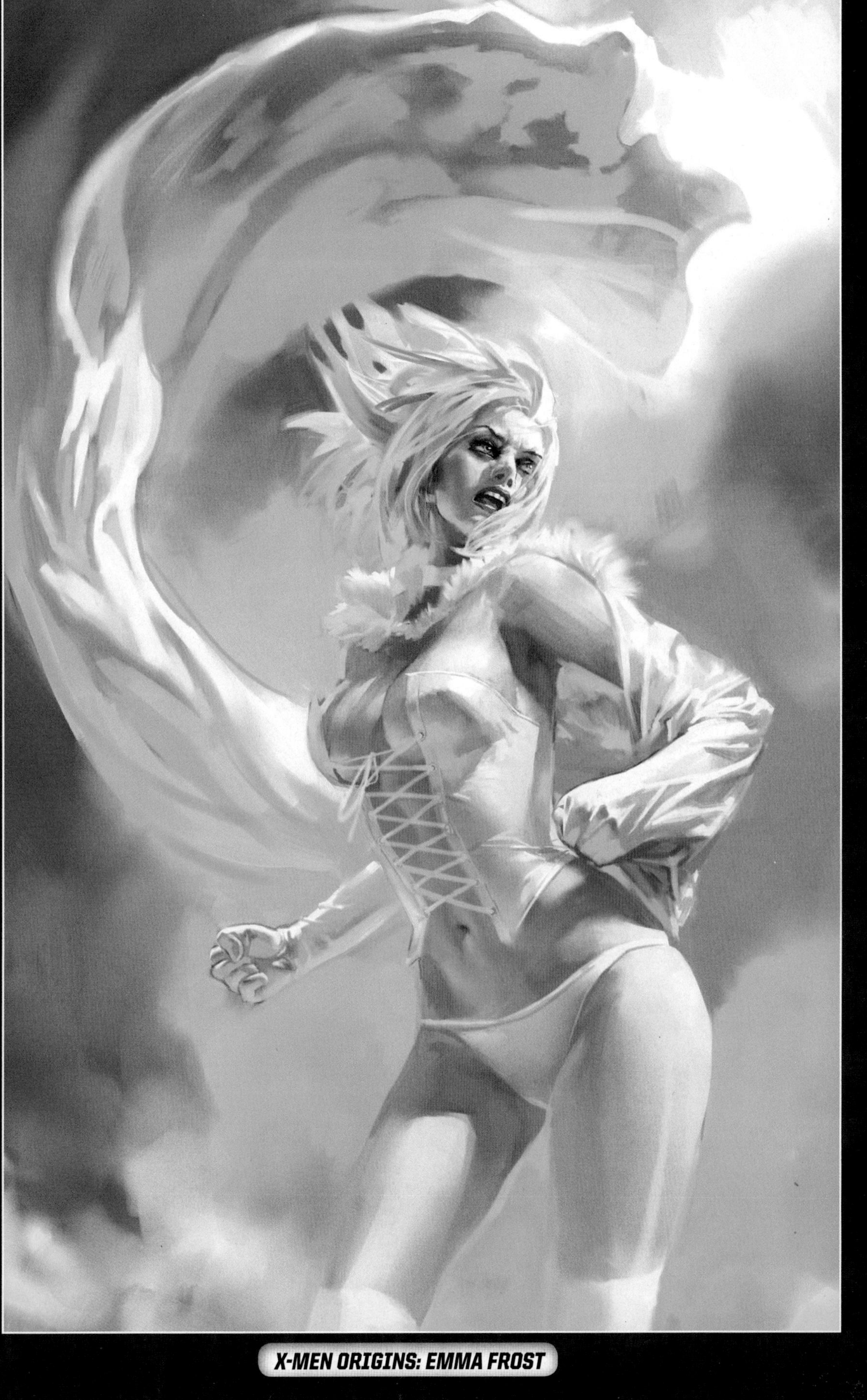

X-MEN ORIGINS: EMMA FROST

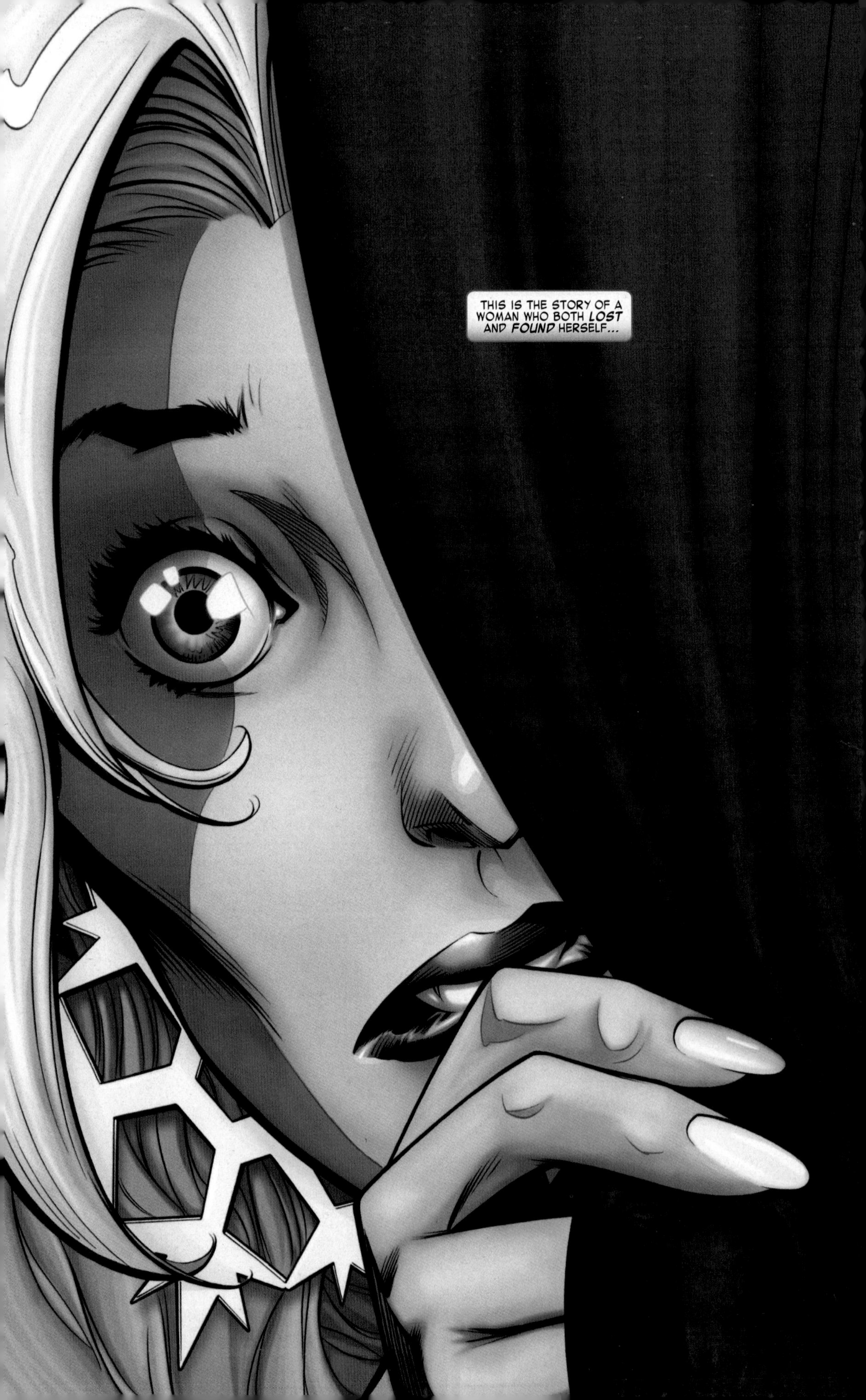
THIS IS THE STORY OF A WOMAN WHO BOTH *LOST* AND *FOUND* HERSELF...

WE HAVE A SPECIAL DANCER IN THE HOUSE TONIGHT, MY DEVILS AND DANDIES...
AND SHE'S GUARANTEED TO WAKE YOU UP QUICKER THAN A COLD SHOWER!
THINK OF IT AS SORT OF A FAIRY TALE...
Hellfire Cabaret
MAKING HER HELLFIRE DEBUT...
I GIVE YOU...THE ICE PRINCESS!
A PARABLE...
YOUR TASTY AND LURID CELEBRITY STORY OF THE WEEK...
WHAT IS THIS $%#?
BUT WHATEVER YOU DO...
S-SORRY...
WHATEVER JUDGMENTS YOU CARE TO MAKE...

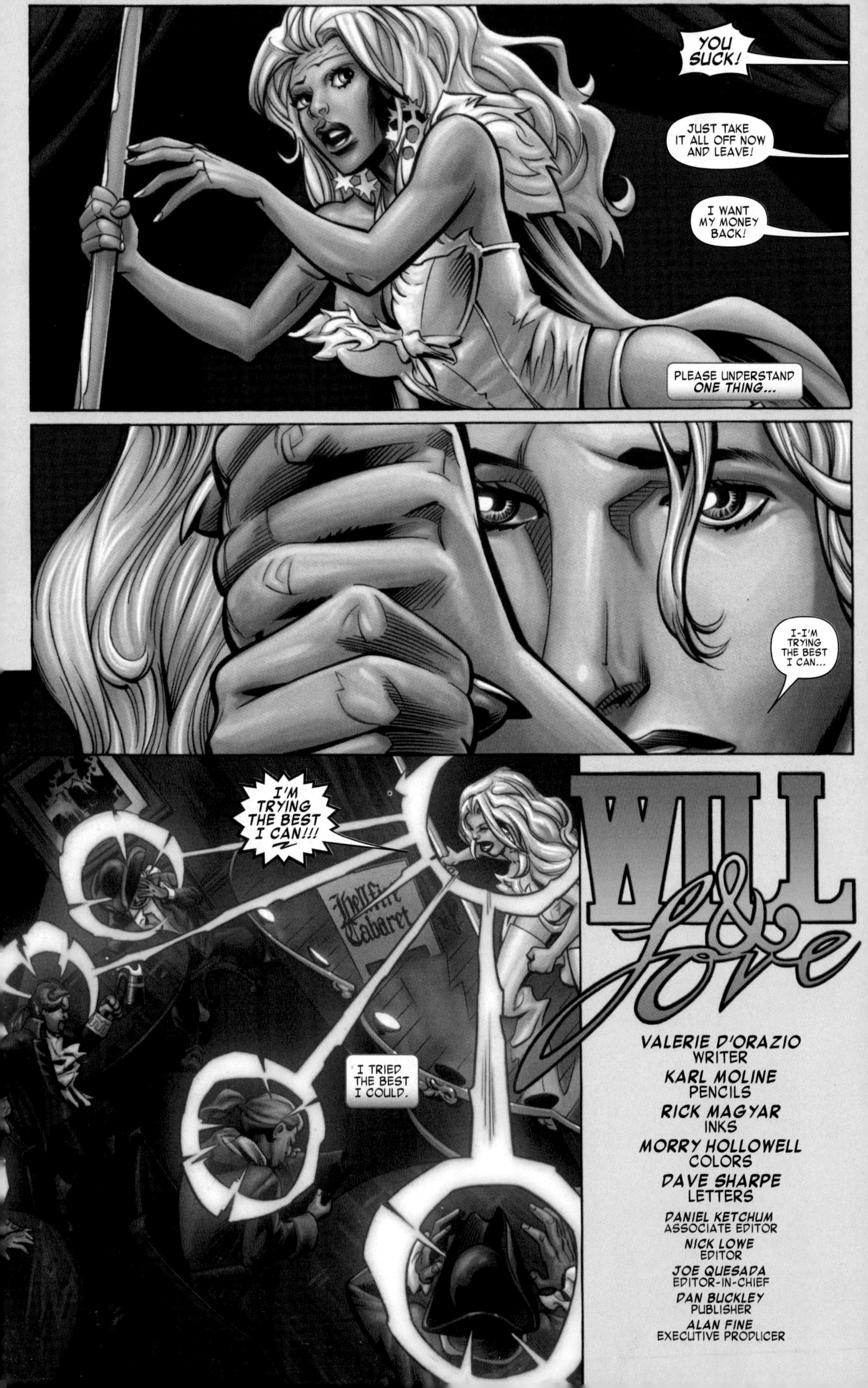
YOU SUCK!
JUST TAKE IT ALL OFF NOW AND LEAVE!
I WANT MY MONEY BACK!
PLEASE UNDERSTAND ONE THING...
I-I'M TRYING THE BEST I CAN...
I'M TRYING THE BEST I CAN!!!
I TRIED THE BEST I COULD.
WILL & Love
VALERIE D'ORAZIO WRITER
KARL MOLINE PENCILS
RICK MAGYAR INKS
MORRY HOLLOWELL COLORS
DAVE SHARPE LETTERS
DANIEL KETCHUM ASSOCIATE EDITOR
NICK LOWE EDITOR
JOE QUESADA EDITOR-IN-CHIEF
DAN BUCKLEY PUBLISHER
ALAN FINE EXECUTIVE PRODUCER

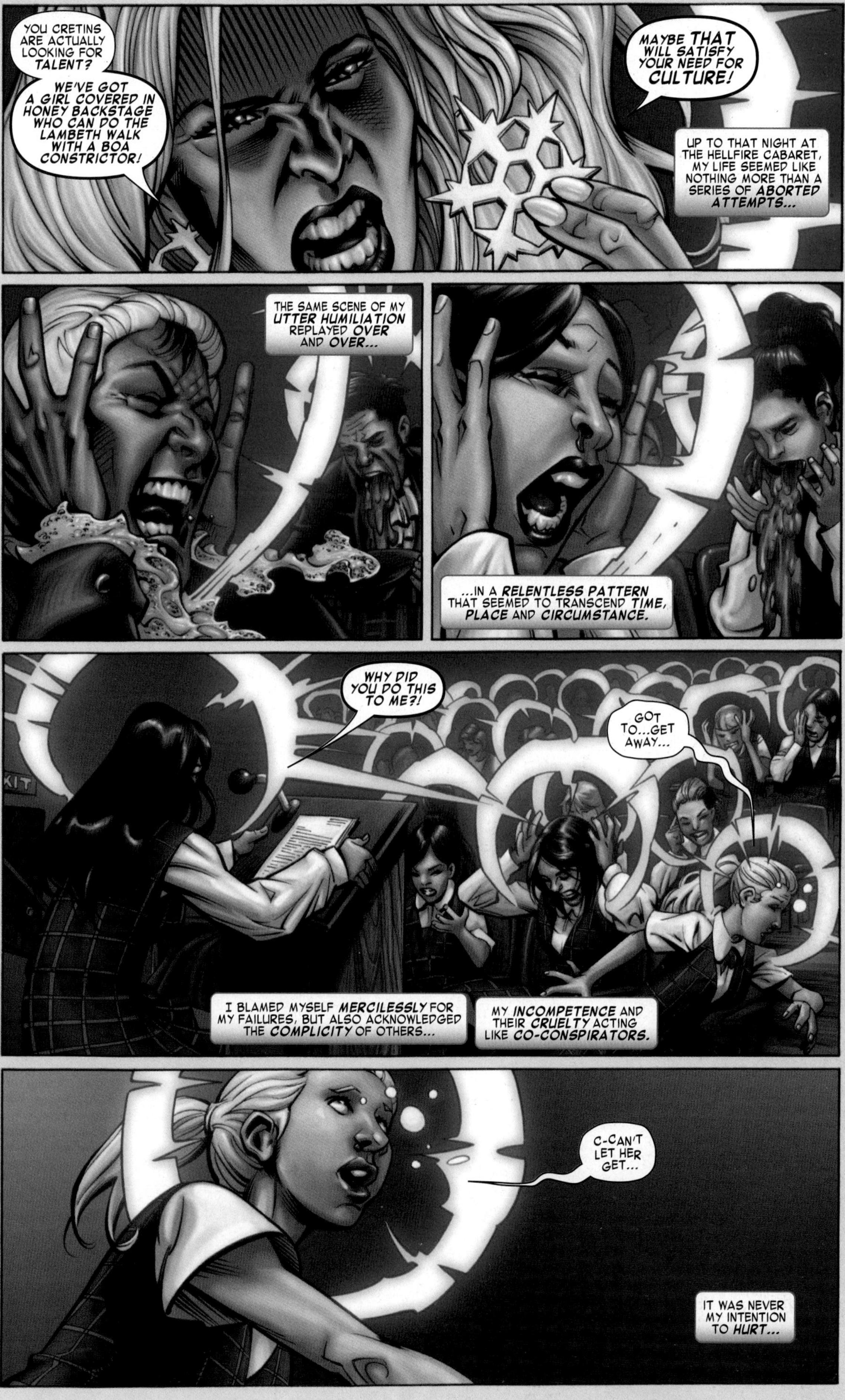
YOU CRETINS ARE ACTUALLY LOOKING FOR TALENT?
WE'VE GOT A GIRL COVERED IN HONEY BACKSTAGE WHO CAN DO THE LAMBETH WALK WITH A BOA CONSTRICTOR!
MAYBE THAT WILL SATISFY YOUR NEED FOR CULTURE!
UP TO THAT NIGHT AT THE HELLFIRE CABARET, MY LIFE SEEMED LIKE NOTHING MORE THAN A SERIES OF ABORTED ATTEMPTS...
THE SAME SCENE OF MY UTTER HUMILIATION REPLAYED OVER AND OVER...
...IN A RELENTLESS PATTERN THAT SEEMED TO TRANSCEND TIME, PLACE AND CIRCUMSTANCE.
WHY DID YOU DO THIS TO ME?!
GOT TO...GET AWAY...
I BLAMED MYSELF MERCILESSLY FOR MY FAILURES, BUT ALSO ACKNOWLEDGED THE COMPLICITY OF OTHERS...
MY INCOMPETENCE AND THEIR CRUELTY ACTING LIKE CO-CONSPIRATORS.
C-CAN'T LET HER GET...
IT WAS NEVER MY INTENTION TO HURT...

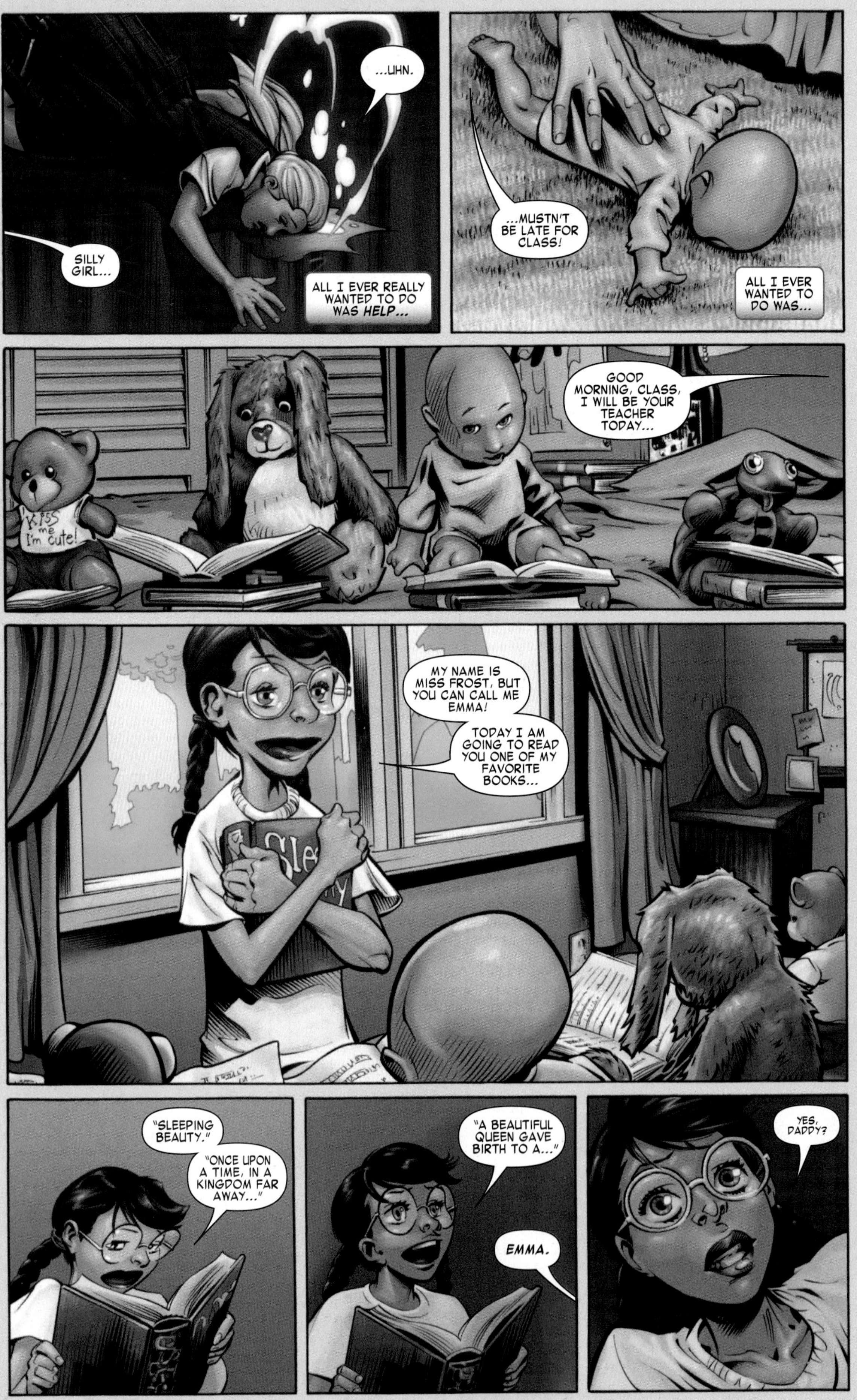
...UHN.
SILLY GIRL...
ALL I EVER REALLY WANTED TO DO WAS HELP...
...MUSTN'T BE LATE FOR CLASS!
ALL I EVER WANTED TO DO WAS...
GOOD MORNING, CLASS, I WILL BE YOUR TEACHER TODAY...
KISS me I'm cute!
MY NAME IS MISS FROST, BUT YOU CAN CALL ME EMMA!
TODAY I AM GOING TO READ YOU ONE OF MY FAVORITE BOOKS...
"SLEEPING BEAUTY."
"ONCE UPON A TIME, IN A KINGDOM FAR AWAY..."
"A BEAUTIFUL QUEEN GAVE BIRTH TO A..."
EMMA.
YES, DADDY?

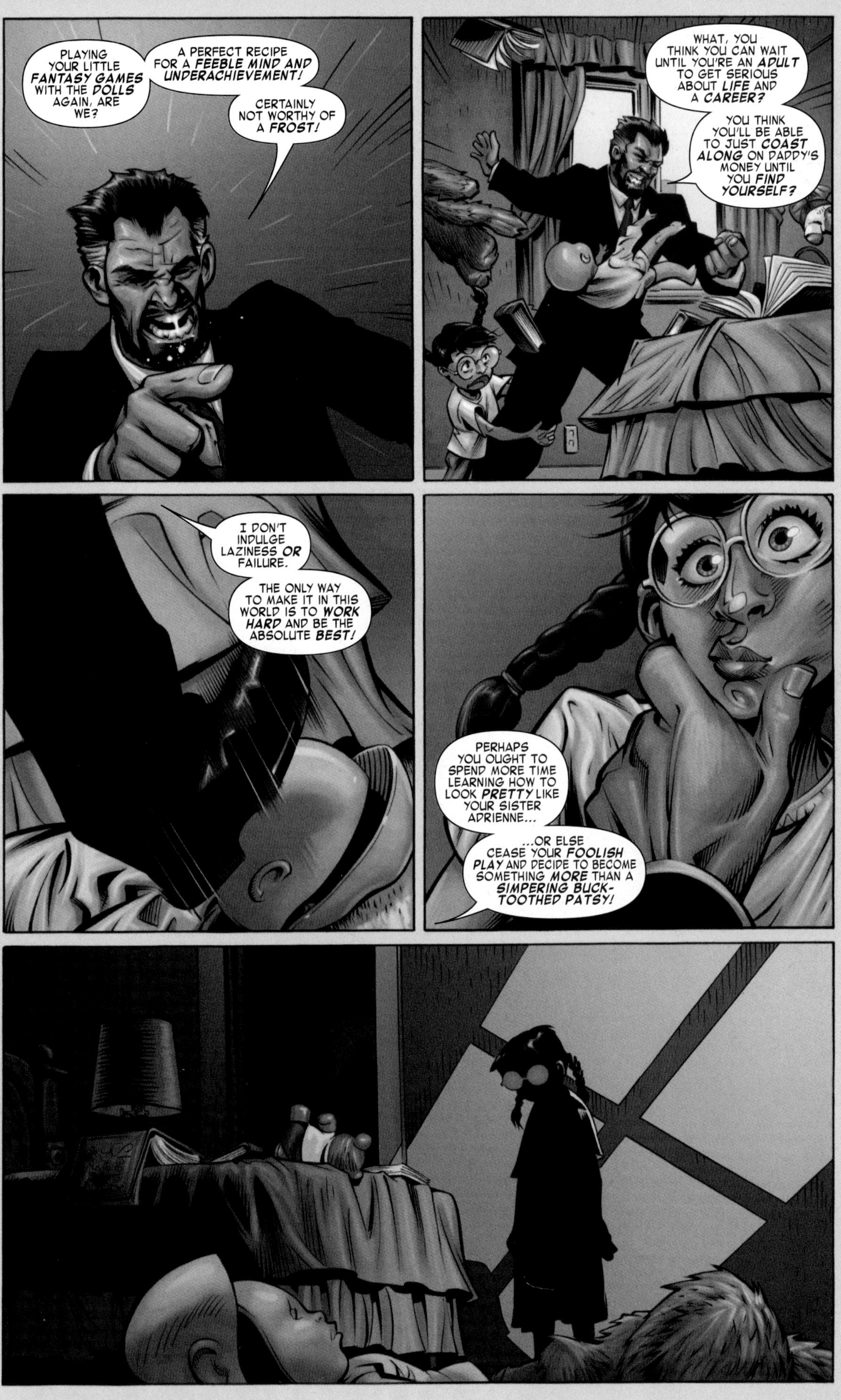

PLAYING YOUR LITTLE FANTASY GAMES WITH THE DOLLS AGAIN, ARE WE?
A PERFECT RECIPE FOR A FEEBLE MIND AND UNDERACHIEVEMENT!
CERTAINLY NOT WORTHY OF A FROST!
WHAT, YOU THINK YOU CAN WAIT UNTIL YOU'RE AN ADULT TO GET SERIOUS ABOUT LIFE AND A CAREER?
YOU THINK YOU'LL BE ABLE TO JUST COAST ALONG ON DADDY'S MONEY UNTIL YOU FIND YOURSELF?
I DON'T INDULGE LAZINESS OR FAILURE.
THE ONLY WAY TO MAKE IT IN THIS WORLD IS TO WORK HARD AND BE THE ABSOLUTE BEST!
PERHAPS YOU OUGHT TO SPEND MORE TIME LEARNING HOW TO LOOK PRETTY LIKE YOUR SISTER ADRIENNE...
...OR ELSE CEASE YOUR FOOLISH PLAY AND DECIDE TO BECOME SOMETHING MORE THAN A SIMPERING BUCK-TOOTHED PATSY!

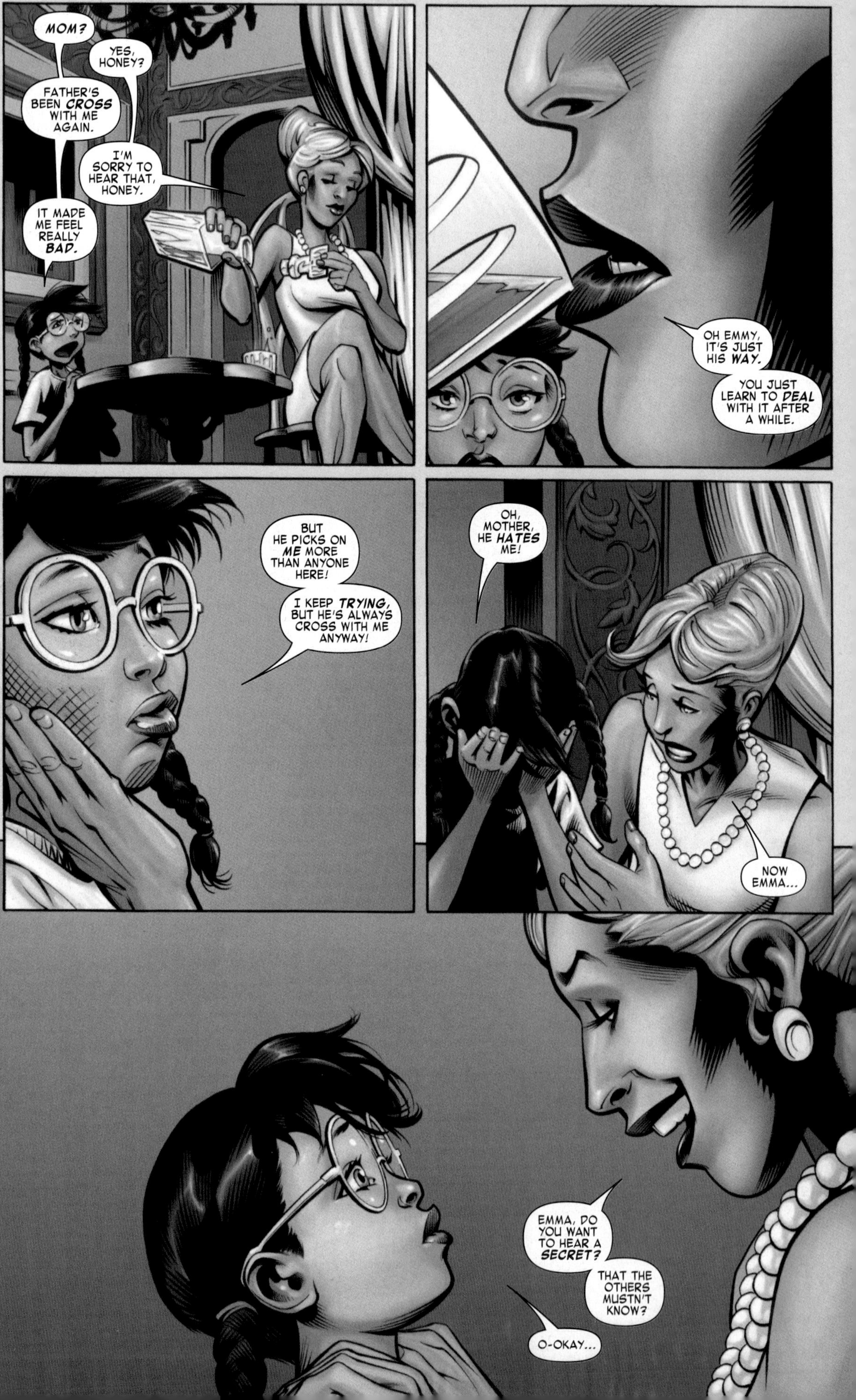
MOM?
YES, HONEY?
FATHER'S BEEN CROSS WITH ME AGAIN.
I'M SORRY TO HEAR THAT, HONEY.
IT MADE ME FEEL REALLY BAD.
OH EMMY, IT'S JUST HIS WAY.
YOU JUST LEARN TO DEAL WITH IT AFTER A WHILE.
BUT HE PICKS ON ME MORE THAN ANYONE HERE!
I KEEP TRYING, BUT HE'S ALWAYS CROSS WITH ME ANYWAY!
OH, MOTHER, HE HATES ME!
NOW EMMA...
EMMA, DO YOU WANT TO HEAR A SECRET?
THAT THE OTHERS MUSTN'T KNOW?
O-OKAY...

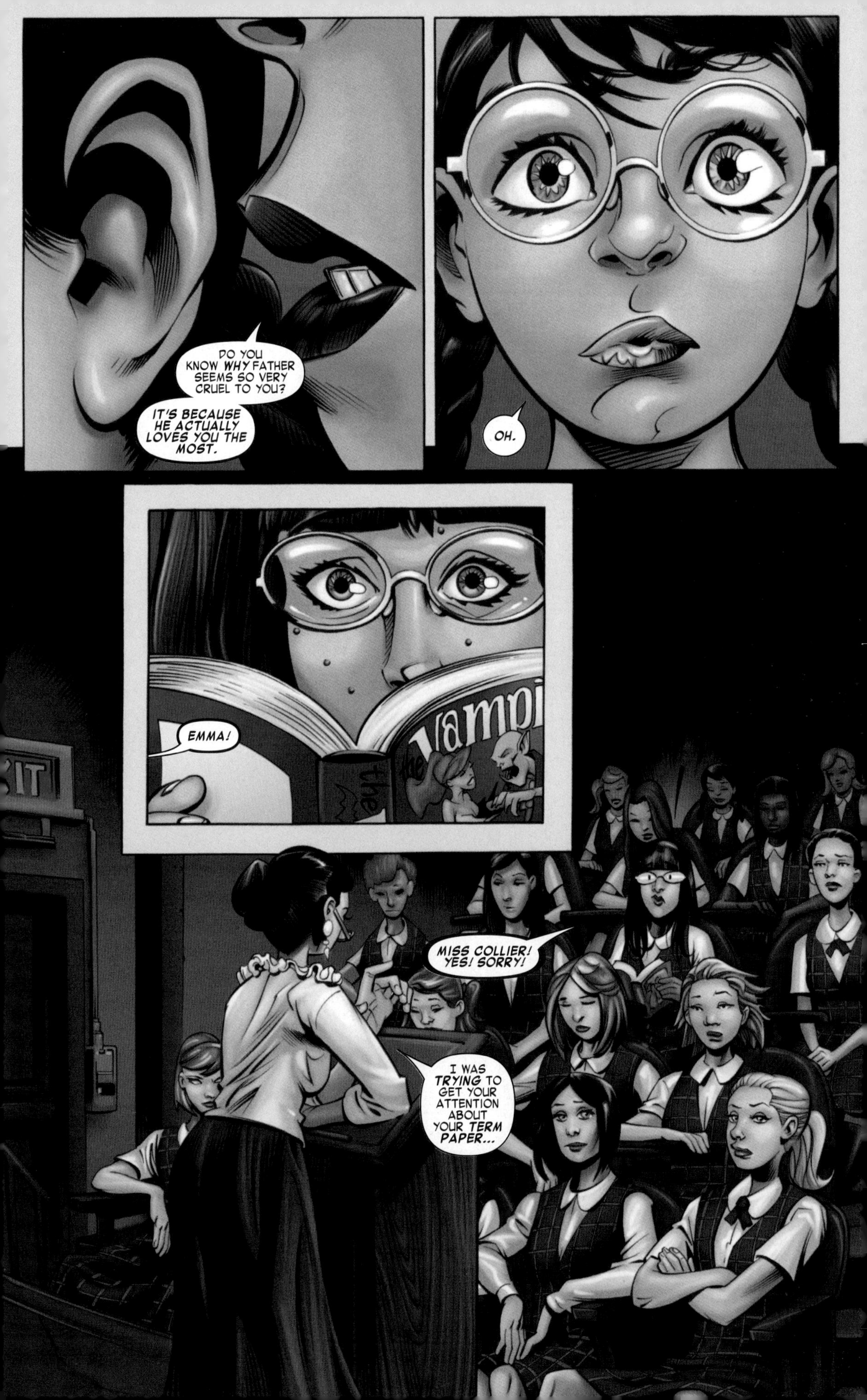
DO YOU KNOW WHY FATHER SEEMS SO VERY CRUEL TO YOU?
IT'S BECAUSE HE ACTUALLY LOVES YOU THE MOST.
OH.
EMMA!
MISS COLLIER! YES! SORRY!
I WAS TRYING TO GET YOUR ATTENTION ABOUT YOUR TERM PAPER...

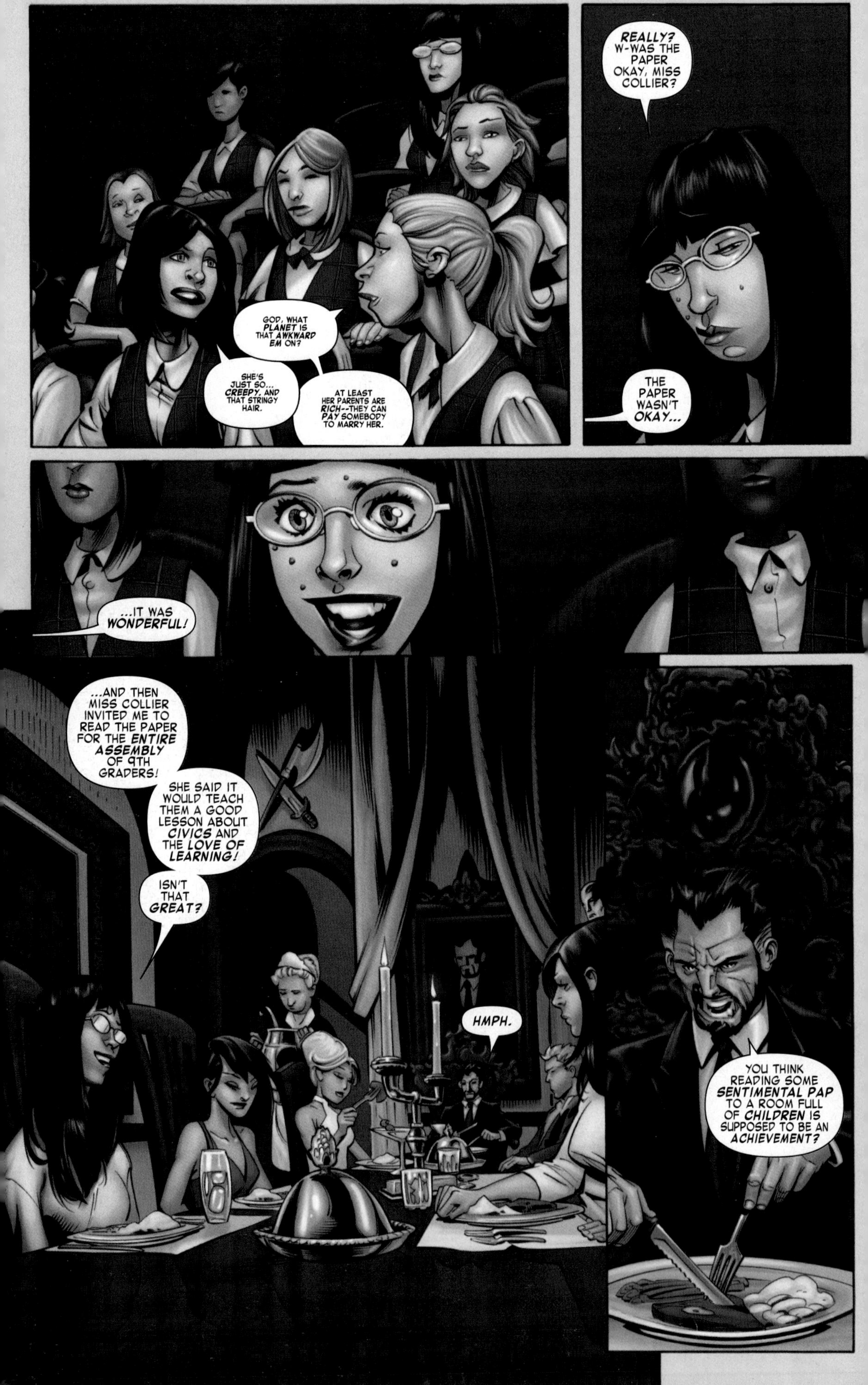

GOD, WHAT PLANET IS THAT AWKWARD EM ON?
SHE'S JUST SO... CREEPY. AND THAT STRINGY HAIR.
AT LEAST HER PARENTS ARE RICH--THEY CAN PAY SOMEBODY TO MARRY HER.
REALLY? W-WAS THE PAPER OKAY, MISS COLLIER?
THE PAPER WASN'T OKAY...
...IT WAS WONDERFUL!
...AND THEN MISS COLLIER INVITED ME TO READ THE PAPER FOR THE ENTIRE ASSEMBLY OF 9TH GRADERS!
SHE SAID IT WOULD TEACH THEM A GOOD LESSON ABOUT CIVICS AND THE LOVE OF LEARNING!
ISN'T THAT GREAT?
HMPH.
YOU THINK READING SOME SENTIMENTAL PAP TO A ROOM FULL OF CHILDREN IS SUPPOSED TO BE AN ACHIEVEMENT?

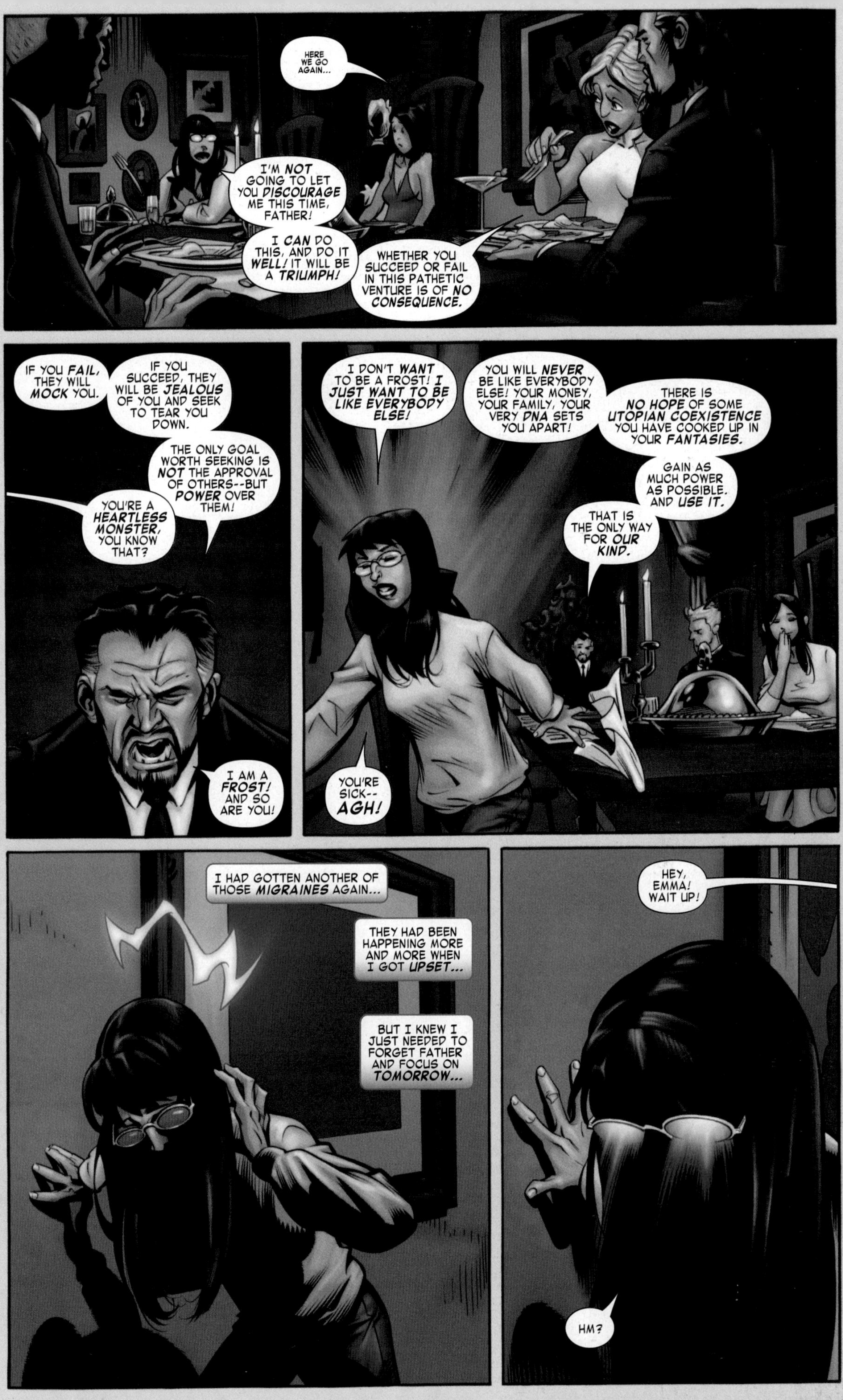
HERE WE GO AGAIN...
I'M NOT GOING TO LET YOU DISCOURAGE ME THIS TIME, FATHER!
I CAN DO THIS, AND DO IT WELL! IT WILL BE A TRIUMPH!
WHETHER YOU SUCCEED OR FAIL IN THIS PATHETIC VENTURE IS OF NO CONSEQUENCE.
IF YOU FAIL, THEY WILL MOCK YOU.
IF YOU SUCCEED, THEY WILL BE JEALOUS OF YOU AND SEEK TO TEAR YOU DOWN.
THE ONLY GOAL WORTH SEEKING IS NOT THE APPROVAL OF OTHERS--BUT POWER OVER THEM!
YOU'RE A HEARTLESS MONSTER, YOU KNOW THAT?
I AM A FROST! AND SO ARE YOU!
I DON'T WANT TO BE A FROST! I JUST WANT TO BE LIKE EVERYBODY ELSE!
YOU WILL NEVER BE LIKE EVERYBODY ELSE! YOUR MONEY, YOUR FAMILY, YOUR VERY DNA SETS YOU APART!
THERE IS NO HOPE OF SOME UTOPIAN COEXISTENCE YOU HAVE COOKED UP IN YOUR FANTASIES.
GAIN AS MUCH POWER AS POSSIBLE. AND USE IT.
THAT IS THE ONLY WAY FOR OUR KIND.
YOU'RE SICK--AGH!
I HAD GOTTEN ANOTHER OF THOSE MIGRAINES AGAIN...
THEY HAD BEEN HAPPENING MORE AND MORE WHEN I GOT UPSET...
BUT I KNEW I JUST NEEDED TO FORGET FATHER AND FOCUS ON TOMORROW...
HEY, EMMA! WAIT UP!
HM?

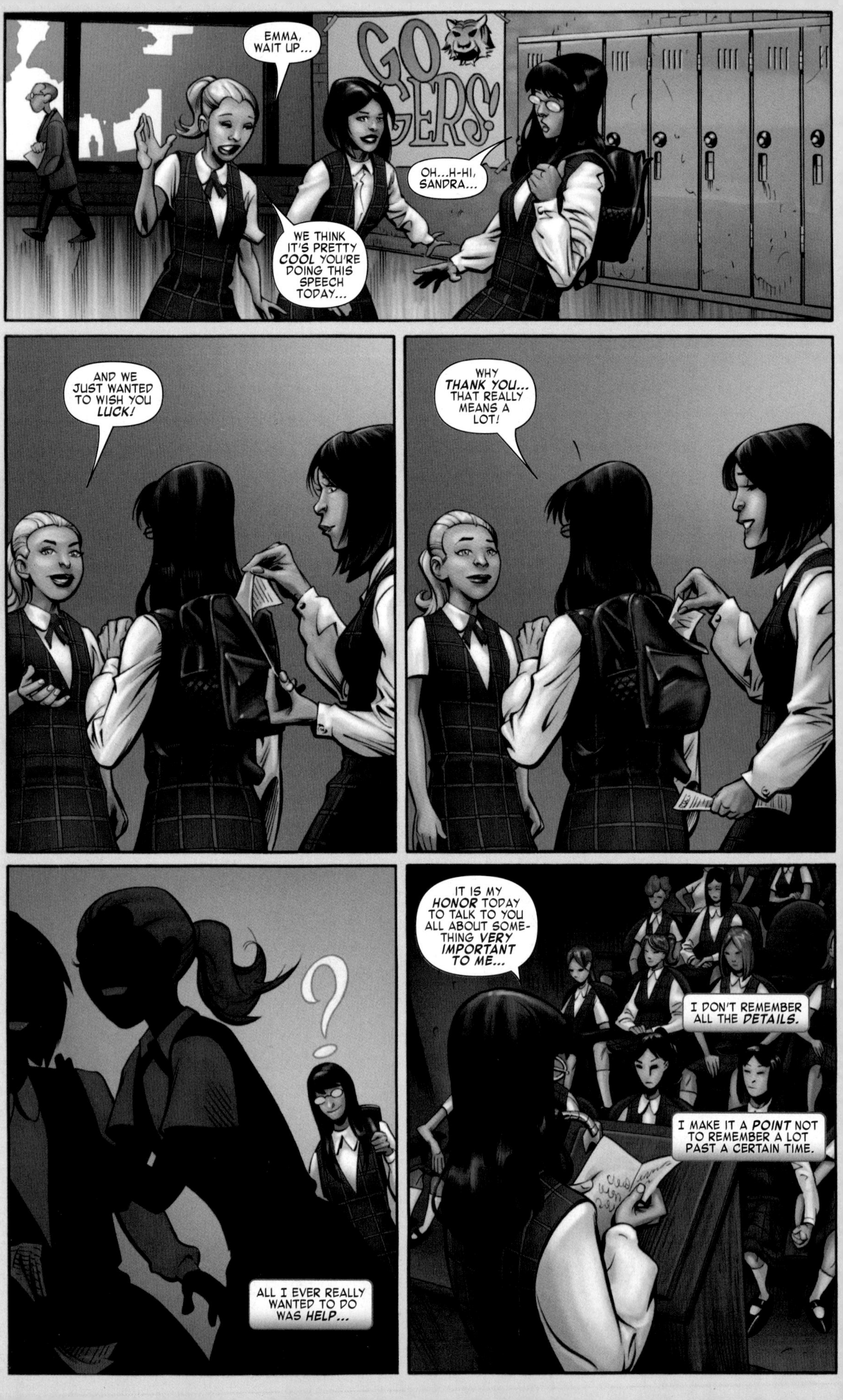
EMMA, WAIT UP...
GO GERS!
OH...H-HI, SANDRA...
WE THINK IT'S PRETTY COOL YOU'RE DOING THIS SPEECH TODAY...
AND WE JUST WANTED TO WISH YOU LUCK!
WHY THANK YOU... THAT REALLY MEANS A LOT!
?
ALL I EVER REALLY WANTED TO DO WAS HELP...
IT IS MY HONOR TODAY TO TALK TO YOU ALL ABOUT SOMETHING VERY IMPORTANT TO ME...
I DON'T REMEMBER ALL THE DETAILS.
I MAKE IT A POINT NOT TO REMEMBER A LOT PAST A CERTAIN TIME.

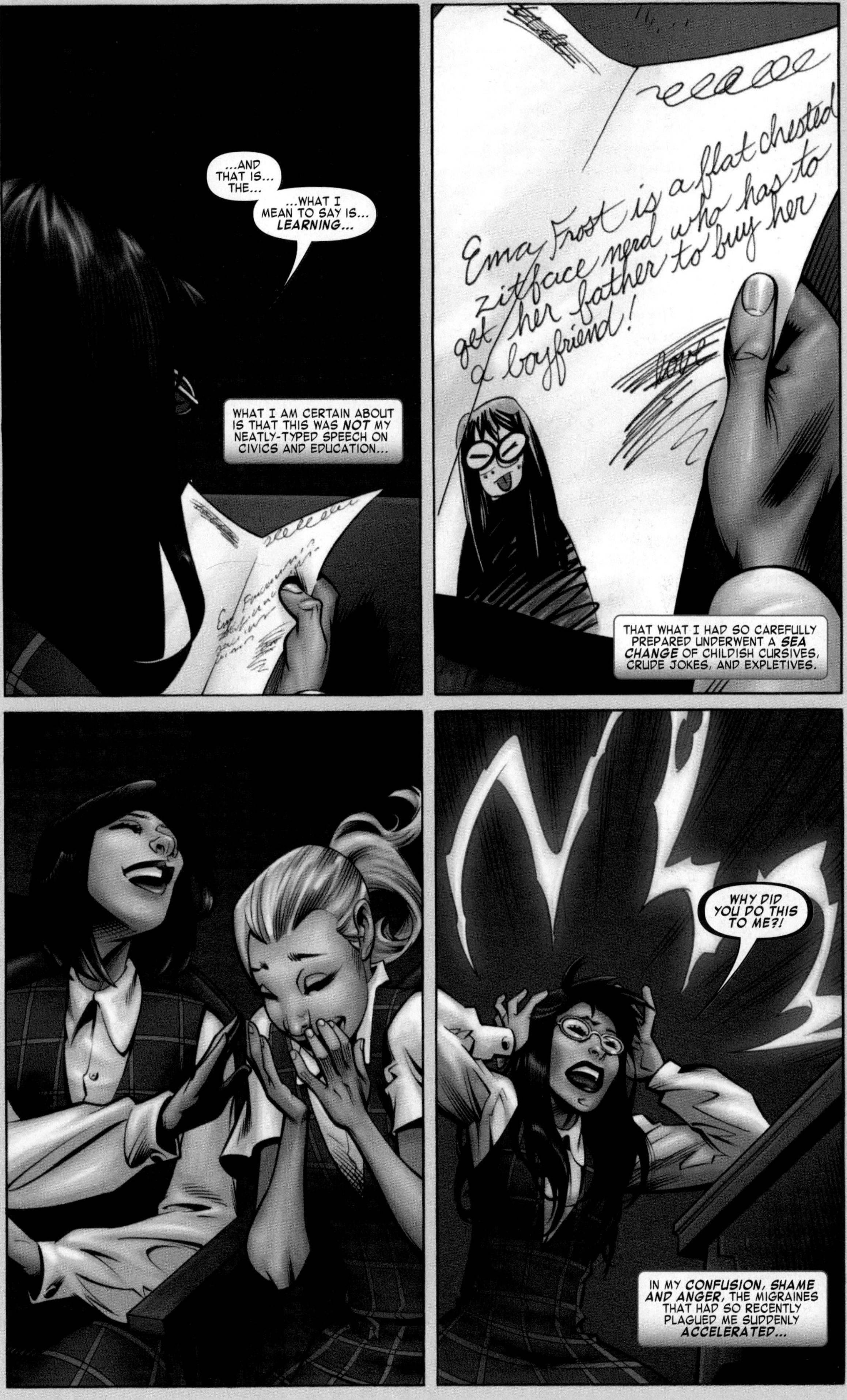
...AND THAT IS... THE...
...WHAT I MEAN TO SAY IS... LEARNING...
WHAT I AM CERTAIN ABOUT IS THAT THIS WAS NOT MY NEATLY-TYPED SPEECH ON CIVICS AND EDUCATION...
Ema Frost is a flat chested zitface nerd who has to get her father to buy her a boyfriend!
THAT WHAT I HAD SO CAREFULLY PREPARED UNDERWENT A SEA CHANGE OF CHILDISH CURSIVES, CRUDE JOKES, AND EXPLETIVES.
WHY DID YOU DO THIS TO ME?!
IN MY CONFUSION, SHAME AND ANGER, THE MIGRAINES THAT HAD SO RECENTLY PLAGUED ME SUDDENLY ACCELERATED...

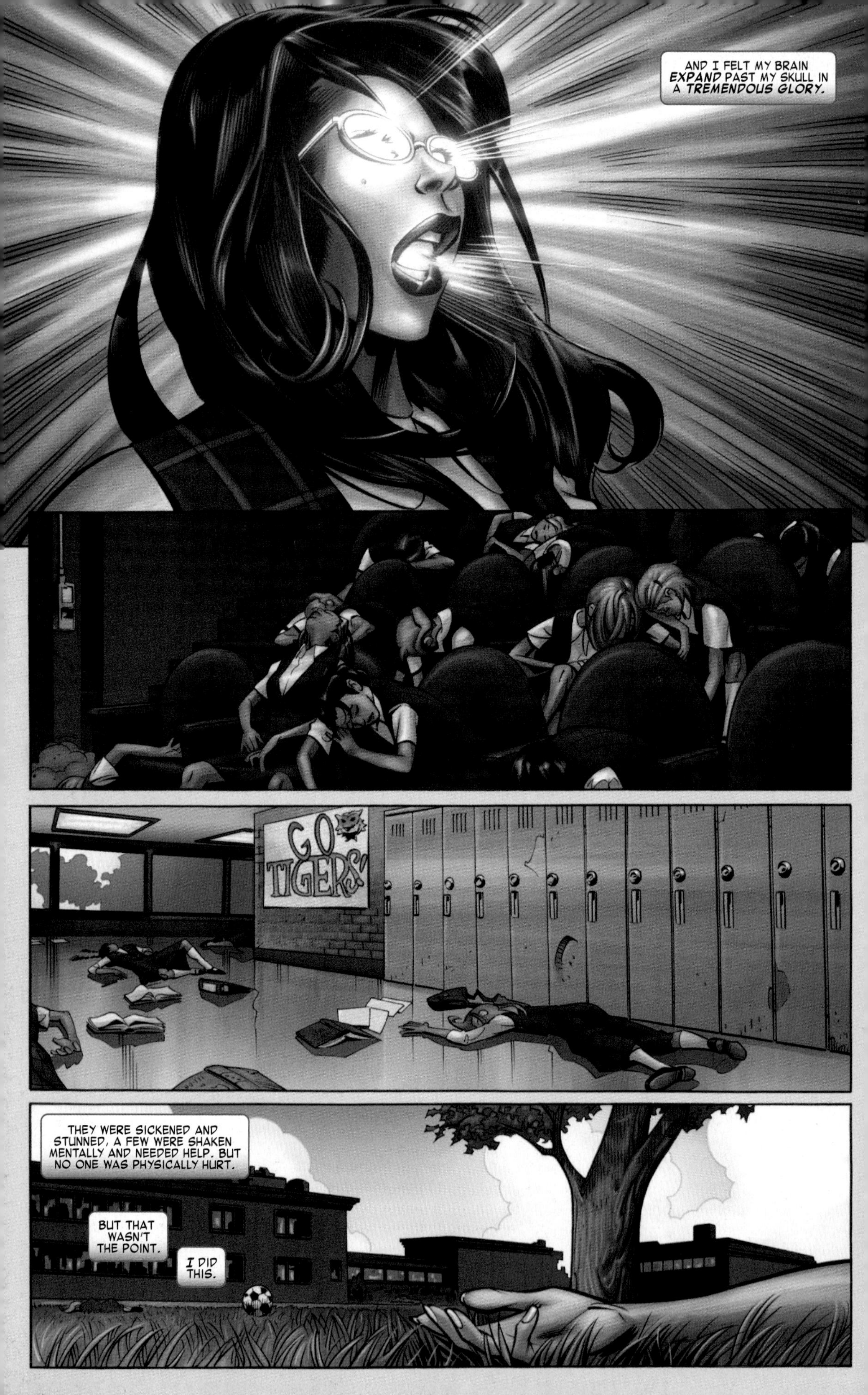

AND I FELT MY BRAIN EXPAND PAST MY SKULL IN A TREMENDOUS GLORY.
GO TIGERS!
THEY WERE SICKENED AND STUNNED, A FEW WERE SHAKEN MENTALLY AND NEEDED HELP. BUT NO ONE WAS PHYSICALLY HURT.
BUT THAT WASN'T THE POINT.
I DID THIS.

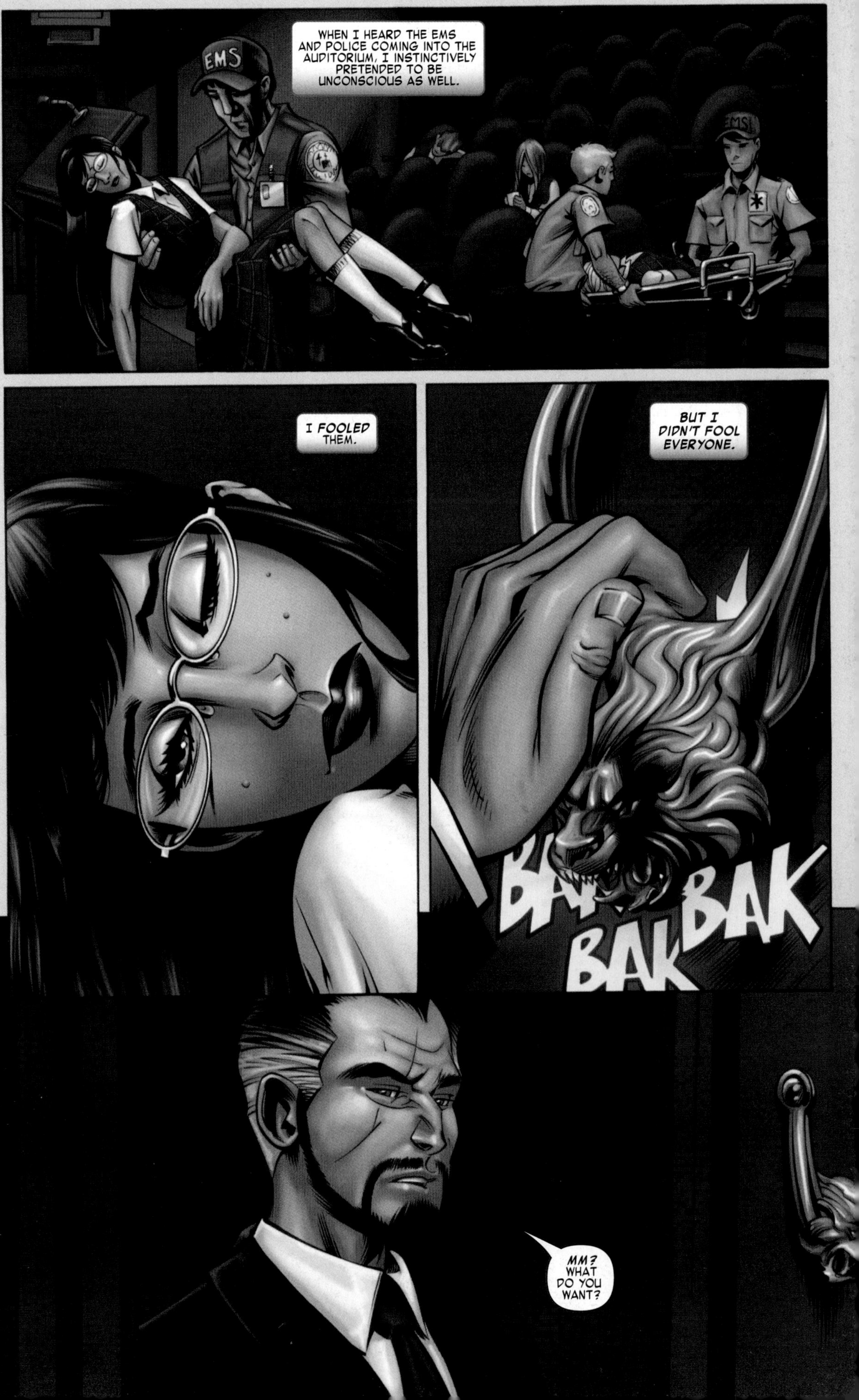
WHEN I HEARD THE EMS AND POLICE COMING INTO THE AUDITORIUM, I INSTINCTIVELY PRETENDED TO BE UNCONSCIOUS AS WELL.
EMS
I FOOLED THEM.
BUT I DIDN'T FOOL EVERYONE.
BAK BAK BAK
MM? WHAT DO YOU WANT?

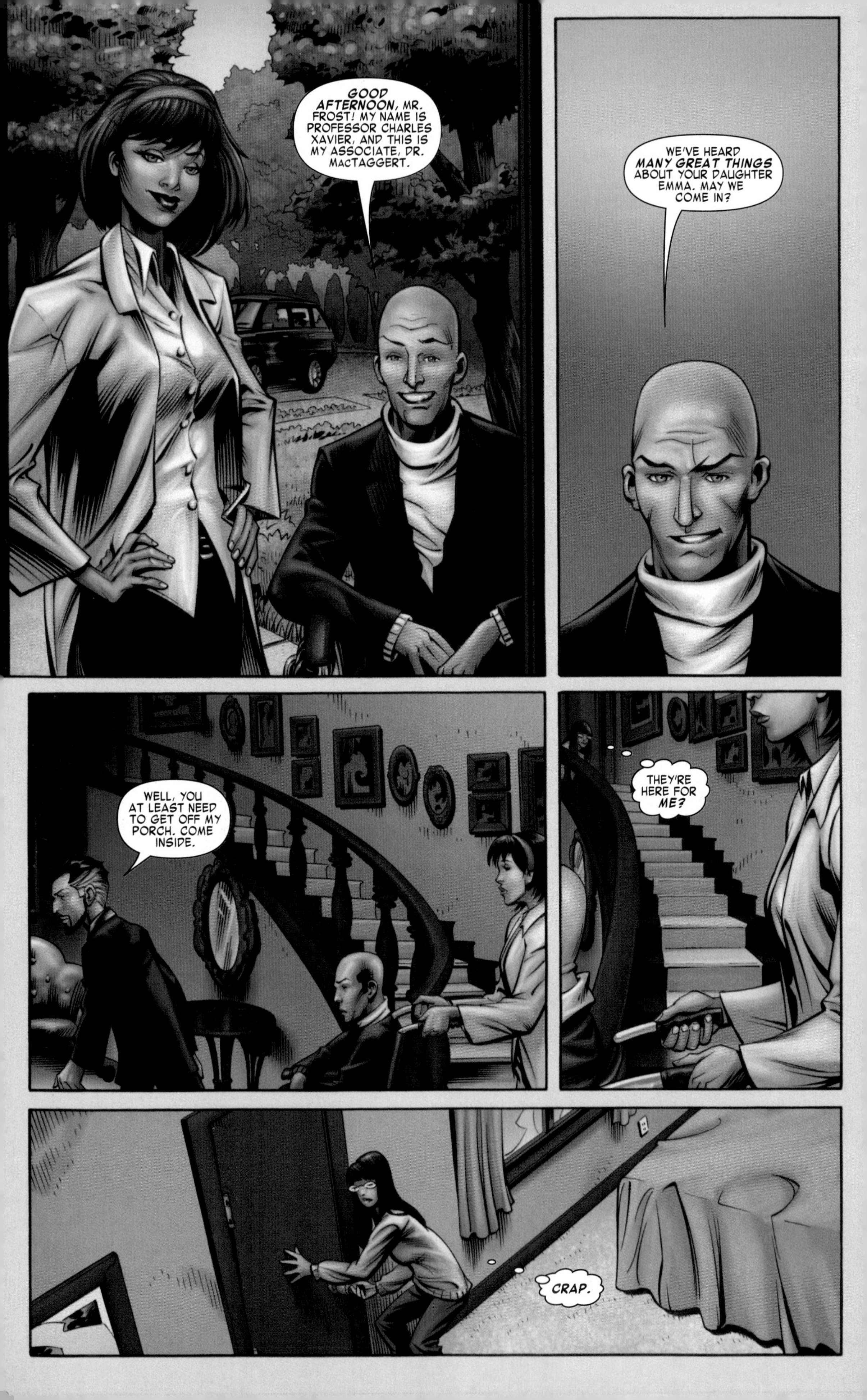
GOOD AFTERNOON, MR. FROST! MY NAME IS PROFESSOR CHARLES XAVIER, AND THIS IS MY ASSOCIATE, DR. MacTAGGERT.
WE'VE HEARD MANY GREAT THINGS ABOUT YOUR DAUGHTER EMMA. MAY WE COME IN?
WELL, YOU AT LEAST NEED TO GET OFF MY PORCH. COME INSIDE.
THEY'RE HERE FOR ME?
CRAP.

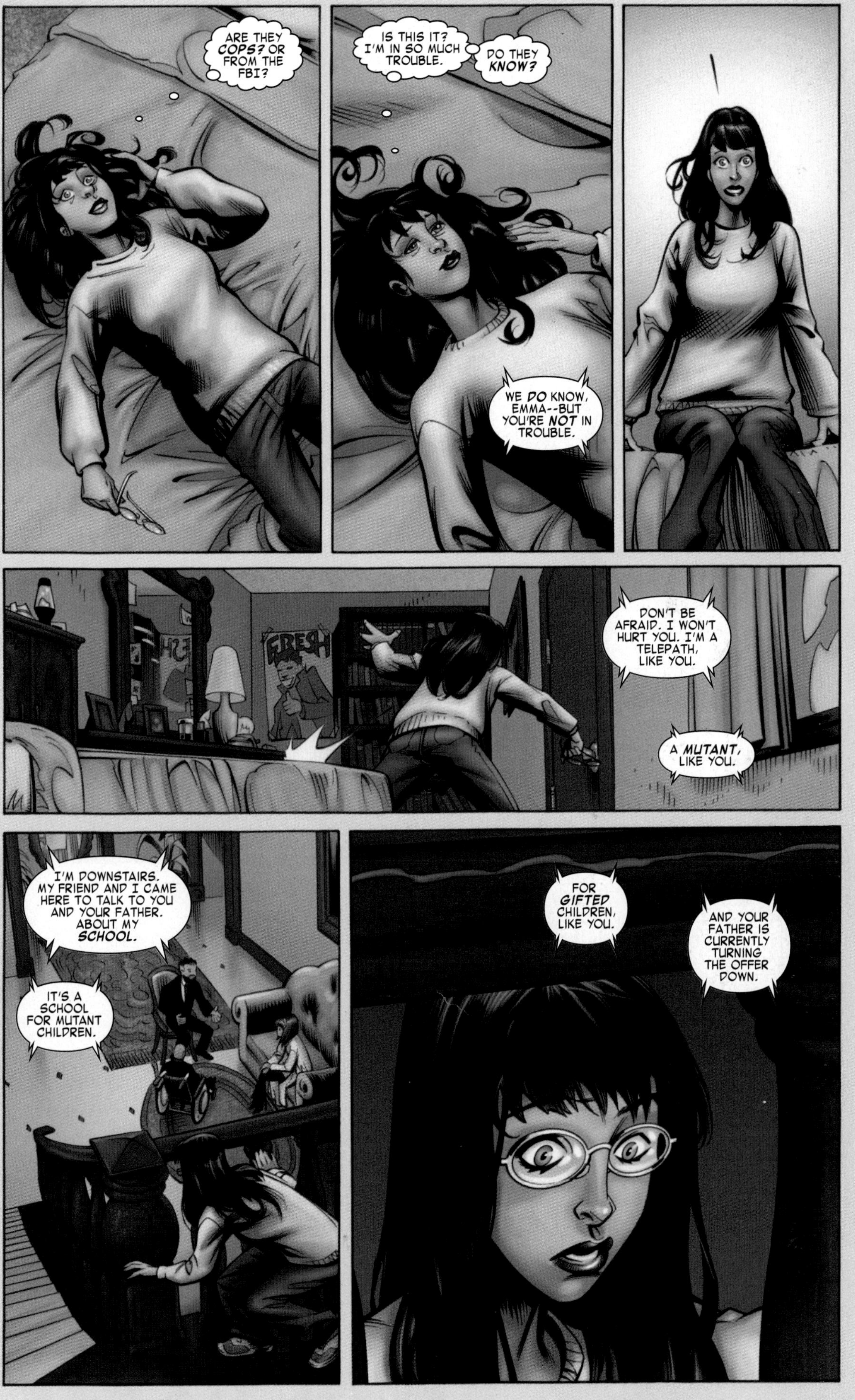
ARE THEY COPS? OR FROM THE FBI?
IS THIS IT? I'M IN SO MUCH TROUBLE.
DO THEY KNOW?
WE DO KNOW, EMMA--BUT YOU'RE NOT IN TROUBLE.
!
DON'T BE AFRAID. I WON'T HURT YOU. I'M A TELEPATH, LIKE YOU.
A MUTANT, LIKE YOU.
FRESH
I'M DOWNSTAIRS. MY FRIEND AND I CAME HERE TO TALK TO YOU AND YOUR FATHER. ABOUT MY SCHOOL.
IT'S A SCHOOL FOR MUTANT CHILDREN.
FOR GIFTED CHILDREN, LIKE YOU.
AND YOUR FATHER IS CURRENTLY TURNING THE OFFER DOWN.

A STRANGER PRESUMES HE KNOWS MY CHILD BETTER THAN I?

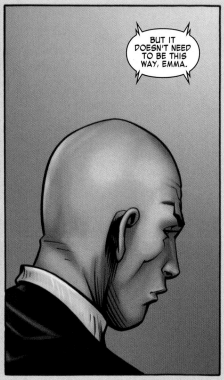

BUT IT DOESN'T NEED TO BE THIS WAY, EMMA.

EMMA, YOU HAVE AN *INCREDIBLE* AMOUNT OF POWER INSIDE OF YOU.

BUT THAT POWER NEEDS TRAINING. HONING. AND WITH THAT, I CAN HELP YOU.

YOU KNOW ENOUGH OF HOW OUR POWERS WORK TO KNOW THAT I CAN CHANGE YOUR FATHER'S MIND.

I CAN SHOW HIM THE ERROR OF HIS WAYS.

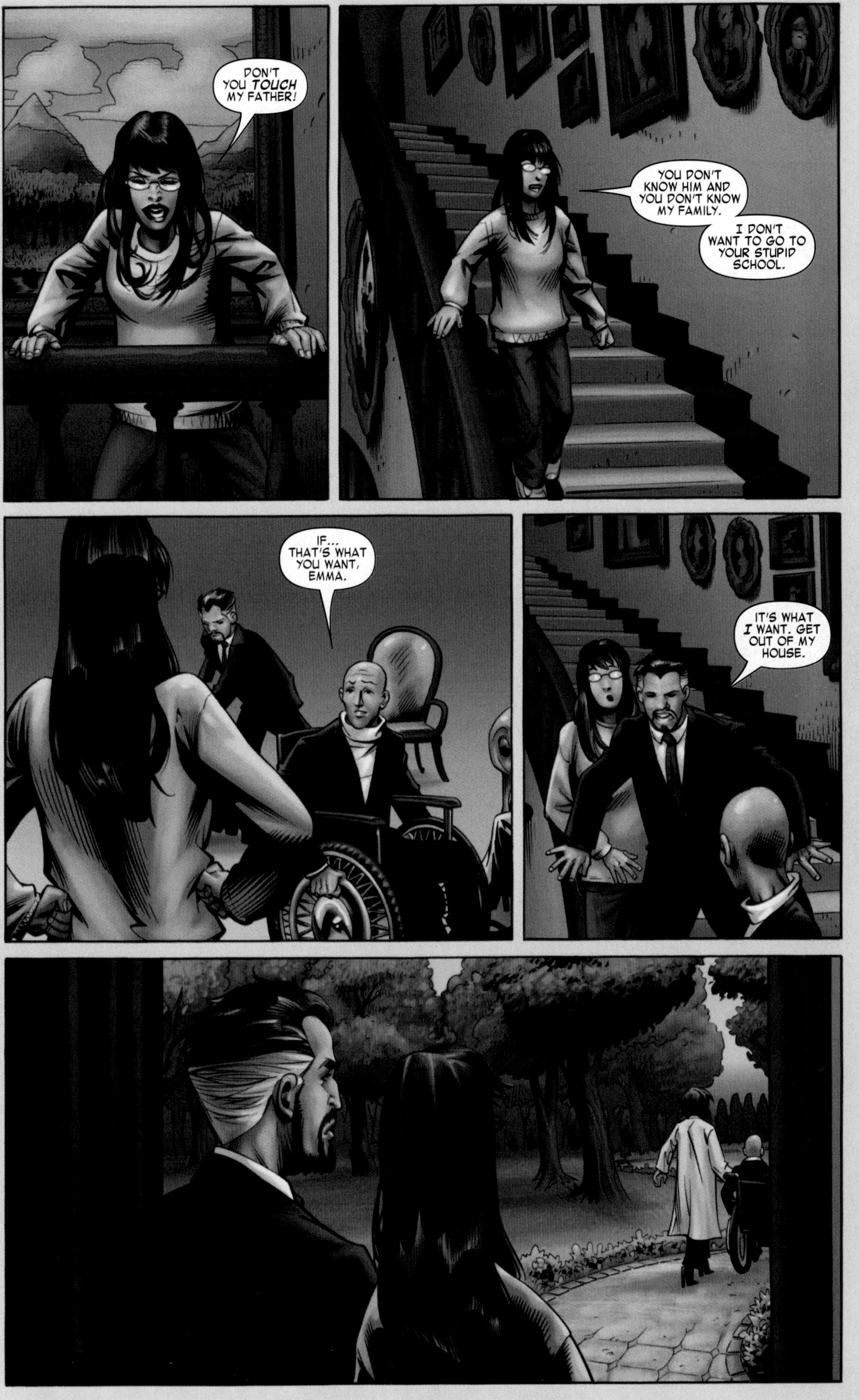
DON'T YOU TOUCH MY FATHER!
YOU DON'T KNOW HIM AND YOU DON'T KNOW MY FAMILY.
I DON'T WANT TO GO TO YOUR STUPID SCHOOL.
IF... THAT'S WHAT YOU WANT, EMMA.
IT'S WHAT I WANT. GET OUT OF MY HOUSE.

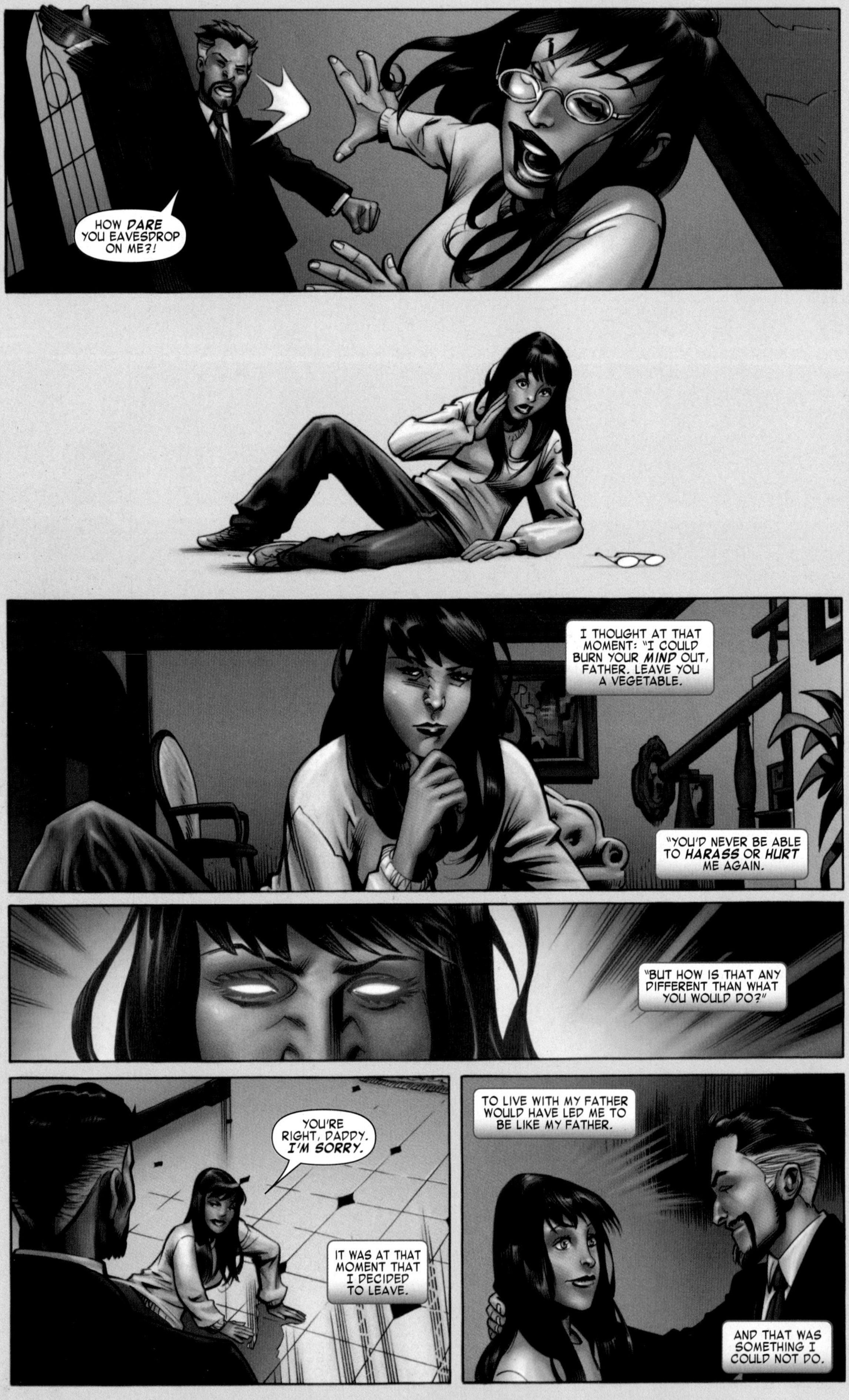
HOW DARE YOU EAVESDROP ON ME?!
I THOUGHT AT THAT MOMENT: "I COULD BURN YOUR MIND OUT, FATHER. LEAVE YOU A VEGETABLE.
"YOU'D NEVER BE ABLE TO HARASS OR HURT ME AGAIN.
"BUT HOW IS THAT ANY DIFFERENT THAN WHAT YOU WOULD DO?"
YOU'RE RIGHT, DADDY. I'M SORRY.
IT WAS AT THAT MOMENT THAT I DECIDED TO LEAVE.
TO LIVE WITH MY FATHER WOULD HAVE LED ME TO BE LIKE MY FATHER.
AND THAT WAS SOMETHING I COULD NOT DO.

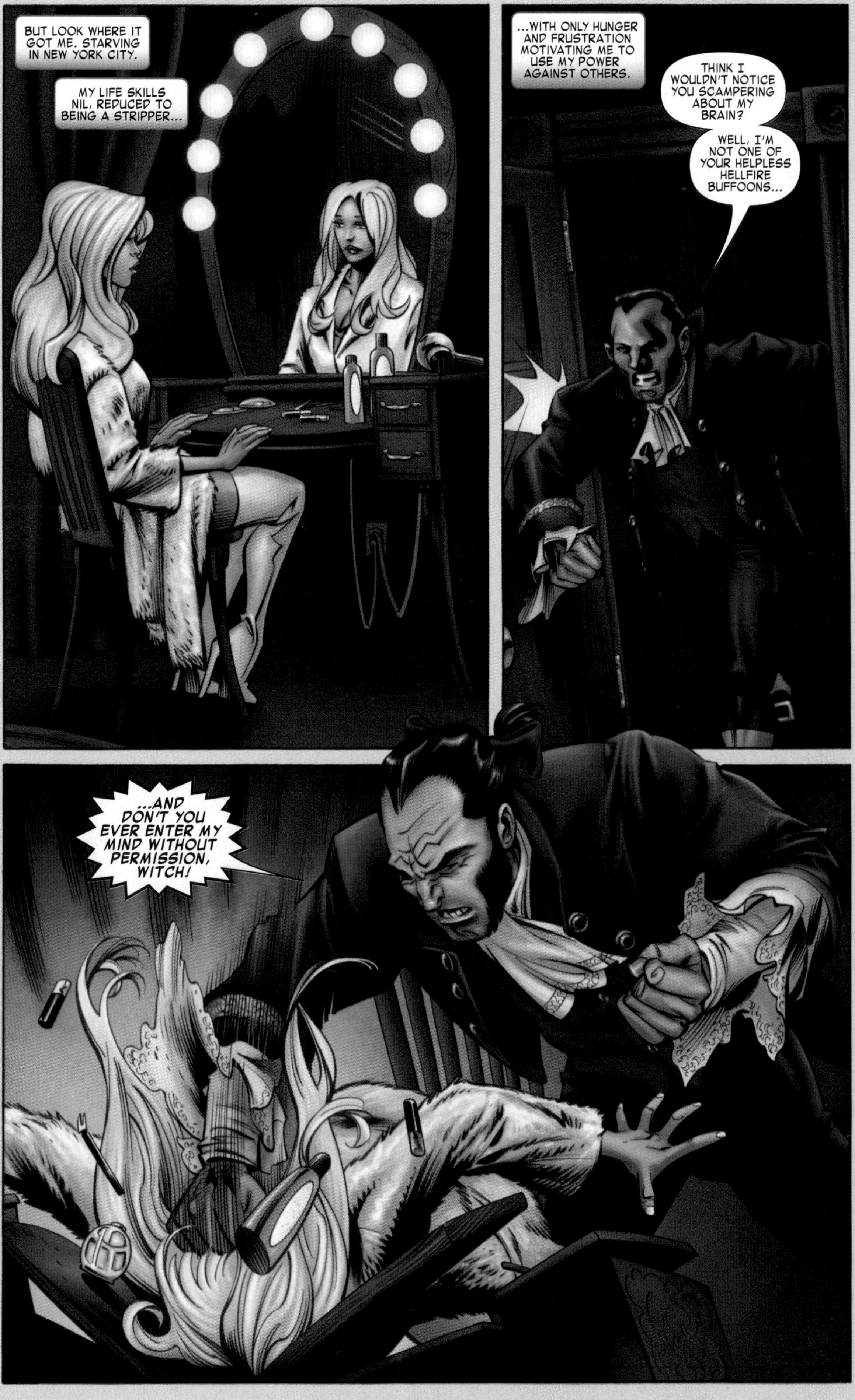
BUT LOOK WHERE IT GOT ME. STARVING IN NEW YORK CITY.
MY LIFE SKILLS NIL, REDUCED TO BEING A STRIPPER...
...WITH ONLY HUNGER AND FRUSTRATION MOTIVATING ME TO USE MY POWER AGAINST OTHERS.
THINK I WOULDN'T NOTICE YOU SCAMPERING ABOUT MY BRAIN?
WELL, I'M NOT ONE OF YOUR HELPLESS HELLFIRE BUFFOONS...
...AND DON'T YOU EVER ENTER MY MIND WITHOUT PERMISSION, WITCH!

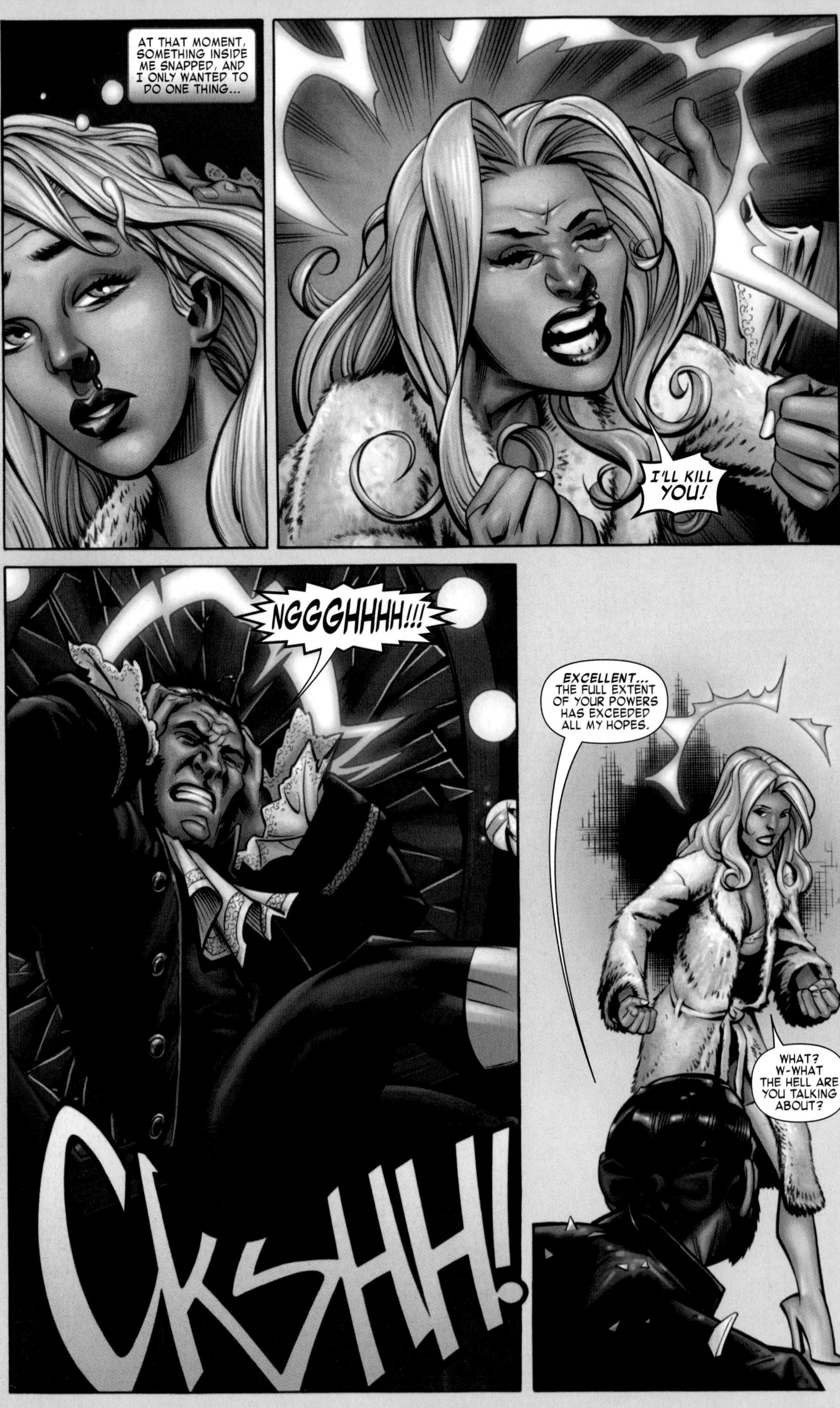
AT THAT MOMENT, SOMETHING INSIDE ME SNAPPED, AND I ONLY WANTED TO DO ONE THING...
I'LL KILL YOU!
NGGGHHHH!!!
CKSHH!
EXCELLENT... THE FULL EXTENT OF YOUR POWERS HAS EXCEEDED ALL MY HOPES.
WHAT? W-WHAT THE HELL ARE YOU TALKING ABOUT?

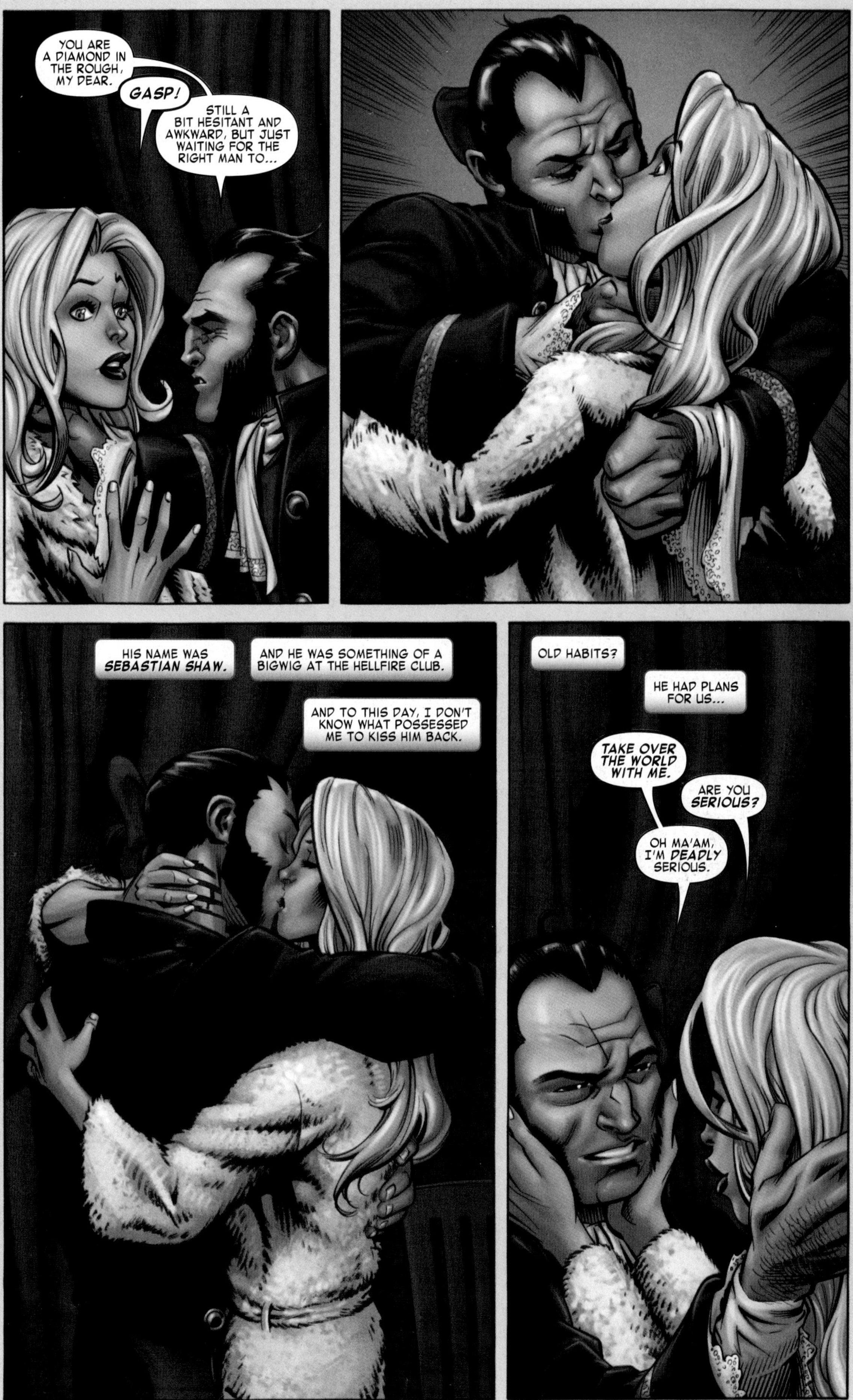
YOU ARE A DIAMOND IN THE ROUGH, MY DEAR.
GASP!
STILL A BIT HESITANT AND AWKWARD, BUT JUST WAITING FOR THE RIGHT MAN TO...
HIS NAME WAS SEBASTIAN SHAW.
AND HE WAS SOMETHING OF A BIGWIG AT THE HELLFIRE CLUB.
AND TO THIS DAY, I DON'T KNOW WHAT POSSESSED ME TO KISS HIM BACK.
OLD HABITS?
HE HAD PLANS FOR US...
TAKE OVER THE WORLD WITH ME.
ARE YOU SERIOUS?
OH MA'AM, I'M DEADLY SERIOUS.

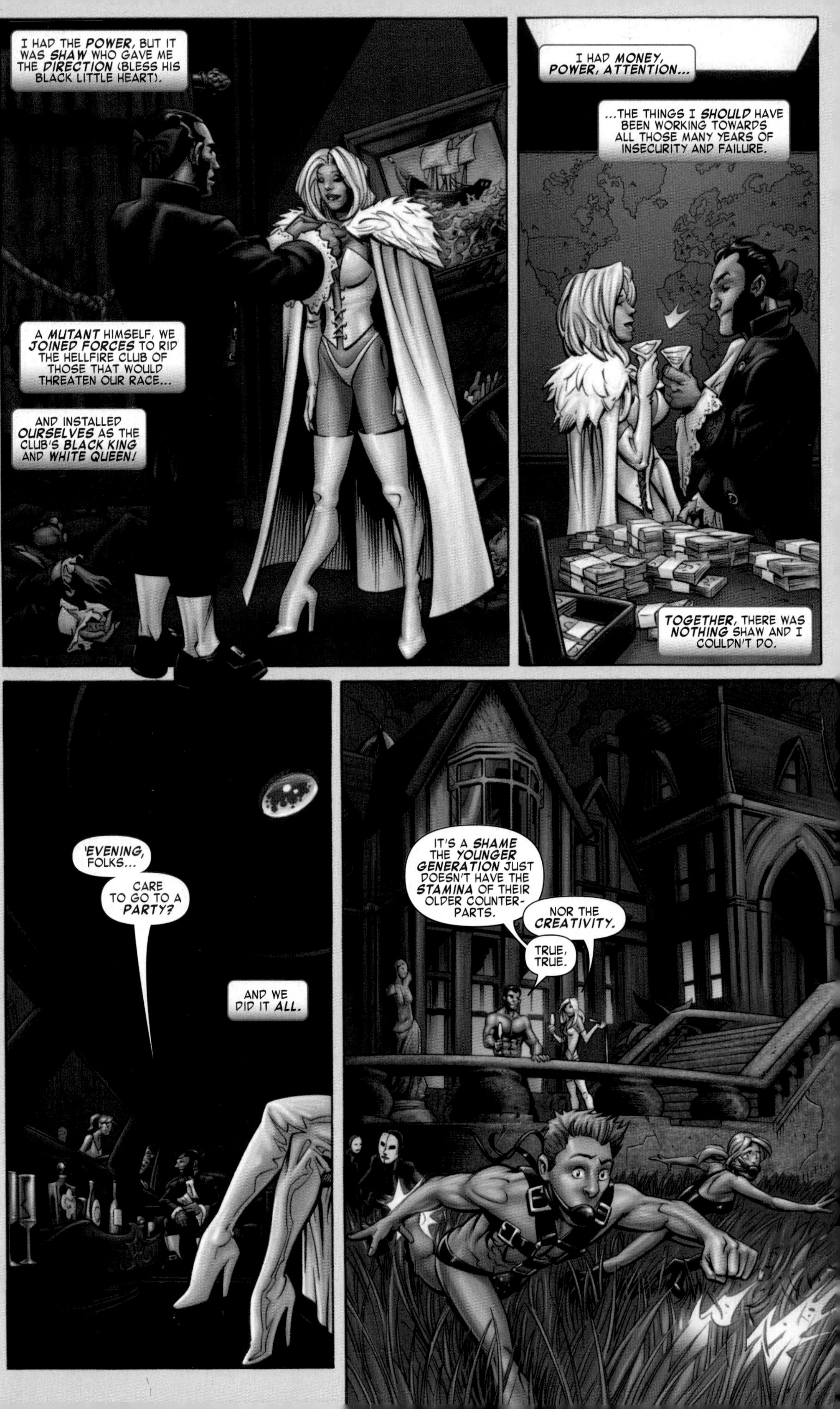
I HAD THE POWER, BUT IT WAS SHAW WHO GAVE ME THE DIRECTION (BLESS HIS BLACK LITTLE HEART).
A MUTANT HIMSELF, WE JOINED FORCES TO RID THE HELLFIRE CLUB OF THOSE THAT WOULD THREATEN OUR RACE...
AND INSTALLED OURSELVES AS THE CLUB'S BLACK KING AND WHITE QUEEN!
I HAD MONEY, POWER, ATTENTION...
...THE THINGS I SHOULD HAVE BEEN WORKING TOWARDS ALL THOSE MANY YEARS OF INSECURITY AND FAILURE.
TOGETHER, THERE WAS NOTHING SHAW AND I COULDN'T DO.
'EVENING, FOLKS...
CARE TO GO TO A PARTY?
AND WE DID IT ALL.
IT'S A SHAME THE YOUNGER GENERATION JUST DOESN'T HAVE THE STAMINA OF THEIR OLDER COUNTER-PARTS.
NOR THE CREATIVITY.
TRUE, TRUE.

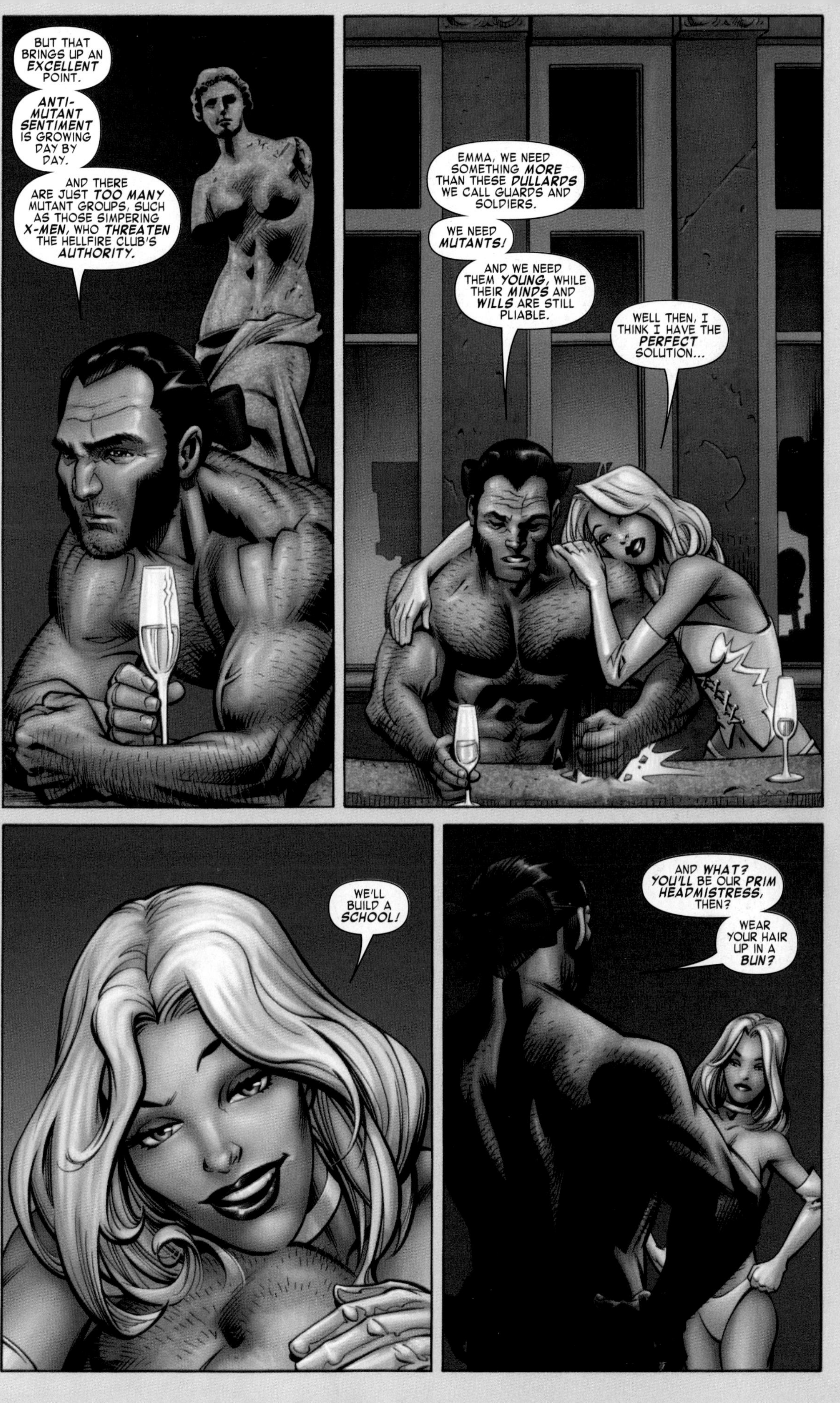
BUT THAT BRINGS UP AN EXCELLENT POINT.
ANTI-MUTANT SENTIMENT IS GROWING DAY BY DAY.
AND THERE ARE JUST TOO MANY MUTANT GROUPS, SUCH AS THOSE SIMPERING X-MEN, WHO THREATEN THE HELLFIRE CLUB'S AUTHORITY.
EMMA, WE NEED SOMETHING MORE THAN THESE DULLARDS WE CALL GUARDS AND SOLDIERS.
WE NEED MUTANTS!
AND WE NEED THEM YOUNG, WHILE THEIR MINDS AND WILLS ARE STILL PLIABLE.
WELL THEN, I THINK I HAVE THE PERFECT SOLUTION...
WE'LL BUILD A SCHOOL!
AND WHAT? YOU'LL BE OUR PRIM HEADMISTRESS, THEN?
WEAR YOUR HAIR UP IN A BUN?

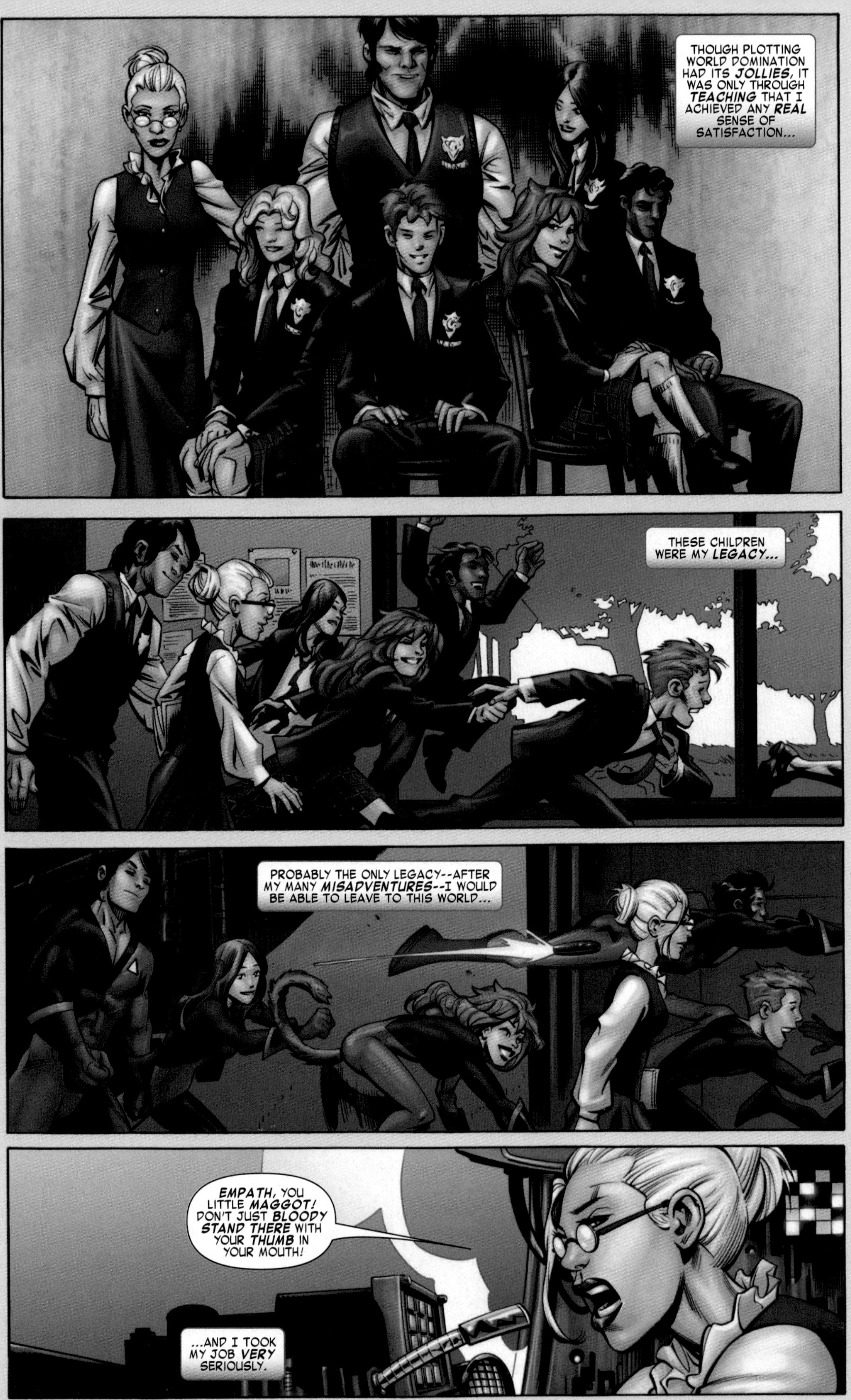
THOUGH PLOTTING WORLD DOMINATION HAD ITS JOLLIES, IT WAS ONLY THROUGH TEACHING THAT I ACHIEVED ANY REAL SENSE OF SATISFACTION...
THESE CHILDREN WERE MY LEGACY...
PROBABLY THE ONLY LEGACY--AFTER MY MANY MISADVENTURES--I WOULD BE ABLE TO LEAVE TO THIS WORLD...
EMPATH, YOU LITTLE MAGGOT! DON'T JUST BLOODY STAND THERE WITH YOUR THUMB IN YOUR MOUTH!
...AND I TOOK MY JOB VERY SERIOUSLY.

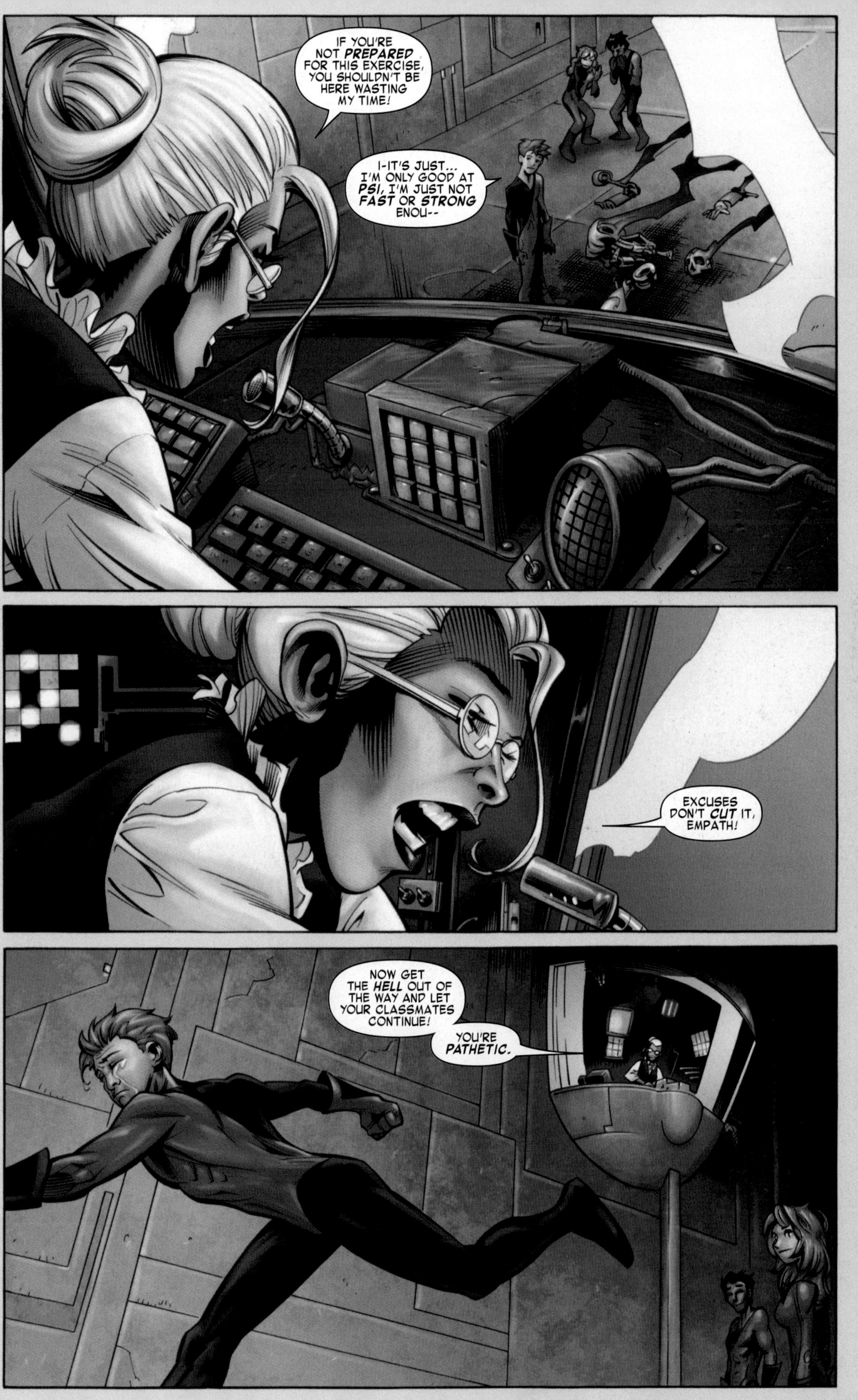
IF YOU'RE NOT PREPARED FOR THIS EXERCISE, YOU SHOULDN'T BE HERE WASTING MY TIME!
I-IT'S JUST... I'M ONLY GOOD AT PSI, I'M JUST NOT FAST OR STRONG ENOU--
EXCUSES DON'T CUT IT, EMPATH!
NOW GET THE HELL OUT OF THE WAY AND LET YOUR CLASSMATES CONTINUE!
YOU'RE PATHETIC.

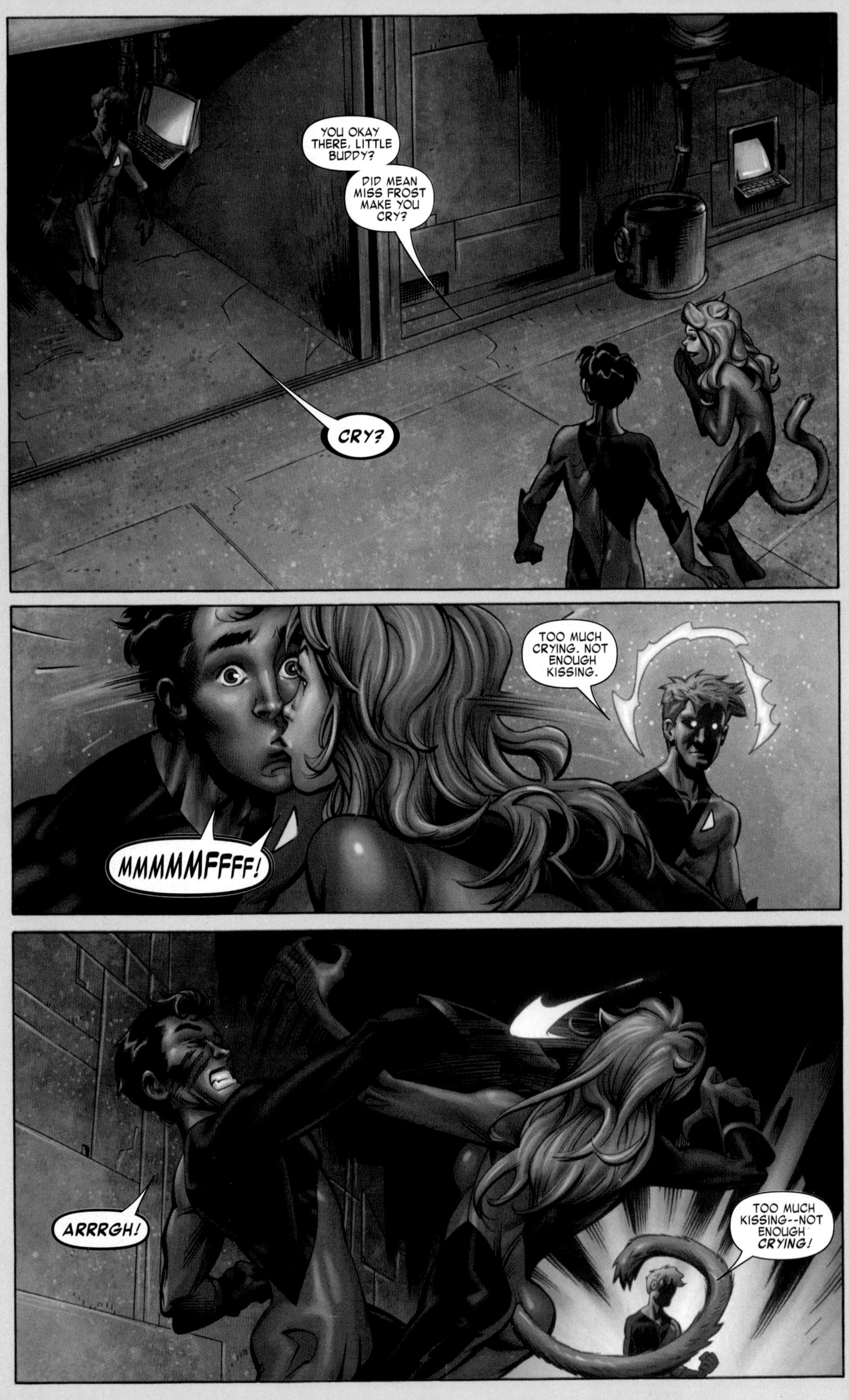
YOU OKAY THERE, LITTLE BUDDY?
DID MEAN MISS FROST MAKE YOU CRY?
CRY?
TOO MUCH CRYING. NOT ENOUGH KISSING.
MMMMMFFFF!
ARRRGH!
TOO MUCH KISSING--NOT ENOUGH CRYING!

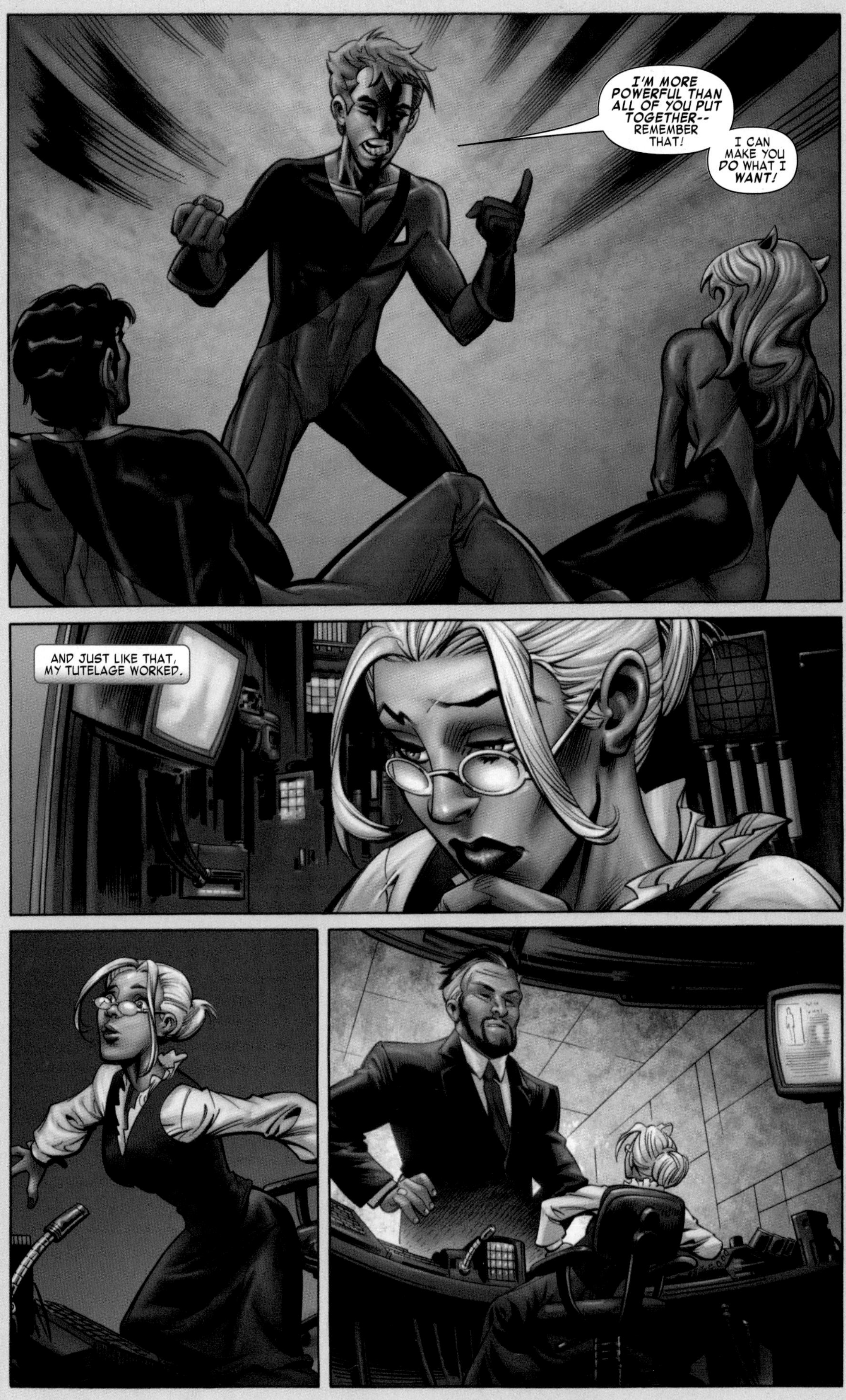
I'M MORE POWERFUL THAN ALL OF YOU PUT TOGETHER-- REMEMBER THAT!
I CAN MAKE YOU DO WHAT I WANT!
AND JUST LIKE THAT, MY TUTELAGE WORKED.

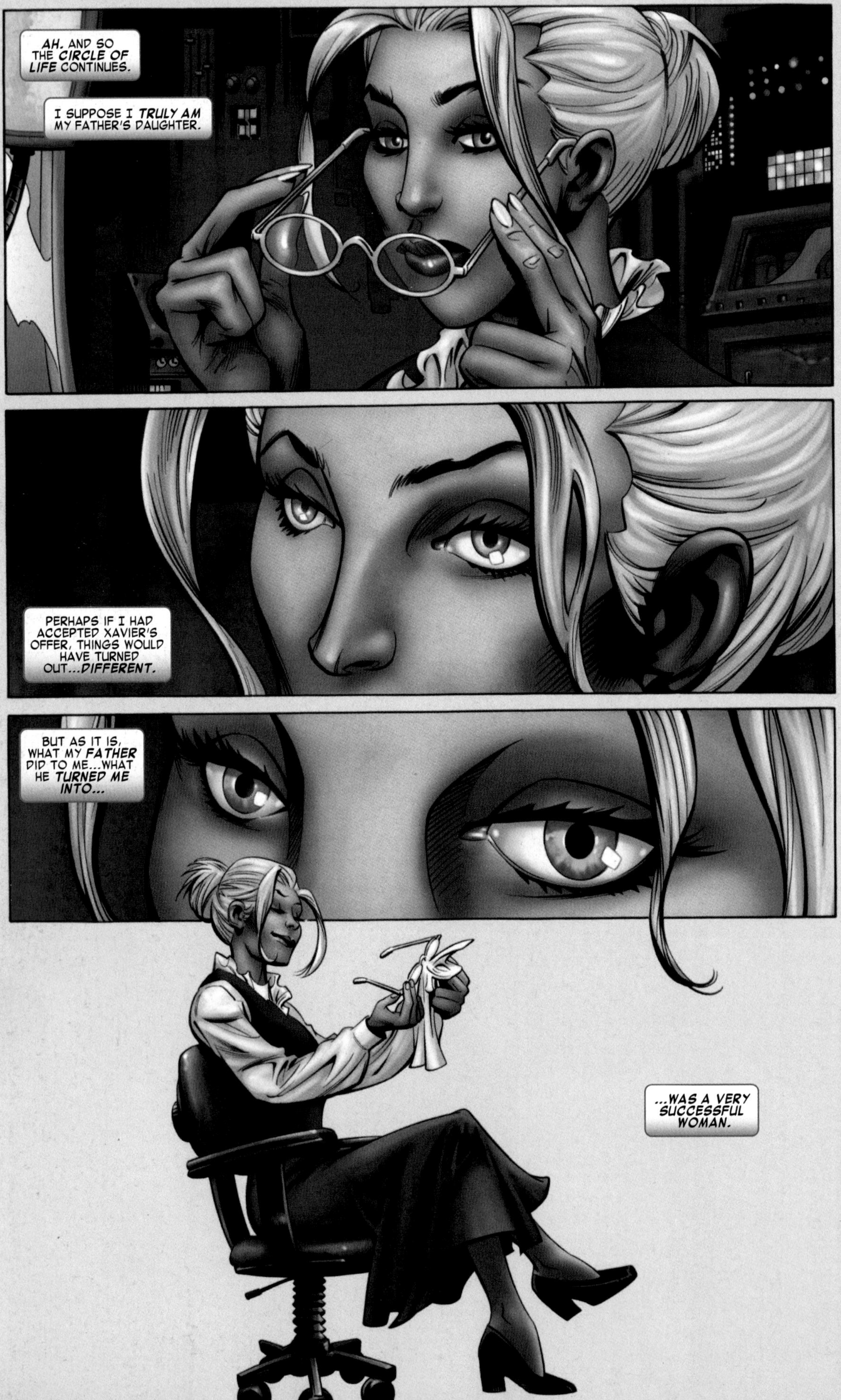
AH. AND SO THE CIRCLE OF LIFE CONTINUES.
I SUPPOSE I TRULY AM MY FATHER'S DAUGHTER.
PERHAPS IF I HAD ACCEPTED XAVIER'S OFFER, THINGS WOULD HAVE TURNED OUT...DIFFERENT.
BUT AS IT IS, WHAT MY FATHER DID TO ME...WHAT HE TURNED ME INTO...
...WAS A VERY SUCCESSFUL WOMAN.

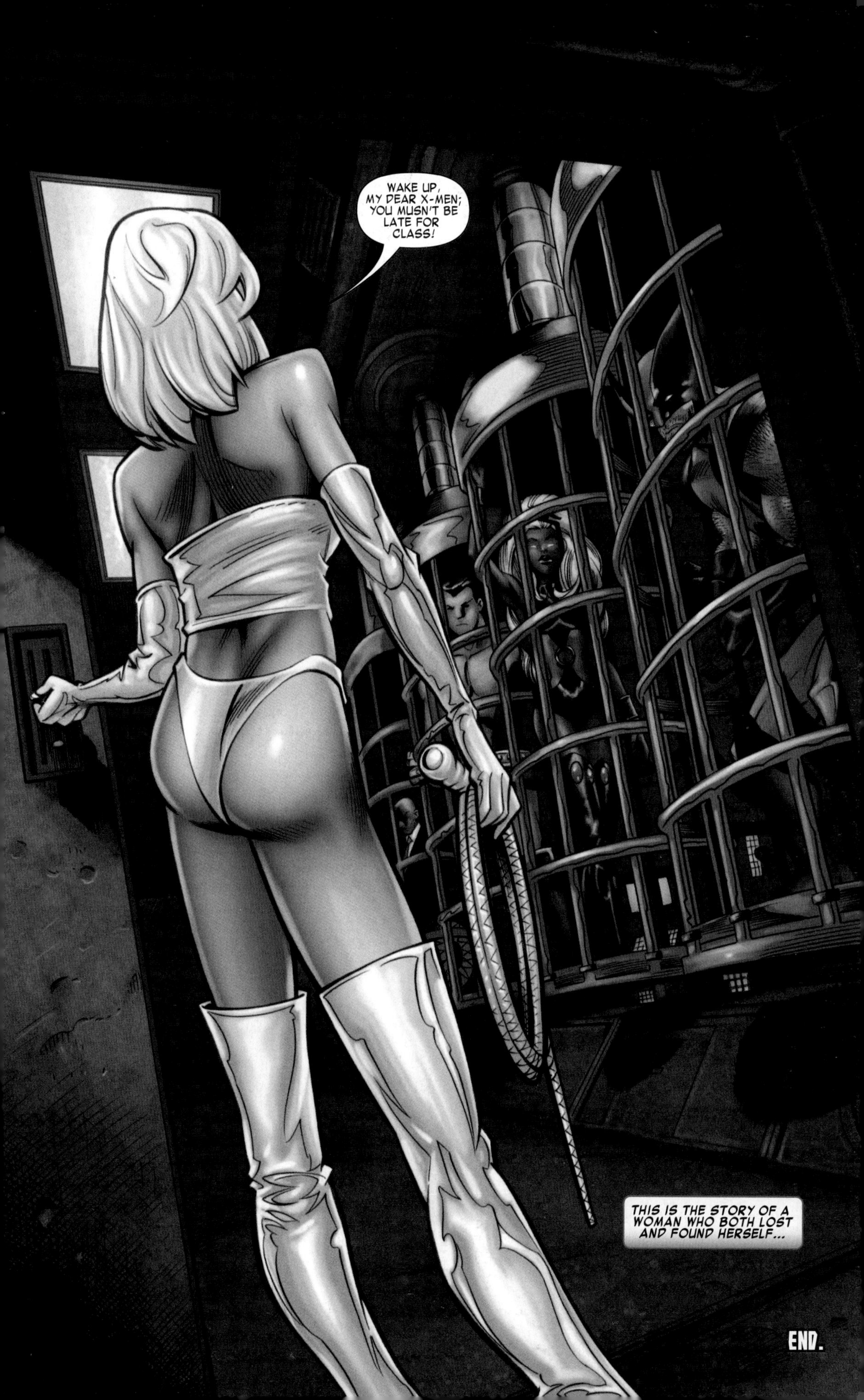
WAKE UP, MY DEAR X-MEN; YOU MUSN'T BE LATE FOR CLASS!
THIS IS THE STORY OF A WOMAN WHO BOTH LOST AND FOUND HERSELF...
END.

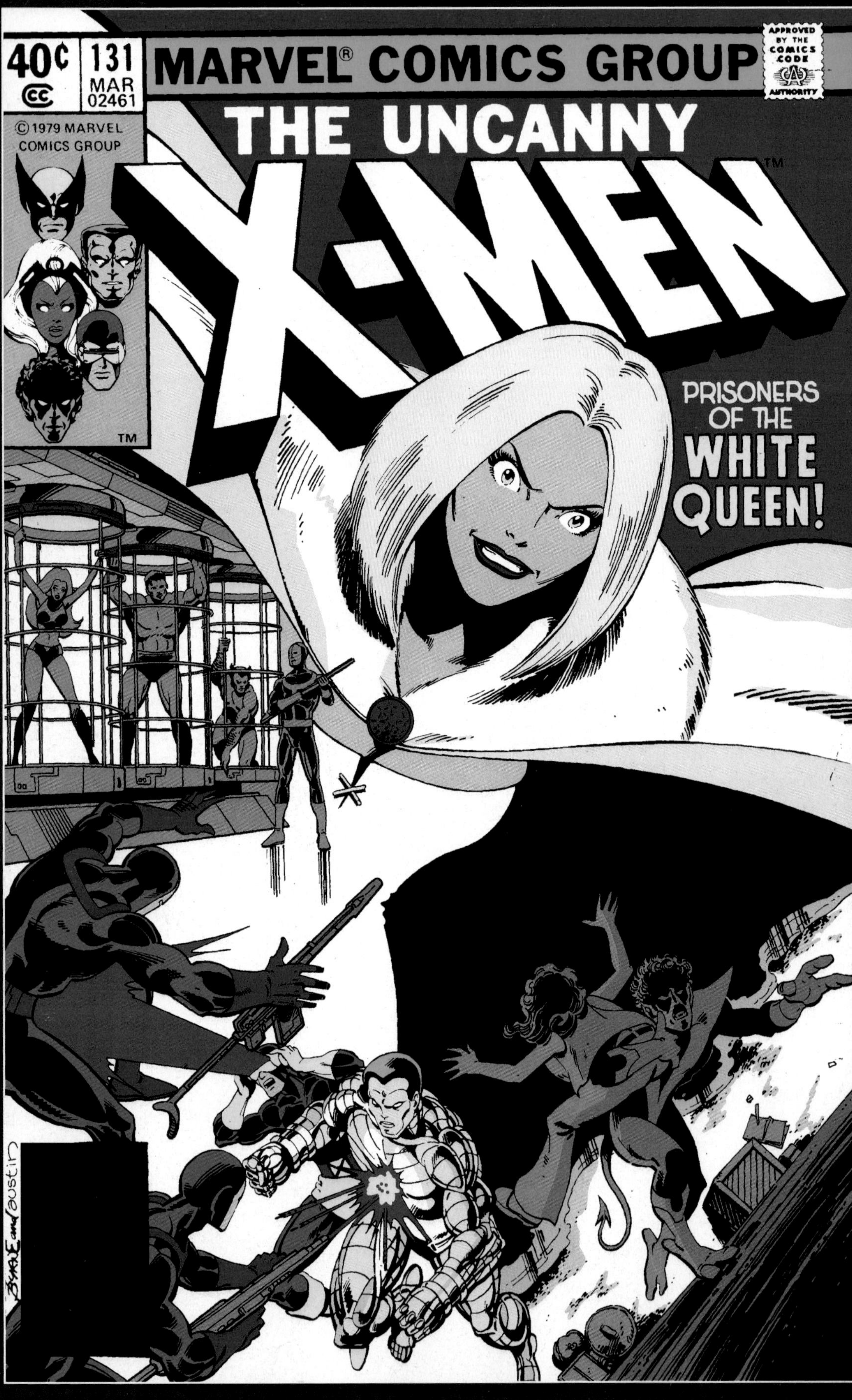
40¢
131
MAR
02461
CC
MARVEL® COMICS GROUP
APPROVED BY THE COMICS CODE AUTHORITY
©1979 MARVEL COMICS GROUP
TM
THE UNCANNY
X-MEN
TM
PRISONERS OF THE WHITE QUEEN!
BYRNE and austin

BONUS: AN EXCERPT FROM EMMA FROST'S FIRST RUN-IN WITH THE X-MEN!

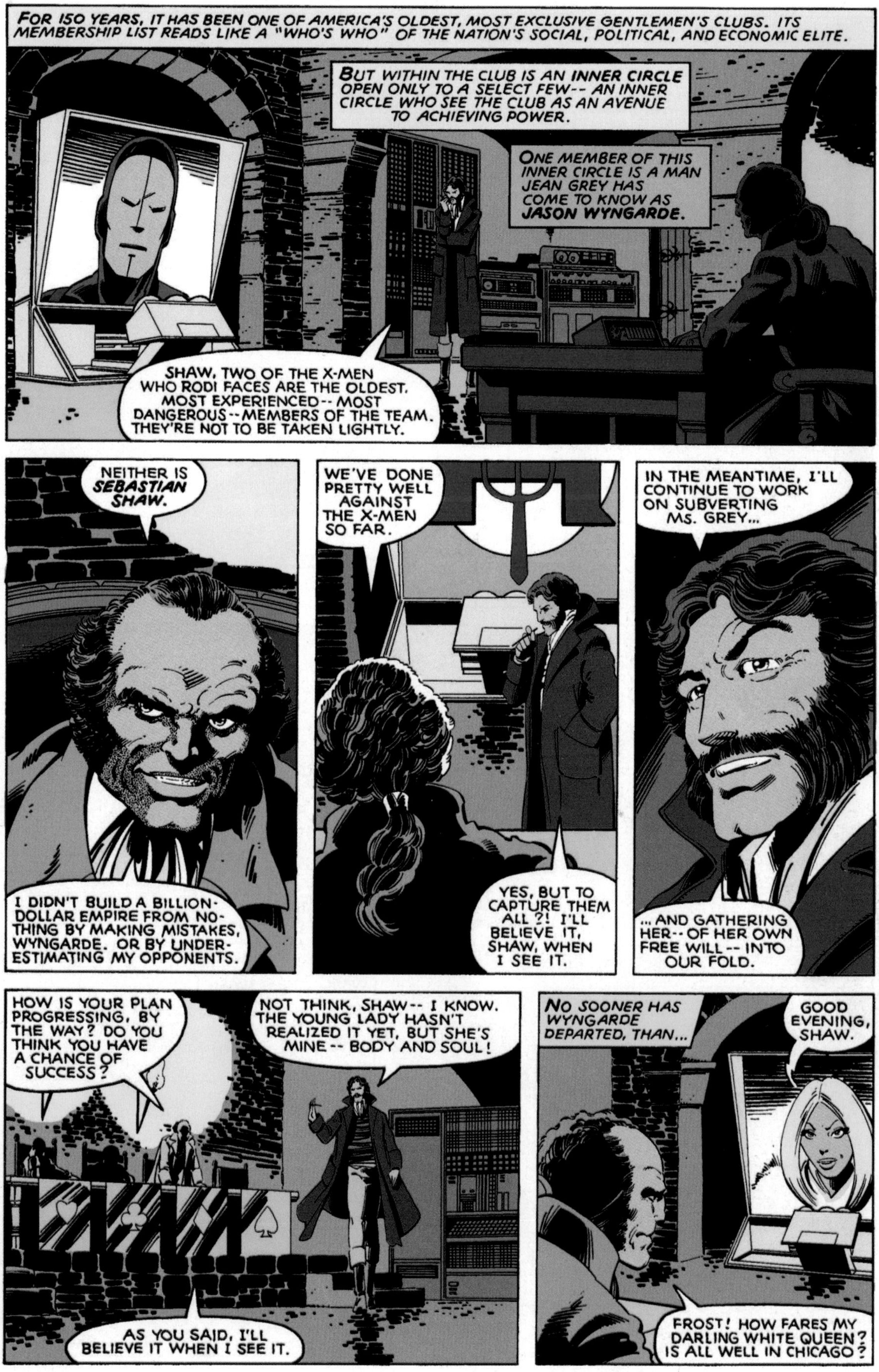
FOR 150 YEARS, IT HAS BEEN ONE OF AMERICA'S OLDEST, MOST EXCLUSIVE GENTLEMEN'S CLUBS. ITS MEMBERSHIP LIST READS LIKE A "WHO'S WHO" OF THE NATION'S SOCIAL, POLITICAL, AND ECONOMIC ELITE.
BUT WITHIN THE CLUB IS AN INNER CIRCLE OPEN ONLY TO A SELECT FEW-- AN INNER CIRCLE WHO SEE THE CLUB AS AN AVENUE TO ACHIEVING POWER.
ONE MEMBER OF THIS INNER CIRCLE IS A MAN JEAN GREY HAS COME TO KNOW AS JASON WYNGARDE.
SHAW, TWO OF THE X-MEN WHO RODI FACES ARE THE OLDEST, MOST EXPERIENCED-- MOST DANGEROUS--MEMBERS OF THE TEAM. THEY'RE NOT TO BE TAKEN LIGHTLY.
NEITHER IS SEBASTIAN SHAW.
I DIDN'T BUILD A BILLION-DOLLAR EMPIRE FROM NOTHING BY MAKING MISTAKES, WYNGARDE. OR BY UNDERESTIMATING MY OPPONENTS.
WE'VE DONE PRETTY WELL AGAINST THE X-MEN SO FAR.
YES, BUT TO CAPTURE THEM ALL?! I'LL BELIEVE IT, SHAW, WHEN I SEE IT.
IN THE MEANTIME, I'LL CONTINUE TO WORK ON SUBVERTING MS. GREY...
...AND GATHERING HER-- OF HER OWN FREE WILL-- INTO OUR FOLD.
HOW IS YOUR PLAN PROGRESSING, BY THE WAY? DO YOU THINK YOU HAVE A CHANCE OF SUCCESS?
NOT THINK, SHAW-- I KNOW. THE YOUNG LADY HASN'T REALIZED IT YET, BUT SHE'S MINE-- BODY AND SOUL!
AS YOU SAID, I'LL BELIEVE IT WHEN I SEE IT.
NO SOONER HAS WYNGARDE DEPARTED, THAN...
GOOD EVENING, SHAW.
FROST! HOW FARES MY DARLING WHITE QUEEN? IS ALL WELL IN CHICAGO?

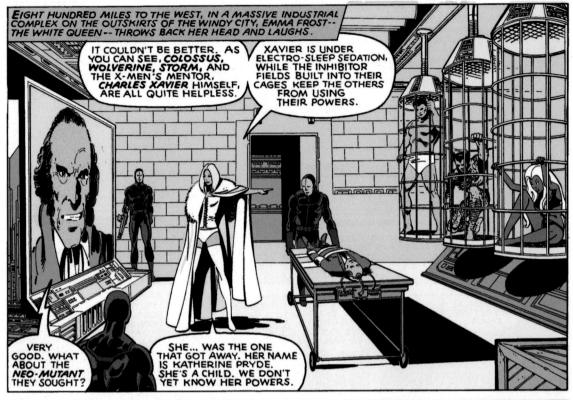

EIGHT HUNDRED MILES TO THE WEST, IN A MASSIVE INDUSTRIAL COMPLEX ON THE OUTSKIRTS OF THE WINDY CITY, EMMA FROST-- THE WHITE QUEEN -- THROWS BACK HER HEAD AND LAUGHS.

IT COULDN'T BE BETTER. AS YOU CAN SEE, *COLOSSUS, WOLVERINE, STORM,* AND THE X-MEN'S MENTOR, *CHARLES XAVIER* HIMSELF, ARE ALL QUITE HELPLESS.

XAVIER IS UNDER ELECTRO-SLEEP SEDATION, WHILE THE INHIBITOR FIELDS BUILT INTO THEIR CAGES KEEP THE OTHERS FROM USING THEIR POWERS.

VERY GOOD. WHAT ABOUT THE *NEO-MUTANT* THEY SOUGHT?

SHE... WAS THE ONE THAT GOT AWAY. HER NAME IS KATHERINE PRYDE. SHE'S A CHILD. WE DON'T YET KNOW HER POWERS.

WE NEEDN'T WORRY ABOUT HER, THOUGH. I THINK I CAN... PERSUADE HER FATHER TO ENROLL HER IN MY MASSACHUSETTS ACADEMY. AFTER ALL, IT IS ONE OF THE MOST PRESTIGIOUS PRIVATE SCHOOLS IN THE COUNTRY.

AND ONCE SHE'S THERE, SHE'S OURS FOR THE TAKING!

AS THE TWO VILLAINS TALK, NO ONE IN THE VAST HOLDING CHAMBER NOTICES A SUDDEN, SLIGHT STIR IN THE AIR...

...THAT HERALDS THE UNORTHODOX ENTRANCE OF KITTY PRYDE.

I DID IT AGAIN!

I THOUGHT REAL HARD-- AN' I WALKED RIGHT THROUGH THAT WALL, LIKE IT WASN'T EVEN THERE! IT GETS EASIER EACH TIME I DO IT, TOO!

OKAY, I'VE SNUCK MY WAY INTO HERE --

-- WHAT THE HECK DO I DO *NOW*???

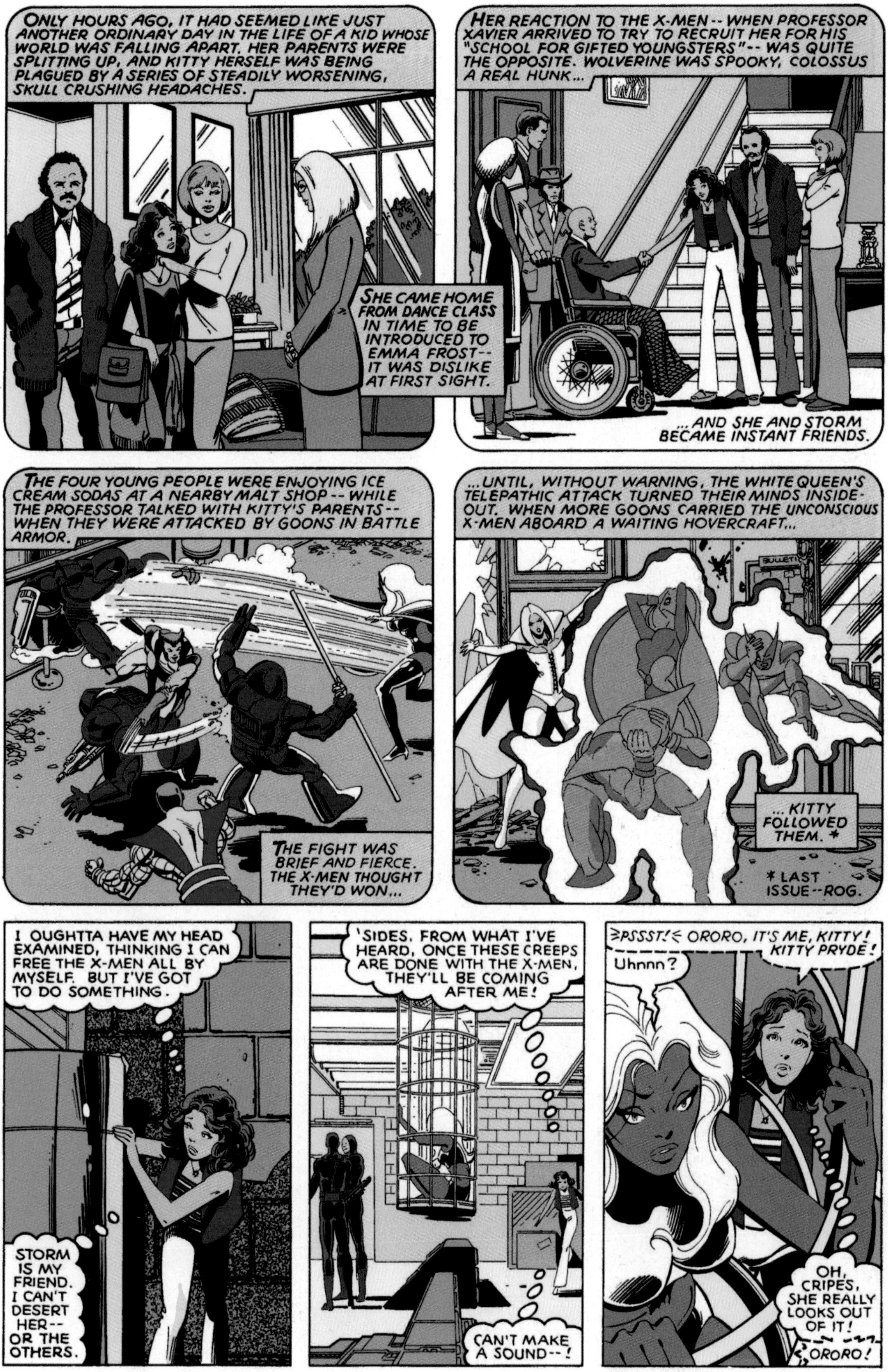

ONLY HOURS AGO, IT HAD SEEMED LIKE JUST ANOTHER ORDINARY DAY IN THE LIFE OF A KID WHOSE WORLD WAS FALLING APART. HER PARENTS WERE SPLITTING UP, AND KITTY HERSELF WAS BEING PLAGUED BY A SERIES OF STEADILY WORSENING, SKULL CRUSHING HEADACHES.
SHE CAME HOME FROM DANCE CLASS IN TIME TO BE INTRODUCED TO EMMA FROST-- IT WAS DISLIKE AT FIRST SIGHT.
HER REACTION TO THE X-MEN -- WHEN PROFESSOR XAVIER ARRIVED TO TRY TO RECRUIT HER FOR HIS "SCHOOL FOR GIFTED YOUNGSTERS" -- WAS QUITE THE OPPOSITE. WOLVERINE WAS SPOOKY, COLOSSUS A REAL HUNK...
...AND SHE AND STORM BECAME INSTANT FRIENDS.
THE FOUR YOUNG PEOPLE WERE ENJOYING ICE CREAM SODAS AT A NEARBY MALT SHOP -- WHILE THE PROFESSOR TALKED WITH KITTY'S PARENTS -- WHEN THEY WERE ATTACKED BY GOONS IN BATTLE ARMOR.
THE FIGHT WAS BRIEF AND FIERCE. THE X-MEN THOUGHT THEY'D WON...
...UNTIL, WITHOUT WARNING, THE WHITE QUEEN'S TELEPATHIC ATTACK TURNED THEIR MINDS INSIDE-OUT. WHEN MORE GOONS CARRIED THE UNCONSCIOUS X-MEN ABOARD A WAITING HOVERCRAFT...
... KITTY FOLLOWED THEM. *
* LAST ISSUE--ROG.
I OUGHTTA HAVE MY HEAD EXAMINED, THINKING I CAN FREE THE X-MEN ALL BY MYSELF. BUT I'VE GOT TO DO SOMETHING.
STORM IS MY FRIEND. I CAN'T DESERT HER-- OR THE OTHERS.
'SIDES. FROM WHAT I'VE HEARD, ONCE THESE CREEPS ARE DONE WITH THE X-MEN, THEY'LL BE COMING AFTER ME!
CAN'T MAKE A SOUND--!
≥PSSST!≤ ORORO, IT'S ME, KITTY! KITTY PRYDE!
Uhnnn?
OH, CRIPES, SHE REALLY LOOKS OUT OF IT!
ORORO!

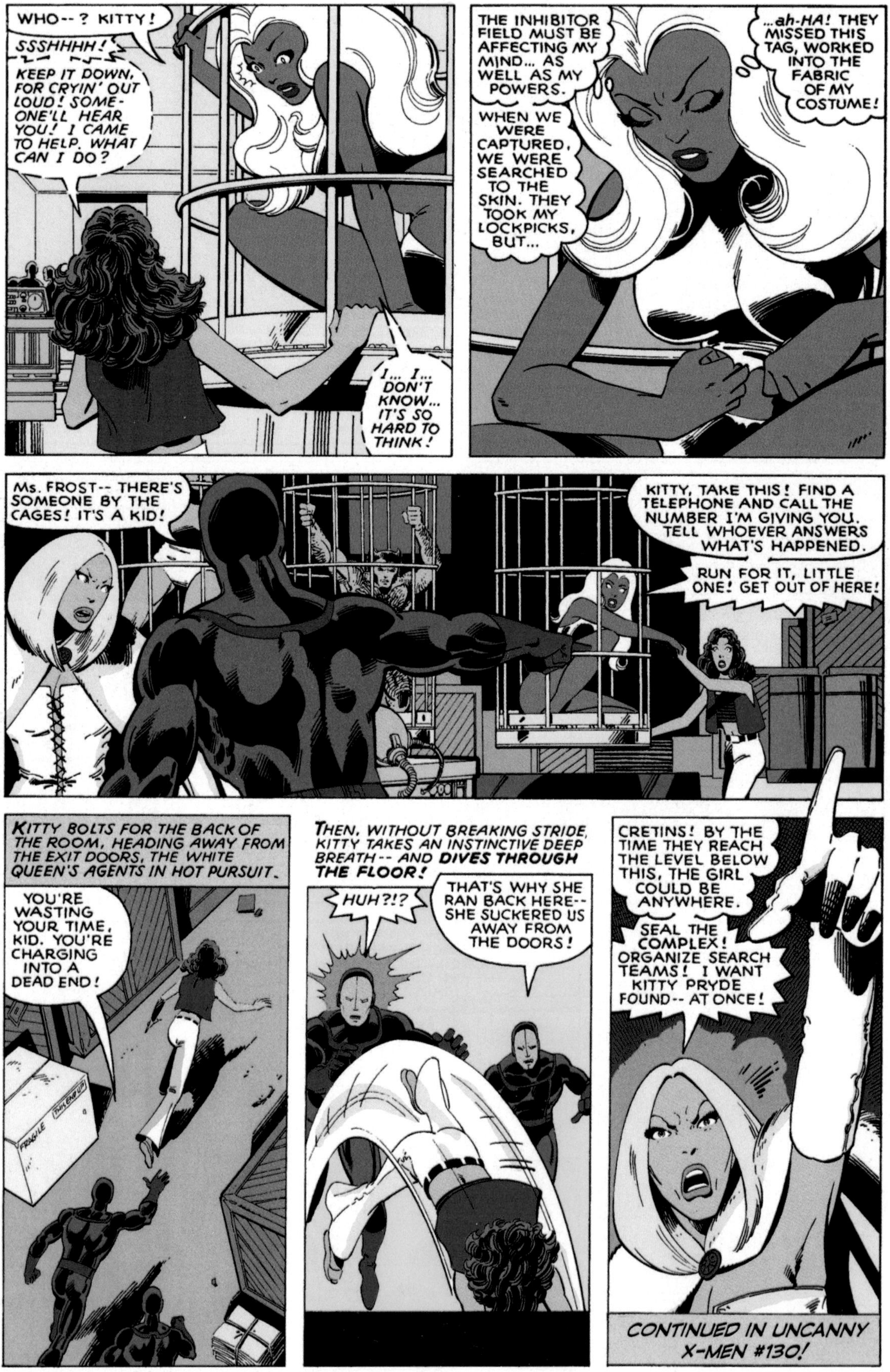
WHO--? KITTY!
SSSHHHH! KEEP IT DOWN, FOR CRYIN' OUT LOUD! SOME-ONE'LL HEAR YOU! I CAME TO HELP. WHAT CAN I DO?
I... I... DON'T KNOW... IT'S SO HARD TO THINK!
THE INHIBITOR FIELD MUST BE AFFECTING MY MIND... AS WELL AS MY POWERS.
WHEN WE WERE CAPTURED, WE WERE SEARCHED TO THE SKIN. THEY TOOK MY LOCKPICKS, BUT...
...ah-HA! THEY MISSED THIS TAG, WORKED INTO THE FABRIC OF MY COSTUME!
Ms. FROST-- THERE'S SOMEONE BY THE CAGES! IT'S A KID!
KITTY, TAKE THIS! FIND A TELEPHONE AND CALL THE NUMBER I'M GIVING YOU. TELL WHOEVER ANSWERS WHAT'S HAPPENED.
RUN FOR IT, LITTLE ONE! GET OUT OF HERE!
KITTY BOLTS FOR THE BACK OF THE ROOM, HEADING AWAY FROM THE EXIT DOORS, THE WHITE QUEEN'S AGENTS IN HOT PURSUIT.
YOU'RE WASTING YOUR TIME, KID. YOU'RE CHARGING INTO A DEAD END!
FRAGILE
THIS END UP
THEN, WITHOUT BREAKING STRIDE, KITTY TAKES AN INSTINCTIVE DEEP BREATH -- AND DIVES THROUGH THE FLOOR!
HUH?!?
THAT'S WHY SHE RAN BACK HERE-- SHE SUCKERED US AWAY FROM THE DOORS!
CRETINS! BY THE TIME THEY REACH THE LEVEL BELOW THIS, THE GIRL COULD BE ANYWHERE.
SEAL THE COMPLEX! ORGANIZE SEARCH TEAMS! I WANT KITTY PRYDE FOUND-- AT ONCE!
CONTINUED IN UNCANNY X-MEN #130!

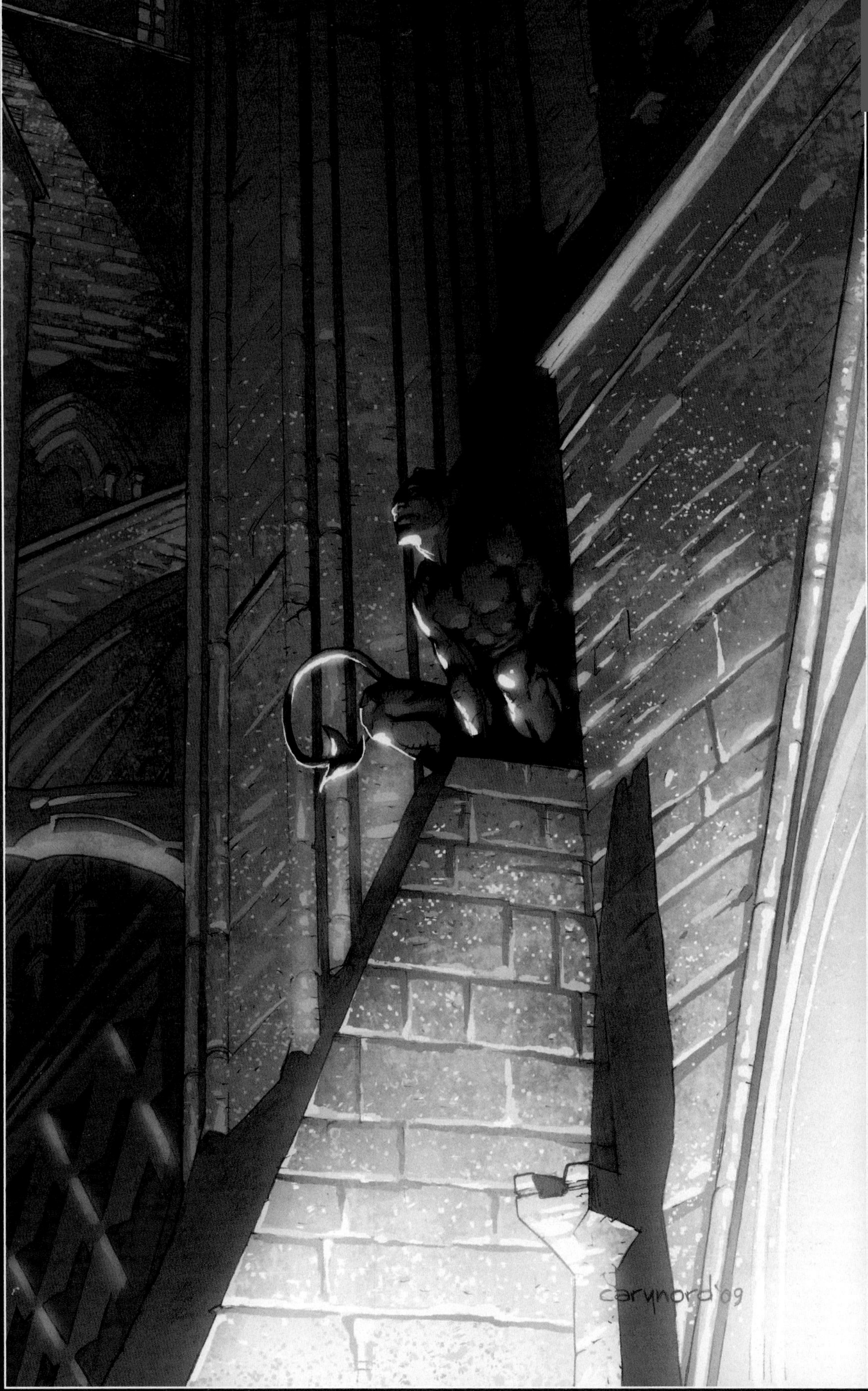
carynord'09

X-MEN ORIGINS: NIGHTCRAWLER

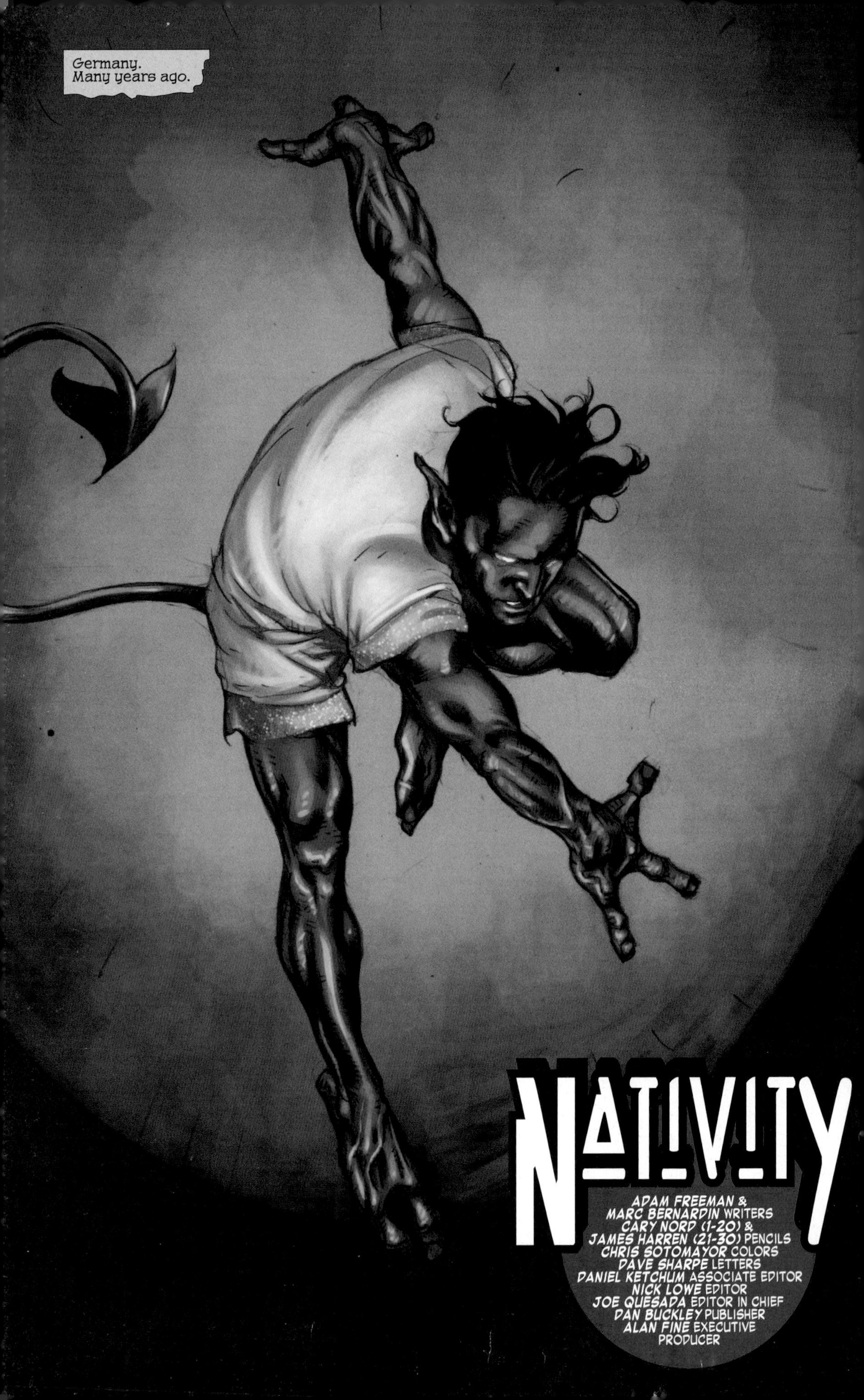
Germany.
Many years ago.
NATIVITY
ADAM FREEMAN &
MARC BERNARDIN WRITERS
CARY NORD (1-20) &
JAMES HARREN (21-30) PENCILS
CHRIS SOTOMAYOR COLORS
DAVE SHARPE LETTERS
DANIEL KETCHUM ASSOCIATE EDITOR
NICK LOWE EDITOR
JOE QUESADA EDITOR IN CHIEF
DAN BUCKLEY PUBLISHER
ALAN FINE EXECUTIVE
PRODUCER

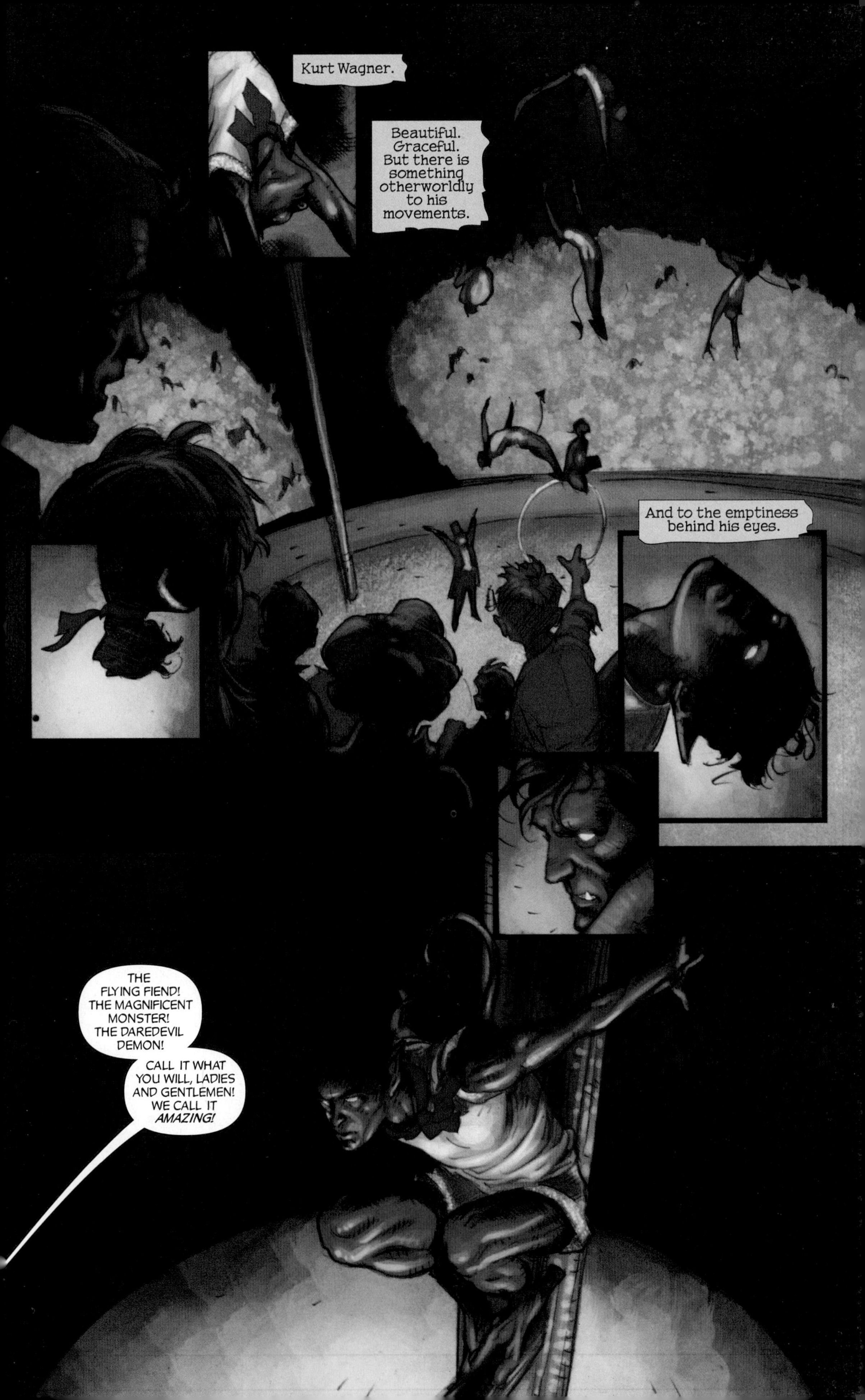

Kurt Wagner.
Beautiful. Graceful. But there is something otherworldly to his movements.
And to the emptiness behind his eyes.
THE FLYING FIEND! THE MAGNIFICENT MONSTER! THE DAREDEVIL DEMON!
CALL IT WHAT YOU WILL, LADIES AND GENTLEMEN! WE CALL IT *AMAZING!*

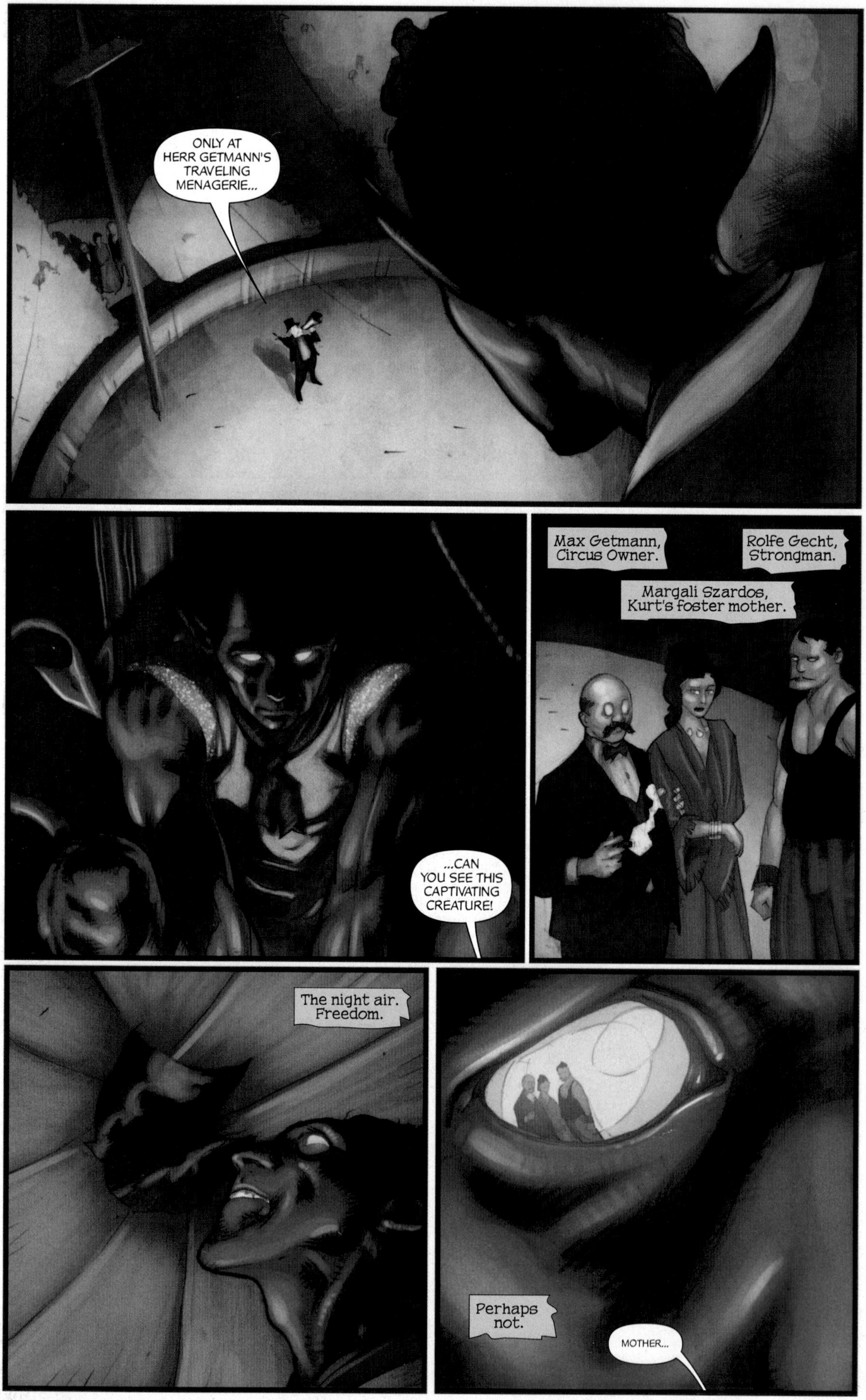
ONLY AT HERR GETMANN'S TRAVELING MENAGERIE...
...CAN YOU SEE THIS CAPTIVATING CREATURE!
Max Getmann, Circus Owner.
Rolfe Gecht, Strongman.
Margali Szardos, Kurt's foster mother.
The night air. Freedom.
Perhaps not.
MOTHER...

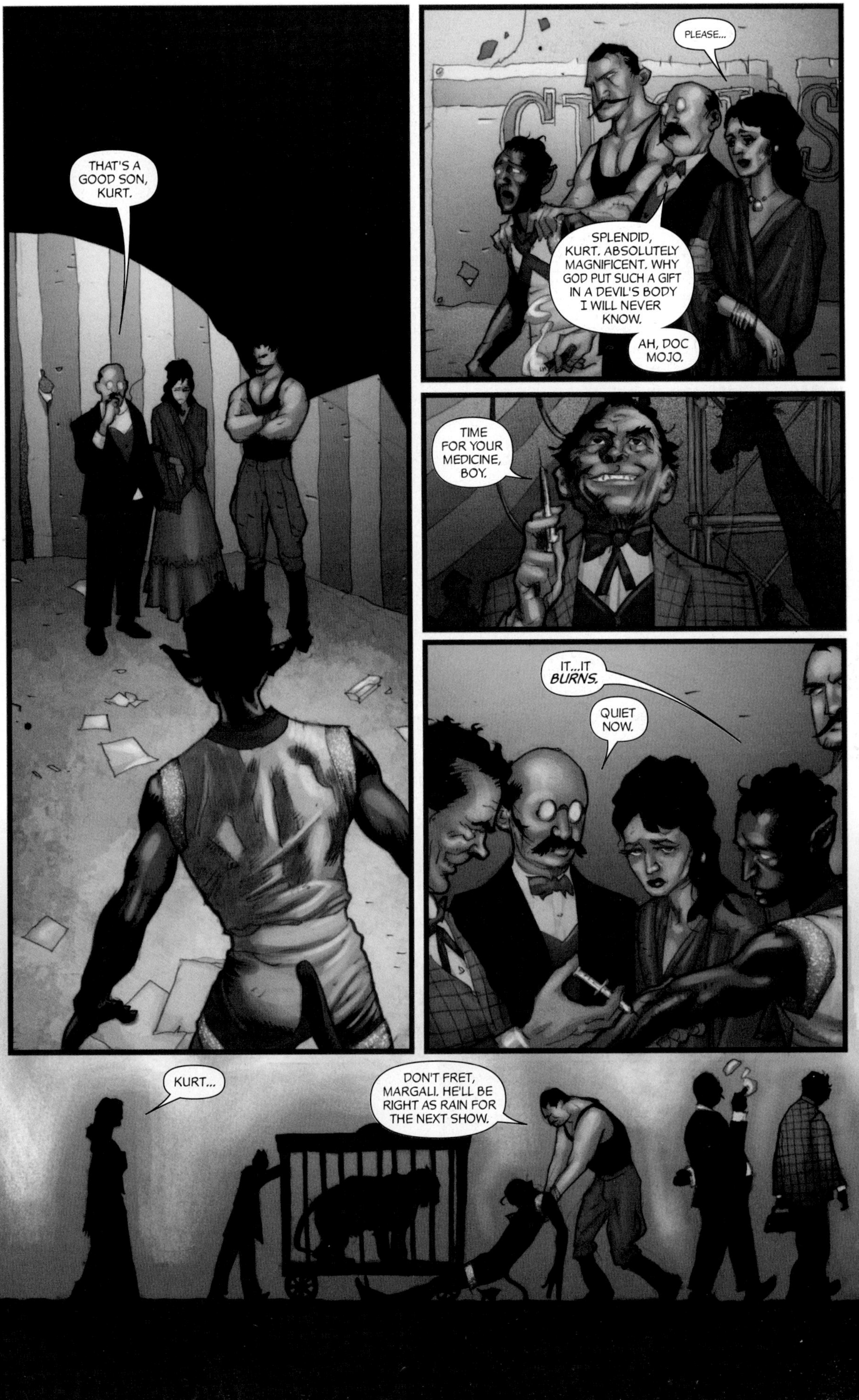

THAT'S A GOOD SON, KURT.
PLEASE...
SPLENDID, KURT. ABSOLUTELY MAGNIFICENT. WHY GOD PUT SUCH A GIFT IN A DEVIL'S BODY I WILL NEVER KNOW.
AH, DOC MOJO.
TIME FOR YOUR MEDICINE, BOY.
IT...IT BURNS.
QUIET NOW.
KURT...
DON'T FRET, MARGALI. HE'LL BE RIGHT AS RAIN FOR THE NEXT SHOW.

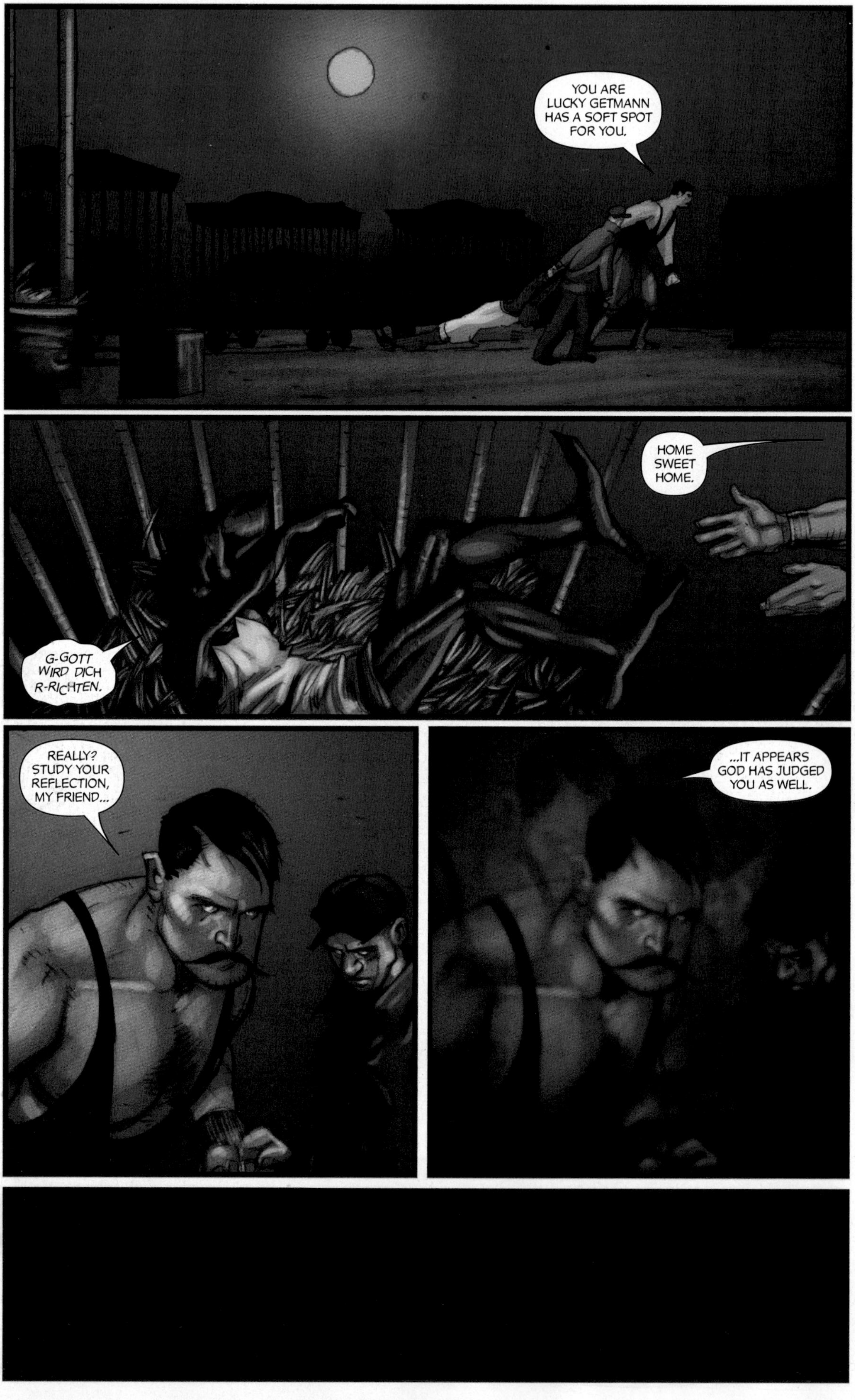

YOU ARE LUCKY GETMANN HAS A SOFT SPOT FOR YOU.
HOME SWEET HOME.
G-GOTT WIRD DICH R-RICHTEN.
REALLY? STUDY YOUR REFLECTION, MY FRIEND...
...IT APPEARS GOD HAS JUDGED YOU AS WELL.

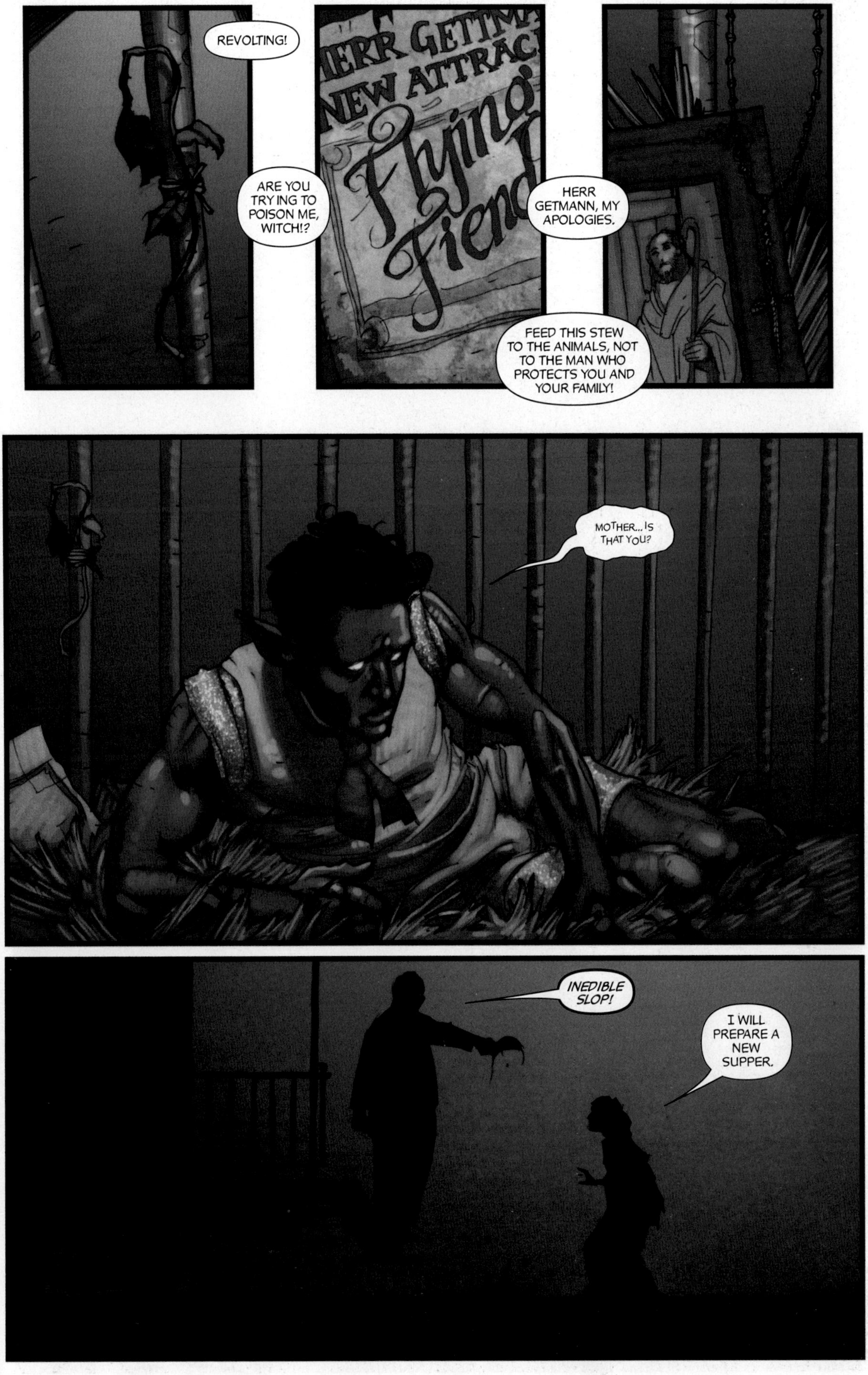
REVOLTING!
ARE YOU TRY ING TO POISON ME, WITCH!?
HERR GETTMA
NEW ATTRAC
Flying
Fiend
HERR GETMANN, MY APOLOGIES.
FEED THIS STEW TO THE ANIMALS, NOT TO THE MAN WHO PROTECTS YOU AND YOUR FAMILY!
MOTHER... IS THAT YOU?
INEDIBLE SLOP!
I WILL PREPARE A NEW SUPPER.

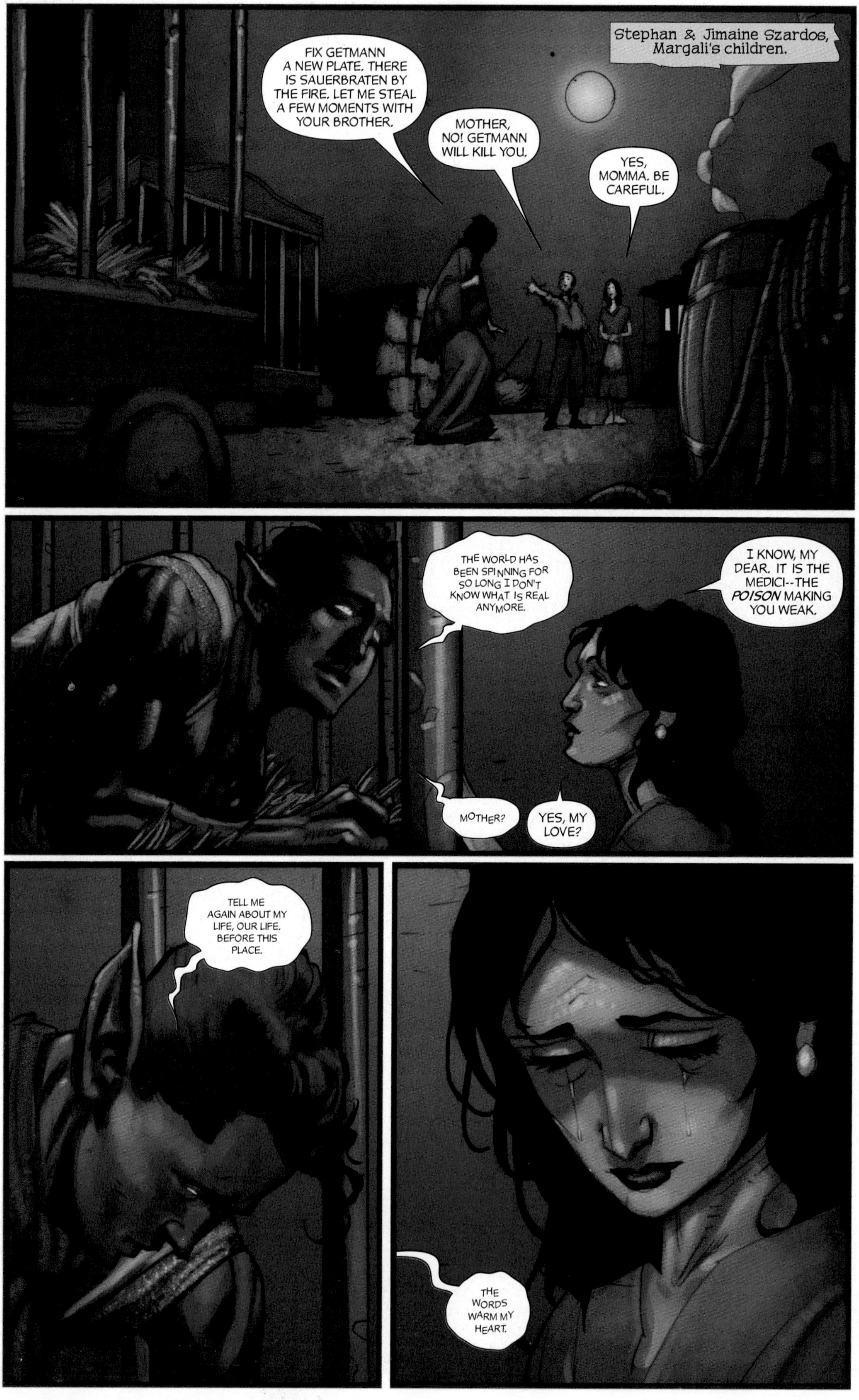
Stephan & Jimaine Szardos, Margali's children.
FIX GETMANN A NEW PLATE. THERE IS SAUERBRATEN BY THE FIRE. LET ME STEAL A FEW MOMENTS WITH YOUR BROTHER.
MOTHER, NO! GETMANN WILL KILL YOU.
YES, MOMMA. BE CAREFUL.
THE WORLD HAS BEEN SPINNING FOR SO LONG I DON'T KNOW WHAT IS REAL ANYMORE.
I KNOW, MY DEAR. IT IS THE MEDICI--THE POISON MAKING YOU WEAK.
MOTHER?
YES, MY LOVE?
TELL ME AGAIN ABOUT MY LIFE, OUR LIFE. BEFORE THIS PLACE.
THE WORDS WARM MY HEART.

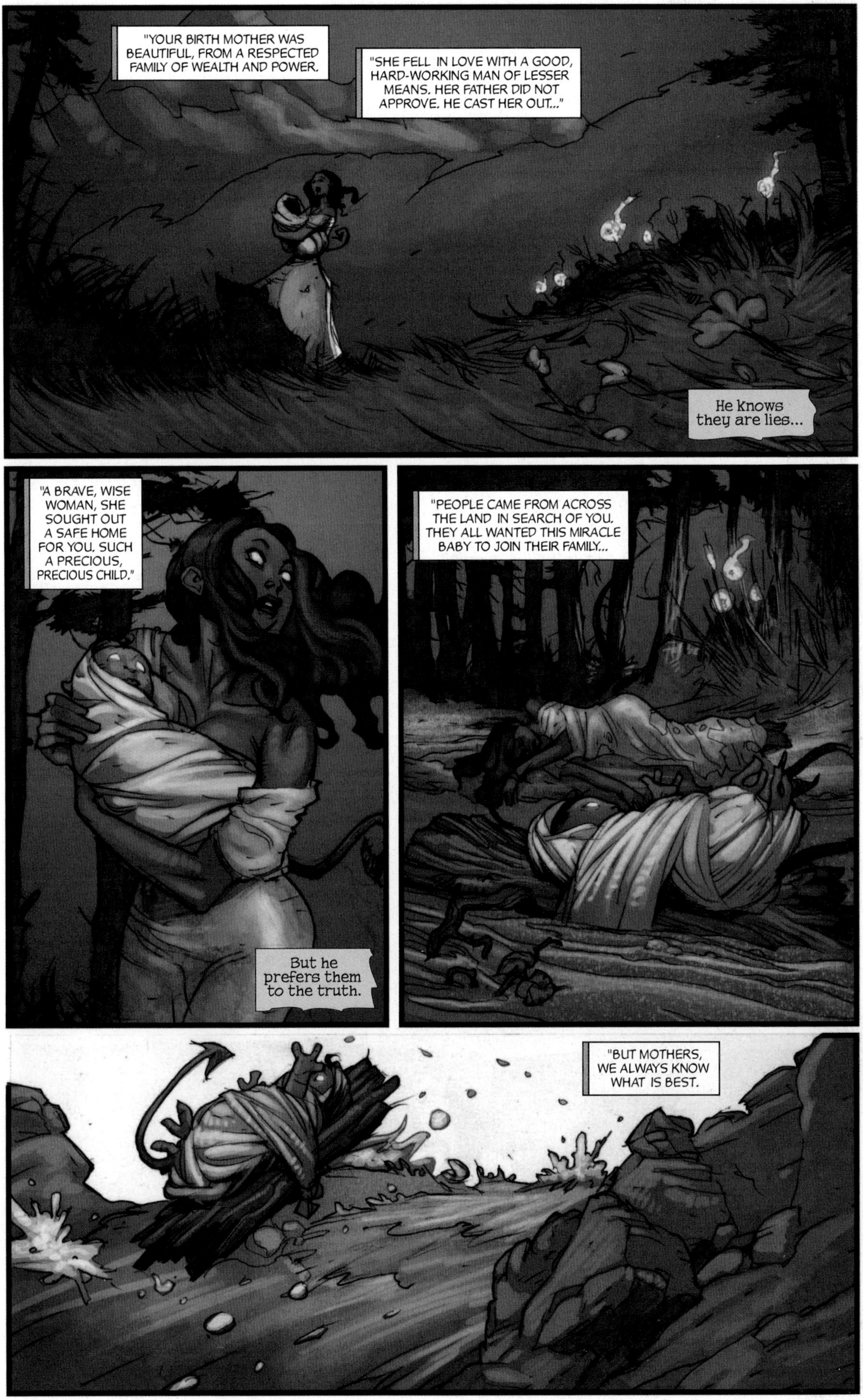
"YOUR BIRTH MOTHER WAS BEAUTIFUL, FROM A RESPECTED FAMILY OF WEALTH AND POWER.
"SHE FELL IN LOVE WITH A GOOD, HARD-WORKING MAN OF LESSER MEANS. HER FATHER DID NOT APPROVE. HE CAST HER OUT..."
He knows they are lies...
"A BRAVE, WISE WOMAN, SHE SOUGHT OUT A SAFE HOME FOR YOU. SUCH A PRECIOUS, PRECIOUS CHILD."
But he prefers them to the truth.
"PEOPLE CAME FROM ACROSS THE LAND IN SEARCH OF YOU. THEY ALL WANTED THIS MIRACLE BABY TO JOIN THEIR FAMILY...
"BUT MOTHERS, WE ALWAYS KNOW WHAT IS BEST.

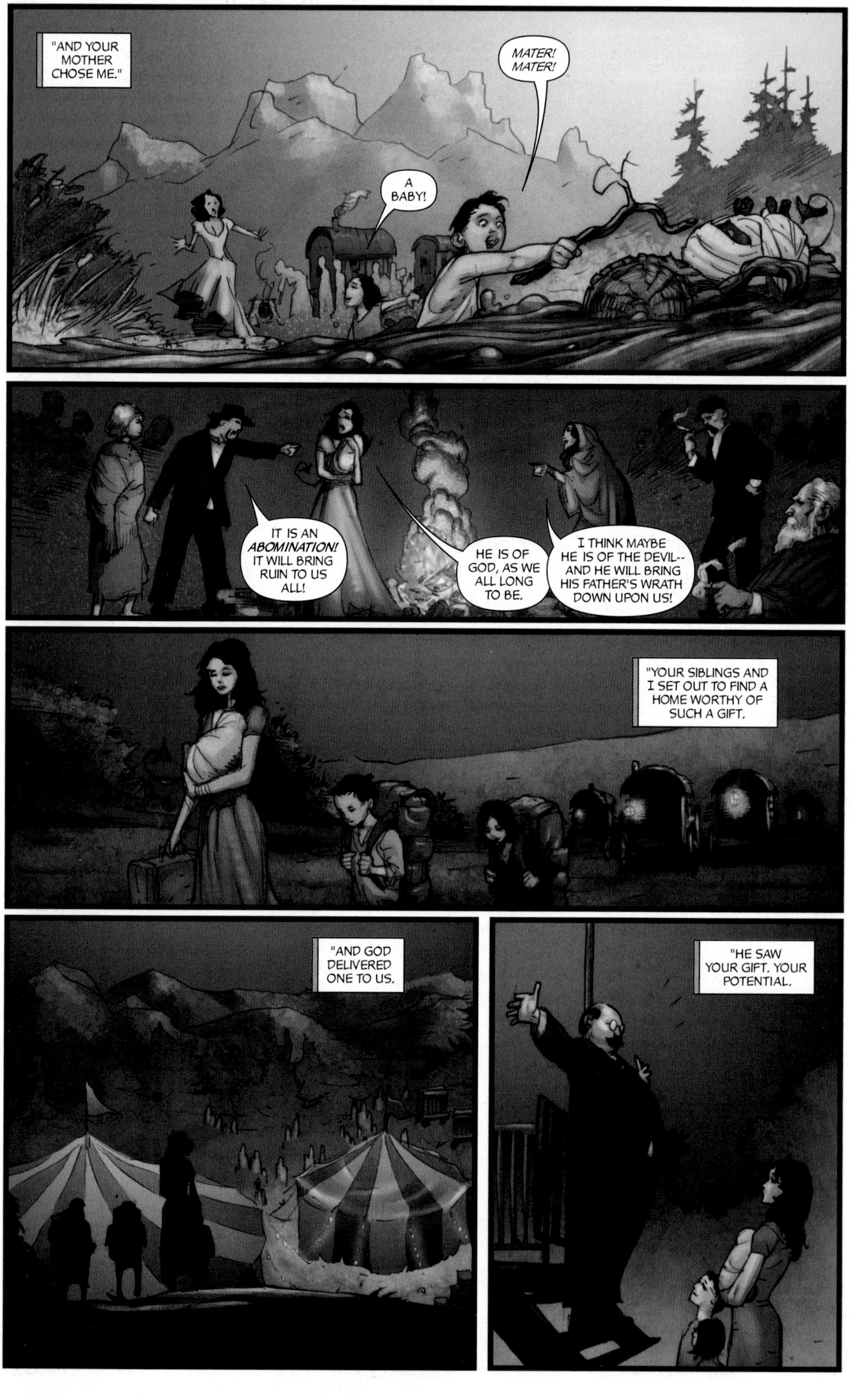
"AND YOUR MOTHER CHOSE ME."
MATER! MATER!
A BABY!
IT IS AN *ABOMINATION!* IT WILL BRING RUIN TO US ALL!
HE IS OF GOD, AS WE ALL LONG TO BE.
I THINK MAYBE HE IS OF THE DEVIL-- AND HE WILL BRING HIS FATHER'S WRATH DOWN UPON US!
"YOUR SIBLINGS AND I SET OUT TO FIND A HOME WORTHY OF SUCH A GIFT.
"AND GOD DELIVERED ONE TO US.
"HE SAW YOUR GIFT. YOUR POTENTIAL.

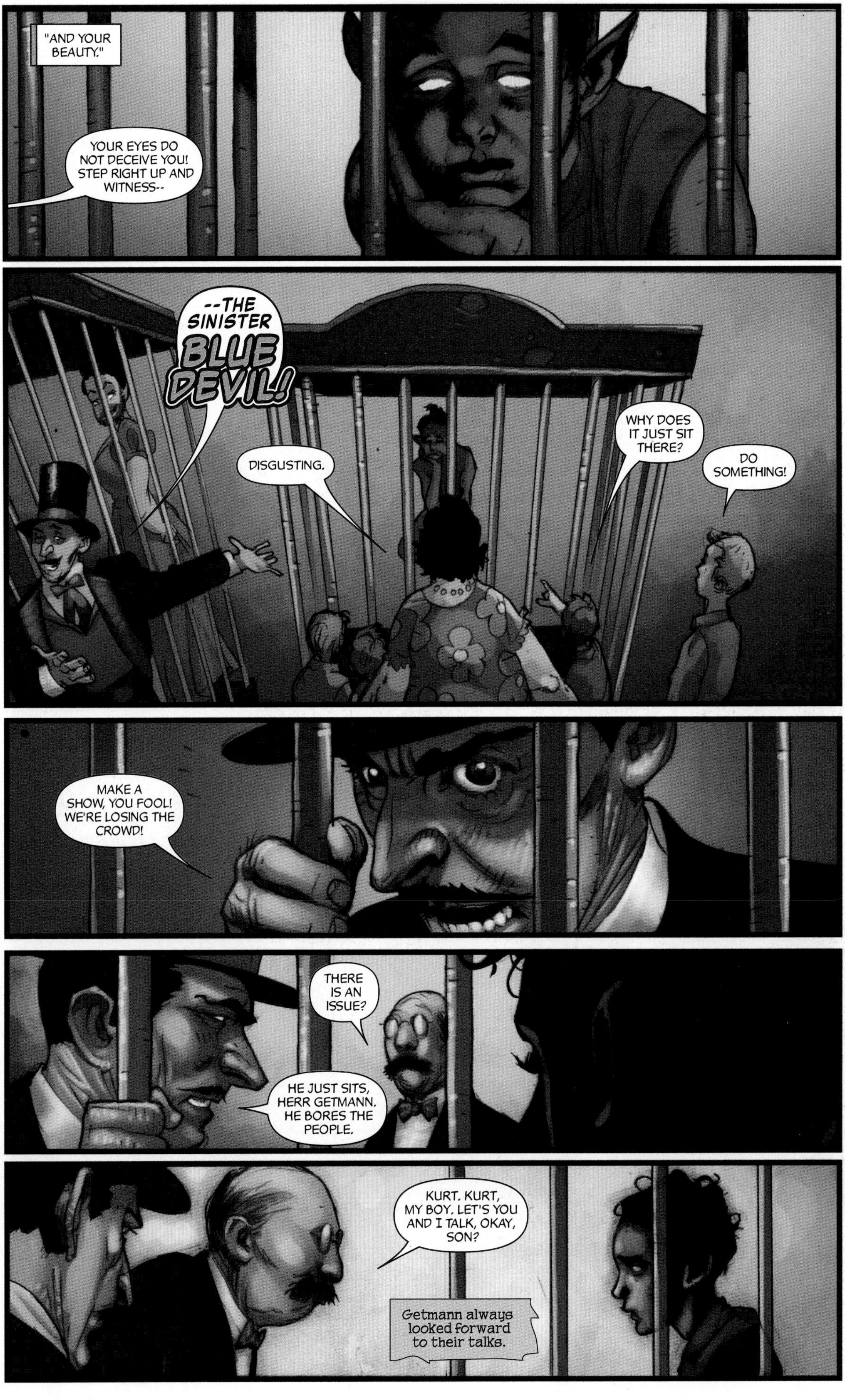
"AND YOUR BEAUTY."
YOUR EYES DO NOT DECEIVE YOU! STEP RIGHT UP AND WITNESS--
--THE SINISTER BLUE DEVIL!
DISGUSTING.
WHY DOES IT JUST SIT THERE?
DO SOMETHING!
MAKE A SHOW, YOU FOOL! WE'RE LOSING THE CROWD!
THERE IS AN ISSUE?
HE JUST SITS, HERR GETMANN. HE BORES THE PEOPLE.
KURT. KURT, MY BOY. LET'S YOU AND I TALK, OKAY, SON?
Getmann always looked forward to their talks.

"GETMANN ALWAYS FOUND A WAY TO SPEAK TO YOU IN A WAY YOU COULD EASILY UNDERSTAND."

FUWWHIPSH!

AAAHHHH!

I TAKE IN YOUR GYPSY WHORE OF A MOTHER AND THIS IS HOW YOU THANK ME?!

I DO NOT RUN A BOARDING HOUSE. I RUN A BUSINESS!

AND IN BUSINESS YOU MUST...

WHSHH!

ARRGGH!

FFWWHSSHH!

...SEIZE...

CRASSH!

...EVERY...

...OPPORTUNITY!

OH, MY DEAR KURT. MY DEAR, DEAR KURT...

HOW WOULD YOU LIKE TO APPEAR IN THE MAIN TENT?

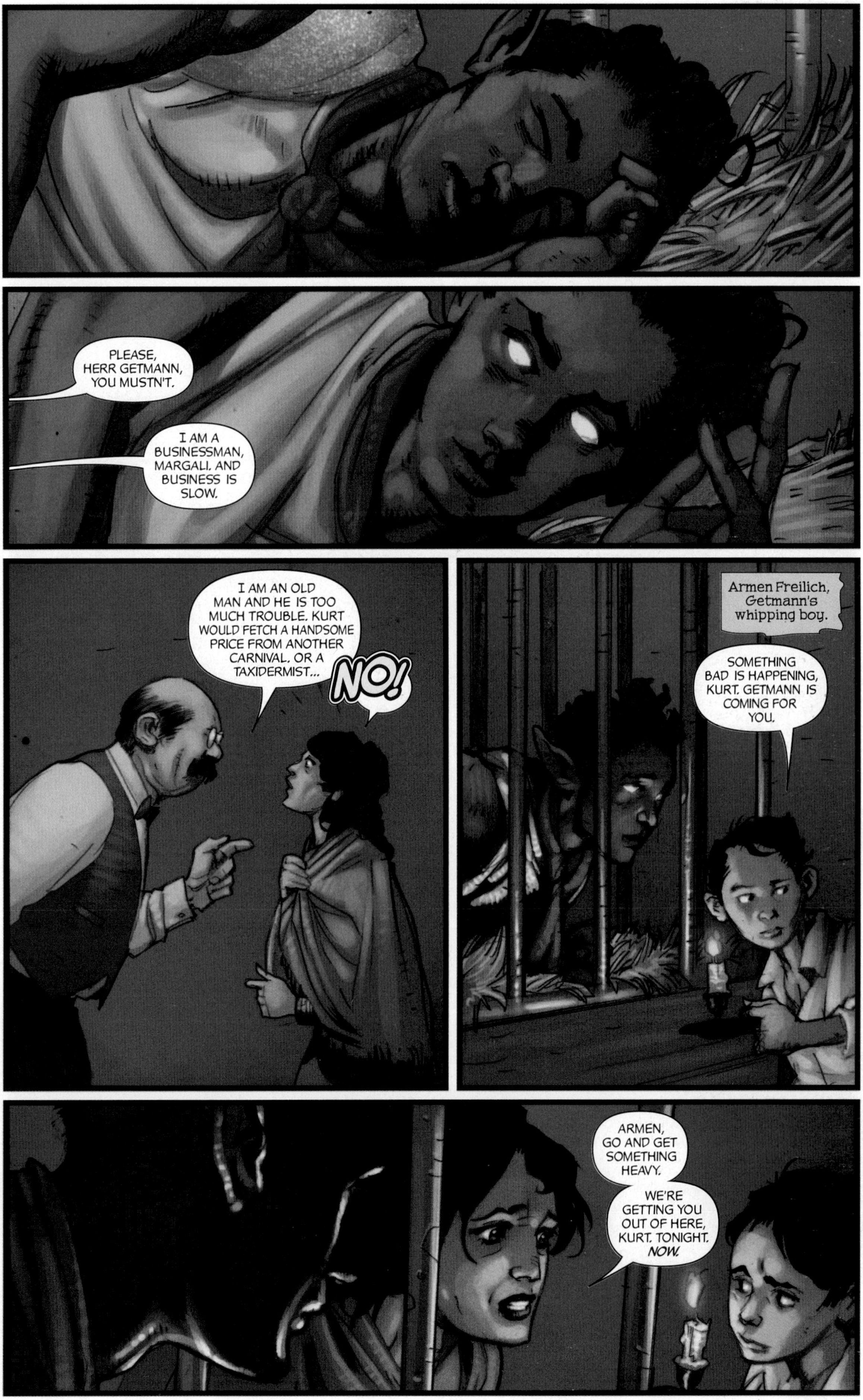
PLEASE, HERR GETMANN, YOU MUSTN'T.
I AM A BUSINESSMAN, MARGALI, AND BUSINESS IS SLOW.
I AM AN OLD MAN AND HE IS TOO MUCH TROUBLE. KURT WOULD FETCH A HANDSOME PRICE FROM ANOTHER CARNIVAL, OR A TAXIDERMIST...
NO!
Armen Freilich, Getmann's whipping boy.
SOMETHING BAD IS HAPPENING, KURT. GETMANN IS COMING FOR YOU.
ARMEN, GO AND GET SOMETHING HEAVY.
WE'RE GETTING YOU OUT OF HERE, KURT. TONIGHT. *NOW.*

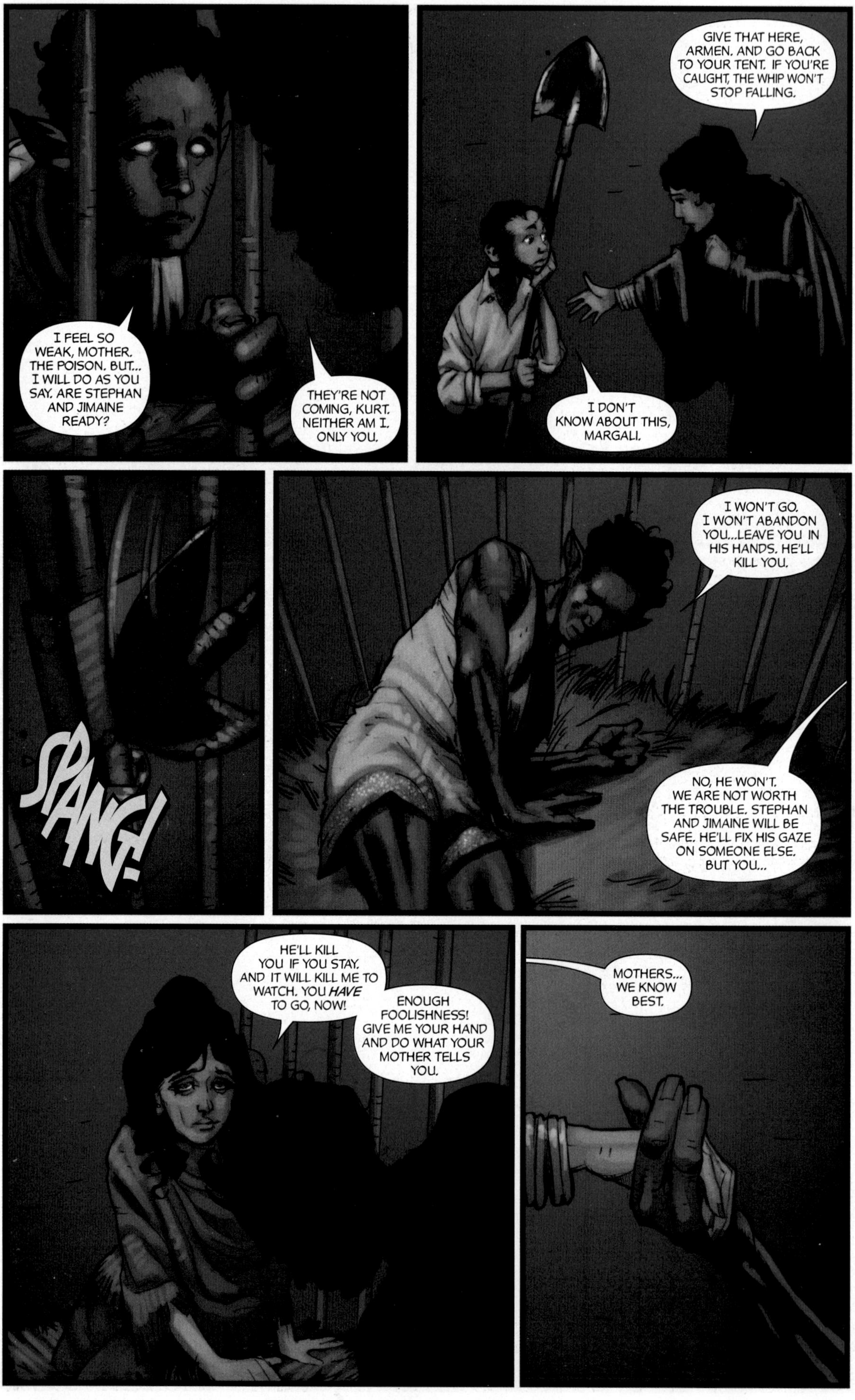
I FEEL SO WEAK, MOTHER. THE POISON. BUT... I WILL DO AS YOU SAY. ARE STEPHAN AND JIMAINE READY?
THEY'RE NOT COMING, KURT. NEITHER AM I. ONLY YOU.
GIVE THAT HERE, ARMEN. AND GO BACK TO YOUR TENT. IF YOU'RE CAUGHT, THE WHIP WON'T STOP FALLING.
I DON'T KNOW ABOUT THIS, MARGALI.
SPANG!
I WON'T GO. I WON'T ABANDON YOU...LEAVE YOU IN HIS HANDS. HE'LL KILL YOU.
NO, HE WON'T. WE ARE NOT WORTH THE TROUBLE. STEPHAN AND JIMAINE WILL BE SAFE. HE'LL FIX HIS GAZE ON SOMEONE ELSE. BUT YOU...
HE'LL KILL YOU IF YOU STAY. AND IT WILL KILL ME TO WATCH. YOU *HAVE* TO GO, NOW!
ENOUGH FOOLISHNESS! GIVE ME YOUR HAND AND DO WHAT YOUR MOTHER TELLS YOU.
MOTHERS... WE KNOW BEST.

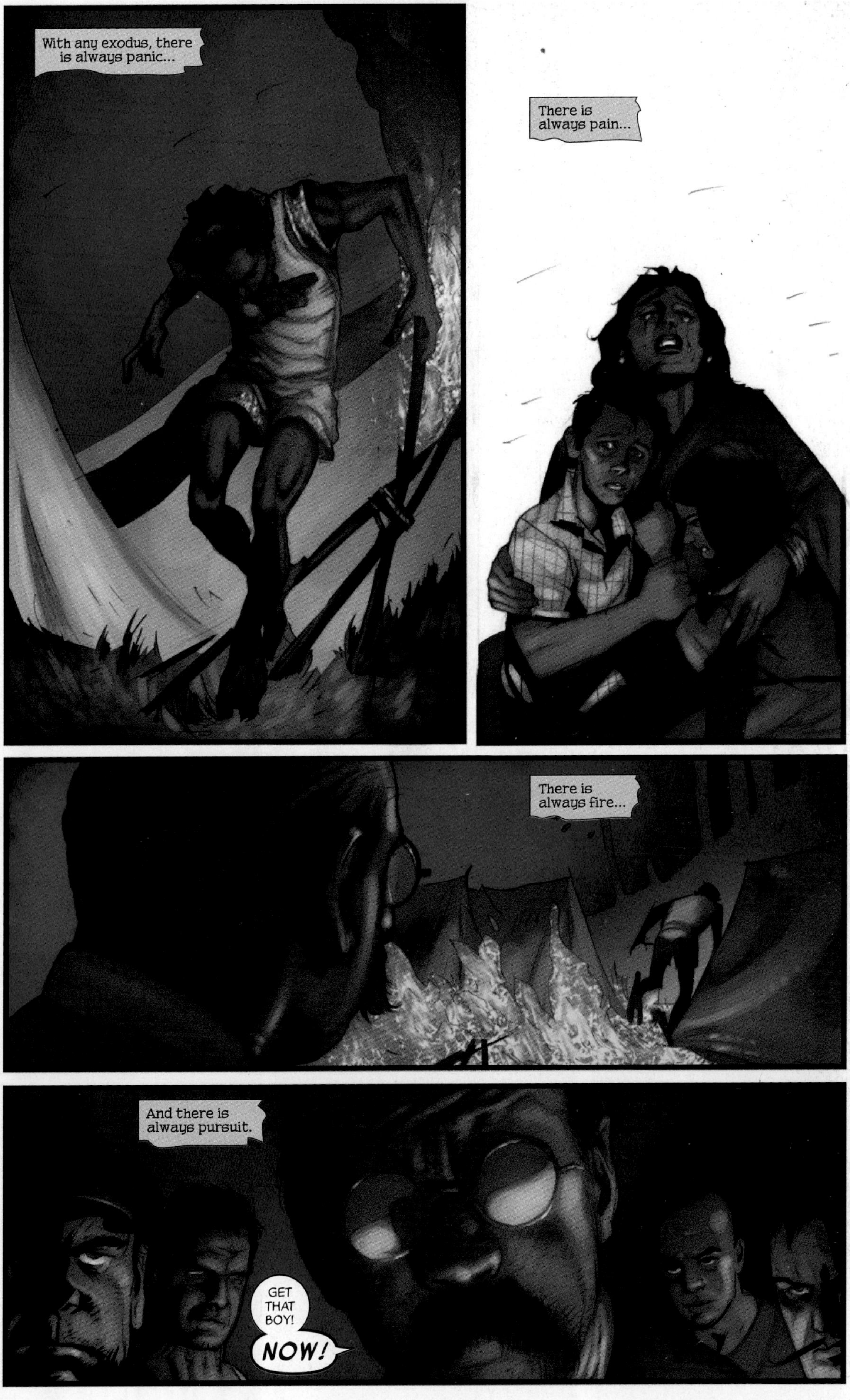
With any exodus, there is always panic...
There is always pain...
There is always fire...
And there is always pursuit.
GET THAT BOY!
NOW!

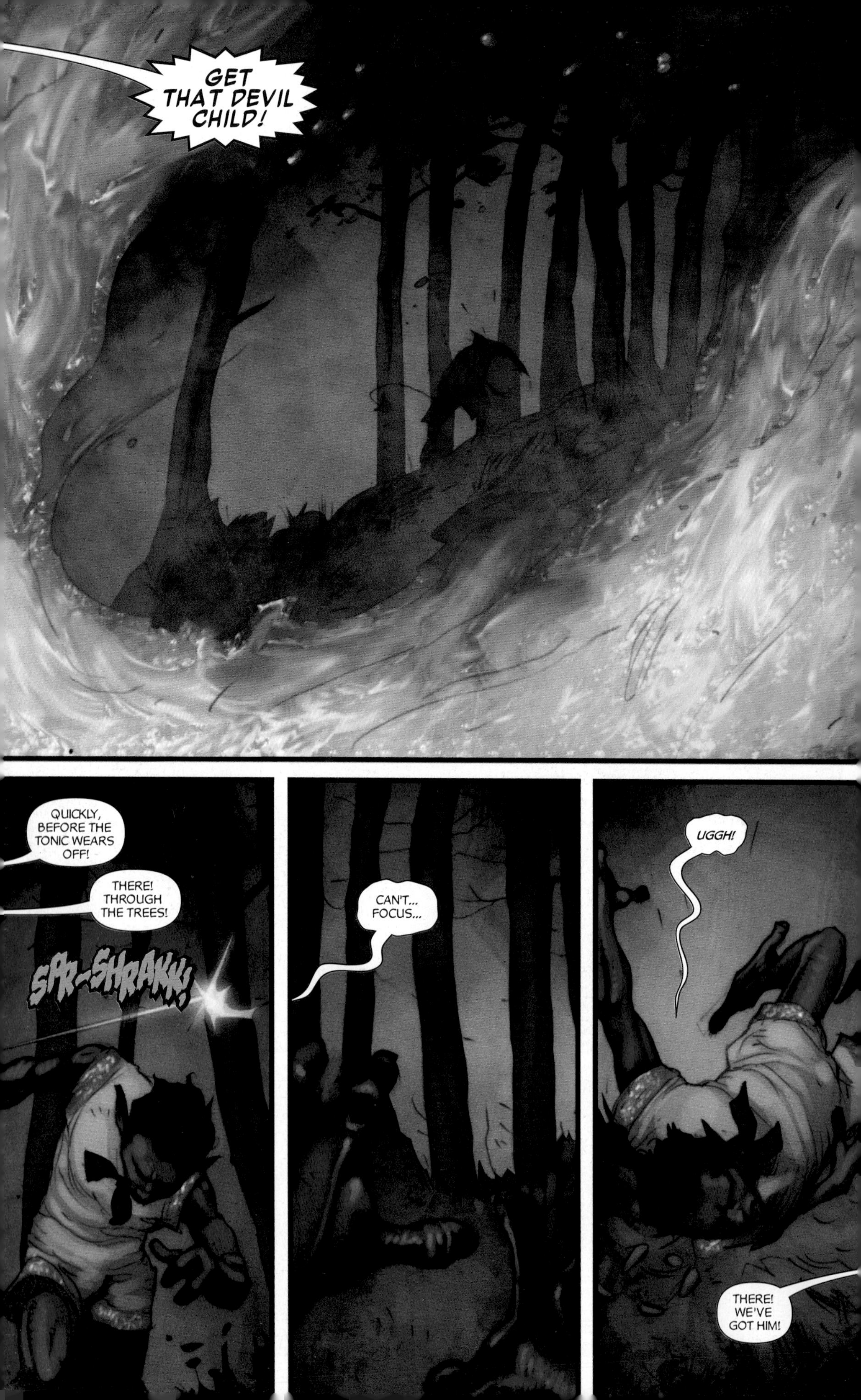
GET THAT DEVIL CHILD!
QUICKLY, BEFORE THE TONIC WEARS OFF!
THERE! THROUGH THE TREES!
SPR-SHRAKK!
CAN'T... FOCUS...
UGGH!
THERE! WE'VE GOT HIM!

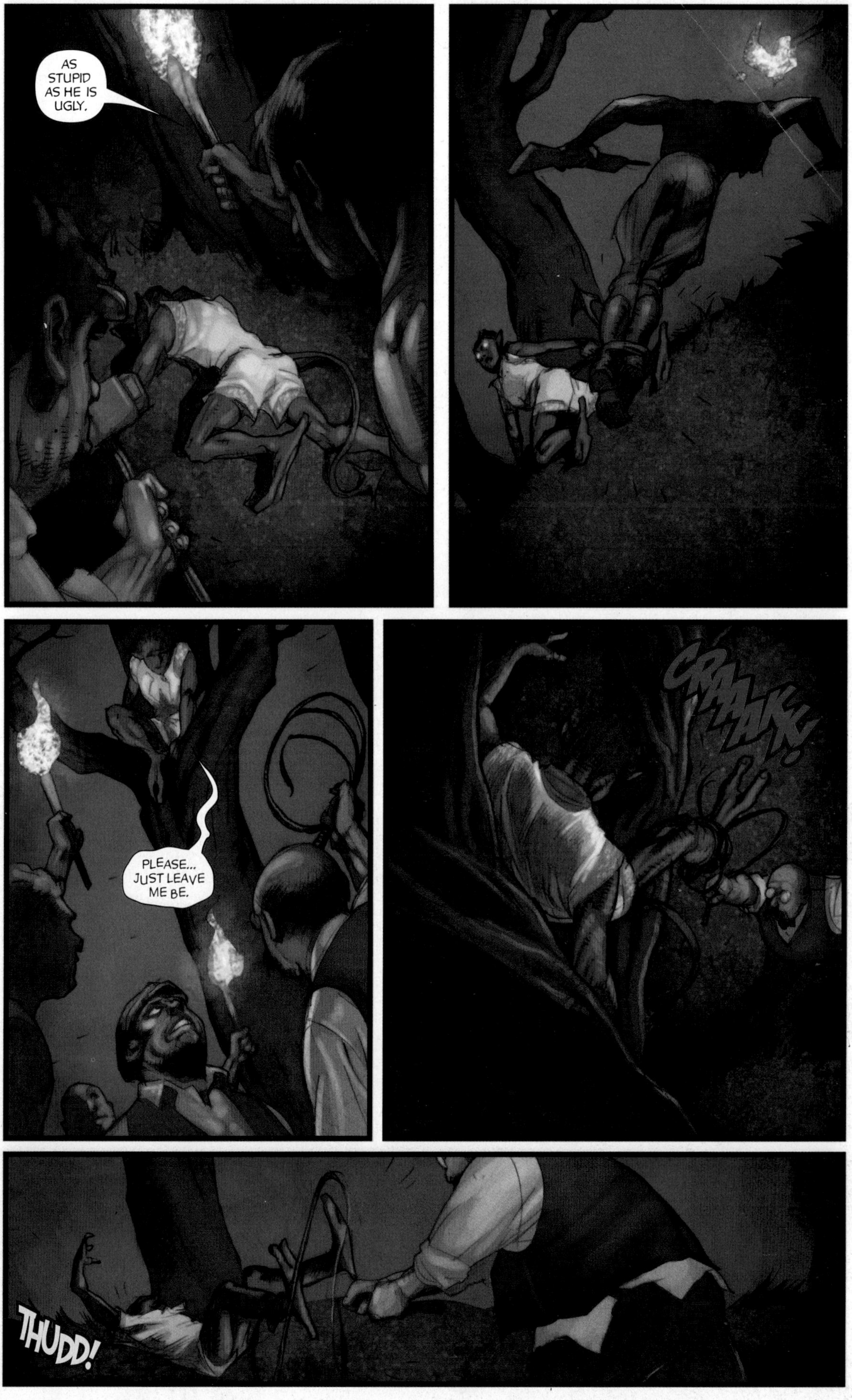
AS STUPID AS HE IS UGLY.
PLEASE... JUST LEAVE ME BE.
CRAAAK!
THUDD!

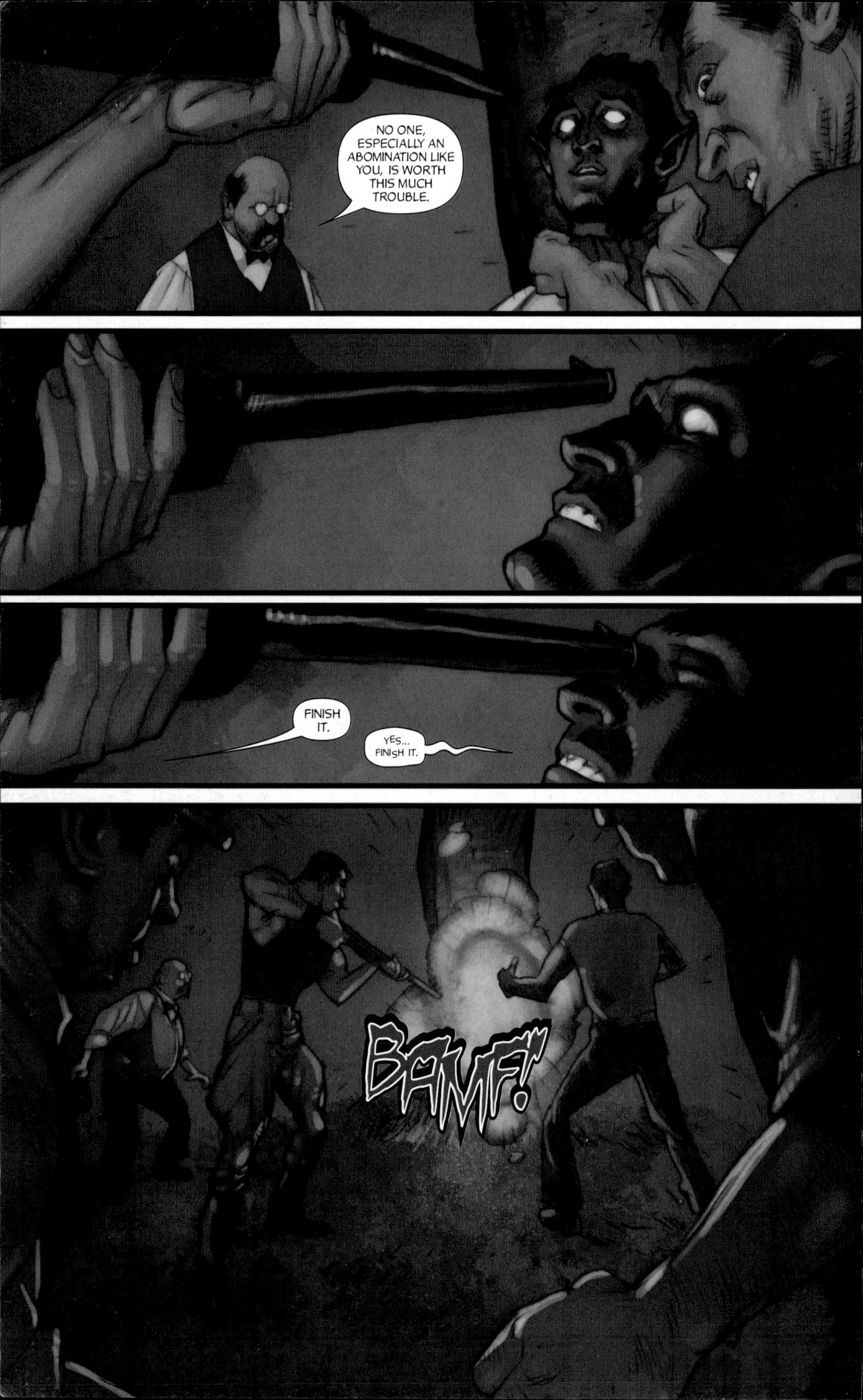
NO ONE, ESPECIALLY AN ABOMINATION LIKE YOU, IS WORTH THIS MUCH TROUBLE.
FINISH IT.
YES... FINISH IT.
BAMF!

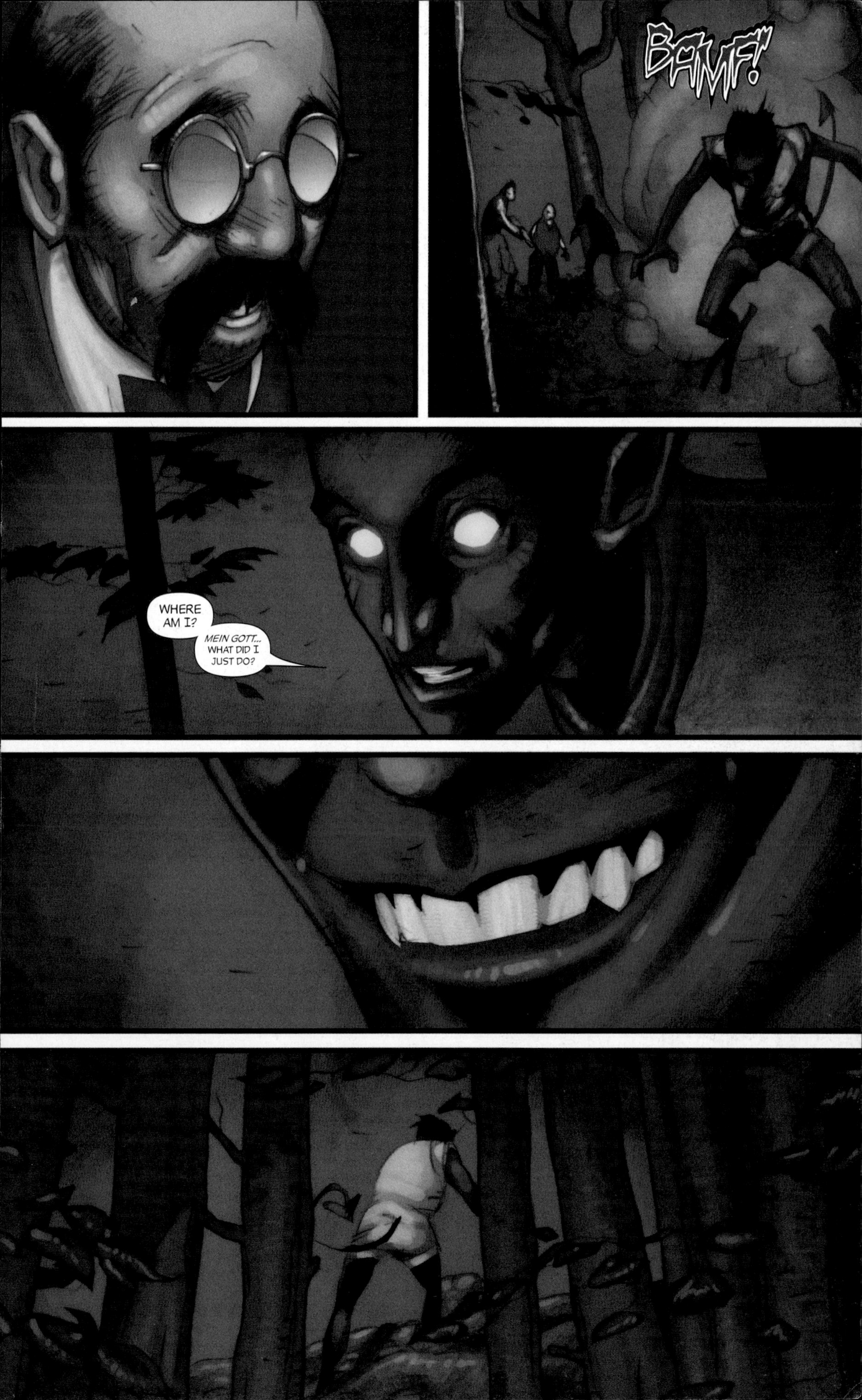
BAMF!
WHERE AM I?
MEIN GOTT... WHAT DID I JUST DO?

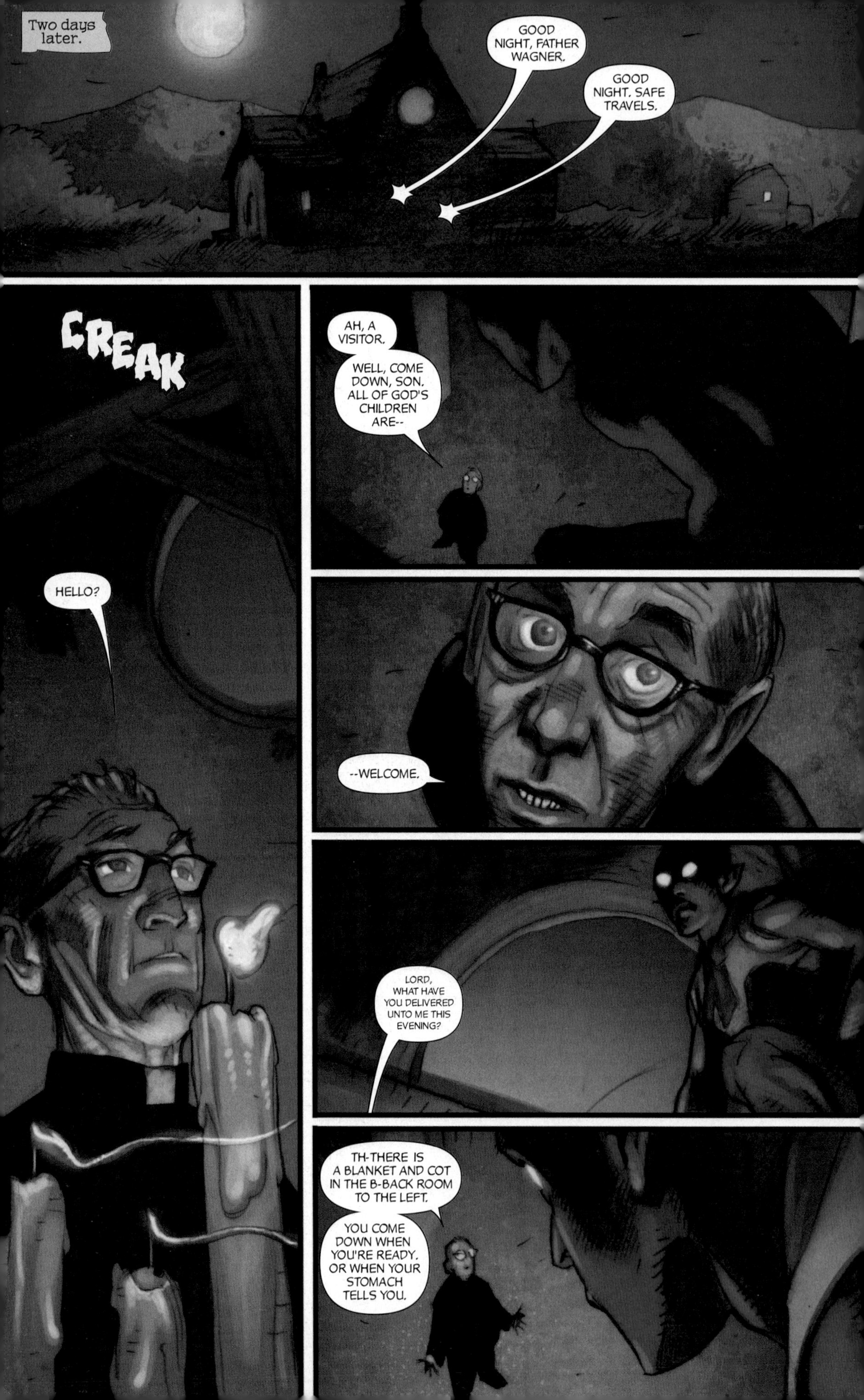
Two days later.
GOOD NIGHT, FATHER WAGNER.
GOOD NIGHT. SAFE TRAVELS.
CREAK
HELLO?
AH, A VISITOR.
WELL, COME DOWN, SON. ALL OF GOD'S CHILDREN ARE--
--WELCOME.
LORD, WHAT HAVE YOU DELIVERED UNTO ME THIS EVENING?
TH-THERE IS A BLANKET AND COT IN THE B-BACK ROOM TO THE LEFT.
YOU COME DOWN WHEN YOU'RE READY. OR WHEN YOUR STOMACH TELLS YOU.

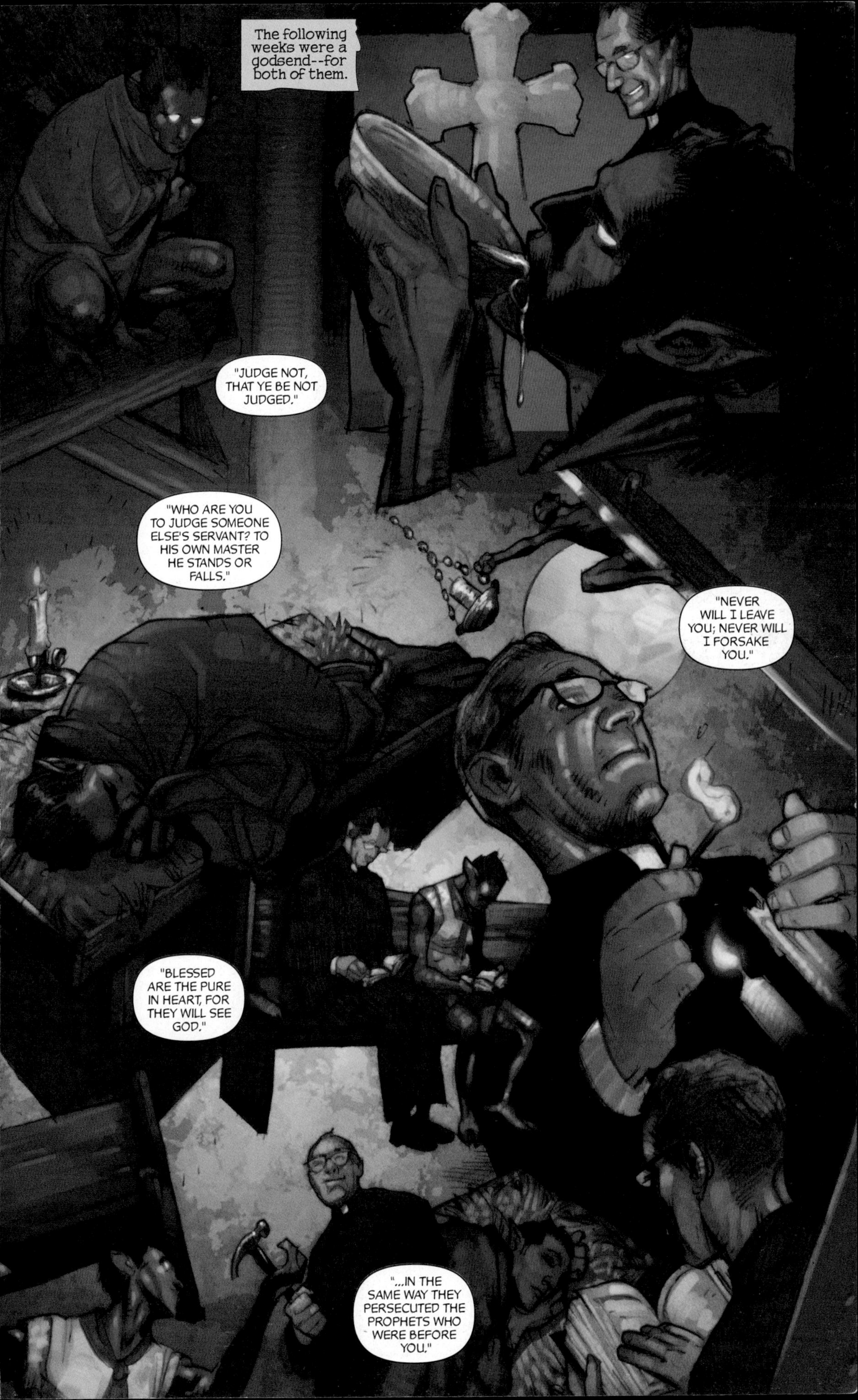
The following weeks were a godsend--for both of them.
"JUDGE NOT, THAT YE BE NOT JUDGED."
"WHO ARE YOU TO JUDGE SOMEONE ELSE'S SERVANT? TO HIS OWN MASTER HE STANDS OR FALLS."
"NEVER WILL I LEAVE YOU; NEVER WILL I FORSAKE YOU."
"BLESSED ARE THE PURE IN HEART, FOR THEY WILL SEE GOD."
"...IN THE SAME WAY THEY PERSECUTED THE PROPHETS WHO WERE BEFORE YOU."

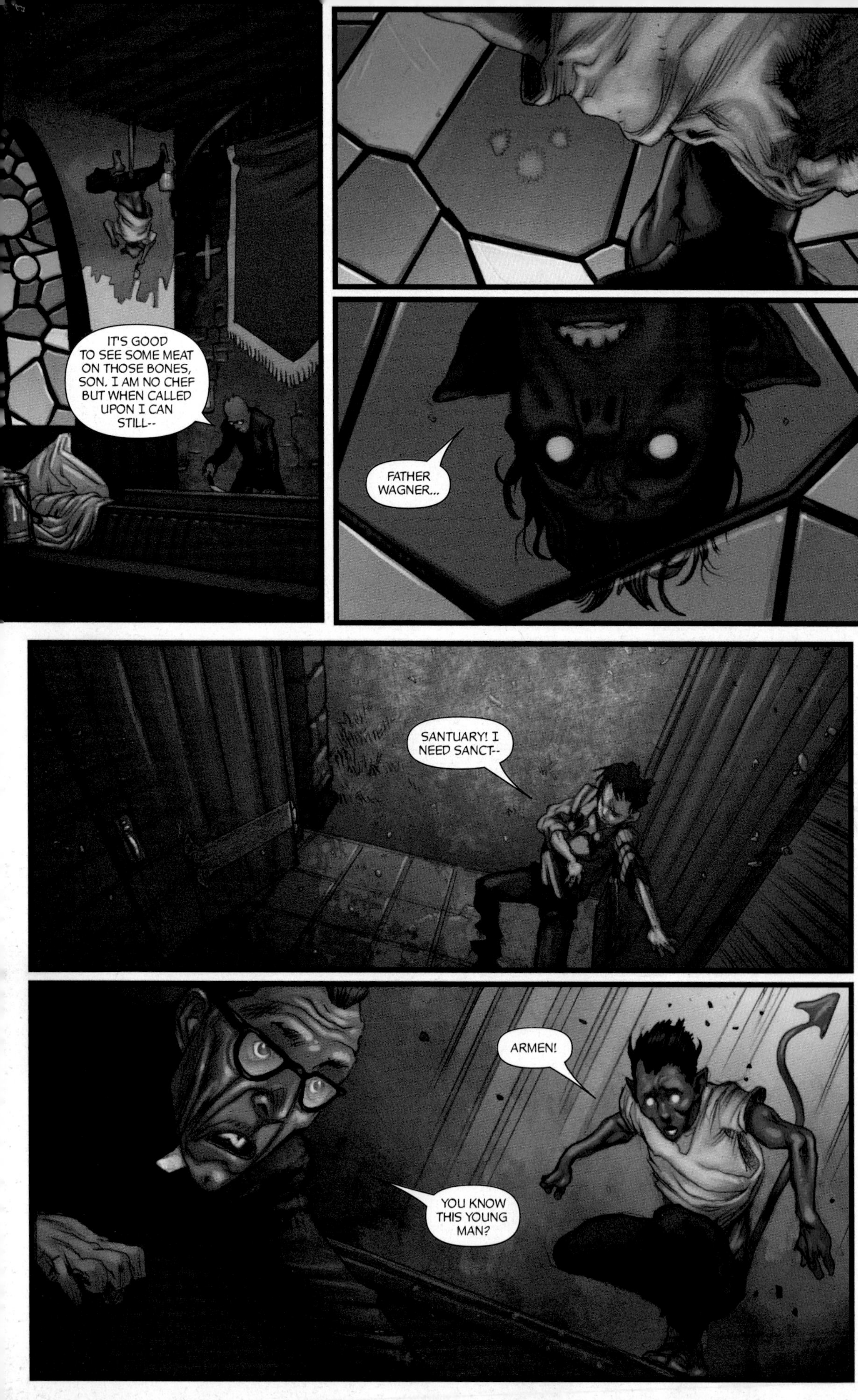

IT'S GOOD TO SEE SOME MEAT ON THOSE BONES, SON. I AM NO CHEF BUT WHEN CALLED UPON I CAN STILL--
FATHER WAGNER...
SANTUARY! I NEED SANCT--
ARMEN!
YOU KNOW THIS YOUNG MAN?

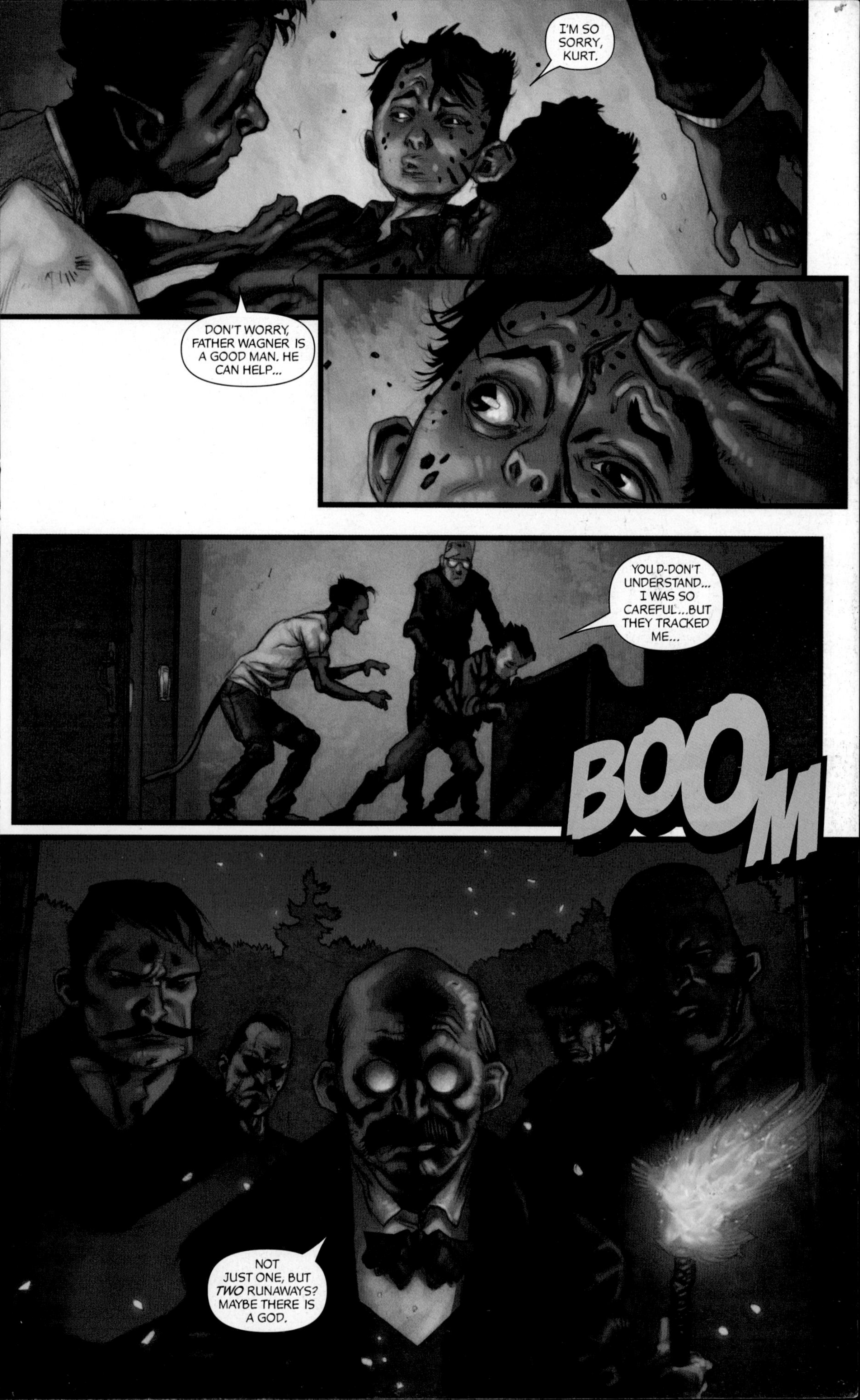
I'M SO SORRY, KURT.
DON'T WORRY, FATHER WAGNER IS A GOOD MAN. HE CAN HELP...
YOU D-DON'T UNDERSTAND... I WAS SO CAREFUL...BUT THEY TRACKED ME...
BOOM
NOT JUST ONE, BUT *TWO* RUNAWAYS? MAYBE THERE IS A GOD.

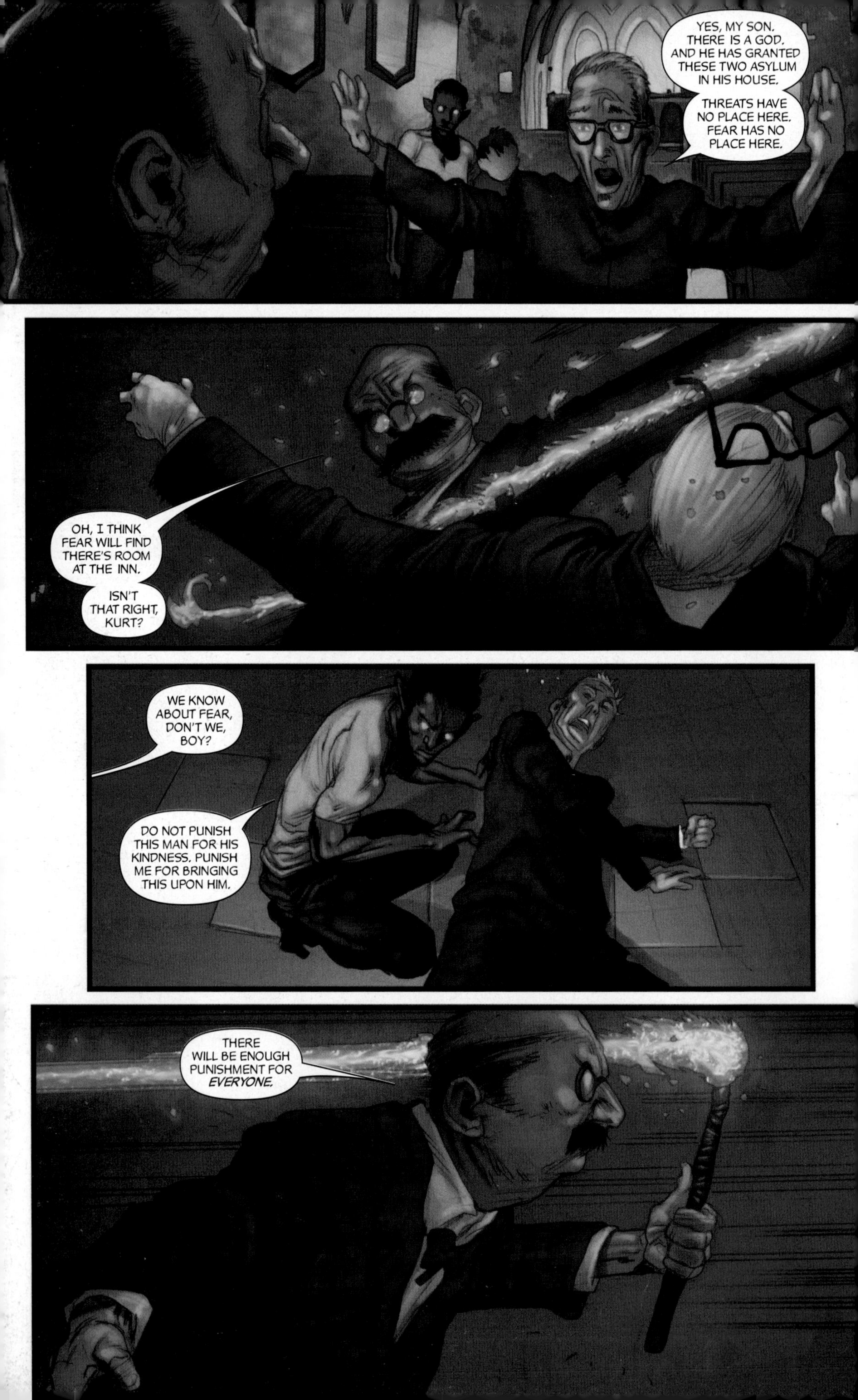
YES, MY SON. THERE IS A GOD. AND HE HAS GRANTED THESE TWO ASYLUM IN HIS HOUSE.
THREATS HAVE NO PLACE HERE. FEAR HAS NO PLACE HERE.
OH, I THINK FEAR WILL FIND THERE'S ROOM AT THE INN.
ISN'T THAT RIGHT, KURT?
WE KNOW ABOUT FEAR, DON'T WE, BOY?
DO NOT PUNISH THIS MAN FOR HIS KINDNESS. PUNISH ME FOR BRINGING THIS UPON HIM.
THERE WILL BE ENOUGH PUNISHMENT FOR *EVERYONE.*

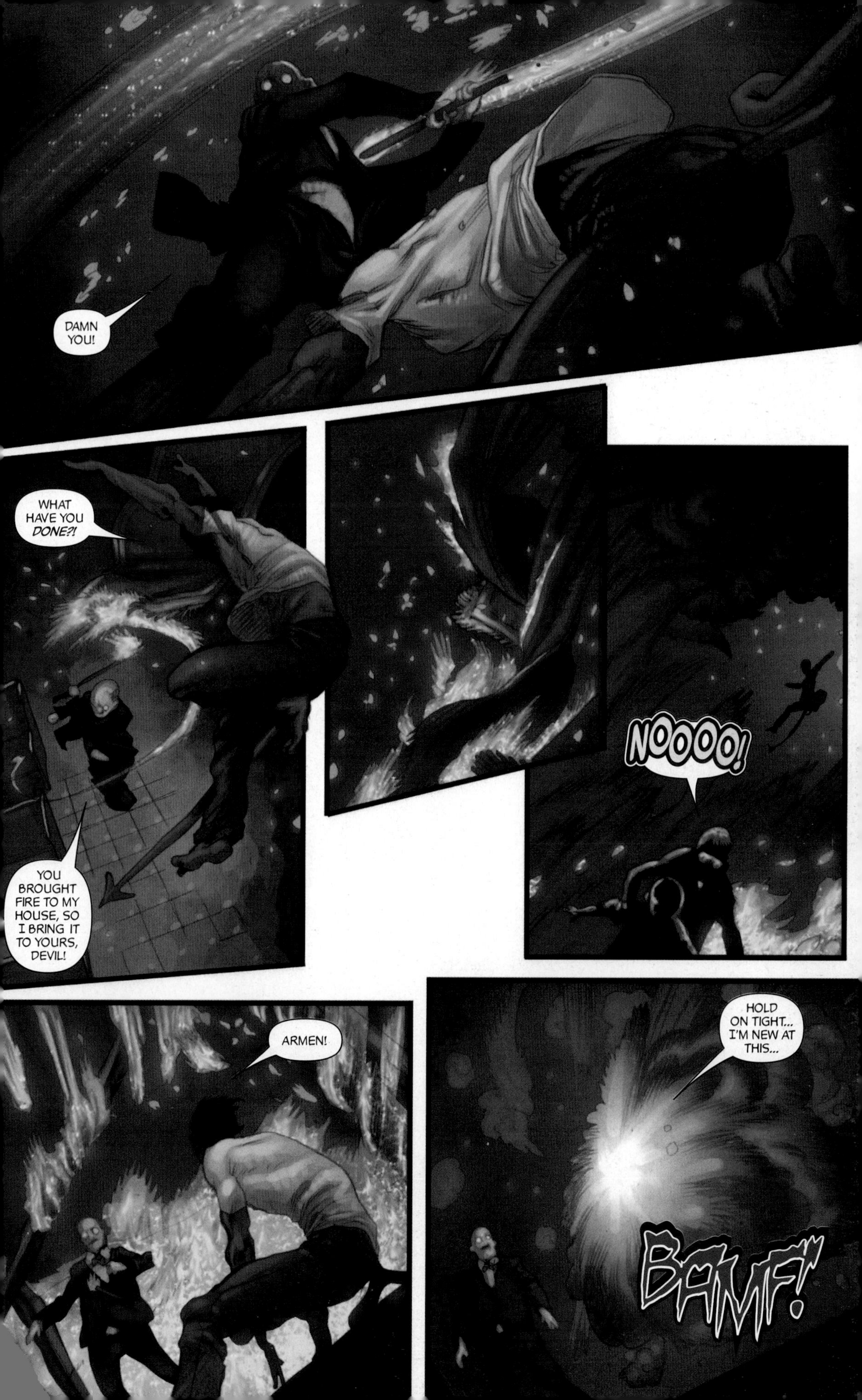
DAMN YOU!
WHAT HAVE YOU *DONE?!*
YOU BROUGHT FIRE TO MY HOUSE, SO I BRING IT TO YOURS, DEVIL!
NOOOO!
ARMEN!
HOLD ON TIGHT... I'M NEW AT THIS...
BAMF!

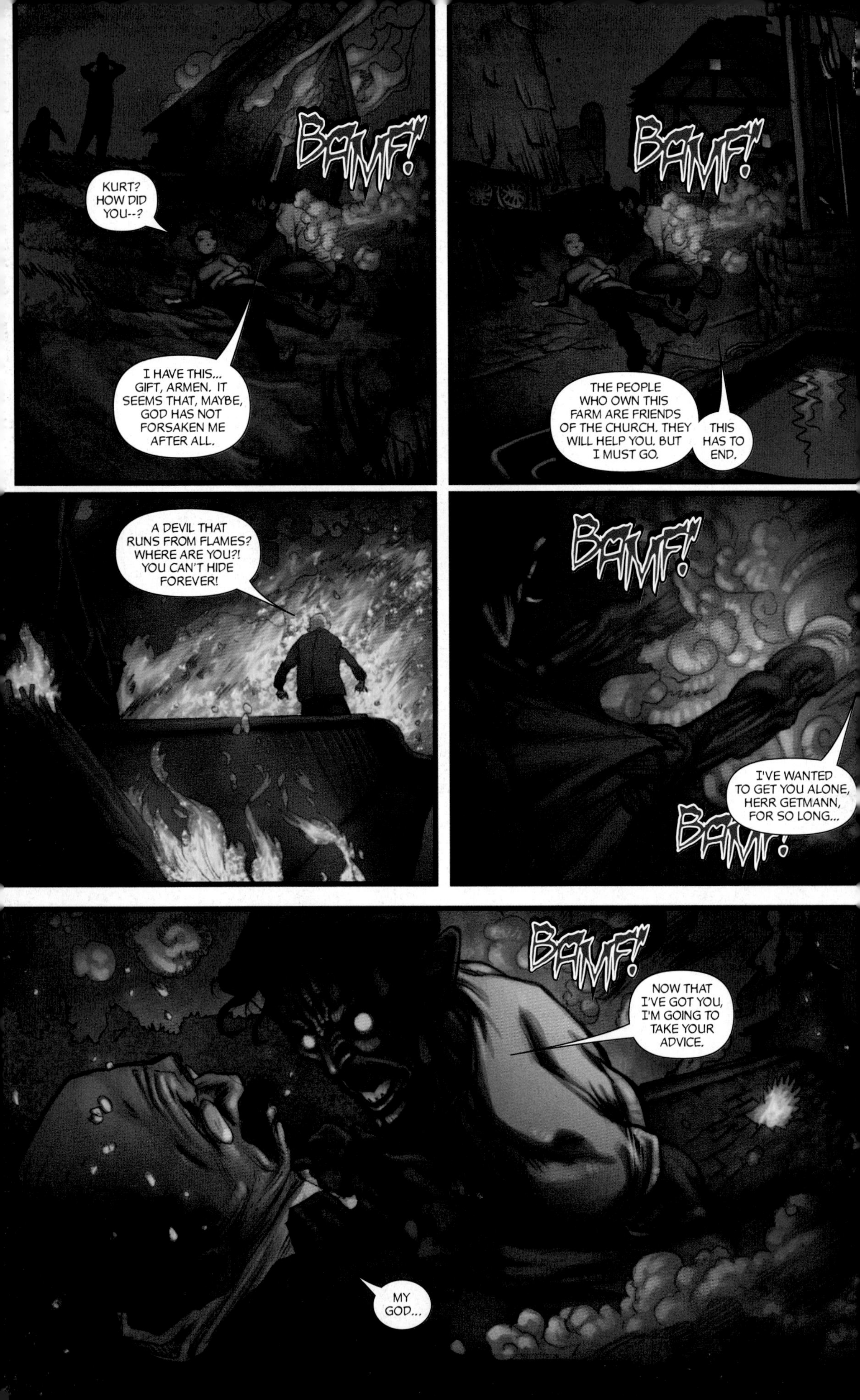
BAMF!
KURT? HOW DID YOU--?
I HAVE THIS... GIFT, ARMEN. IT SEEMS THAT, MAYBE, GOD HAS NOT FORSAKEN ME AFTER ALL.
BAMF!
THE PEOPLE WHO OWN THIS FARM ARE FRIENDS OF THE CHURCH. THEY WILL HELP YOU. BUT I MUST GO.
THIS HAS TO END.
A DEVIL THAT RUNS FROM FLAMES? WHERE ARE YOU?! YOU CAN'T HIDE FOREVER!
BAMF!
I'VE WANTED TO GET YOU ALONE, HERR GETMANN, FOR SO LONG...
BAMF!
BAMF!
NOW THAT I'VE GOT YOU, I'M GOING TO TAKE YOUR ADVICE.
MY GOD...

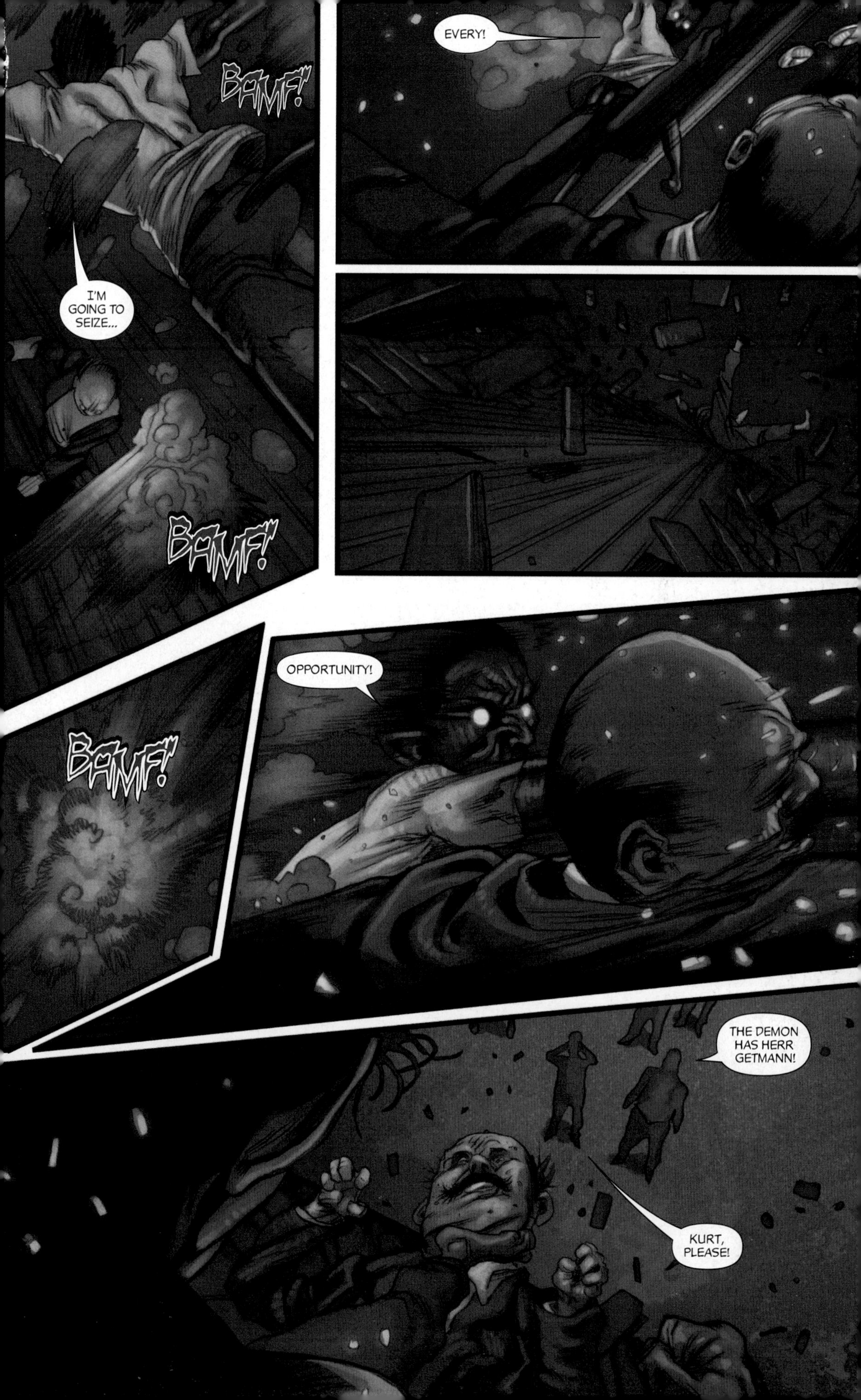
BAMF!
I'M GOING TO SEIZE...
BAMF!
EVERY!
BAMF!
OPPORTUNITY!
THE DEMON HAS HERR GETMANN!
KURT, PLEASE!

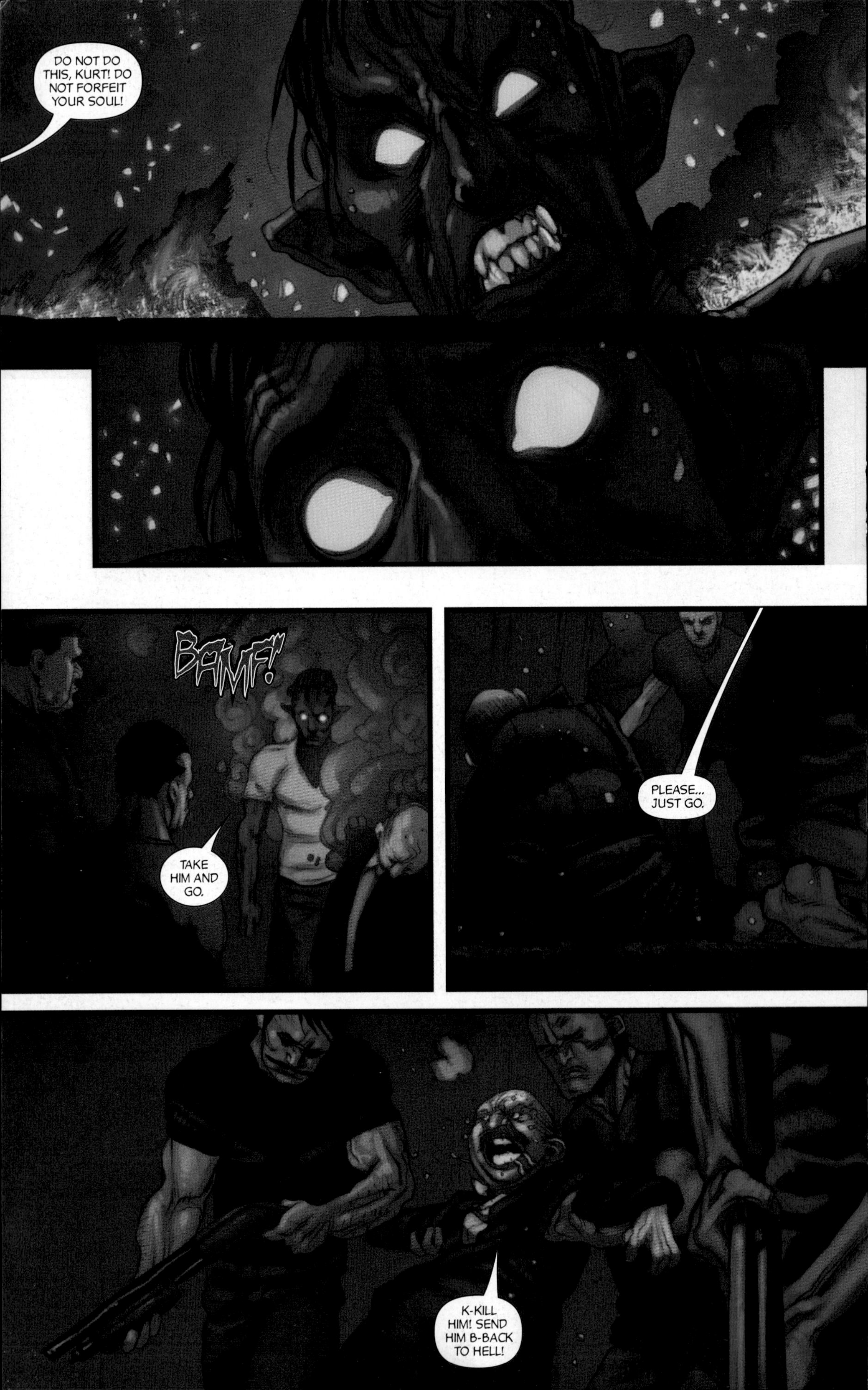
DO NOT DO THIS, KURT! DO NOT FORFEIT YOUR SOUL!
BAMF!
TAKE HIM AND GO.
PLEASE... JUST GO.
K-KILL HIM! SEND HIM B-BACK TO HELL!

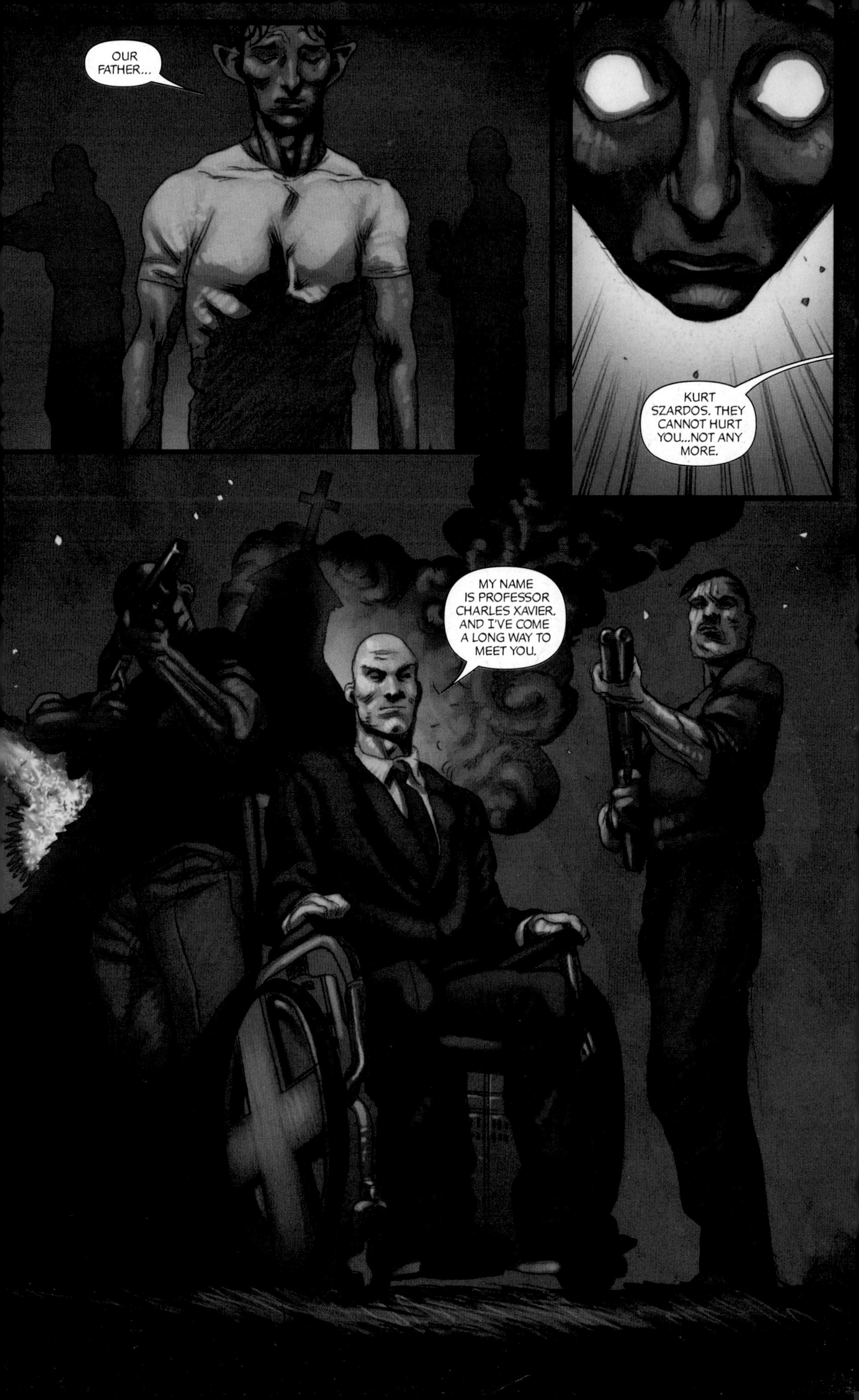
OUR FATHER...
KURT SZARDOS. THEY CANNOT HURT YOU...NOT ANY MORE.
MY NAME IS PROFESSOR CHARLES XAVIER, AND I'VE COME A LONG WAY TO MEET YOU.

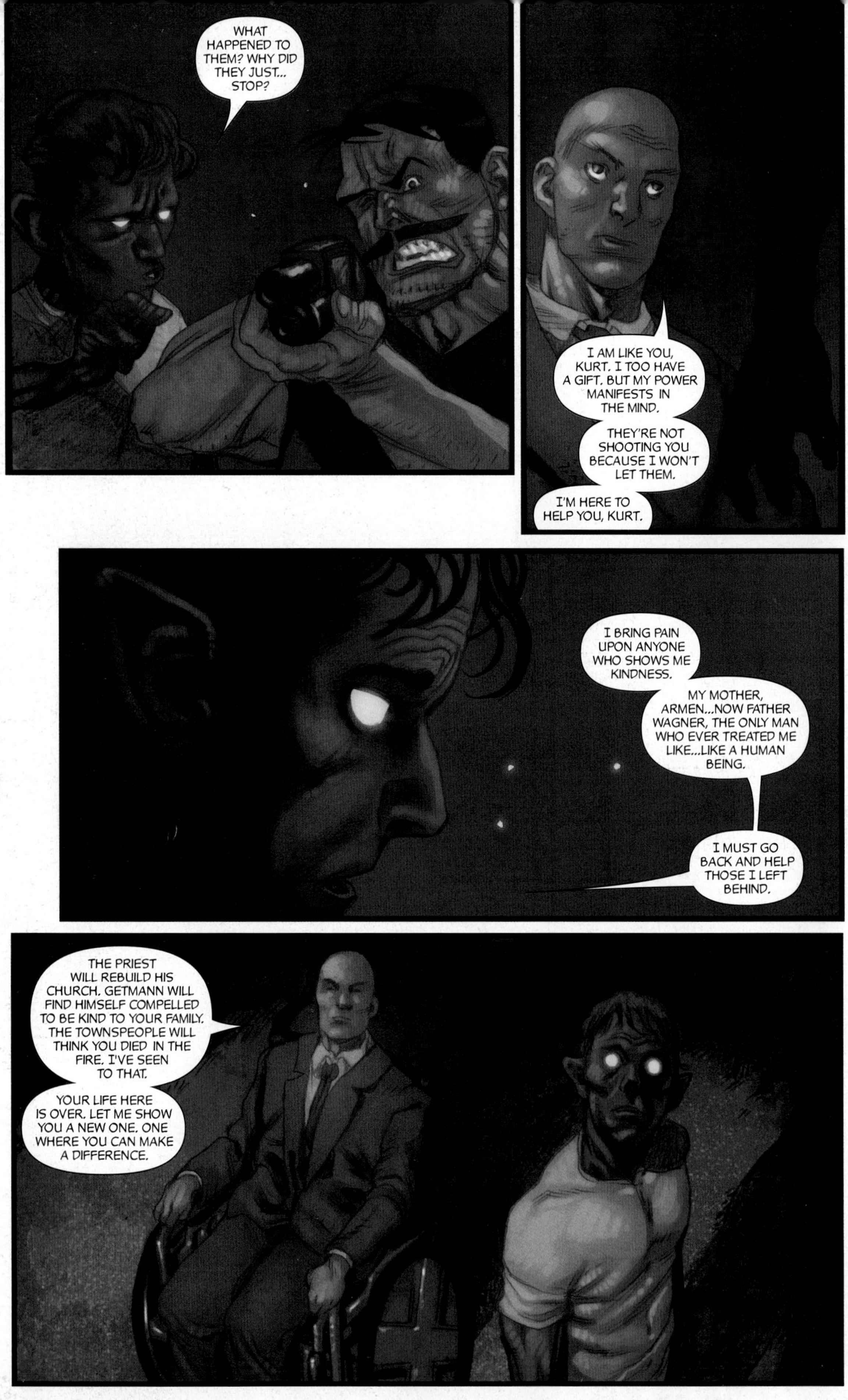
WHAT HAPPENED TO THEM? WHY DID THEY JUST... STOP?
I AM LIKE YOU, KURT. I TOO HAVE A GIFT. BUT MY POWER MANIFESTS IN THE MIND.
THEY'RE NOT SHOOTING YOU BECAUSE I WON'T LET THEM.
I'M HERE TO HELP YOU, KURT.
I BRING PAIN UPON ANYONE WHO SHOWS ME KINDNESS.
MY MOTHER, ARMEN...NOW FATHER WAGNER, THE ONLY MAN WHO EVER TREATED ME LIKE...LIKE A HUMAN BEING.
I MUST GO BACK AND HELP THOSE I LEFT BEHIND.
THE PRIEST WILL REBUILD HIS CHURCH. GETMANN WILL FIND HIMSELF COMPELLED TO BE KIND TO YOUR FAMILY. THE TOWNSPEOPLE WILL THINK YOU DIED IN THE FIRE. I'VE SEEN TO THAT.
YOUR LIFE HERE IS OVER. LET ME SHOW YOU A NEW ONE. ONE WHERE YOU CAN MAKE A DIFFERENCE.

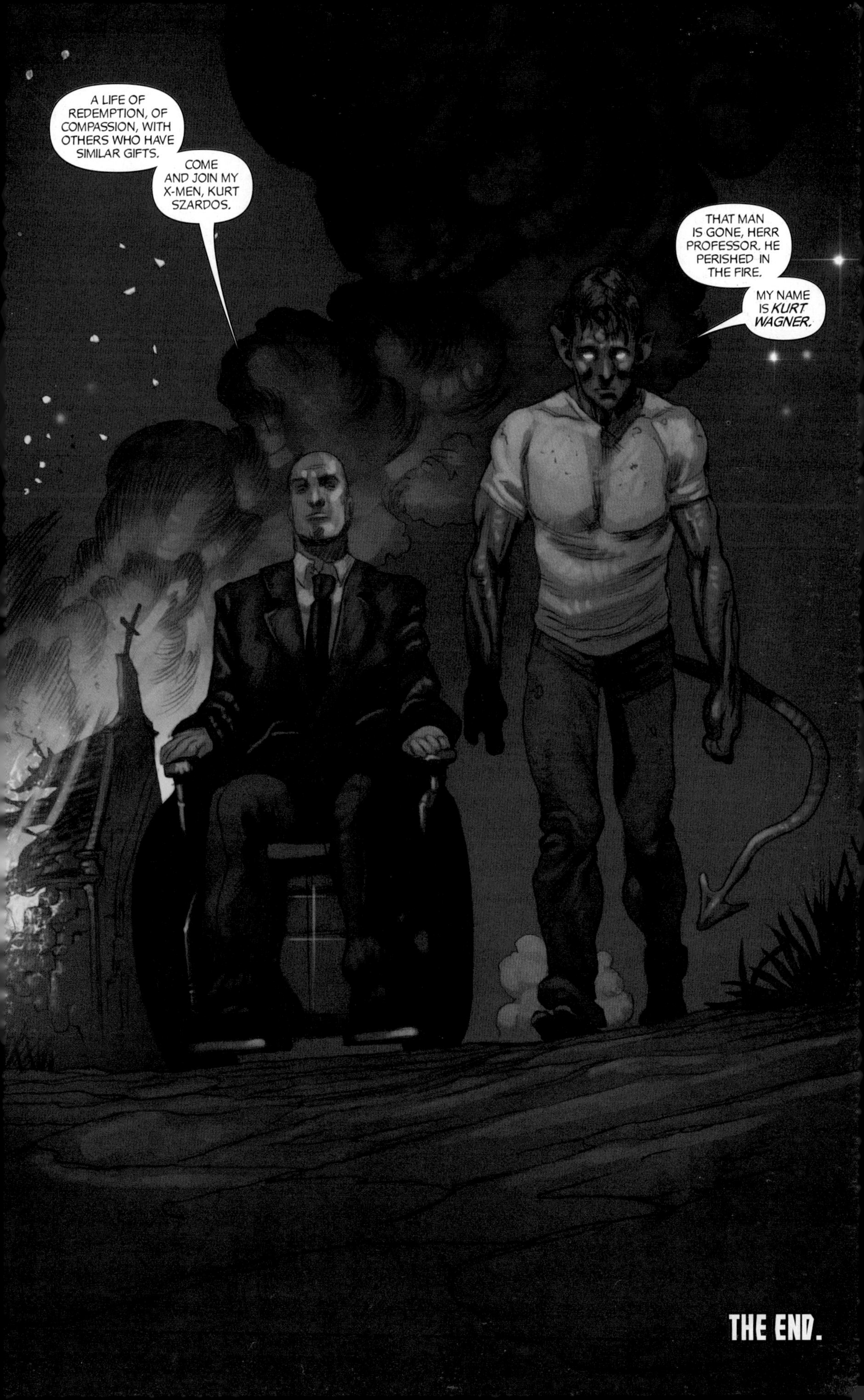
A LIFE OF REDEMPTION, OF COMPASSION, WITH OTHERS WHO HAVE SIMILAR GIFTS.
COME AND JOIN MY X-MEN, KURT SZARDOS.
THAT MAN IS GONE, HERR PROFESSOR. HE PERISHED IN THE FIRE.
MY NAME IS *KURT WAGNER*.
THE END.

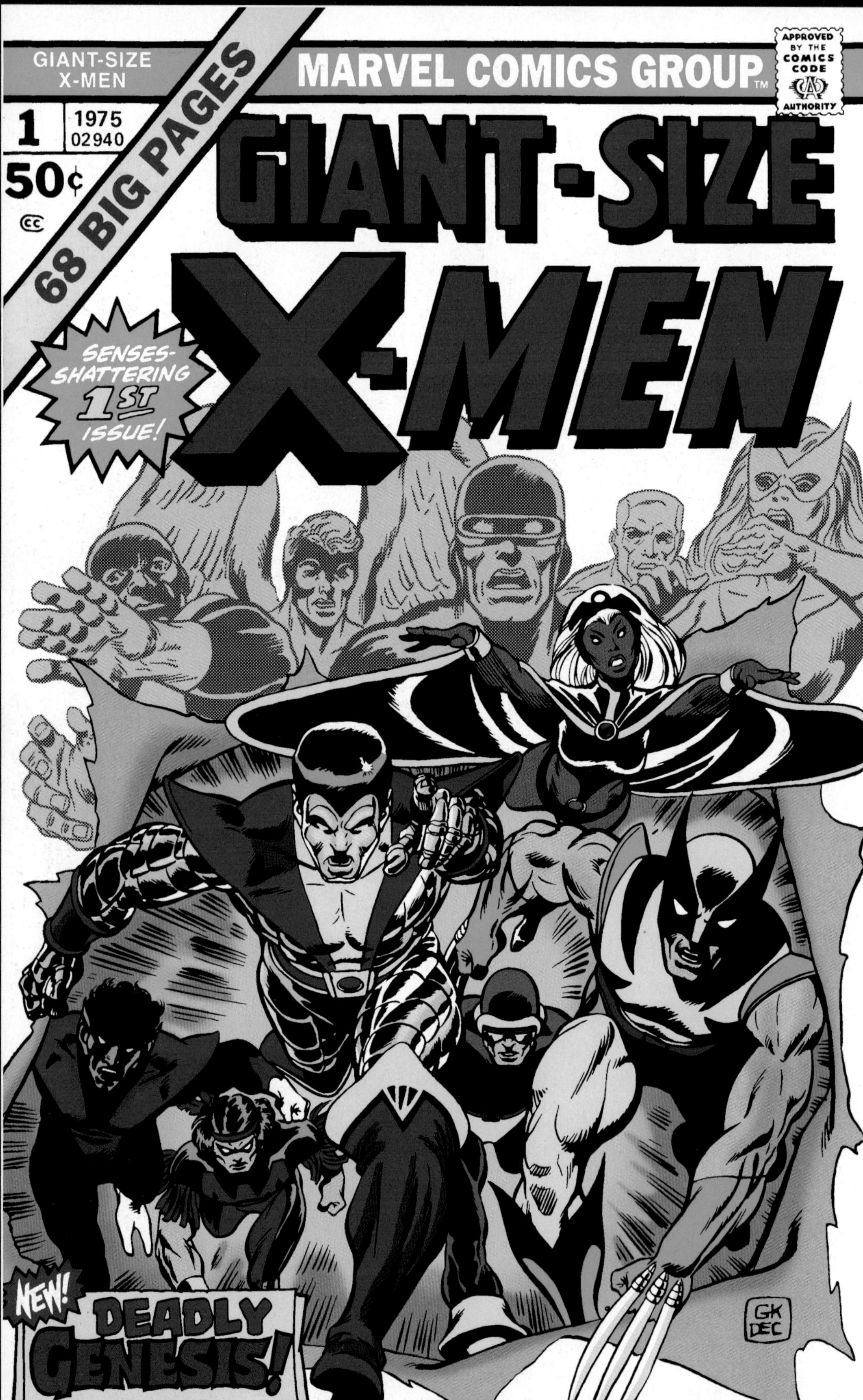

BONUS: NIGHTCRAWLER'S FIRST APPEARANCE IN GIANT-SIZE X-MEN #1!

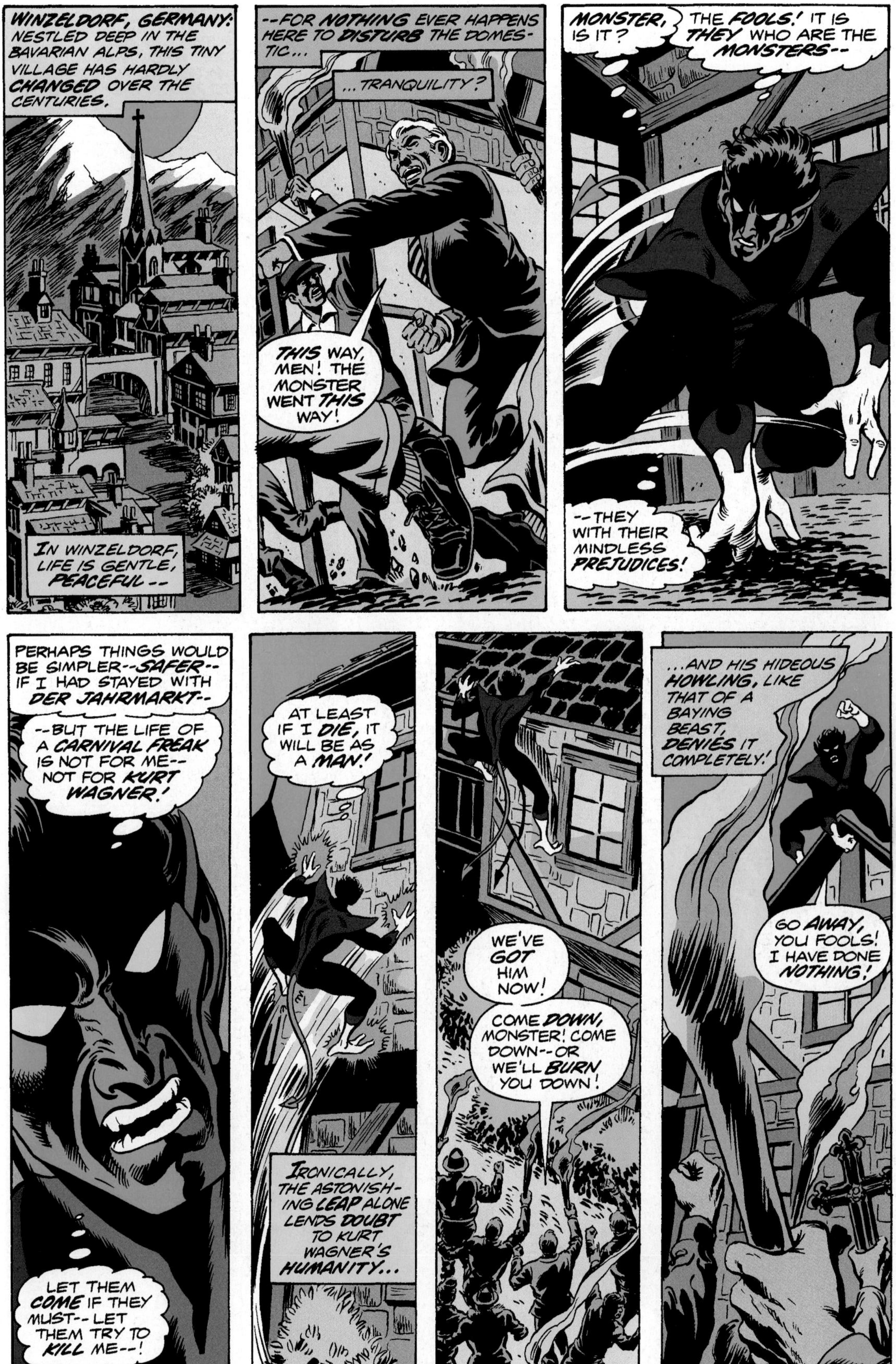
WINZELDORF, GERMANY: NESTLED DEEP IN THE BAVARIAN ALPS, THIS TINY VILLAGE HAS HARDLY CHANGED OVER THE CENTURIES.
IN WINZELDORF, LIFE IS GENTLE, PEACEFUL--
--FOR NOTHING EVER HAPPENS HERE TO DISTURB THE DOMESTIC...
...TRANQUILITY?
THIS WAY, MEN! THE MONSTER WENT THIS WAY!
MONSTER, IS IT?
THE FOOLS! IT IS THEY WHO ARE THE MONSTERS--
--THEY WITH THEIR MINDLESS PREJUDICES!
PERHAPS THINGS WOULD BE SIMPLER--SAFER--IF I HAD STAYED WITH DER JAHRMARKT--
--BUT THE LIFE OF A CARNIVAL FREAK IS NOT FOR ME--NOT FOR KURT WAGNER!
LET THEM COME IF THEY MUST--LET THEM TRY TO KILL ME--!
AT LEAST IF I DIE, IT WILL BE AS A MAN!
IRONICALLY, THE ASTONISHING LEAP ALONE LENDS DOUBT TO KURT WAGNER'S HUMANITY...
WE'VE GOT HIM NOW!
COME DOWN, MONSTER! COME DOWN--OR WE'LL BURN YOU DOWN!
...AND HIS HIDEOUS HOWLING, LIKE THAT OF A BAYING BEAST, DENIES IT COMPLETELY!
GO AWAY, YOU FOOLS! I HAVE DONE NOTHING!

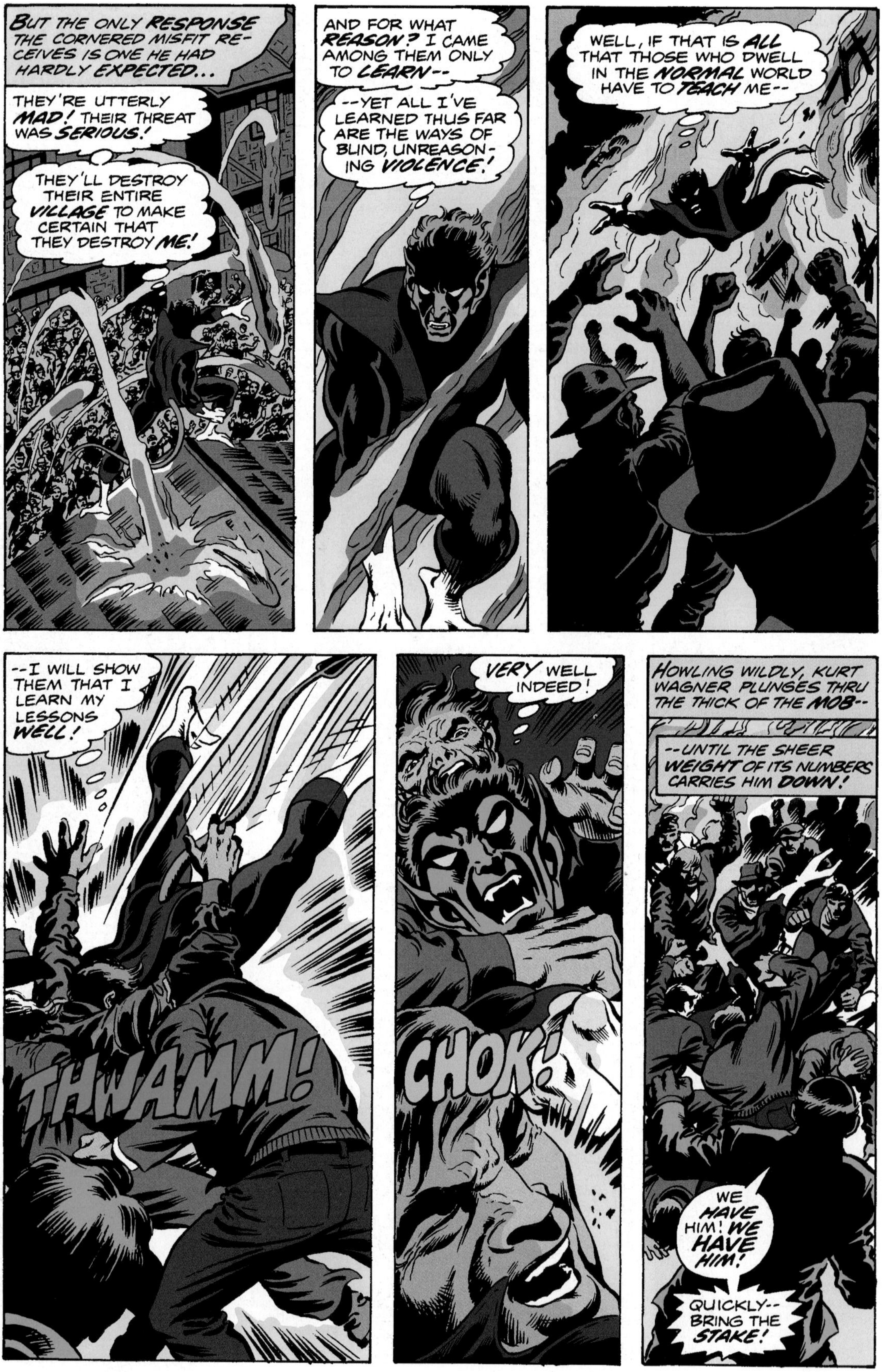
BUT THE ONLY RESPONSE THE CORNERED MISFIT RECEIVES IS ONE HE HAD HARDLY EXPECTED...
THEY'RE UTTERLY MAD! THEIR THREAT WAS SERIOUS!
THEY'LL DESTROY THEIR ENTIRE VILLAGE TO MAKE CERTAIN THAT THEY DESTROY ME!
AND FOR WHAT REASON? I CAME AMONG THEM ONLY TO LEARN--
--YET ALL I'VE LEARNED THUS FAR ARE THE WAYS OF BLIND, UNREASONING VIOLENCE!
WELL, IF THAT IS ALL THAT THOSE WHO DWELL IN THE NORMAL WORLD HAVE TO TEACH ME--
--I WILL SHOW THEM THAT I LEARN MY LESSONS WELL!
THWAMM!
VERY WELL INDEED!
CHOK!
HOWLING WILDLY, KURT WAGNER PLUNGES THRU THE THICK OF THE MOB--
--UNTIL THE SHEER WEIGHT OF ITS NUMBERS CARRIES HIM DOWN!
WE HAVE HIM! WE HAVE HIM!
QUICKLY--BRING THE STAKE!

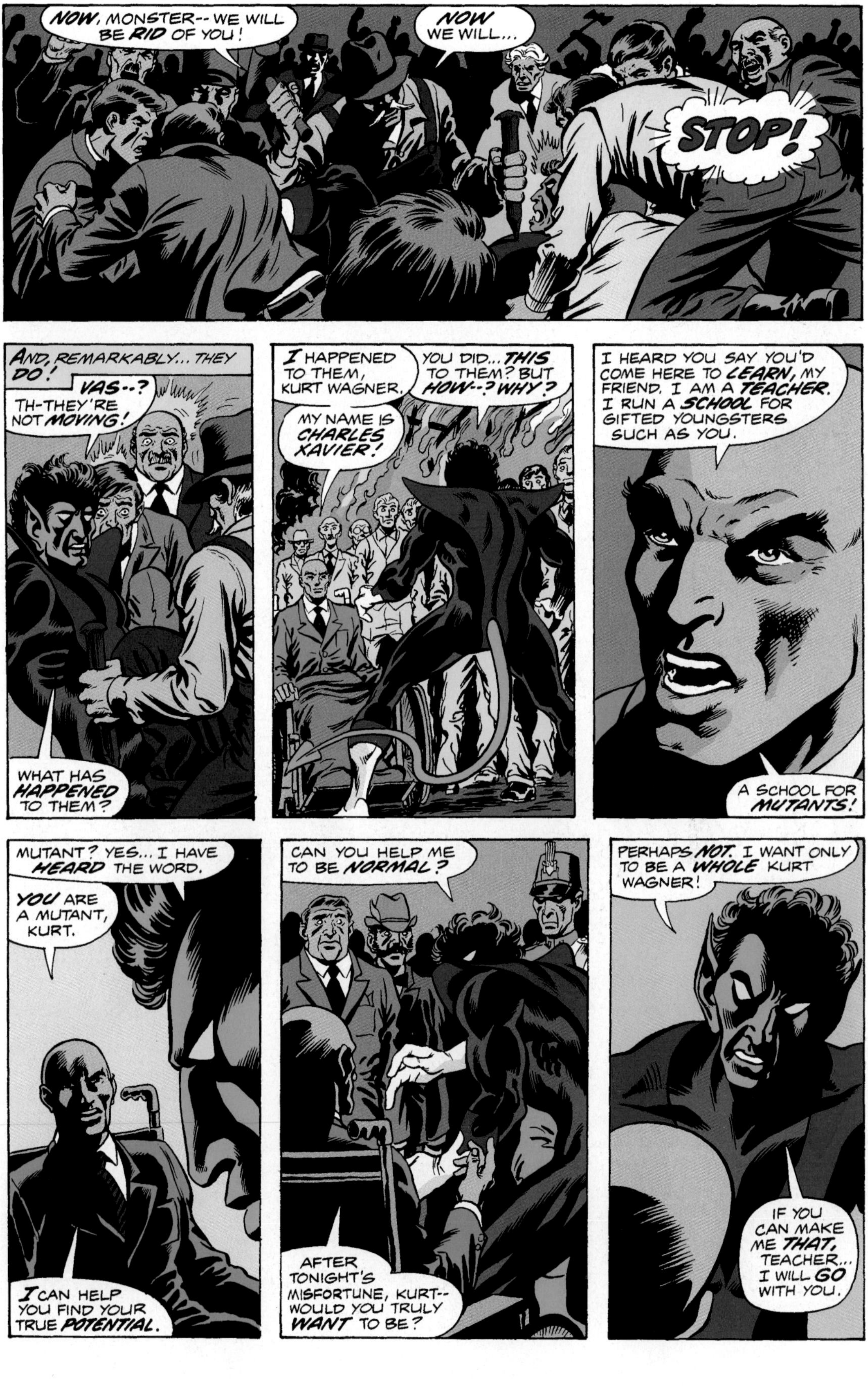
NOW, MONSTER-- WE WILL BE RID OF YOU!
NOW WE WILL...
STOP!
AND, REMARKABLY... THEY DO!
VAS--? TH-THEY'RE NOT MOVING!
WHAT HAS HAPPENED TO THEM?
I HAPPENED TO THEM, KURT WAGNER.
YOU DID... THIS TO THEM? BUT HOW--? WHY?
MY NAME IS CHARLES XAVIER!
I HEARD YOU SAY YOU'D COME HERE TO LEARN, MY FRIEND. I AM A TEACHER. I RUN A SCHOOL FOR GIFTED YOUNGSTERS SUCH AS YOU.
A SCHOOL FOR MUTANTS!
MUTANT? YES... I HAVE HEARD THE WORD.
YOU ARE A MUTANT, KURT.
I CAN HELP YOU FIND YOUR TRUE POTENTIAL.
CAN YOU HELP ME TO BE NORMAL?
AFTER TONIGHT'S MISFORTUNE, KURT-- WOULD YOU TRULY WANT TO BE?
PERHAPS NOT. I WANT ONLY TO BE A WHOLE KURT WAGNER!
IF YOU CAN MAKE ME THAT, TEACHER... I WILL GO WITH YOU.

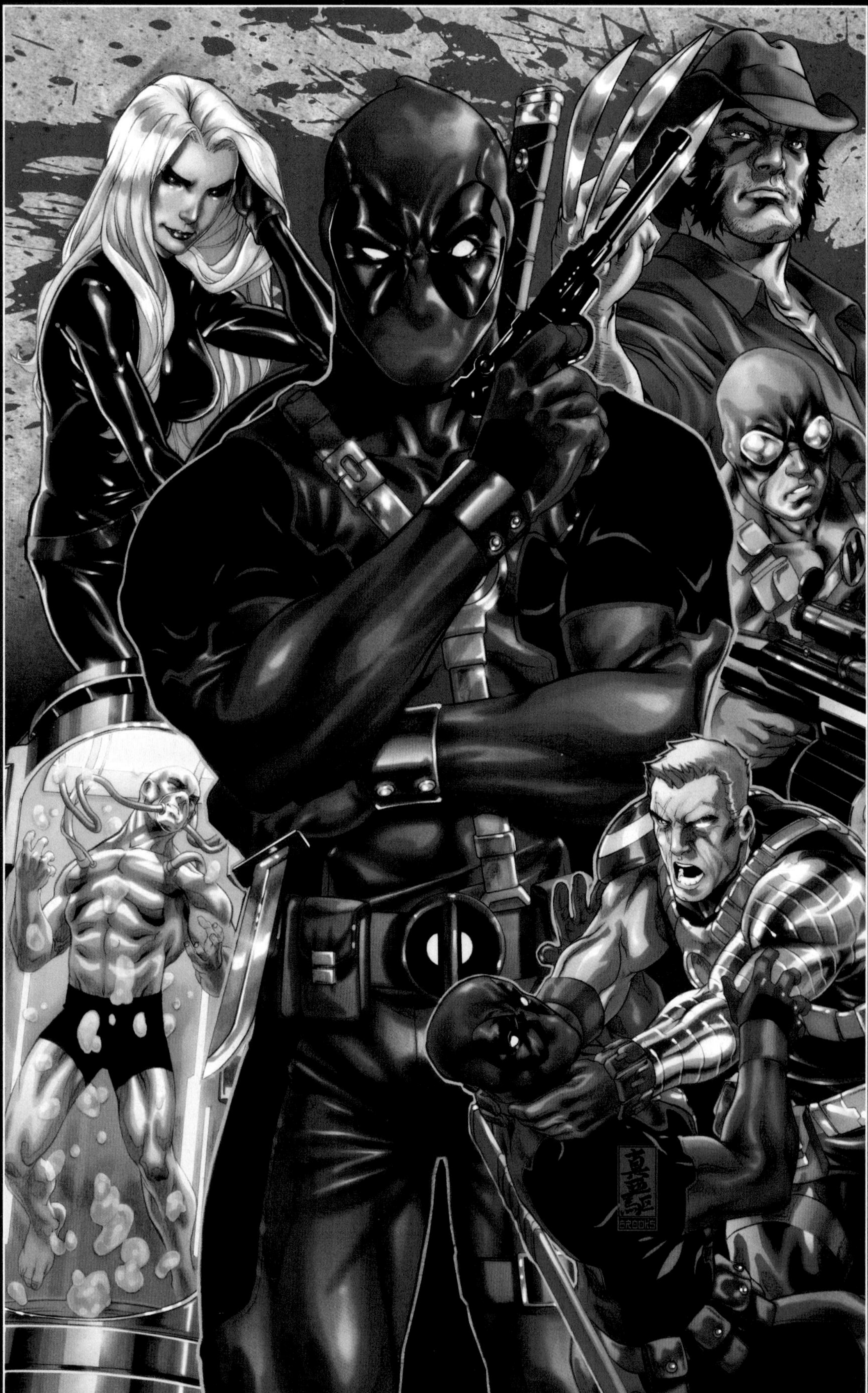

X-MEN ORIGINS: DEADPOOL

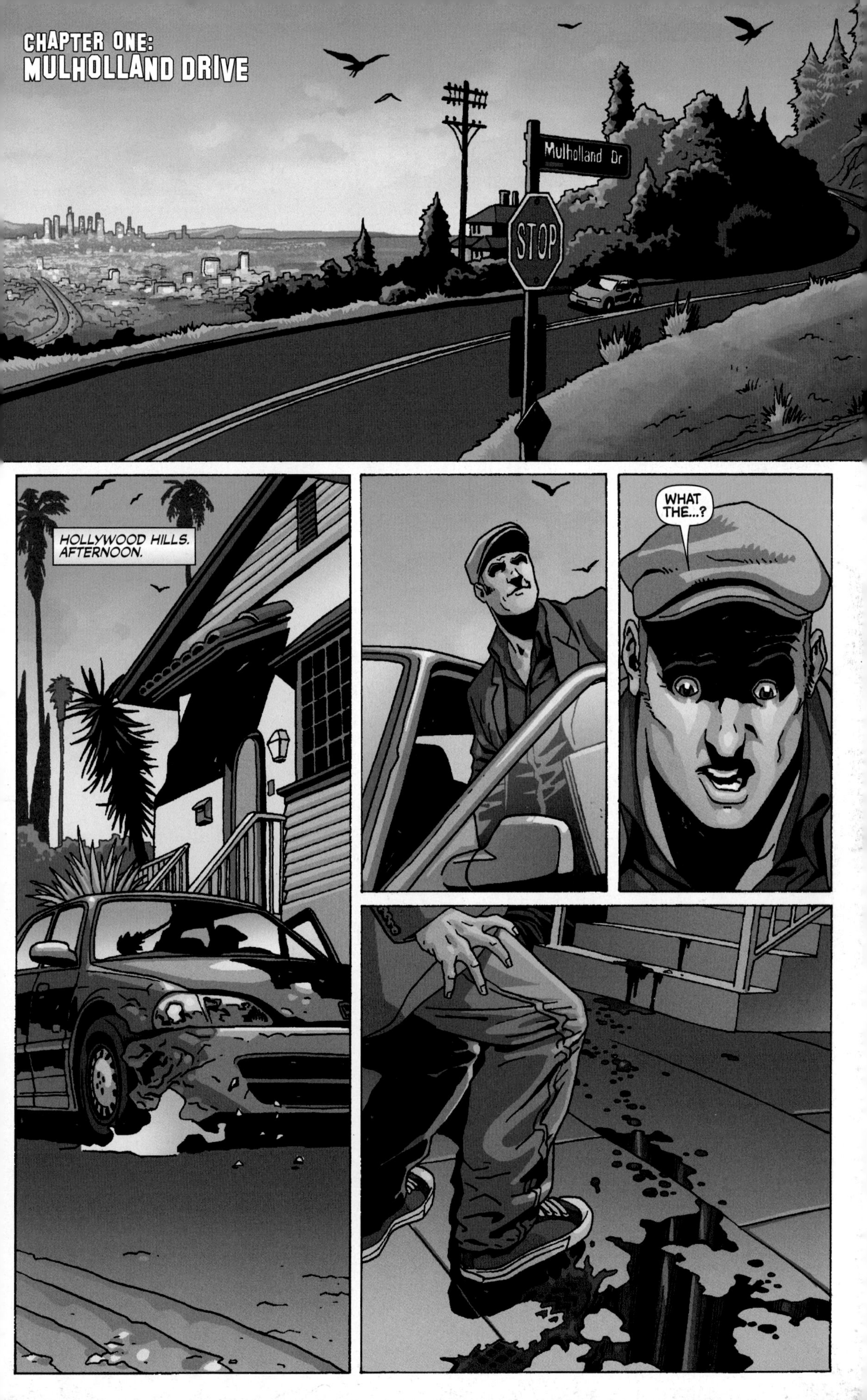
CHAPTER ONE:
MULHOLLAND DRIVE
Mulholland Dr
STOP
HOLLYWOOD HILLS. AFTERNOON.
WHAT THE...?

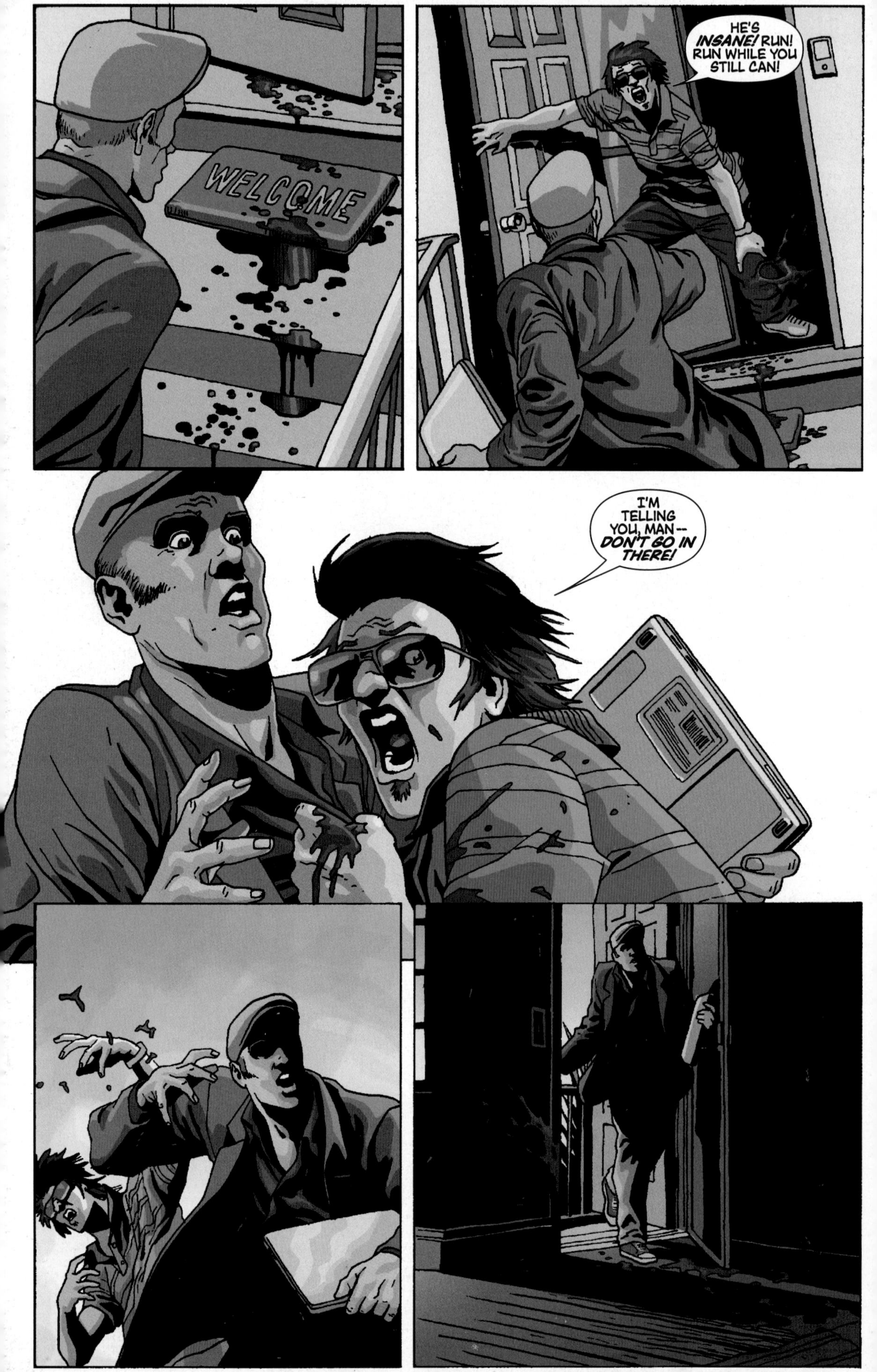
WELCOME
HE'S INSANE! RUN! RUN WHILE YOU STILL CAN!
I'M TELLING YOU, MAN-- DON'T GO IN THERE!

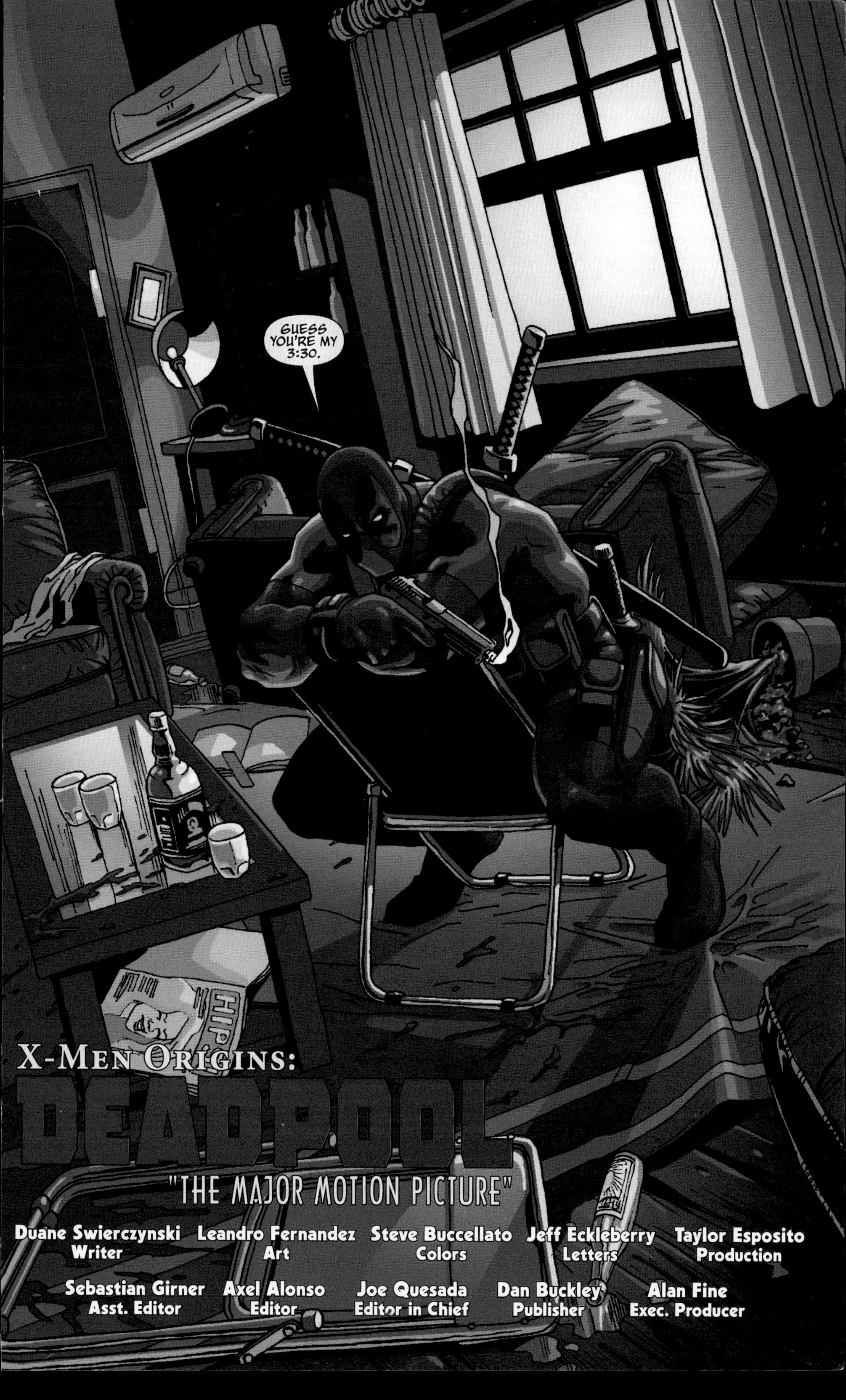
GUESS YOU'RE MY 3:30.

X-MEN ORIGINS: DEADPOOL

"THE MAJOR MOTION PICTURE"

Duane Swierczynski Writer
Leandro Fernandez Art
Steve Buccellato Colors
Jeff Eckleberry Letters
Taylor Esposito Production
Sebastian Girner Asst. Editor
Axel Alonso Editor
Joe Quesada Editor in Chief
Dan Buckley Publisher
Alan Fine Exec. Producer

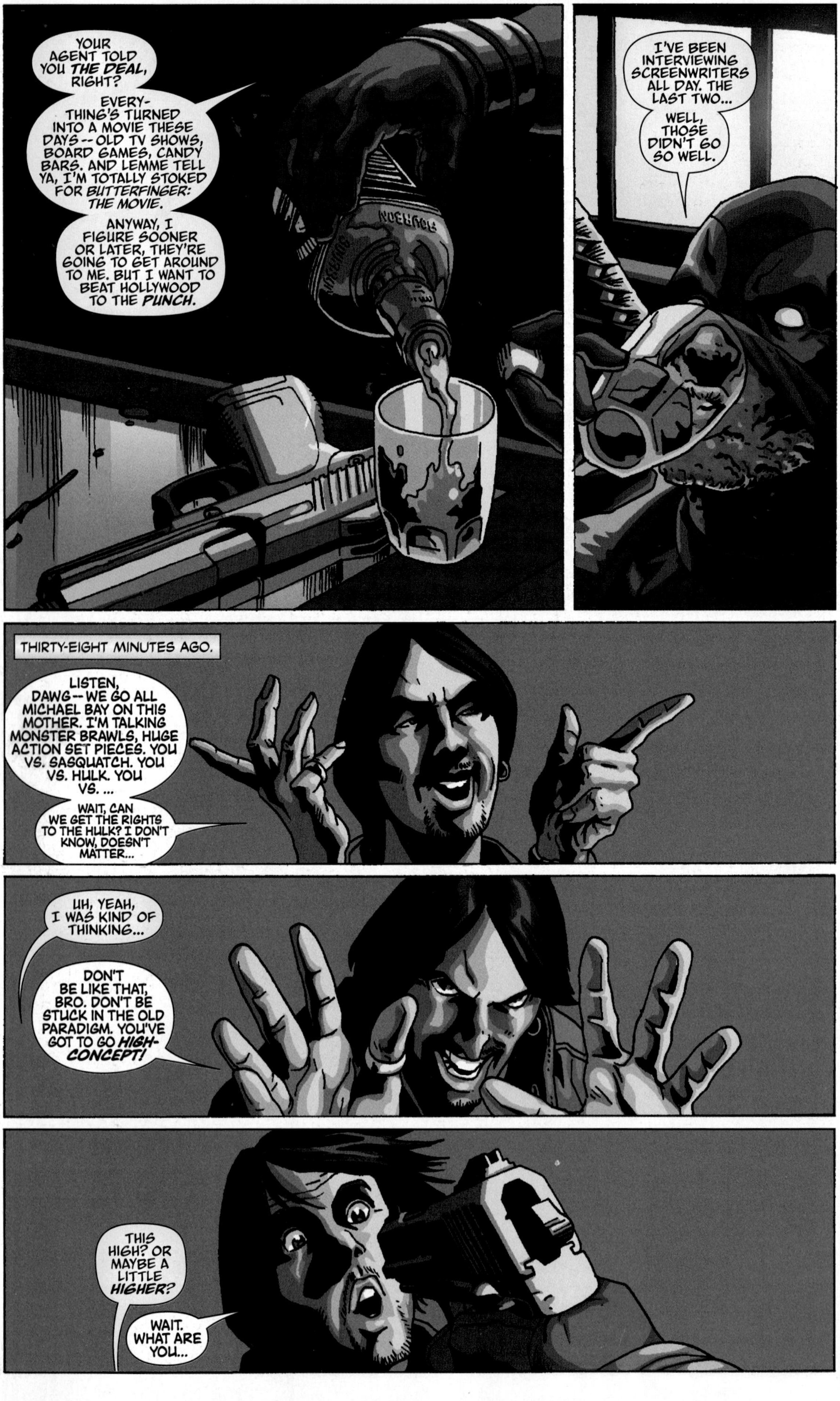
YOUR AGENT TOLD YOU THE DEAL, RIGHT?
EVERY-THING'S TURNED INTO A MOVIE THESE DAYS -- OLD TV SHOWS, BOARD GAMES, CANDY BARS. AND LEMME TELL YA, I'M TOTALLY STOKED FOR BUTTERFINGER: THE MOVIE.
ANYWAY, I FIGURE SOONER OR LATER, THEY'RE GOING TO GET AROUND TO ME. BUT I WANT TO BEAT HOLLYWOOD TO THE PUNCH.
I'VE BEEN INTERVIEWING SCREENWRITERS ALL DAY. THE LAST TWO...
WELL, THOSE DIDN'T GO SO WELL.
THIRTY-EIGHT MINUTES AGO.
LISTEN, DAWG -- WE GO ALL MICHAEL BAY ON THIS MOTHER. I'M TALKING MONSTER BRAWLS, HUGE ACTION SET PIECES. YOU VS. SASQUATCH. YOU VS. HULK. YOU VS. ...
WAIT, CAN WE GET THE RIGHTS TO THE HULK? I DON'T KNOW, DOESN'T MATTER...
UH, YEAH, I WAS KIND OF THINKING...
DON'T BE LIKE THAT, BRO. DON'T BE STUCK IN THE OLD PARADIGM. YOU'VE GOT TO GO HIGH-CONCEPT!
THIS HIGH? OR MAYBE A LITTLE HIGHER?
WAIT. WHAT ARE YOU...

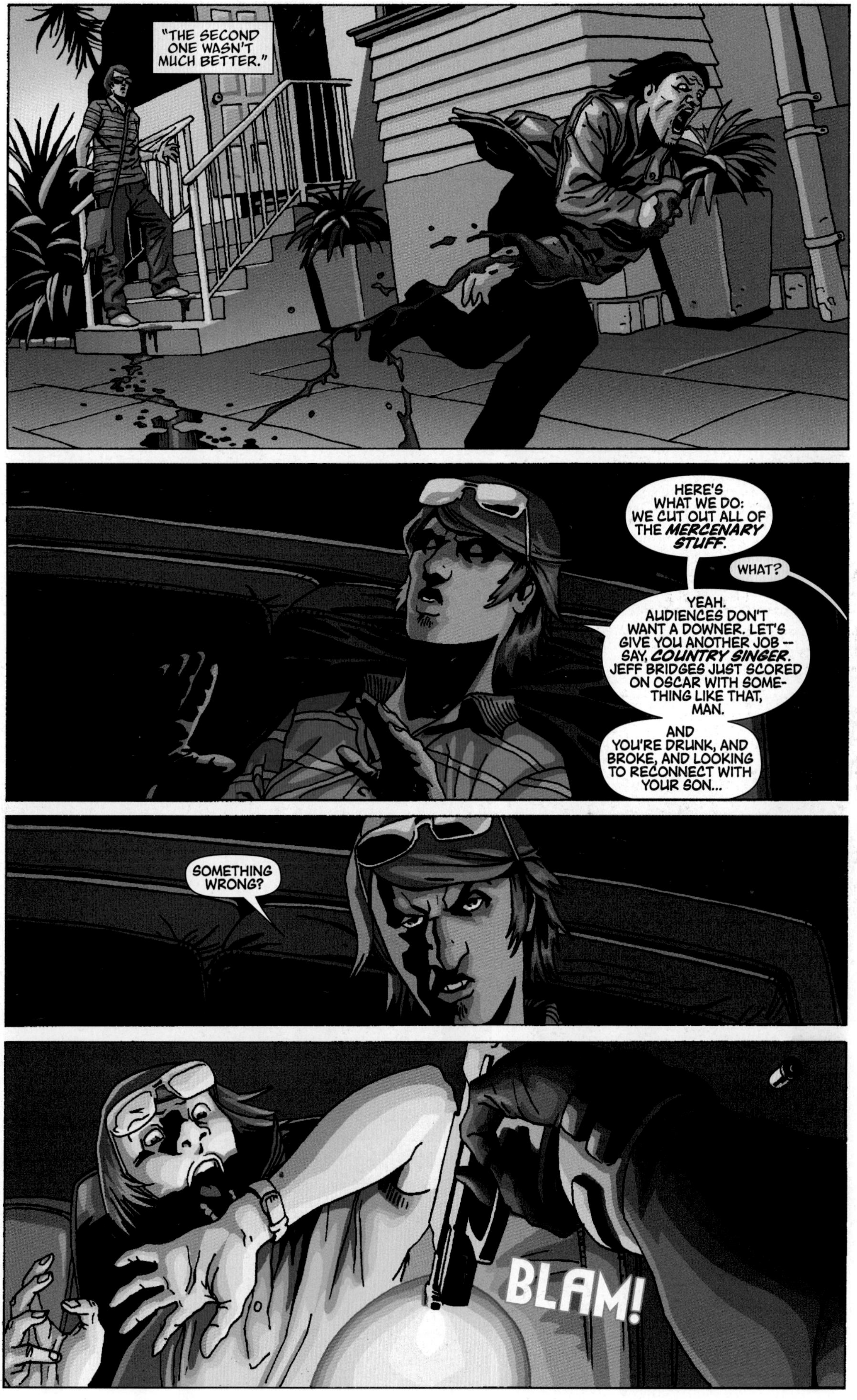
"THE SECOND ONE WASN'T MUCH BETTER."
HERE'S WHAT WE DO: WE CUT OUT ALL OF THE MERCENARY STUFF.
WHAT?
YEAH. AUDIENCES DON'T WANT A DOWNER. LET'S GIVE YOU ANOTHER JOB -- SAY, COUNTRY SINGER. JEFF BRIDGES JUST SCORED ON OSCAR WITH SOMETHING LIKE THAT, MAN.
AND YOU'RE DRUNK, AND BROKE, AND LOOKING TO RECONNECT WITH YOUR SON...
SOMETHING WRONG?
BLAM!

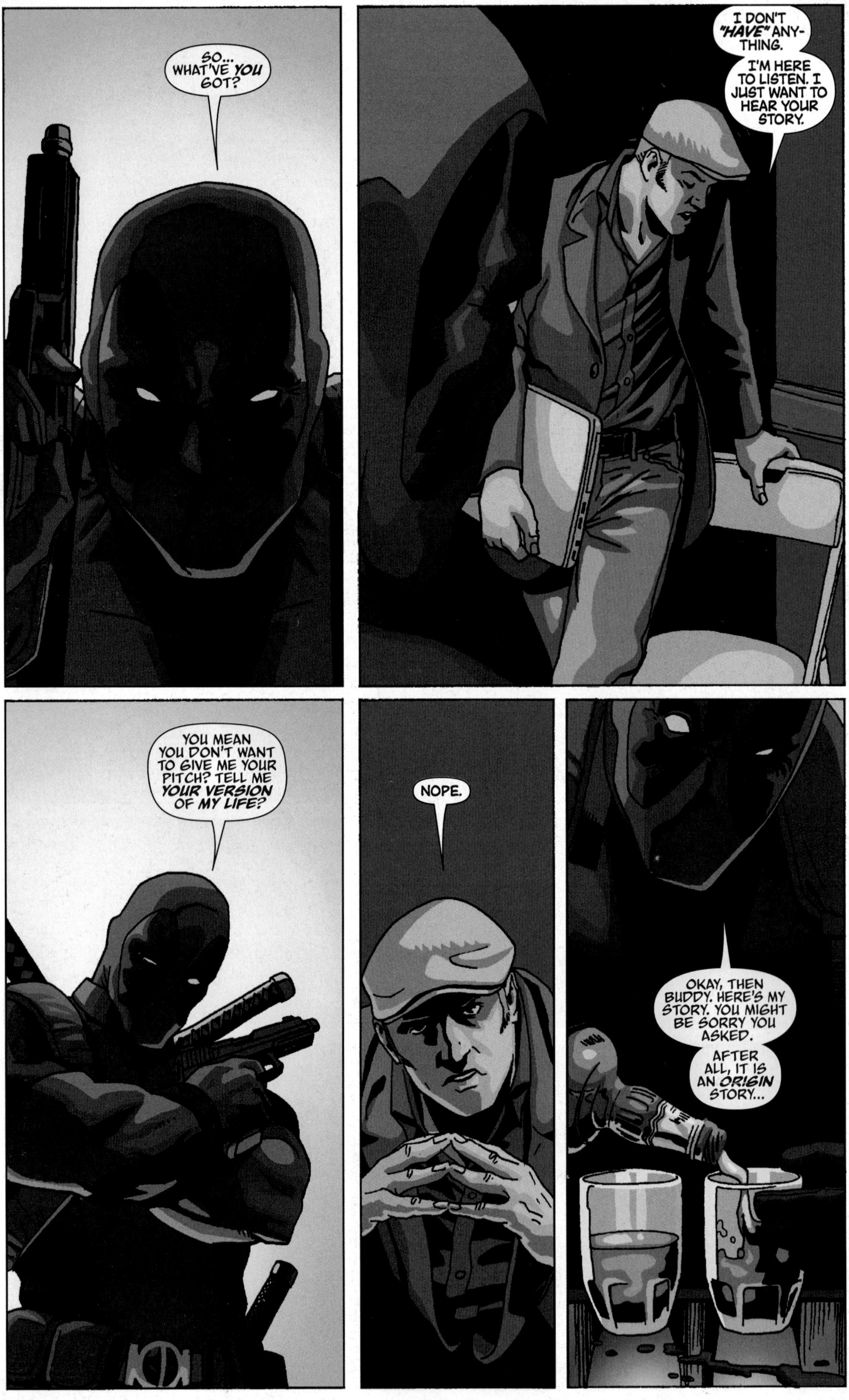
SO... WHAT'VE *YOU* GOT?
I DON'T *"HAVE"* ANYTHING.
I'M HERE TO LISTEN. I JUST WANT TO HEAR YOUR STORY.
YOU MEAN YOU DON'T WANT TO GIVE ME YOUR PITCH? TELL ME *YOUR VERSION* OF *MY LIFE?*
NOPE.
OKAY, THEN BUDDY. HERE'S MY STORY. YOU MIGHT BE SORRY YOU ASKED.
AFTER ALL, IT IS AN *ORIGIN* STORY...

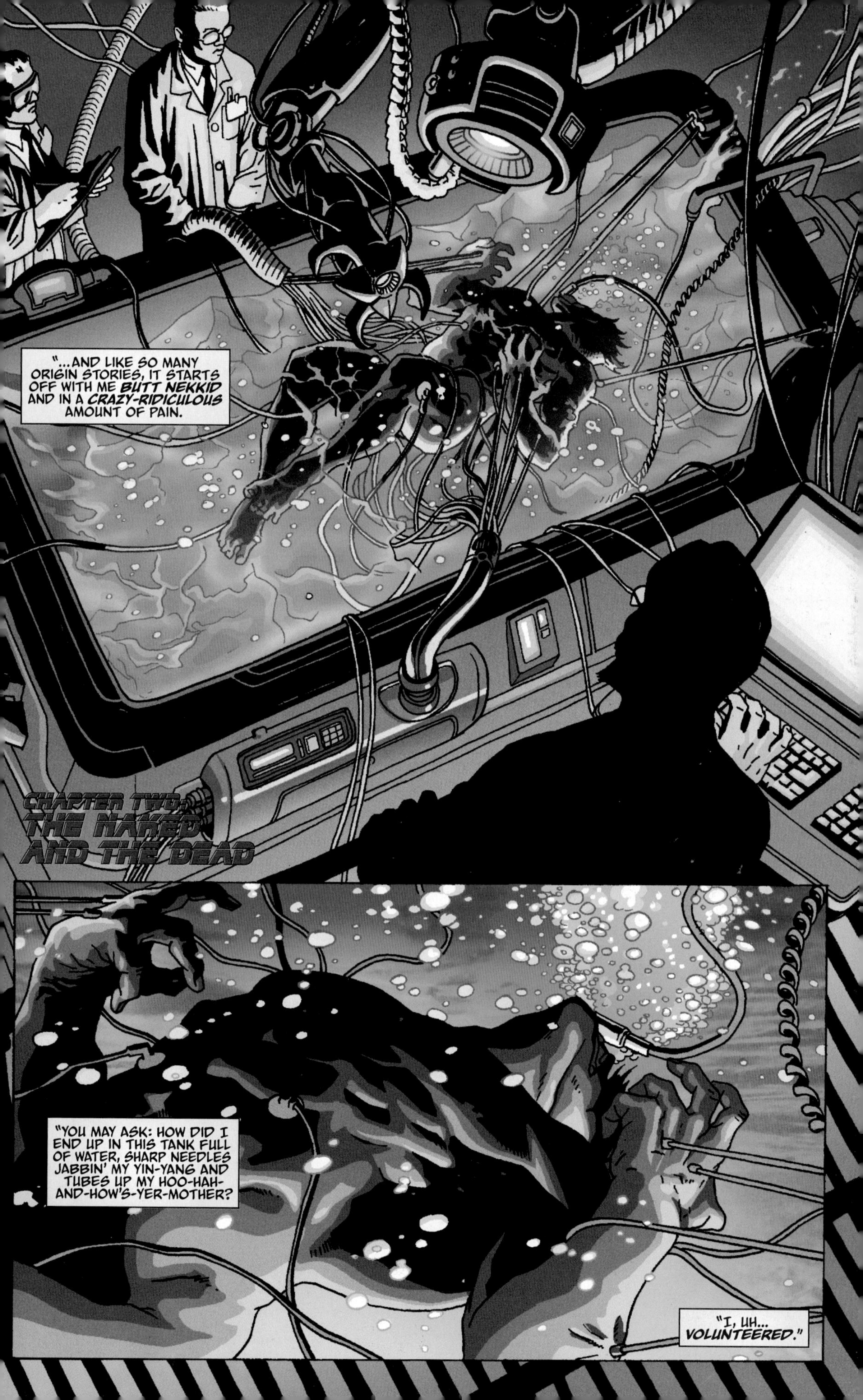
"...AND LIKE SO MANY ORIGIN STORIES, IT STARTS OFF WITH ME BUTT NEKKID AND IN A CRAZY-RIDICULOUS AMOUNT OF PAIN.
CHAPTER TWO: THE NAKED AND THE DEAD
"YOU MAY ASK: HOW DID I END UP IN THIS TANK FULL OF WATER, SHARP NEEDLES JABBIN' MY YIN-YANG AND TUBES UP MY HOO-HAH-AND-HOW'S-YER-MOTHER?
"I, UH... VOLUNTEERED."

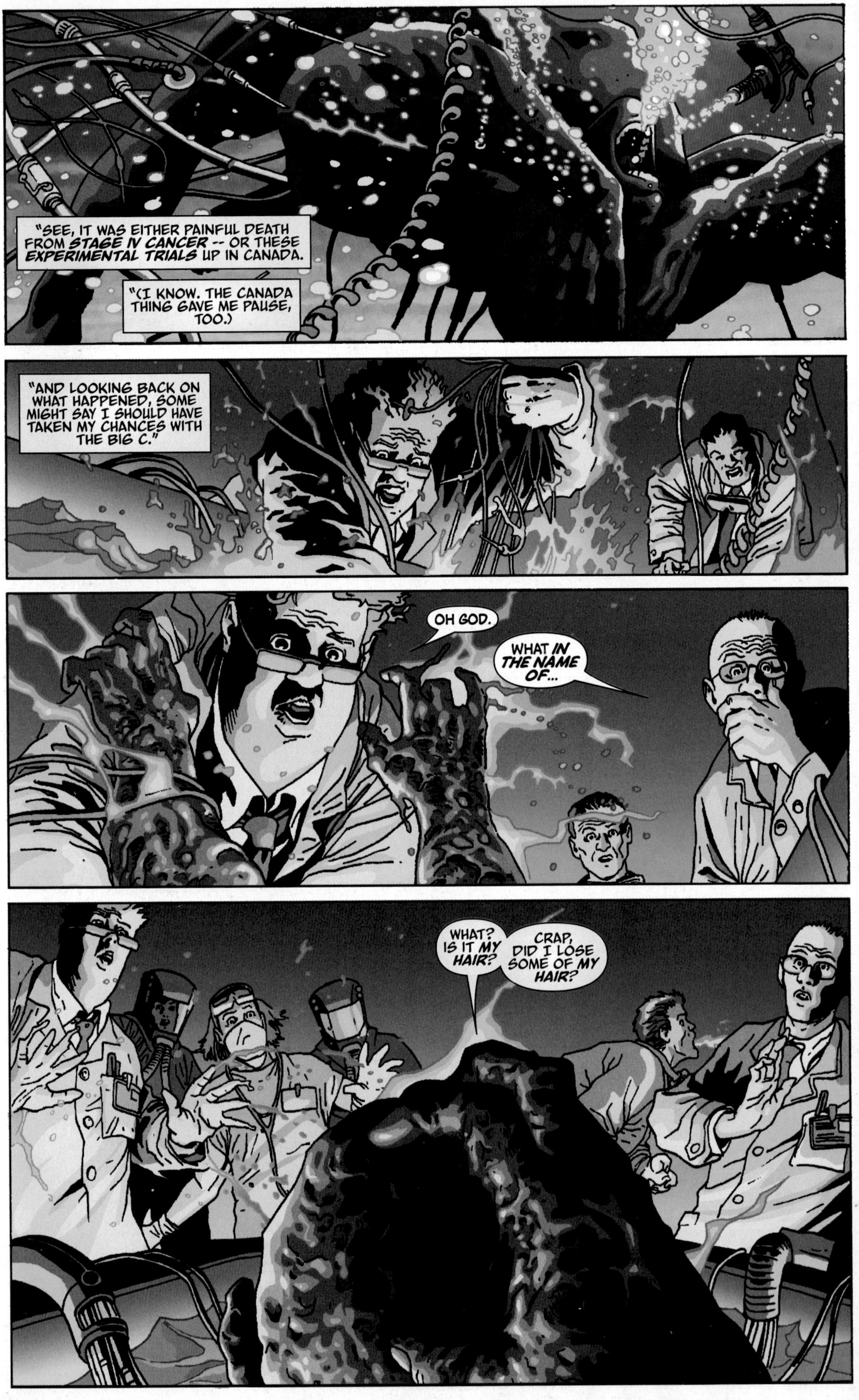
"SEE, IT WAS EITHER PAINFUL DEATH FROM STAGE IV CANCER -- OR THESE EXPERIMENTAL TRIALS UP IN CANADA.
"(I KNOW. THE CANADA THING GAVE ME PAUSE, TOO.)
"AND LOOKING BACK ON WHAT HAPPENED, SOME MIGHT SAY I SHOULD HAVE TAKEN MY CHANCES WITH THE BIG C."
OH GOD.
WHAT IN THE NAME OF...
WHAT? IS IT MY HAIR?
CRAP, DID I LOSE SOME OF MY HAIR?

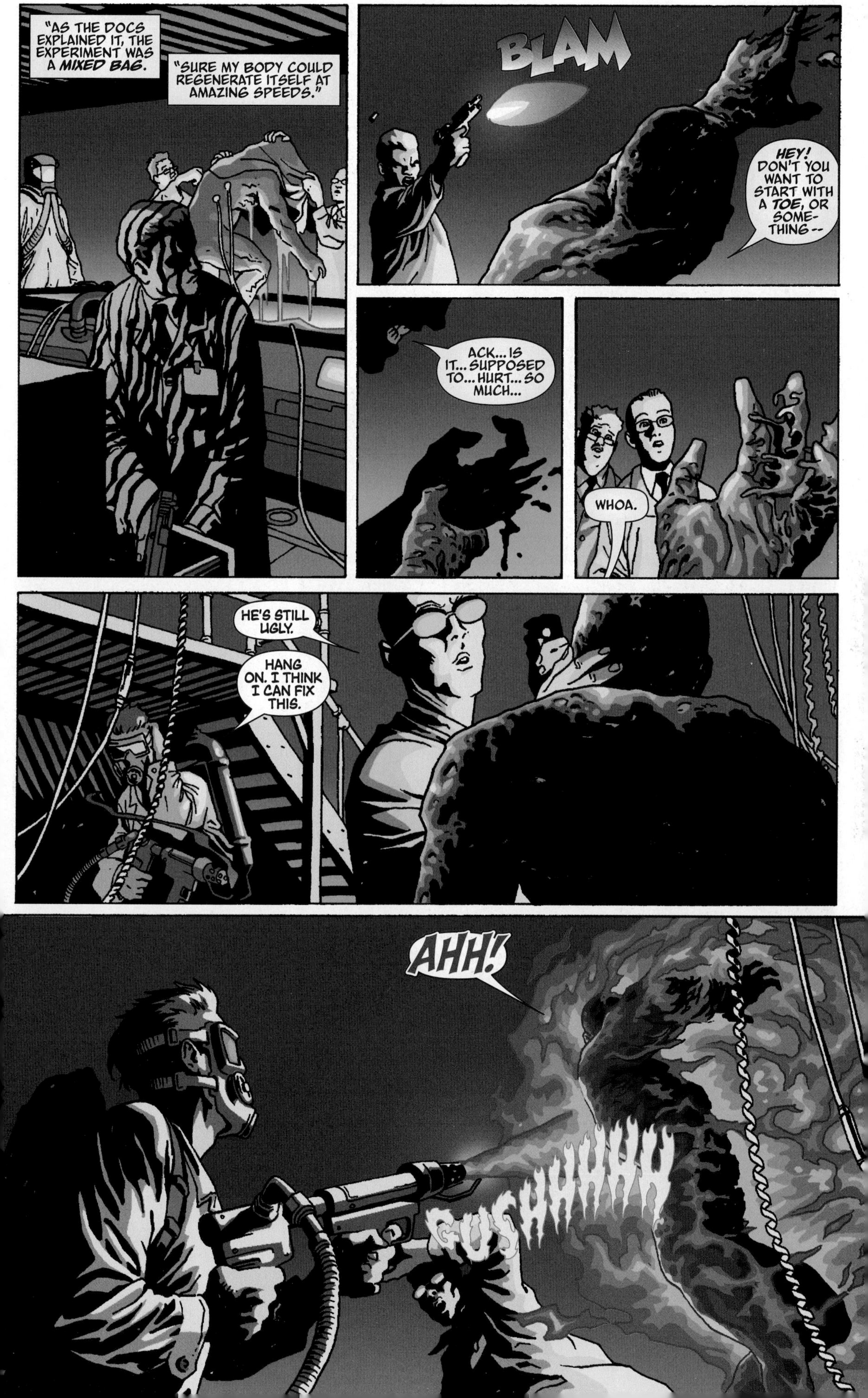
"AS THE DOCS EXPLAINED IT, THE EXPERIMENT WAS A MIXED BAG.
"SURE MY BODY COULD REGENERATE ITSELF AT AMAZING SPEEDS."
BLAM
HEY! DON'T YOU WANT TO START WITH A TOE, OR SOME-THING--
ACK... IS IT... SUPPOSED TO... HURT... SO MUCH...
WHOA.
HE'S STILL UGLY.
HANG ON. I THINK I CAN FIX THIS.
AHH!
GUSHHHHH

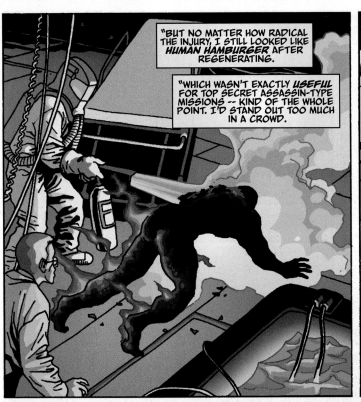

"BUT NO MATTER HOW RADICAL THE INJURY, I STILL LOOKED LIKE *HUMAN HAMBURGER* AFTER REGENERATING.

"WHICH WASN'T EXACTLY *USEFUL* FOR TOP SECRET ASSASSIN-TYPE MISSIONS -- KIND OF THE WHOLE POINT. I'D STAND OUT TOO MUCH IN A CROWD.

"THEY TOLD ME NOT TO WORRY. WHILE THEY SORTED IT OUT, I COULD CHILL OUT AT A *RESORT* TO RECOVER.

"AND IT WAS A REAL *CLUB MED.*

"IF BY CLUB MED YOU MEAN *CLUB FAILED MED-ICAL EXPERIMENTS.*

"ROTTING AWAY IN MY CELL, I REALIZED I SIGNED ON FOR A FATE WORSE THAN CANCER. AT LEAST CANCER ENDS. THIS WENT ON AND ON...POTENTIALLY *FOREVER.*

"I HAD TO FIND A WAY OUT."

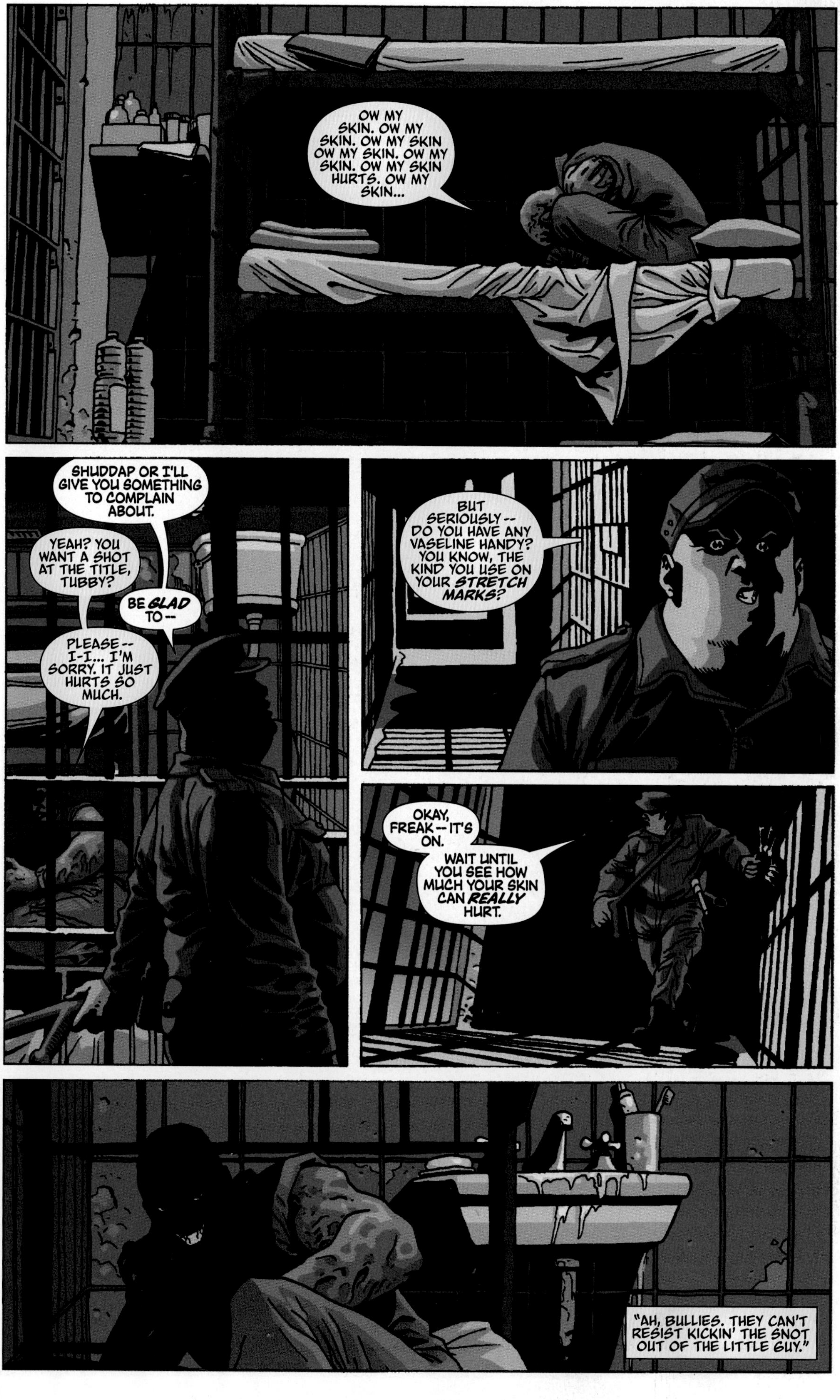
OW MY SKIN. OW MY SKIN. OW MY SKIN OW MY SKIN. OW MY SKIN. OW MY SKIN HURTS. OW MY SKIN...
SHUDDAP OR I'LL GIVE YOU SOMETHING TO COMPLAIN ABOUT.
YEAH? YOU WANT A SHOT AT THE TITLE, TUBBY?
BE GLAD TO--
PLEASE-- I-I... I'M SORRY. IT JUST HURTS SO MUCH.
BUT SERIOUSLY-- DO YOU HAVE ANY VASELINE HANDY? YOU KNOW, THE KIND YOU USE ON YOUR STRETCH MARKS?
OKAY, FREAK--IT'S ON.
WAIT UNTIL YOU SEE HOW MUCH YOUR SKIN CAN REALLY HURT.
"AH, BULLIES. THEY CAN'T RESIST KICKIN' THE SNOT OUT OF THE LITTLE GUY."

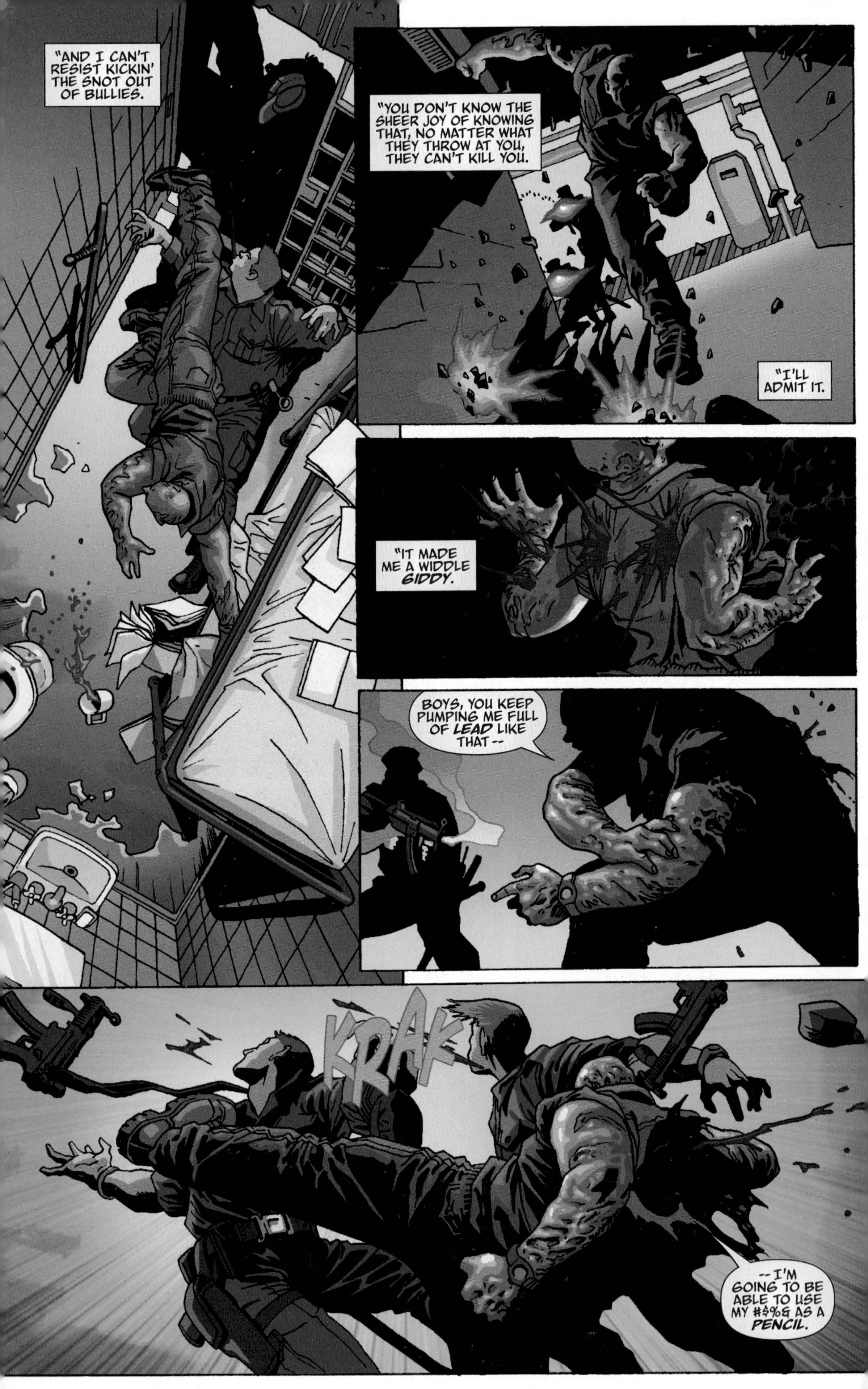
"AND I CAN'T RESIST KICKIN' THE SNOT OUT OF BULLIES.
"YOU DON'T KNOW THE SHEER JOY OF KNOWING THAT, NO MATTER WHAT THEY THROW AT YOU, THEY CAN'T KILL YOU.
"I'LL ADMIT IT.
"IT MADE ME A WIDDLE GIDDY.
BOYS, YOU KEEP PUMPING ME FULL OF LEAD LIKE THAT --
KRAK
-- I'M GOING TO BE ABLE TO USE MY #$%& AS A PENCIL.

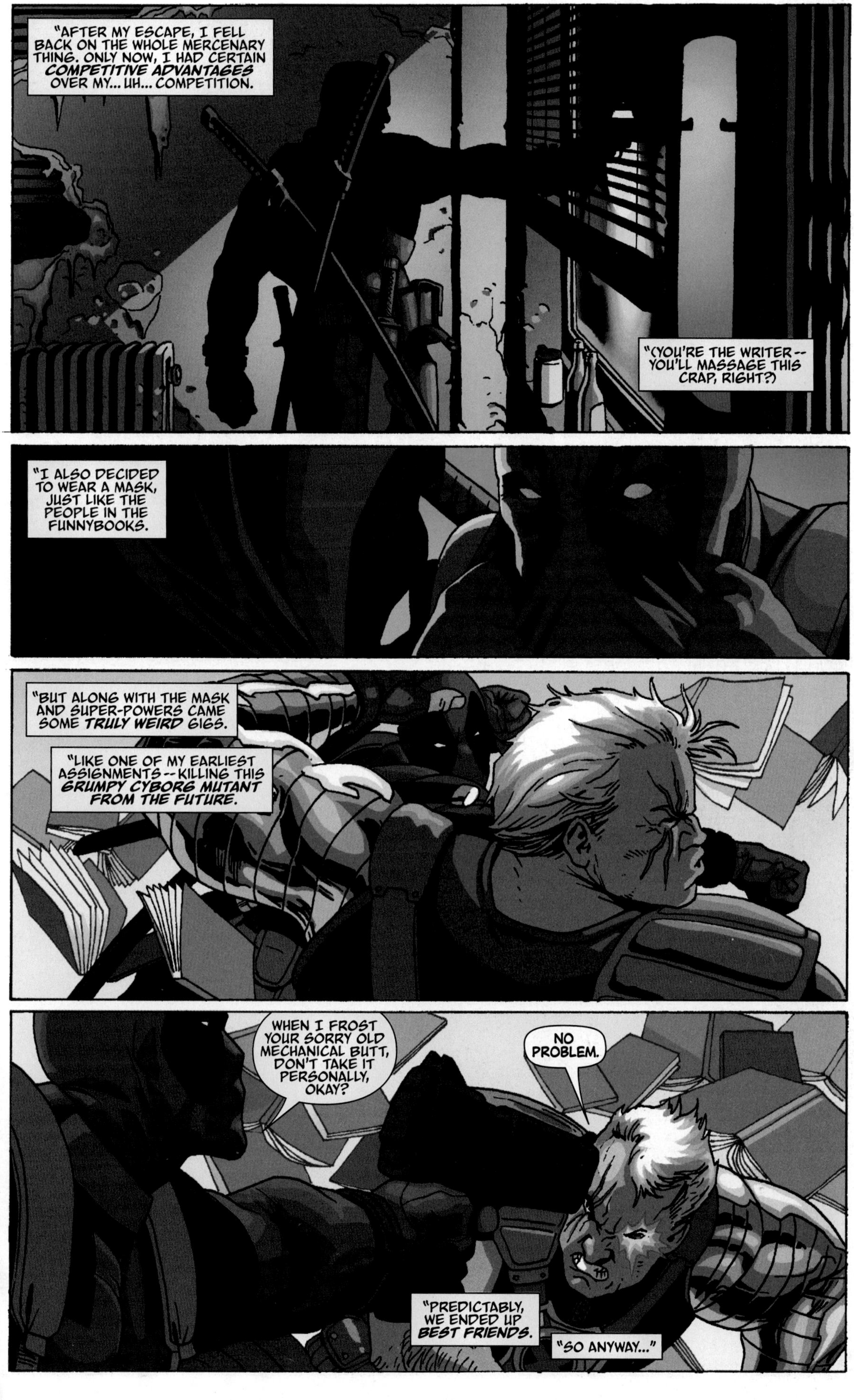
"AFTER MY ESCAPE, I FELL BACK ON THE WHOLE MERCENARY THING. ONLY NOW, I HAD CERTAIN *COMPETITIVE ADVANTAGES* OVER MY... UH... COMPETITION.
"(YOU'RE THE WRITER -- YOU'LL MASSAGE THIS CRAP, RIGHT?)
"I ALSO DECIDED TO WEAR A MASK, JUST LIKE THE PEOPLE IN THE FUNNYBOOKS.
"BUT ALONG WITH THE MASK AND SUPER-POWERS CAME SOME *TRULY WEIRD* GIGS.
"LIKE ONE OF MY EARLIEST ASSIGNMENTS -- KILLING THIS *GRUMPY CYBORG MUTANT FROM THE FUTURE*.
WHEN I FROST YOUR SORRY OLD MECHANICAL BUTT, DON'T TAKE IT PERSONALLY, OKAY?
NO PROBLEM.
"PREDICTABLY, WE ENDED UP *BEST FRIENDS*.
"SO ANYWAY..."

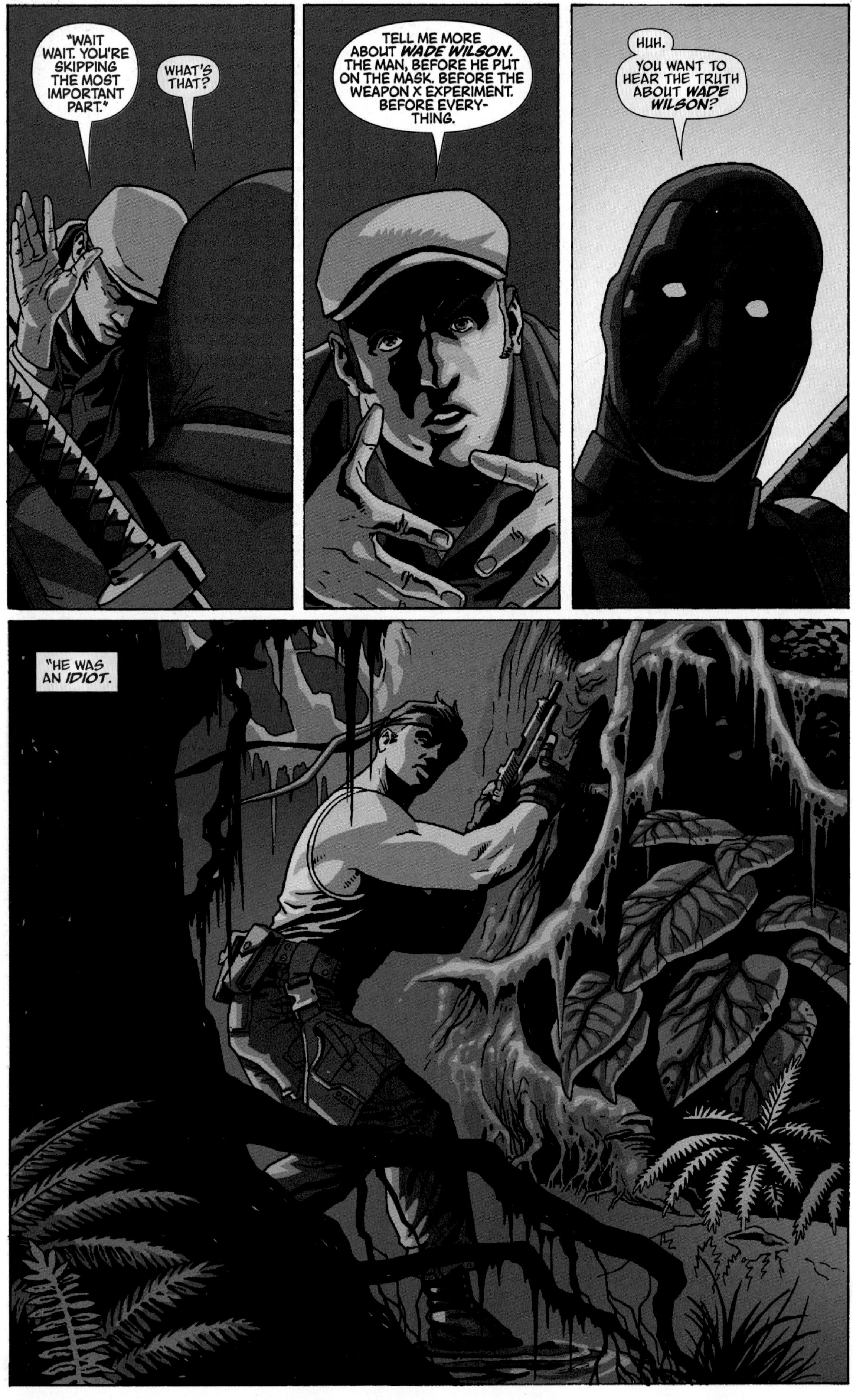
"WAIT WAIT. YOU'RE SKIPPING THE MOST IMPORTANT PART."
WHAT'S THAT?
TELL ME MORE ABOUT *WADE WILSON*. THE MAN, BEFORE HE PUT ON THE MASK. BEFORE THE WEAPON X EXPERIMENT. BEFORE EVERY-THING.
HUH.
YOU WANT TO HEAR THE TRUTH ABOUT *WADE WILSON*?
"HE WAS AN *IDIOT*.

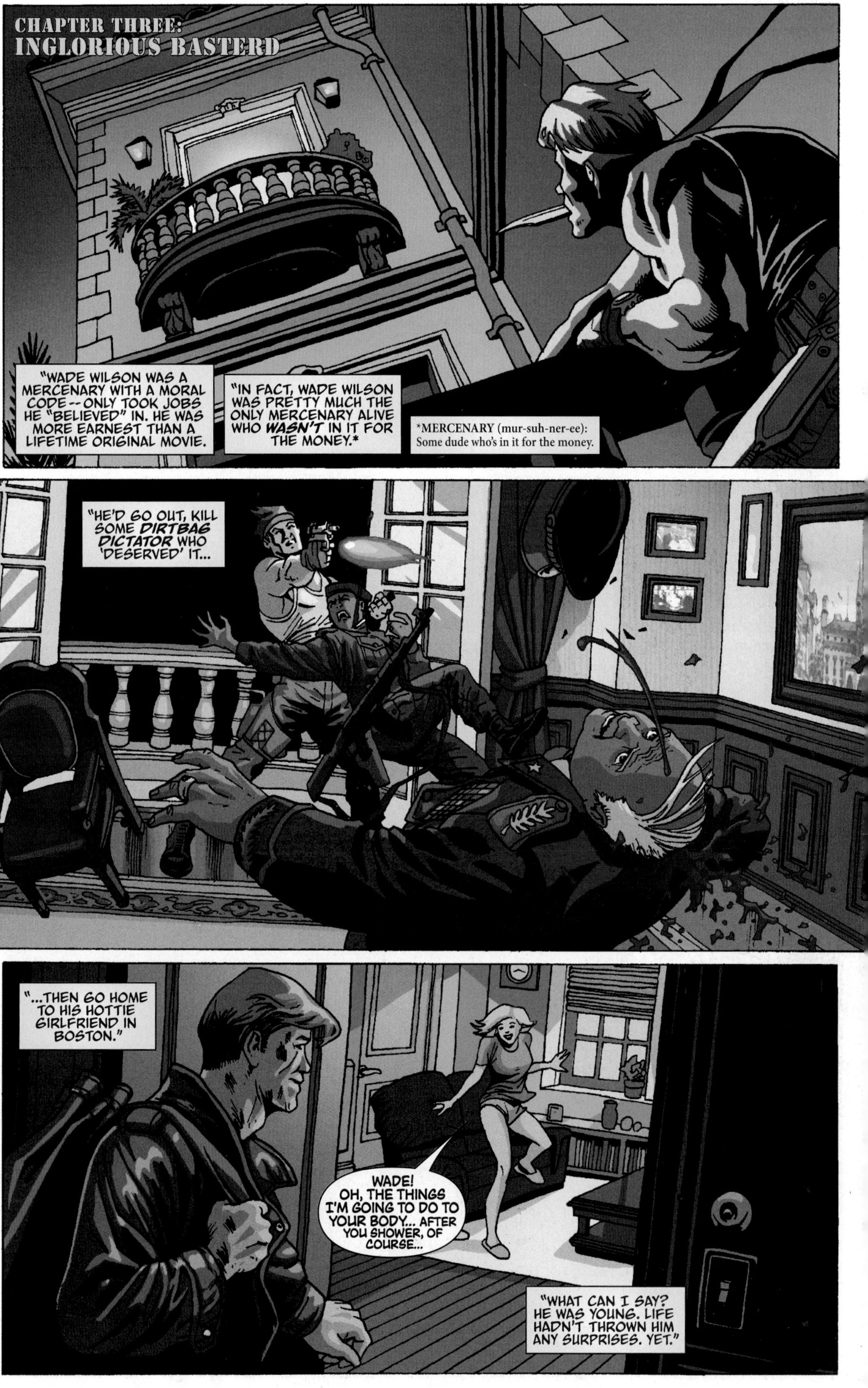
CHAPTER THREE:
INGLORIOUS BASTERD
"WADE WILSON WAS A MERCENARY WITH A MORAL CODE -- ONLY TOOK JOBS HE "BELIEVED" IN. HE WAS MORE EARNEST THAN A LIFETIME ORIGINAL MOVIE.
"IN FACT, WADE WILSON WAS PRETTY MUCH THE ONLY MERCENARY ALIVE WHO WASN'T IN IT FOR THE MONEY.*
*MERCENARY (mur-suh-ner-ee): Some dude who's in it for the money.
"HE'D GO OUT, KILL SOME DIRTBAG DICTATOR WHO 'DESERVED' IT...
"...THEN GO HOME TO HIS HOTTIE GIRLFRIEND IN BOSTON."
WADE! OH, THE THINGS I'M GOING TO DO TO YOUR BODY... AFTER YOU SHOWER, OF COURSE...
"WHAT CAN I SAY? HE WAS YOUNG. LIFE HADN'T THROWN HIM ANY SURPRISES. YET."

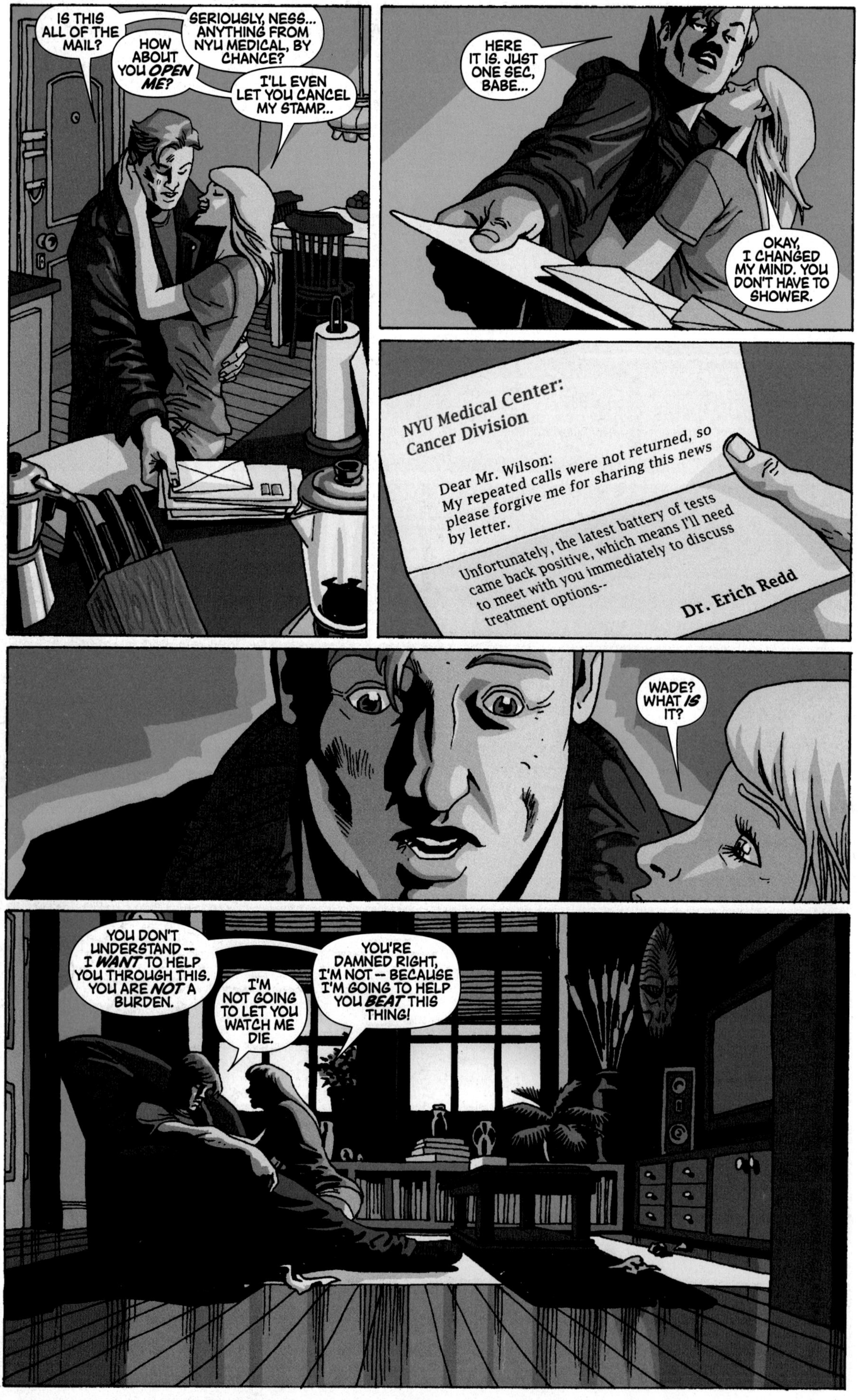
IS THIS ALL OF THE MAIL?
SERIOUSLY, NESS... ANYTHING FROM NYU MEDICAL, BY CHANCE?
HOW ABOUT YOU *OPEN ME*?
I'LL EVEN LET YOU CANCEL MY STAMP...
HERE IT IS. JUST ONE SEC, BABE...
OKAY, I CHANGED MY MIND. YOU DON'T HAVE TO SHOWER.
NYU Medical Center: Cancer Division
Dear Mr. Wilson: My repeated calls were not returned, so please forgive me for sharing this news by letter.
Unfortunately, the latest battery of tests came back positive, which means I'll need to meet with you immediately to discuss treatment options--
Dr. Erich Redd
WADE? WHAT *IS* IT?
YOU DON'T UNDERSTAND -- I *WANT* TO HELP YOU THROUGH THIS. YOU ARE *NOT* A BURDEN.
I'M NOT GOING TO LET YOU WATCH ME DIE.
YOU'RE DAMNED RIGHT, I'M NOT -- BECAUSE I'M GOING TO HELP YOU *BEAT* THIS THING!

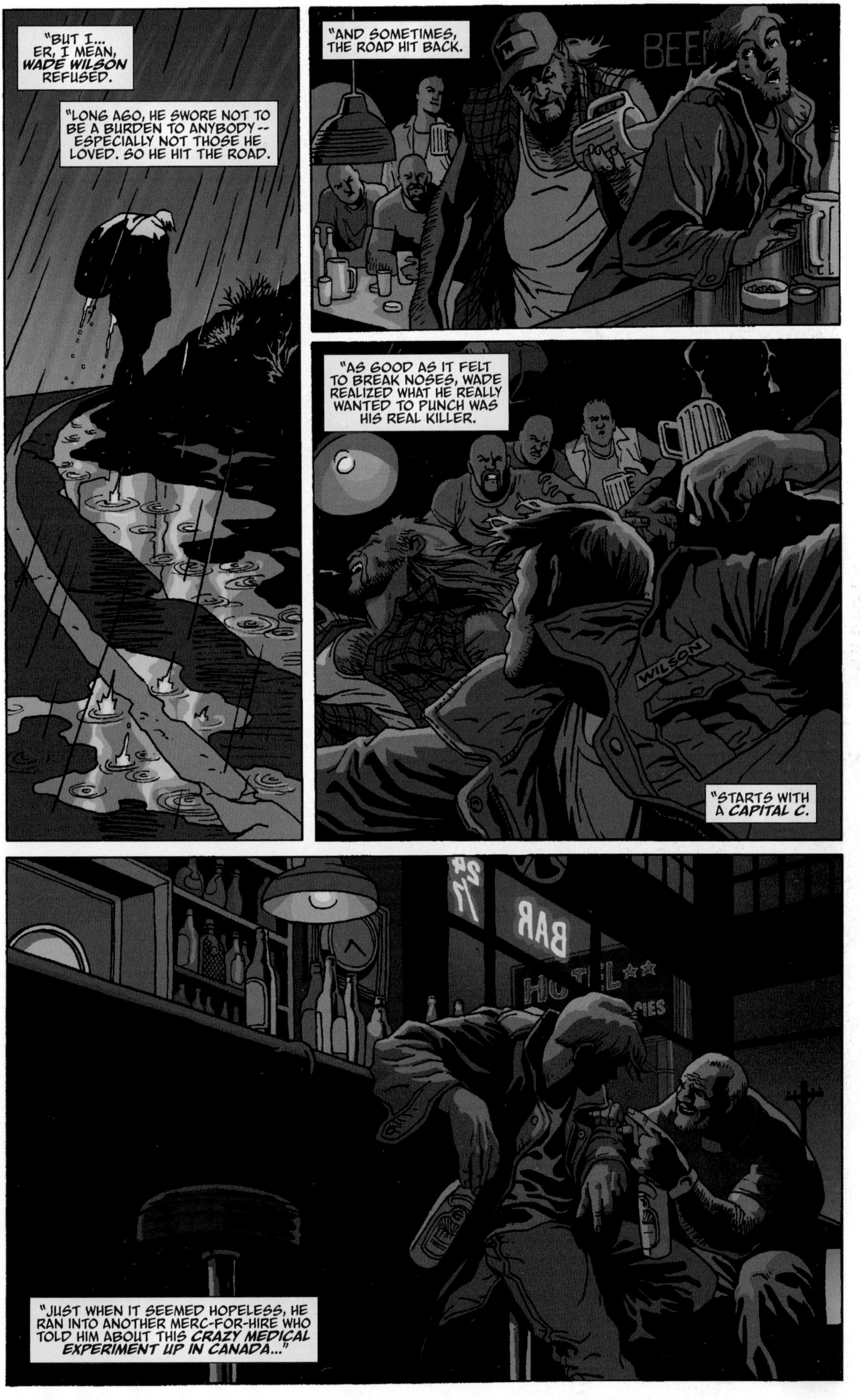
"BUT I... ER, I MEAN, WADE WILSON REFUSED.
"LONG AGO, HE SWORE NOT TO BE A BURDEN TO ANYBODY -- ESPECIALLY NOT THOSE HE LOVED. SO HE HIT THE ROAD.
"AND SOMETIMES, THE ROAD HIT BACK.
"AS GOOD AS IT FELT TO BREAK NOSES, WADE REALIZED WHAT HE REALLY WANTED TO PUNCH WAS HIS REAL KILLER.
WILSON
"STARTS WITH A CAPITAL C.
BAR
"JUST WHEN IT SEEMED HOPELESS, HE RAN INTO ANOTHER MERC-FOR-HIRE WHO TOLD HIM ABOUT THIS CRAZY MEDICAL EXPERIMENT UP IN CANADA..."

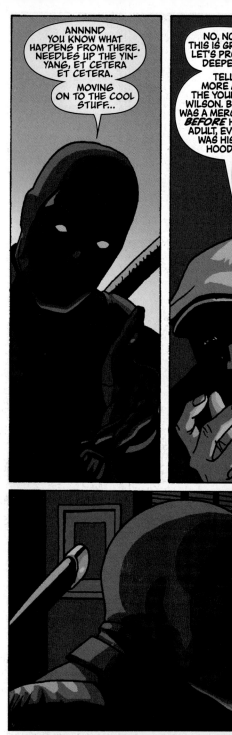

ANNNND YOU KNOW WHAT HAPPENS FROM THERE. NEEDLES UP THE YIN-YANG, ET CETERA ET CETERA.

MOVING ON TO THE COOL STUFF...

NO, NO. THIS IS GREAT. LET'S PROBE DEEPER.

TELL ME MORE ABOUT THE YOUNG WADE WILSON. BEFORE HE WAS A MERC FOR HIRE. *BEFORE* HE WAS AN ADULT, EVEN. WHAT WAS HIS CHILD-HOOD LIKE?

WHAT, IS THIS -- *DIARY OF A WIMPY MERC?* NOBODY WANTS TO HEAR THAT STUFF.

I'M NOT JOKING! THIS IS THE *EMOTIONAL CENTER** OF THE WHOLE MOVIE! CAN'T SEE THAT?

*EMOTIONAL CENTER (e-mo-shun-ul cen-tur): A word screenwriters use to impress chicks.

JOKING, HUH?

MY DAD WAS A REAL KIDDER.

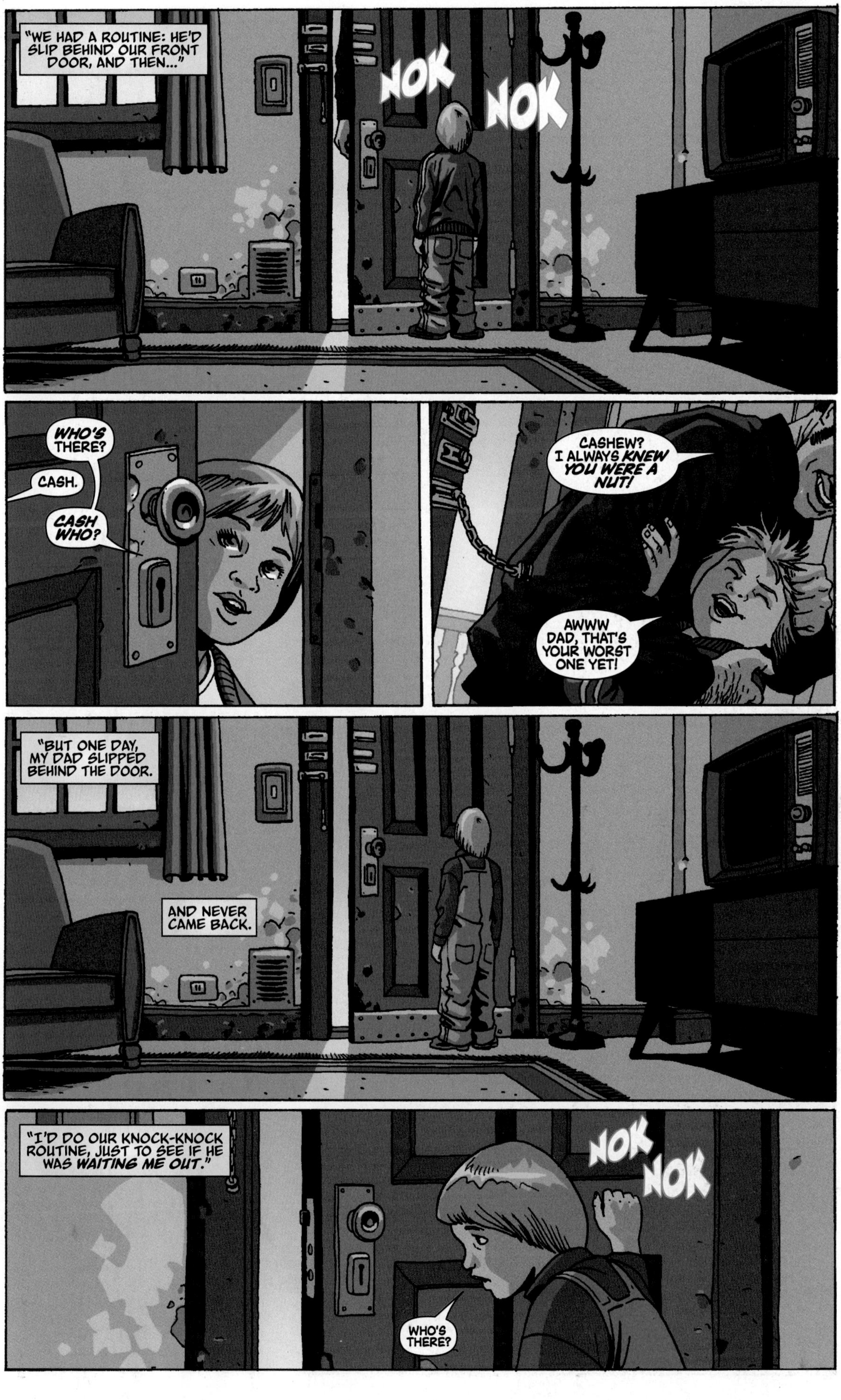
"WE HAD A ROUTINE: HE'D SLIP BEHIND OUR FRONT DOOR, AND THEN..."
NOK
NOK
WHO'S THERE?
CASH.
CASH WHO?
CASHEW? I ALWAYS KNEW YOU WERE A NUT!
AWWW DAD, THAT'S YOUR WORST ONE YET!
"BUT ONE DAY, MY DAD SLIPPED BEHIND THE DOOR.
AND NEVER CAME BACK.
"I'D DO OUR KNOCK-KNOCK ROUTINE, JUST TO SEE IF HE WAS WAITING ME OUT."
NOK
NOK
WHO'S THERE?

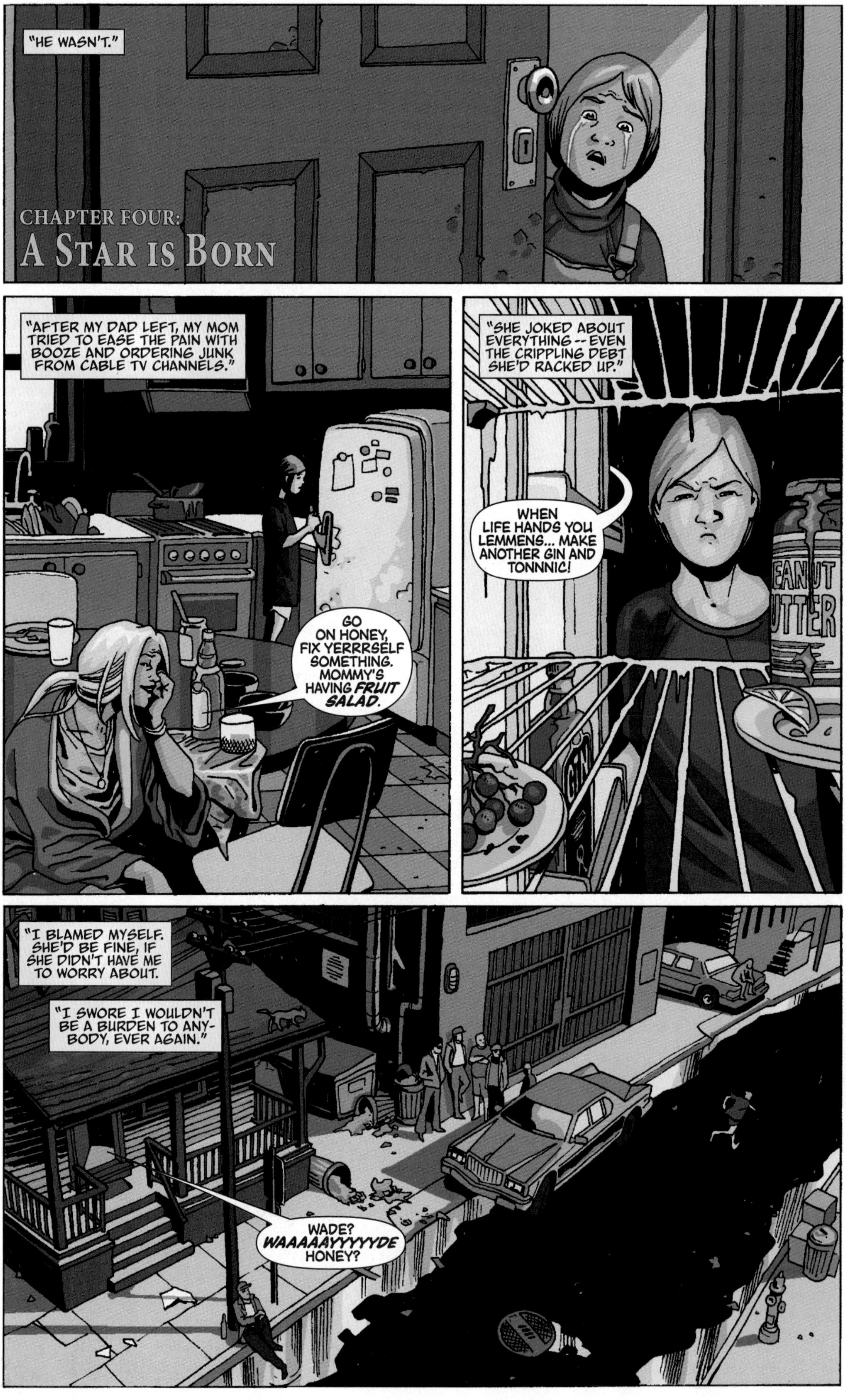
"HE WASN'T."
CHAPTER FOUR:
A STAR IS BORN
"AFTER MY DAD LEFT, MY MOM TRIED TO EASE THE PAIN WITH BOOZE AND ORDERING JUNK FROM CABLE TV CHANNELS."
GO ON HONEY, FIX YERRRSELF SOMETHING. MOMMY'S HAVING FRUIT SALAD.
"SHE JOKED ABOUT EVERYTHING -- EVEN THE CRIPPLING DEBT SHE'D RACKED UP."
WHEN LIFE HANDS YOU LEMMENS... MAKE ANOTHER GIN AND TONNNIC!
EANUT UTTER
"I BLAMED MYSELF. SHE'D BE FINE, IF SHE DIDN'T HAVE ME TO WORRY ABOUT.
"I SWORE I WOULDN'T BE A BURDEN TO ANYBODY, EVER AGAIN."
WADE? WAAAAAYYYYYDE HONEY?

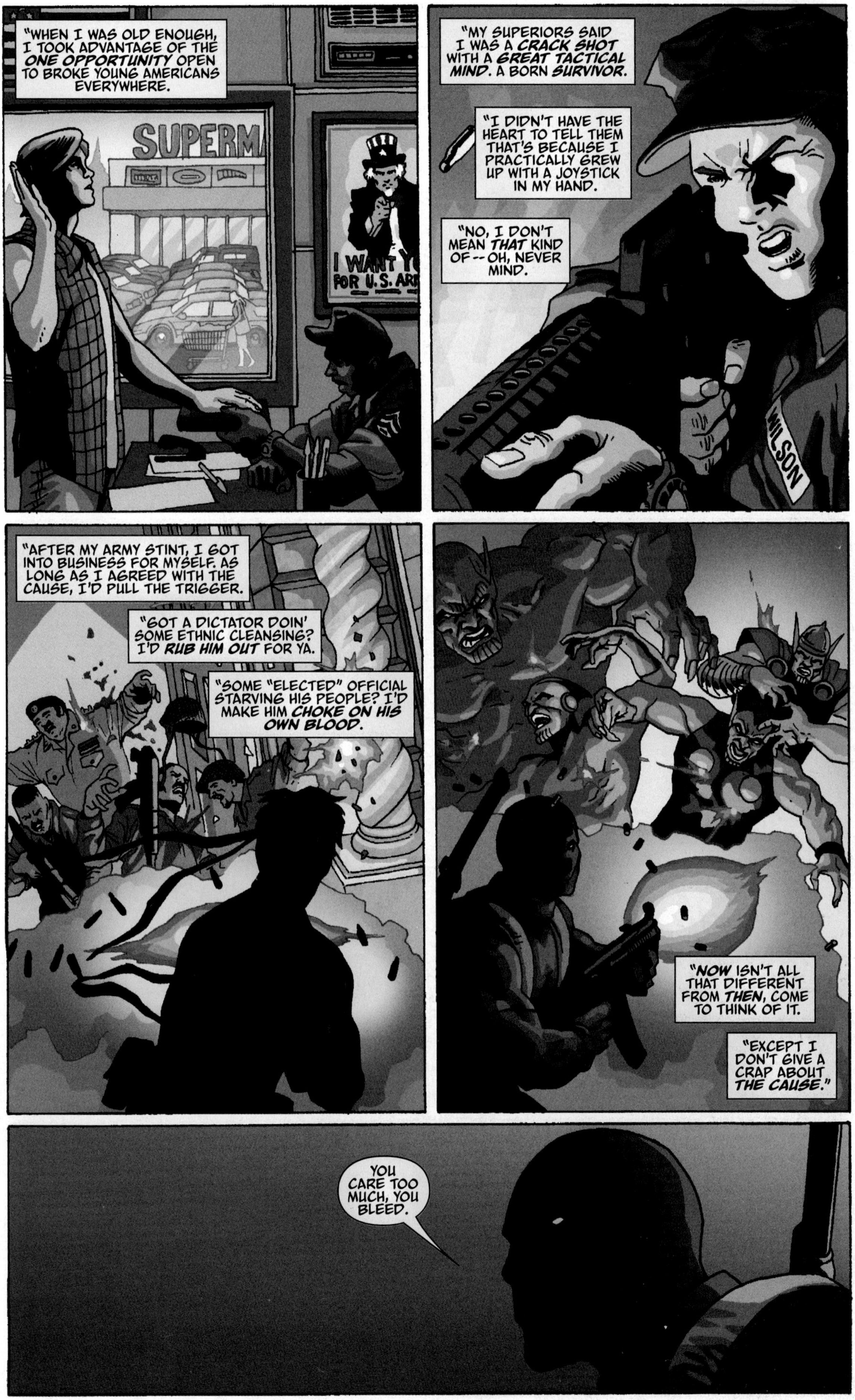

"WHEN I WAS OLD ENOUGH, I TOOK ADVANTAGE OF THE ONE OPPORTUNITY OPEN TO BROKE YOUNG AMERICANS EVERYWHERE.
SUPERM
I WANT YO FOR U.S. AR
"MY SUPERIORS SAID I WAS A CRACK SHOT WITH A GREAT TACTICAL MIND. A BORN SURVIVOR.
"I DIDN'T HAVE THE HEART TO TELL THEM THAT'S BECAUSE I PRACTICALLY GREW UP WITH A JOYSTICK IN MY HAND.
"NO, I DON'T MEAN THAT KIND OF -- OH, NEVER MIND.
WILSON
"AFTER MY ARMY STINT, I GOT INTO BUSINESS FOR MYSELF. AS LONG AS I AGREED WITH THE CAUSE, I'D PULL THE TRIGGER.
"GOT A DICTATOR DOIN' SOME ETHNIC CLEANSING? I'D RUB HIM OUT FOR YA.
"SOME "ELECTED" OFFICIAL STARVING HIS PEOPLE? I'D MAKE HIM CHOKE ON HIS OWN BLOOD.
"NOW ISN'T ALL THAT DIFFERENT FROM THEN, COME TO THINK OF IT.
"EXCEPT I DON'T GIVE A CRAP ABOUT THE CAUSE."
YOU CARE TOO MUCH, YOU BLEED.

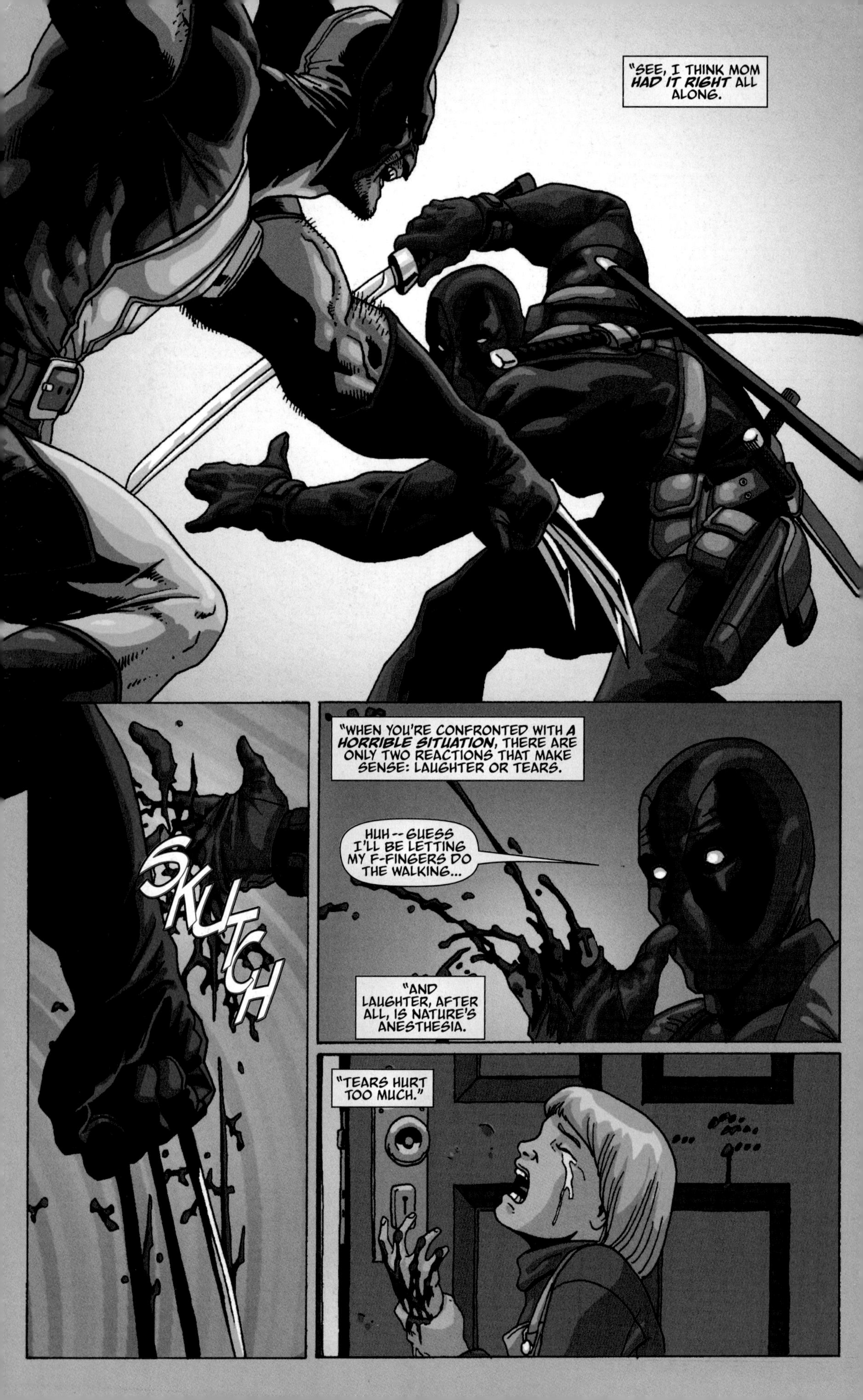
"SEE, I THINK MOM **HAD IT RIGHT** ALL ALONG.
SKUTCH
"WHEN YOU'RE CONFRONTED WITH A **HORRIBLE SITUATION**, THERE ARE ONLY TWO REACTIONS THAT MAKE SENSE: LAUGHTER OR TEARS.
HUH -- GUESS I'LL BE LETTING MY F-FINGERS DO THE WALKING...
"AND LAUGHTER, AFTER ALL, IS NATURE'S ANESTHESIA.
"TEARS HURT TOO MUCH."

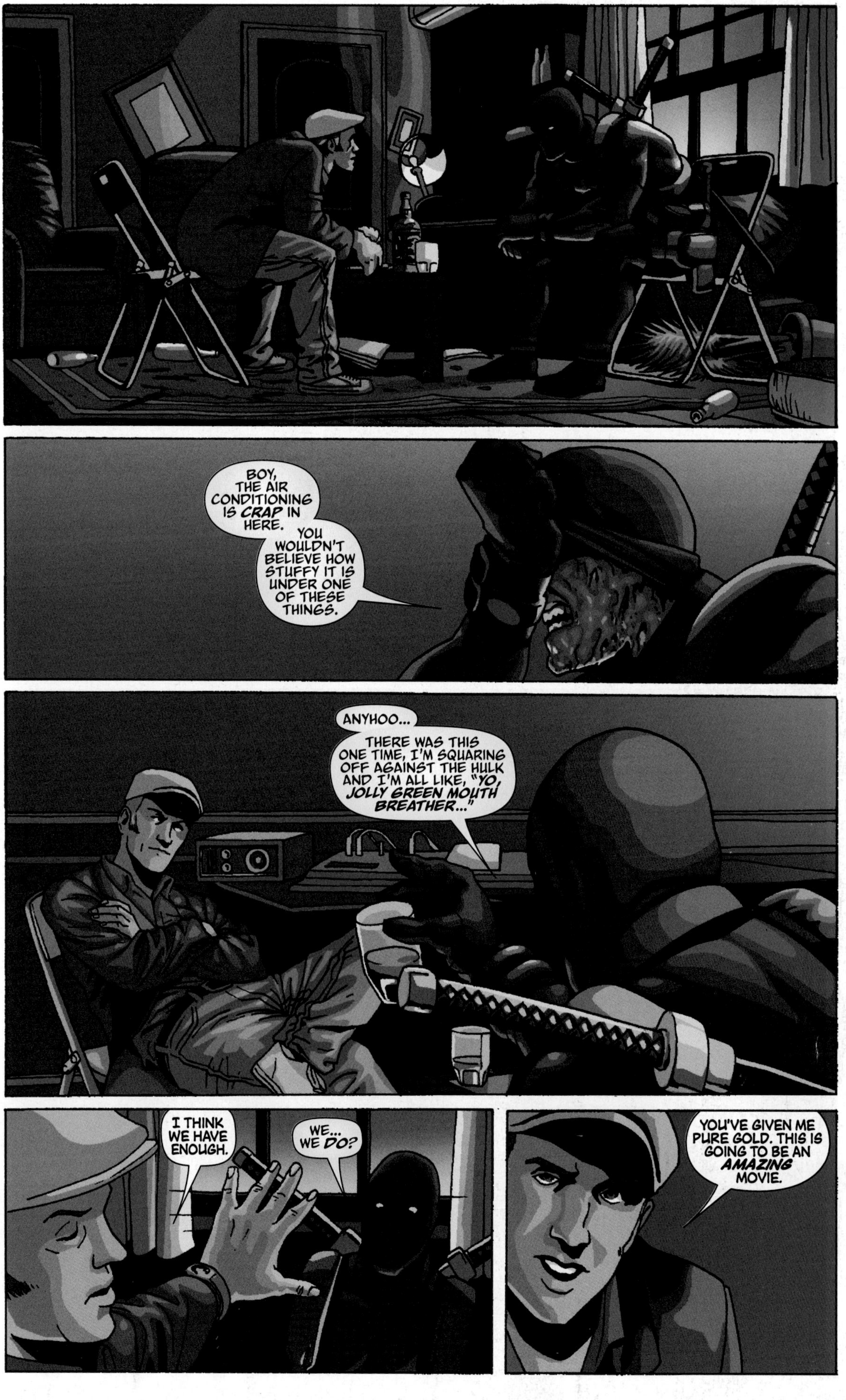
BOY, THE AIR CONDITIONING IS CRAP IN HERE.
YOU WOULDN'T BELIEVE HOW STUFFY IT IS UNDER ONE OF THESE THINGS.
ANYHOO...
THERE WAS THIS ONE TIME, I'M SQUARING OFF AGAINST THE HULK AND I'M ALL LIKE, "YO, JOLLY GREEN MOUTH BREATHER..."
I THINK WE HAVE ENOUGH.
WE... WE DO?
YOU'VE GIVEN ME PURE GOLD. THIS IS GOING TO BE AN AMAZING MOVIE.

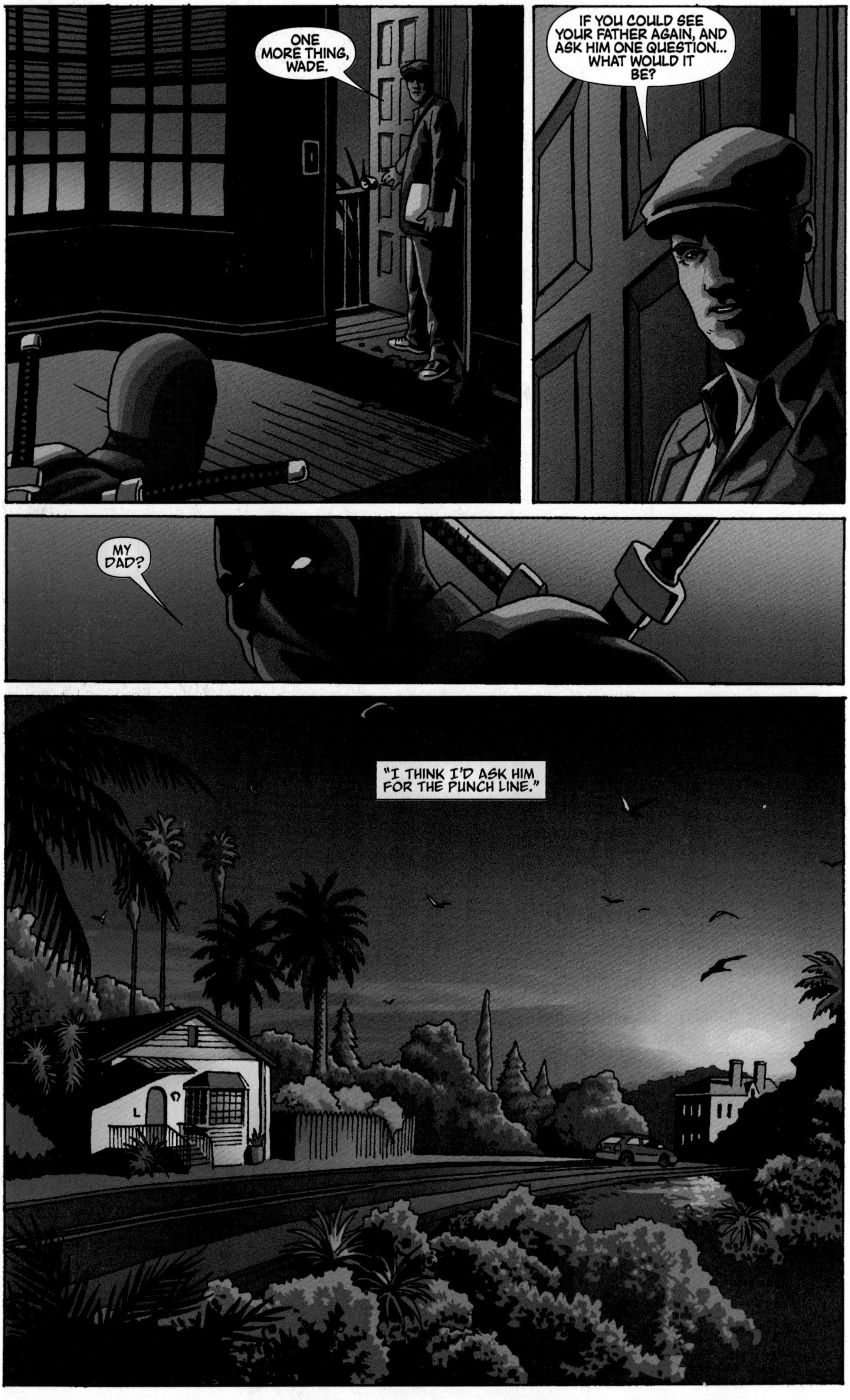
ONE MORE THING, WADE.
IF YOU COULD SEE YOUR FATHER AGAIN, AND ASK HIM ONE QUESTION... WHAT WOULD IT BE?
MY DAD?
"I THINK I'D ASK HIM FOR THE PUNCH LINE."

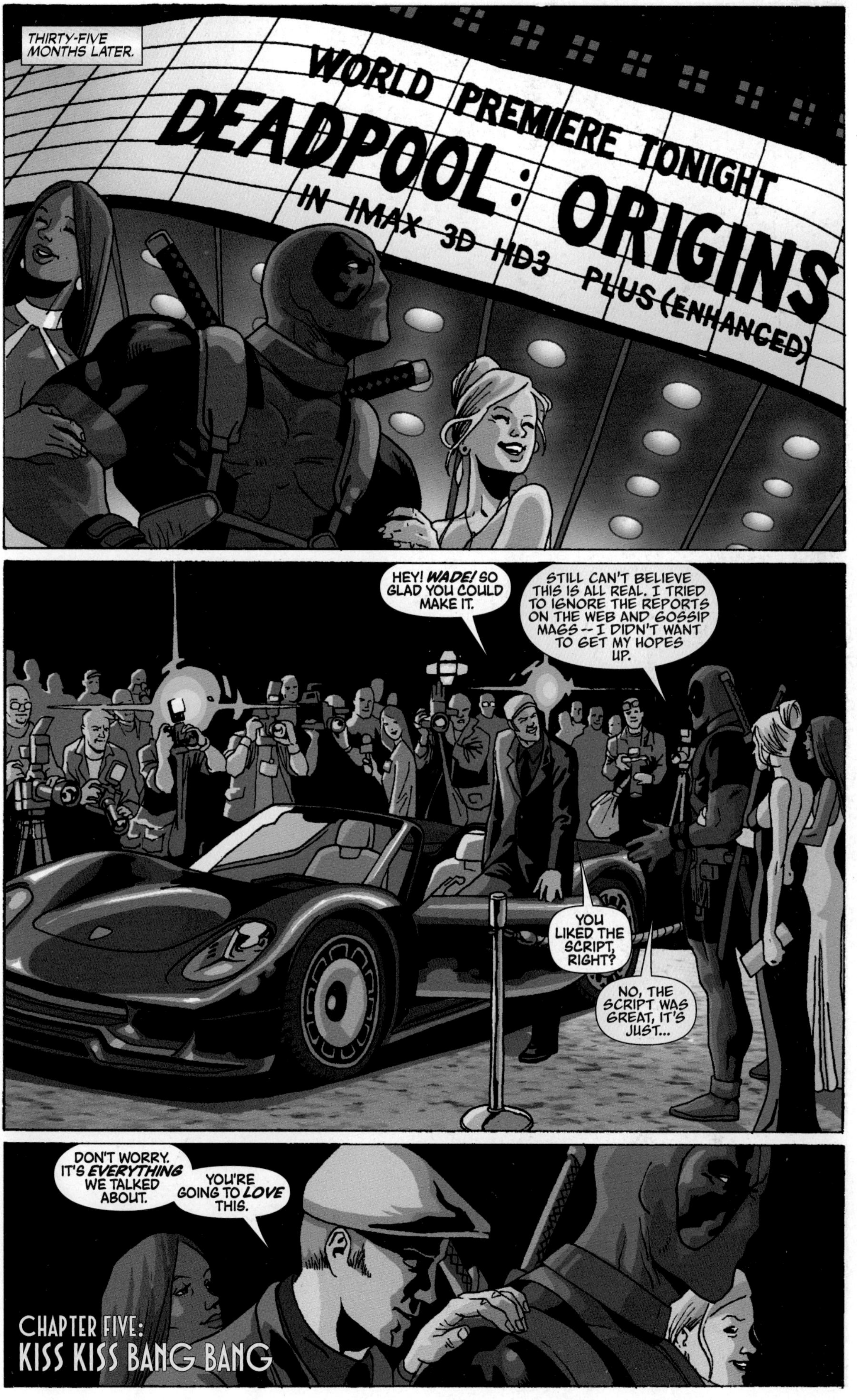
THIRTY-FIVE MONTHS LATER.
WORLD PREMIERE TONIGHT
DEADPOOL: ORIGINS
IN IMAX 3D HD3 PLUS (ENHANCED)
HEY! WADE! SO GLAD YOU COULD MAKE IT.
STILL CAN'T BELIEVE THIS IS ALL REAL. I TRIED TO IGNORE THE REPORTS ON THE WEB AND GOSSIP MAGS -- I DIDN'T WANT TO GET MY HOPES UP.
YOU LIKED THE SCRIPT, RIGHT?
NO, THE SCRIPT WAS GREAT, IT'S JUST...
DON'T WORRY. IT'S EVERYTHING WE TALKED ABOUT.
YOU'RE GOING TO LOVE THIS.
CHAPTER FIVE:
KISS KISS BANG BANG

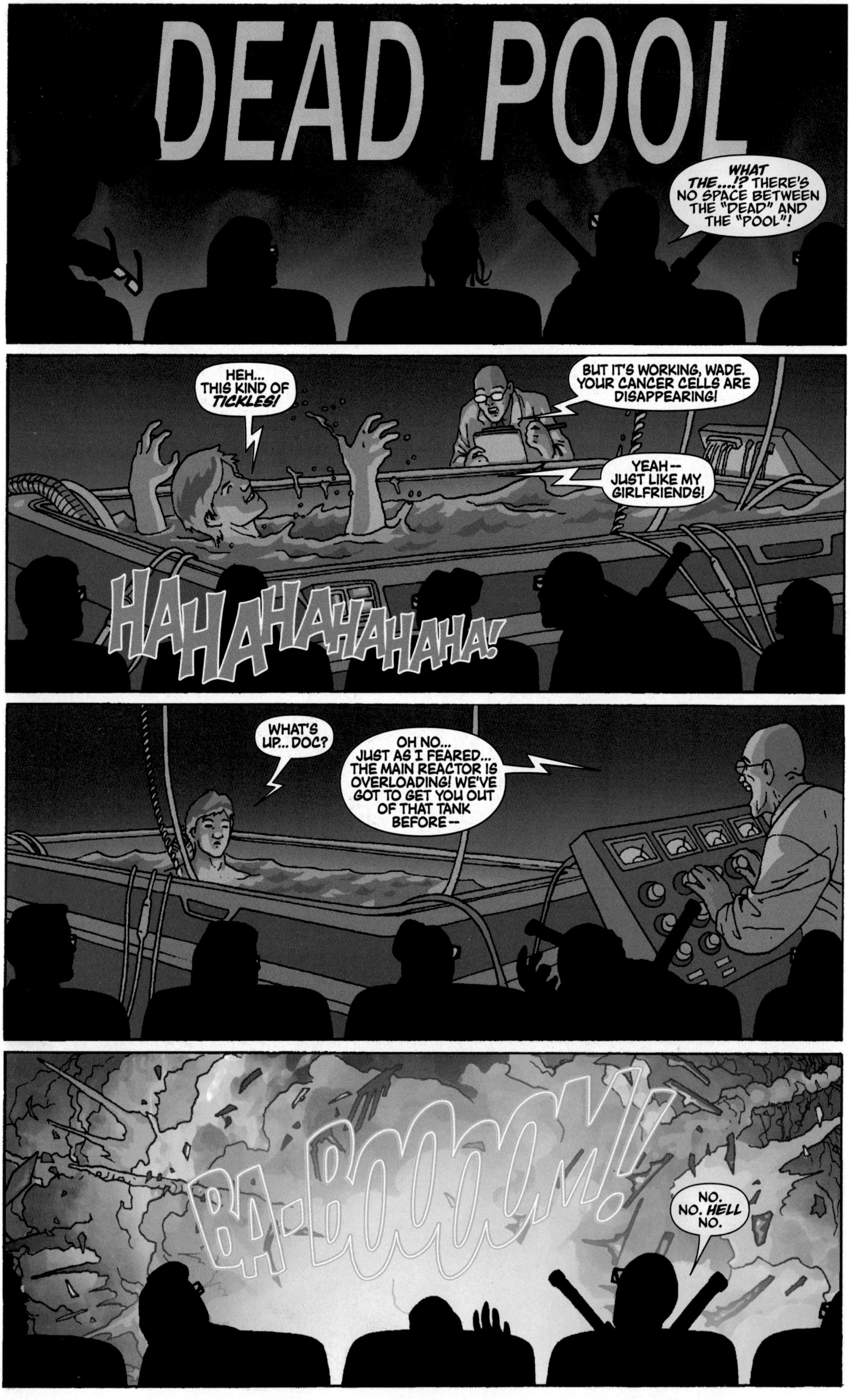
DEAD POOL
WHAT THE...!? THERE'S NO SPACE BETWEEN THE "DEAD" AND THE "POOL"!
HEH... THIS KIND OF TICKLES!
BUT IT'S WORKING, WADE. YOUR CANCER CELLS ARE DISAPPEARING!
YEAH -- JUST LIKE MY GIRLFRIENDS!
HAHAHAHAHAHAHA!
WHAT'S UP... DOC?
OH NO... JUST AS I FEARED... THE MAIN REACTOR IS OVERLOADING! WE'VE GOT TO GET YOU OUT OF THAT TANK BEFORE --
BA-BOOOOM!
NO. NO. HELL NO.

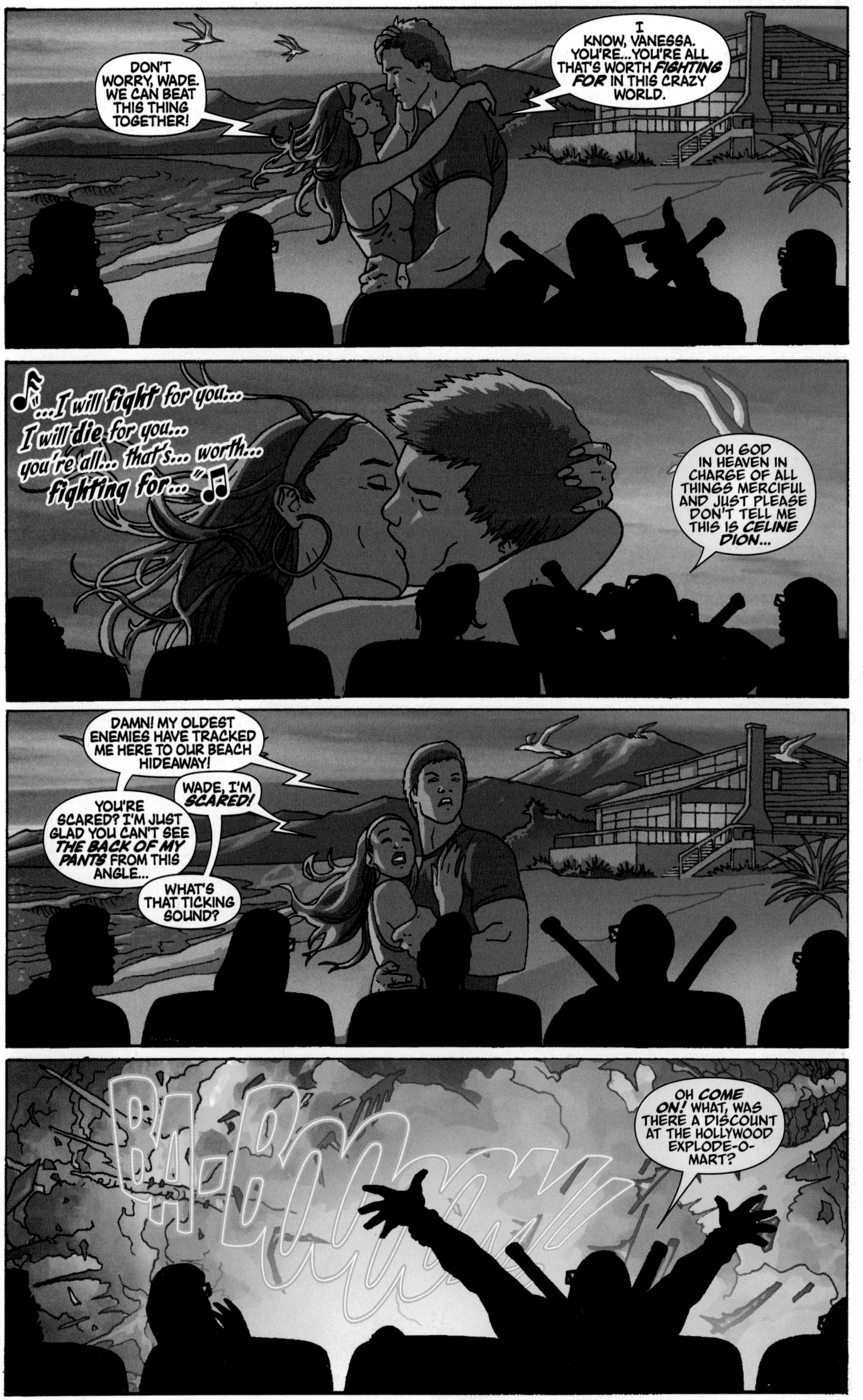
DON'T WORRY, WADE. WE CAN BEAT THIS THING TOGETHER!
I KNOW, VANESSA. YOU'RE...YOU'RE ALL THAT'S WORTH FIGHTING FOR IN THIS CRAZY WORLD.
♪ ...I will fight for you... I will die for you... you're all... that's... worth... fighting for...'' ♫
OH GOD IN HEAVEN IN CHARGE OF ALL THINGS MERCIFUL AND JUST PLEASE DON'T TELL ME THIS IS CELINE DION...
DAMN! MY OLDEST ENEMIES HAVE TRACKED ME HERE TO OUR BEACH HIDEAWAY!
WADE, I'M SCARED!
YOU'RE SCARED? I'M JUST GLAD YOU CAN'T SEE THE BACK OF MY PANTS FROM THIS ANGLE...
WHAT'S THAT TICKING SOUND?
BA-BOOOOM!
OH COME ON! WHAT, WAS THERE A DISCOUNT AT THE HOLLYWOOD EXPLODE-O-MART?

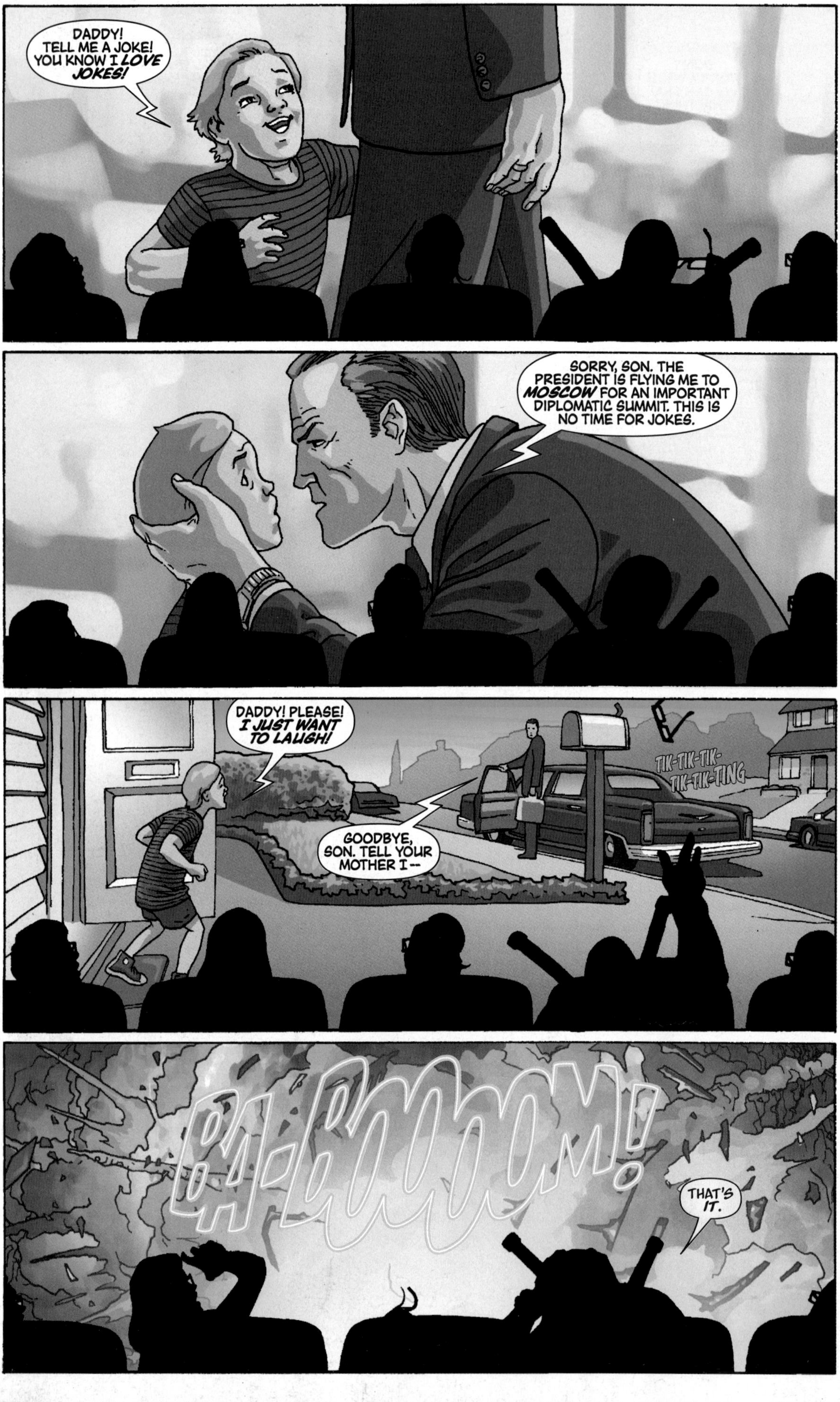
DADDY! TELL ME A JOKE! YOU KNOW I *LOVE* *JOKES!*
SORRY, SON. THE PRESIDENT IS FLYING ME TO *MOSCOW* FOR AN IMPORTANT DIPLOMATIC SUMMIT. THIS IS NO TIME FOR JOKES.
DADDY! PLEASE! *I JUST WANT TO LAUGH!*
TIK-TIK-TIK-TIK-TIK-TING
GOODBYE, SON. TELL YOUR MOTHER I--
KA-BOOOOOM!
THAT'S *IT.*

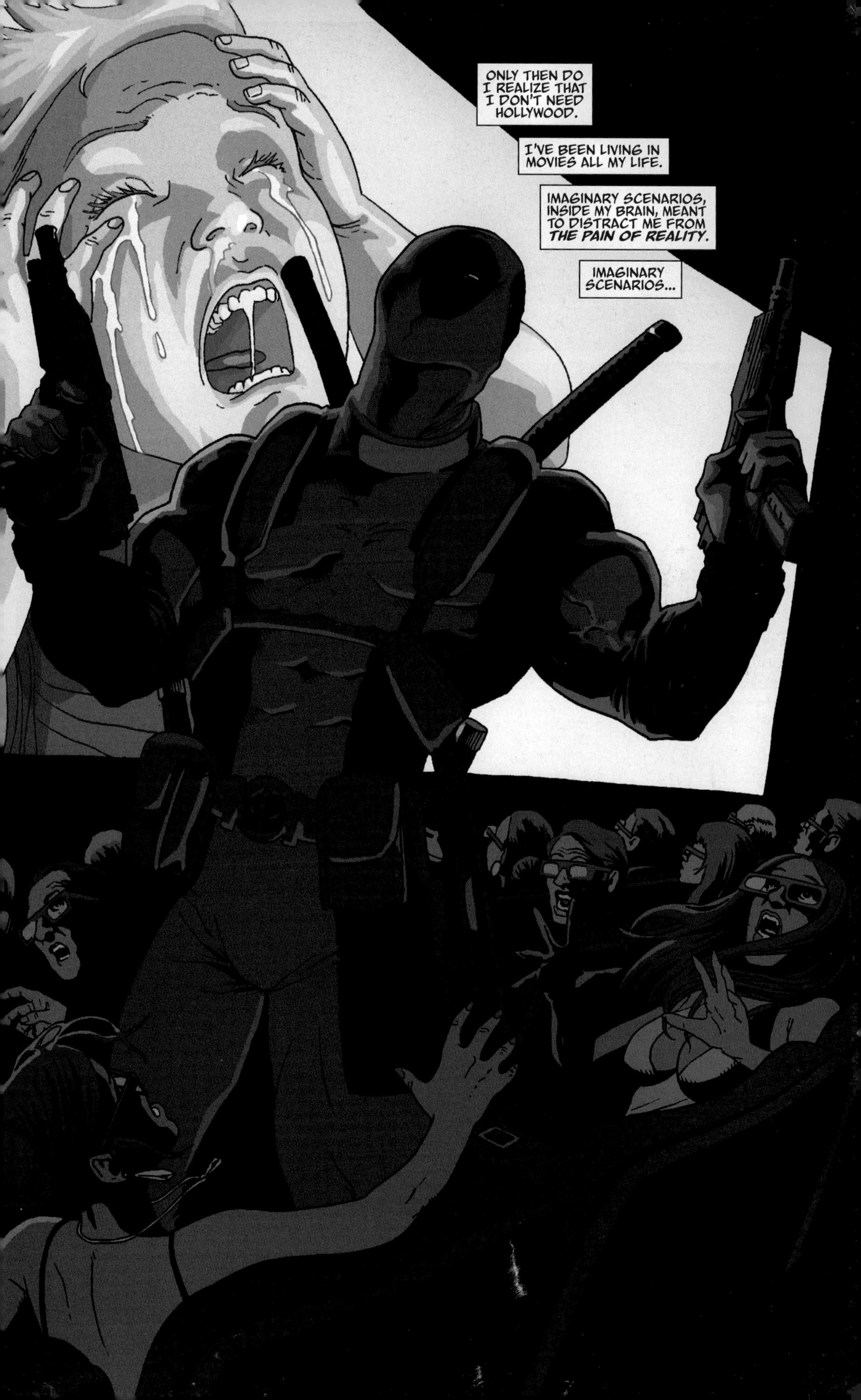
ONLY THEN DO I REALIZE THAT I DON'T NEED HOLLYWOOD.
I'VE BEEN LIVING IN MOVIES ALL MY LIFE.
IMAGINARY SCENARIOS, INSIDE MY BRAIN, MEANT TO DISTRACT ME FROM *THE PAIN OF REALITY*.
IMAGINARY SCENARIOS...

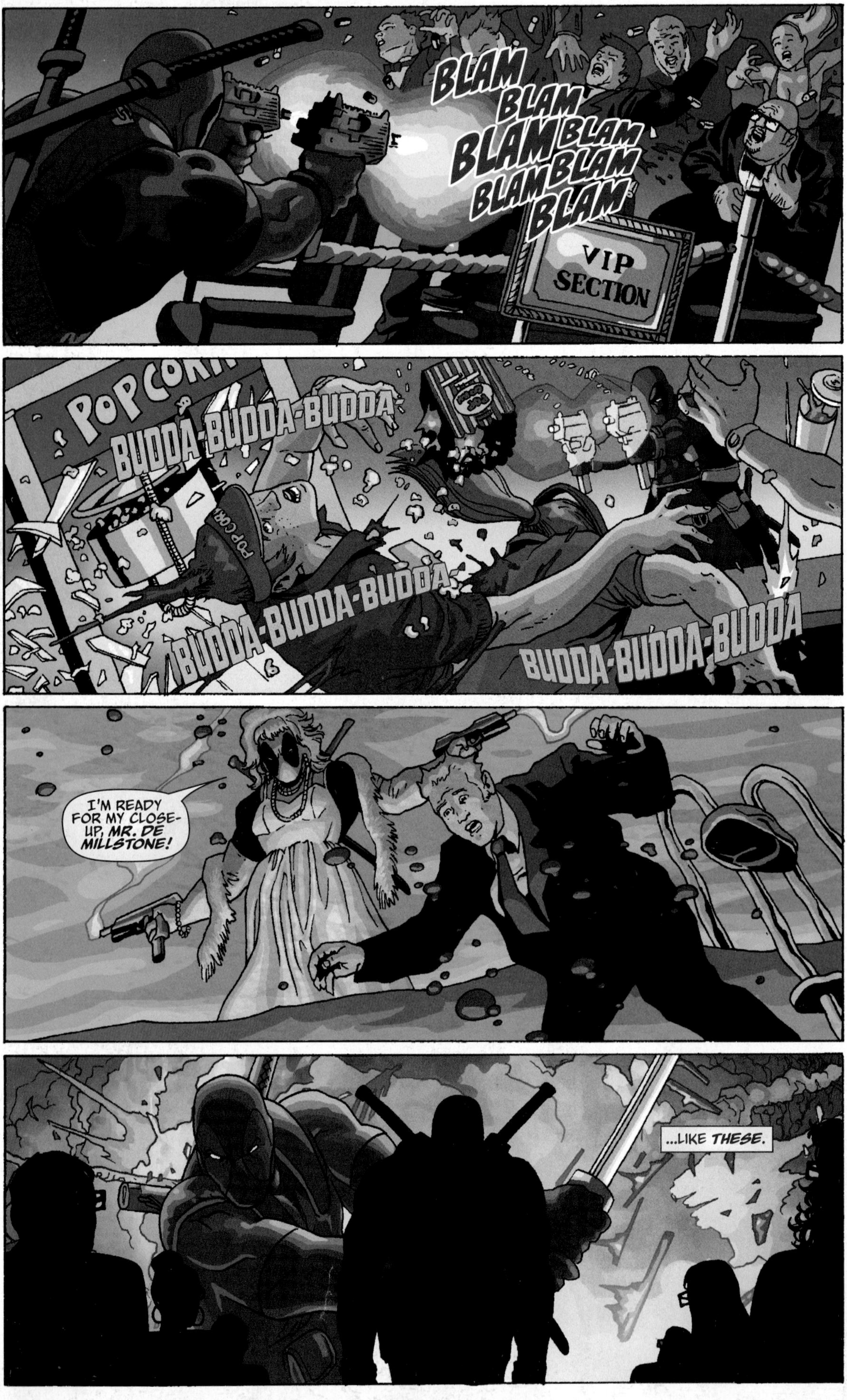
BLAM BLAM BLAM BLAM BLAM BLAM BLAM
VIP SECTION
POPCORN
BUDDA-BUDDA-BUDDA
BUDDA-BUDDA-BUDDA
BUDDA-BUDDA-BUDDA
I'M READY FOR MY CLOSE-UP, MR. DE MILLSTONE!
...LIKE THESE.

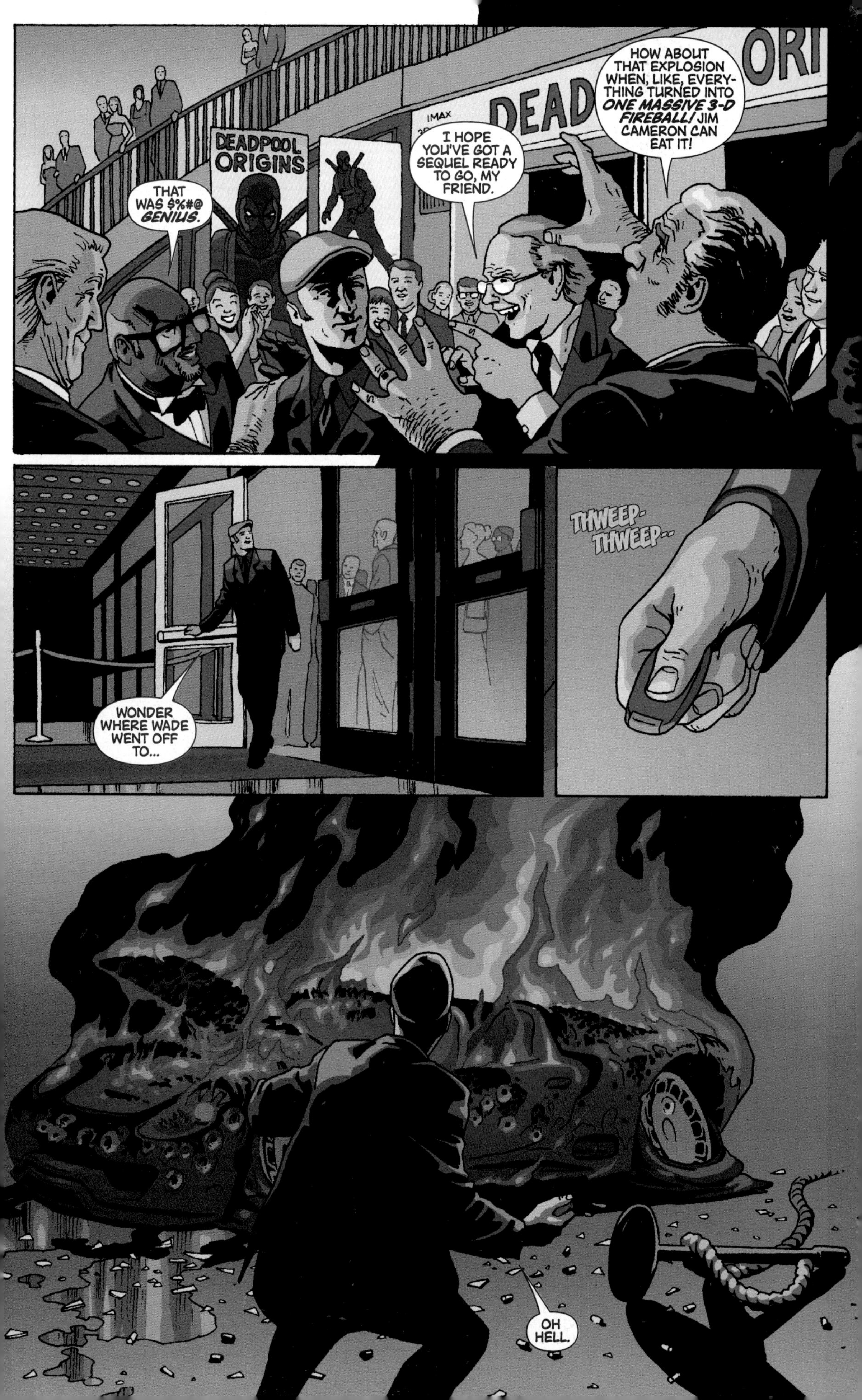
DEADPOOL ORIGINS
IMAX
DEAD ORI
THAT WAS $%#@ GENIUS.
I HOPE YOU'VE GOT A SEQUEL READY TO GO, MY FRIEND.
HOW ABOUT THAT EXPLOSION WHEN, LIKE, EVERYTHING TURNED INTO ONE MASSIVE 3-D FIREBALL! JIM CAMERON CAN EAT IT!
WONDER WHERE WADE WENT OFF TO...
THWEEP-THWEEP..
OH HELL.

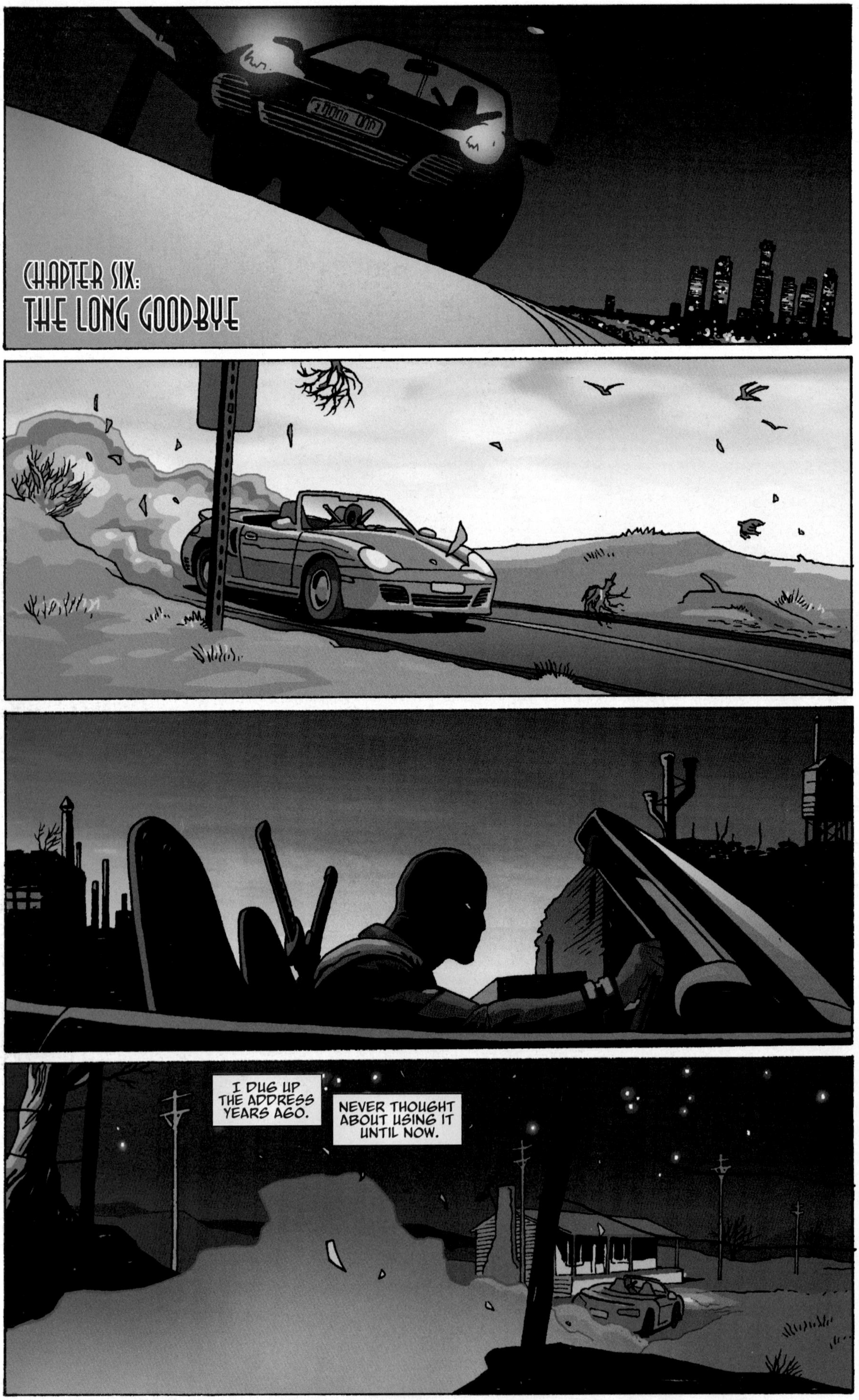
CHAPTER SIX:
THE LONG GOODBYE
I DUG UP THE ADDRESS YEARS AGO.
NEVER THOUGHT ABOUT USING IT UNTIL NOW.

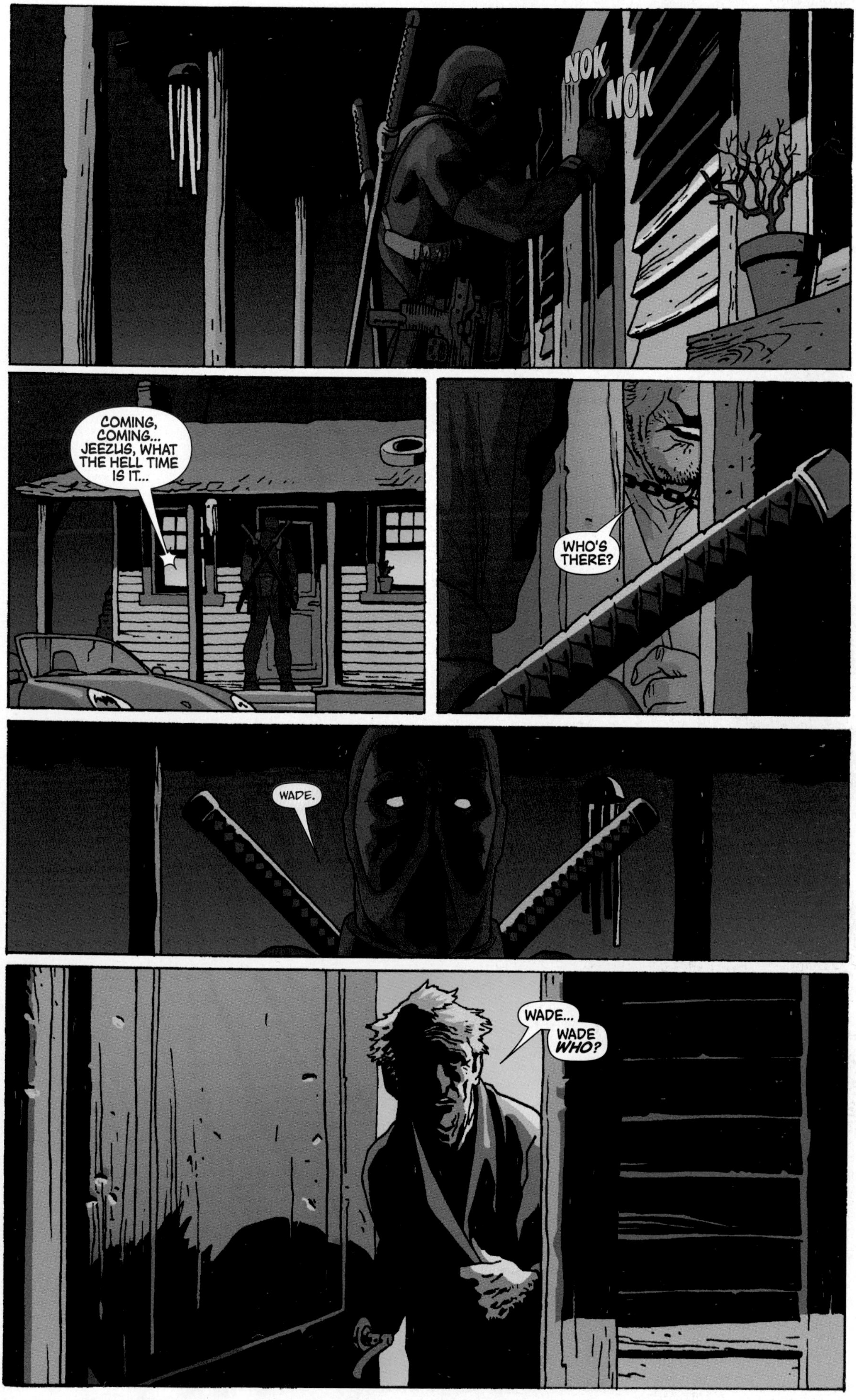
NOK NOK
COMING, COMING... JEEZUS, WHAT THE HELL TIME IS IT...
WHO'S THERE?
WADE.
WADE... WADE *WHO?*

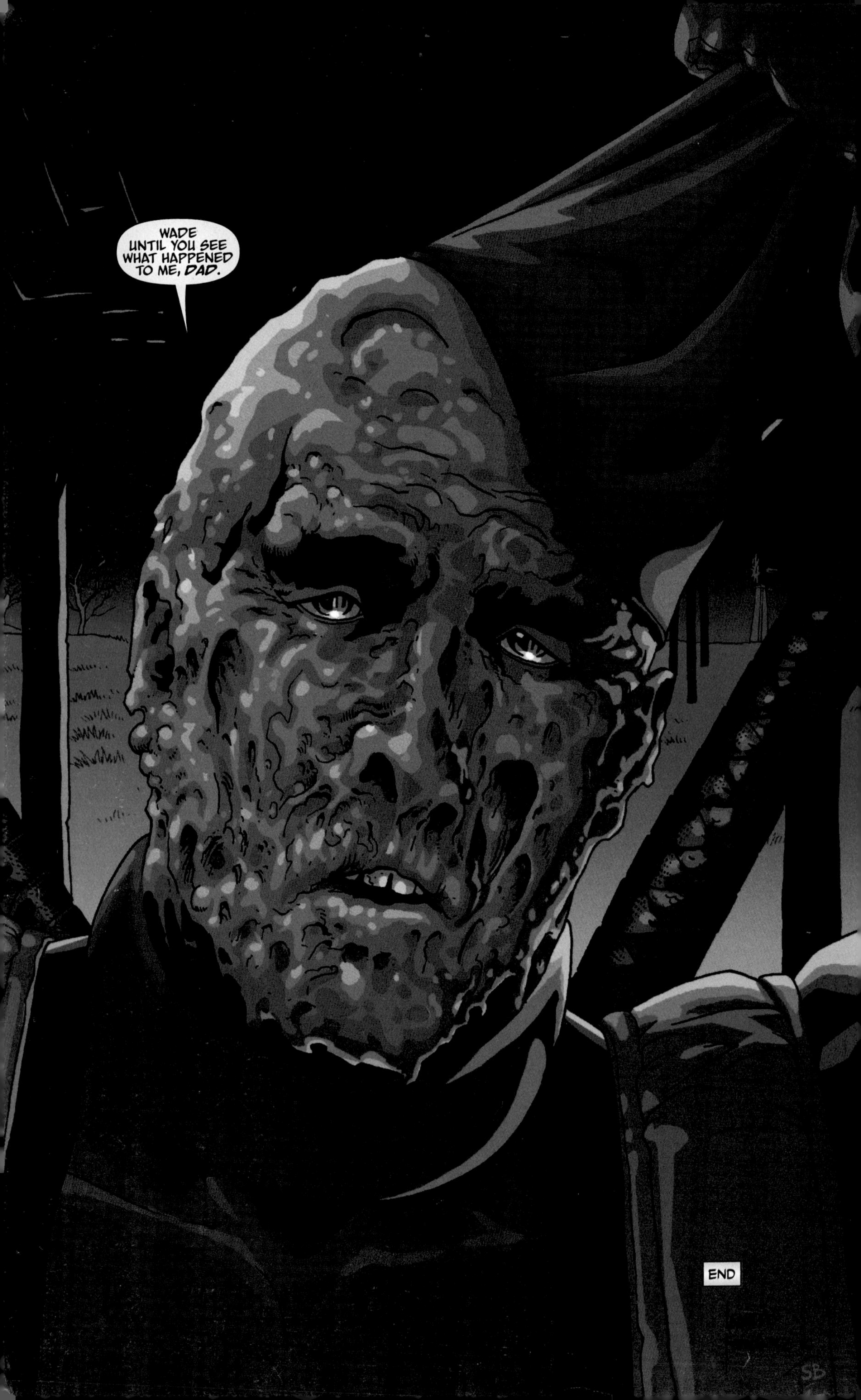
WADE UNTIL YOU SEE WHAT HAPPENED TO ME, DAD.
END
SB

CYCLOPS DESIGN
BY JESSE DELPERDANG

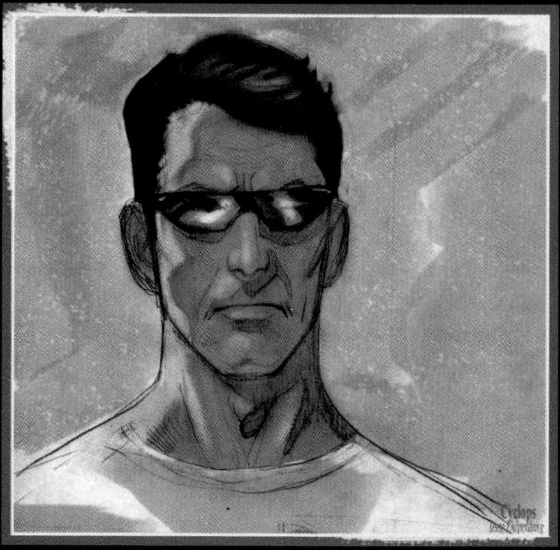

CYCLOPS COVER SKETCHES BY ADI GRANOV

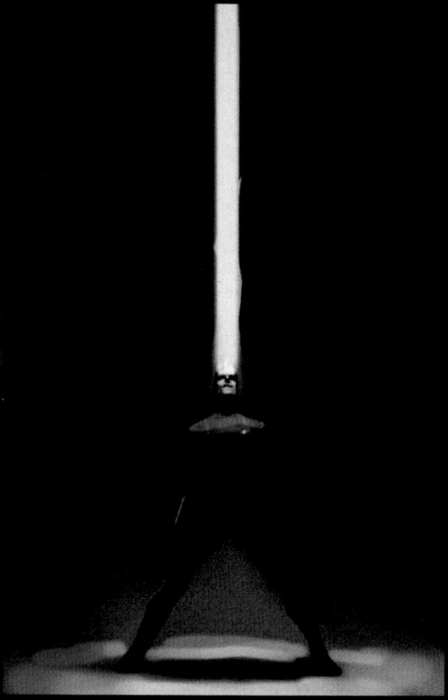

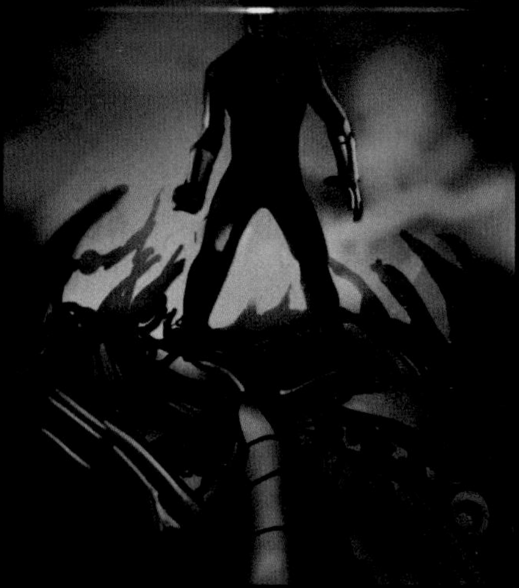

ICEMAN COVER SKETCHES
BY PHIL NOTO

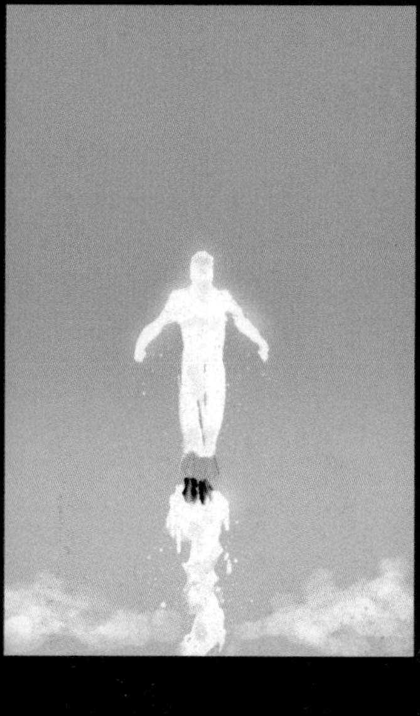

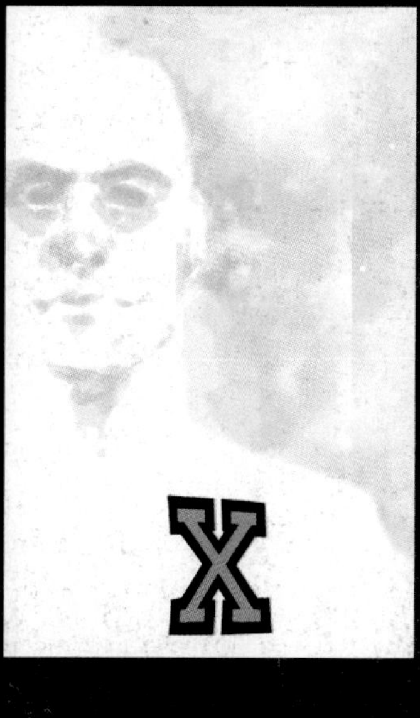

EMMA FROST COVER SKETCHES BY BENJAMIN ZHANG BIN

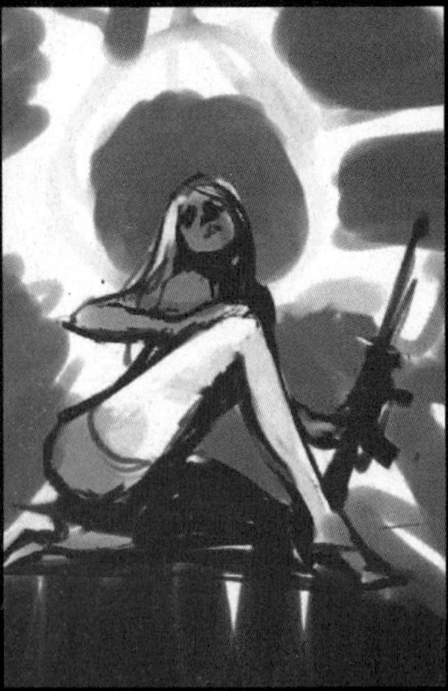

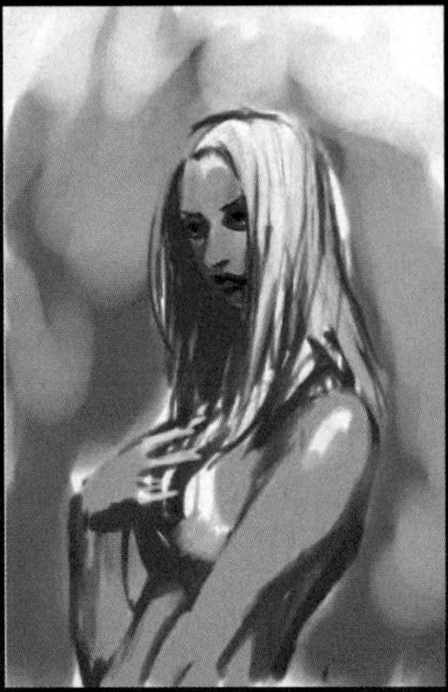

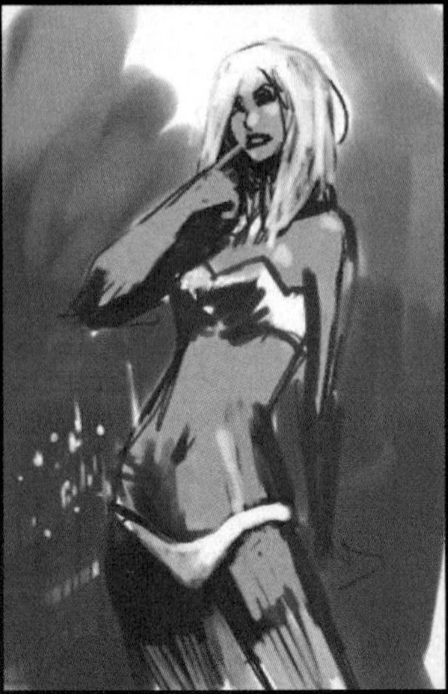

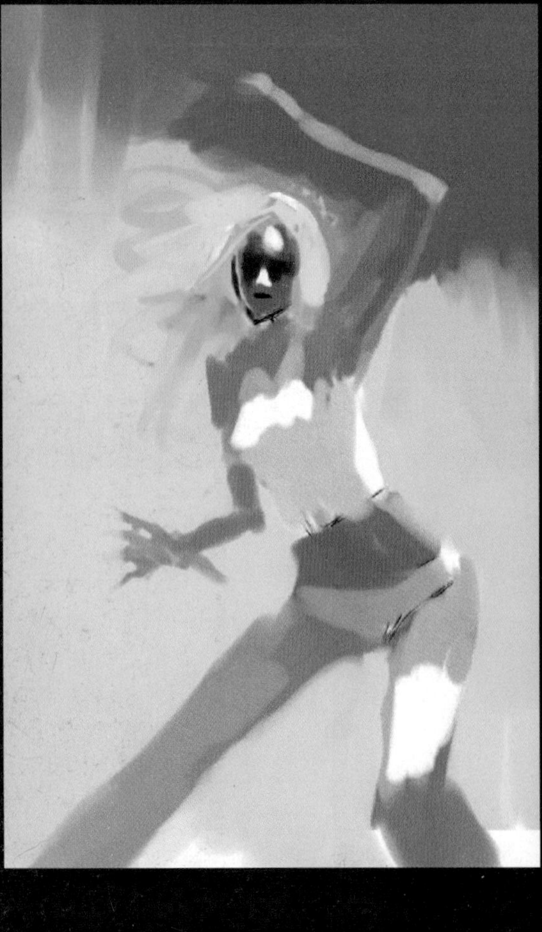

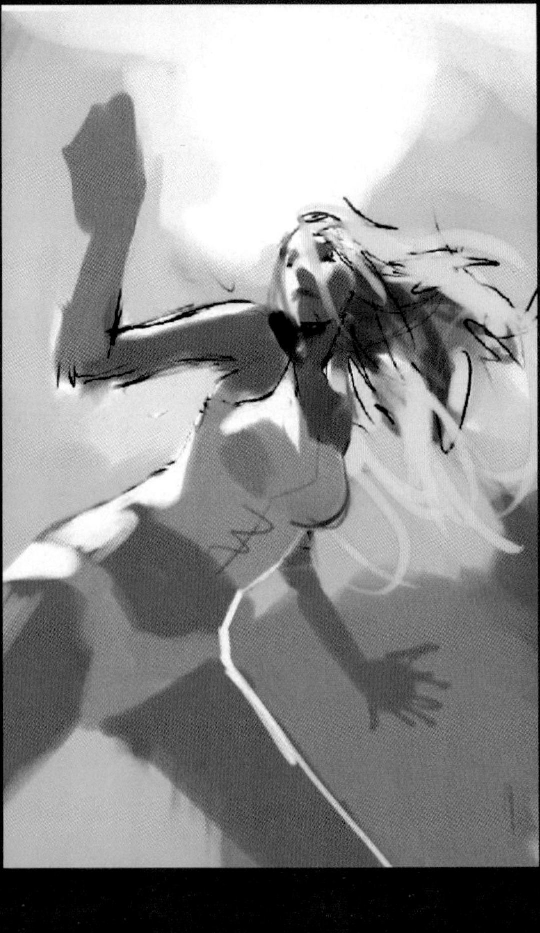

NIGHTCRAWLER COVER SKETCHES & PENCILS BY CARY NORD

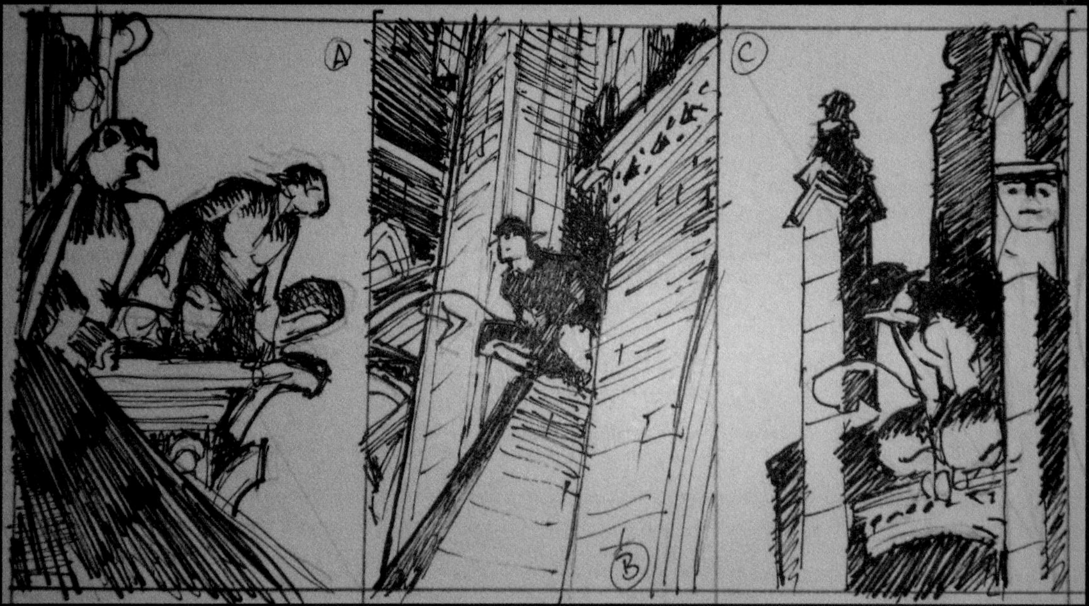
A
B
C

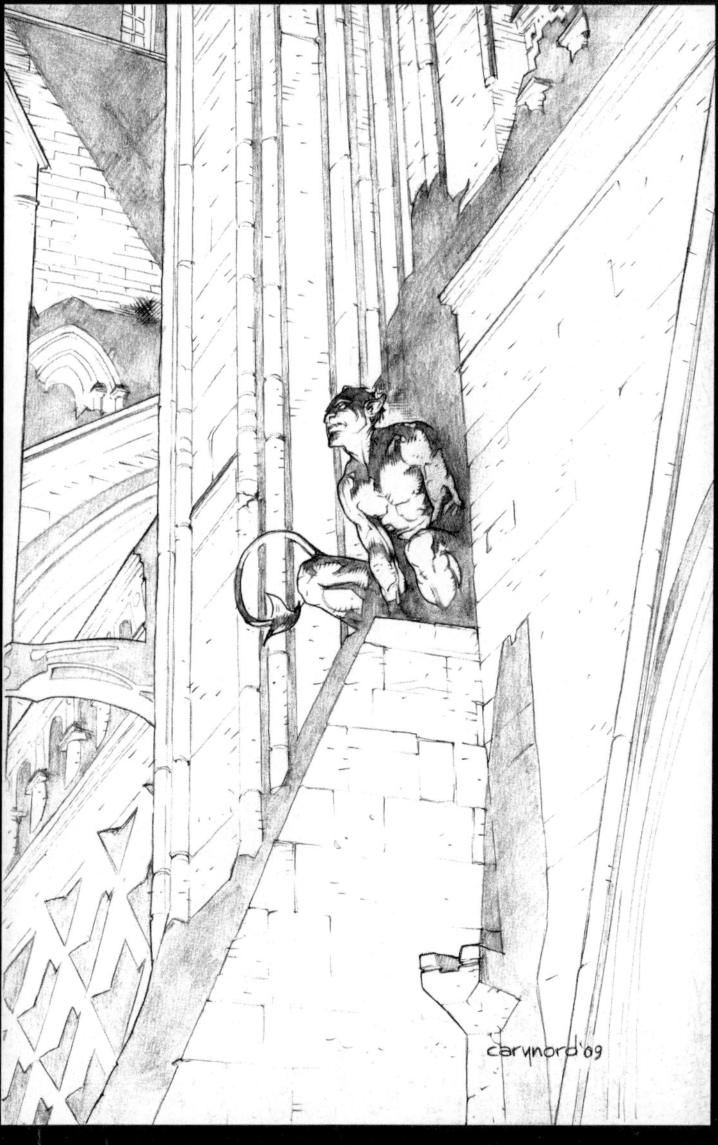
carynord'09

DEADPOOL, PAGE 29 PENCILS & INKS
BY LEANDRO FERNANDEZ

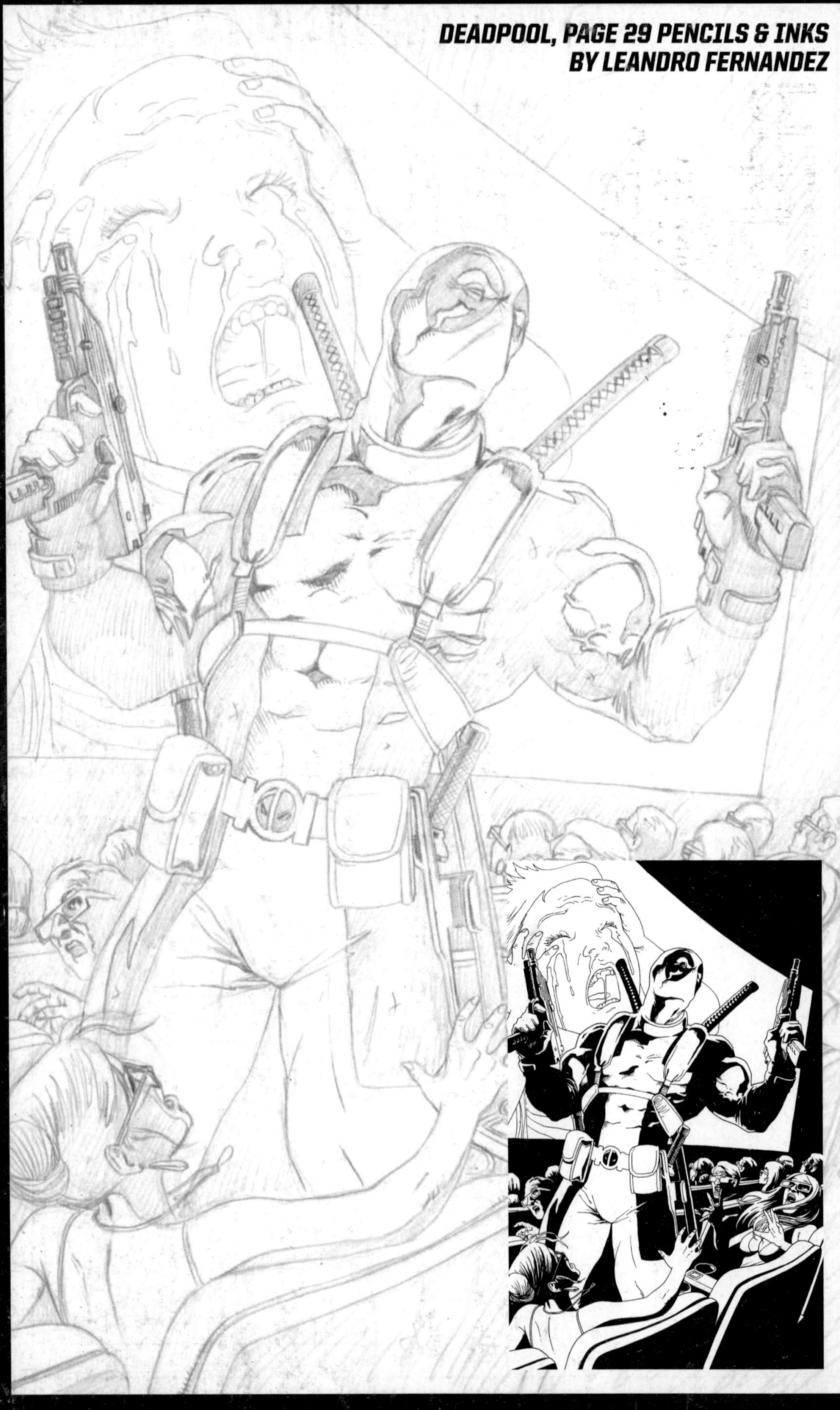